LEGAL CONTROL OF THE MULTINATIONAL ENTERPRISE

LEGAL CONTROL OF THE MULTINATIONAL ENTERPRISE

National Regulatory Techniques and the Prospects for International Controls

Cynthia Day Wallace

1982

MARTINUS NIJHOFF PUBLISHERS

THE HAGUE/BOSTON/LONDON

Distributors:

for the United States and Canada
Kluwer Boston, Inc.
190 Old Derby Street
Hingham, MA 02043
USA

for all other countries
Kluwer Academic Publishers Group
Distribution Center
P.O. Box 322
3300 AH Dordrecht
The Netherlands

Library of Congress Cataloging in Publication Data

Wallace, Cynthia D.
Legal control of the multinational enterprise.

Originally presented as the author's thesis (Ph. D.)--Cambridge University.
Bibliography: p.
Includes index.
1. International business enterprises--law and legislation. I. Title.
K1322.W34 1982 346'.07 82-3598
ISBN 90-247-2668-9 342.67 AACR2

ISBN 90-247-2668-9

PRINTED IN THE NETHERLANDS

To I.H.S. and B.L.H.,
both of whom sustained
me in their respective spheres.

FOREWORD

Although the cascade of publications about multinationals quickens constantly, Dr. Wallace's book has virtues that recommend it to even the busiest reader. Above all, it is free of the awed preconceptions that permeated so much of the early writings on the topic — the *Sovereignty at Bay, Le Défi américain, Global Reach, Invisible Empires* generation of analysis. Since the early 1970's enough has been written to justify the 426 page bibliography patiently assembled by the United Nations Centre on Transnational Corporations. The author is obviously fully aware of that flood, including the very substantial part of it that is only accessible in French and German, but does not leave us to drown in it. Her presentation is compact, though comprehensive, and her style is crisp and lucid.

The unblurred focus of this book is made possible by the decision to concentrate on relations between multinationals and the states of the developed world. Since so much of the writing has been from the perspective of the Third World (even when the author is thoroughly American or European) this comes at first as a shock. Upon reflection one sees that not only is this an entirely workable division of labor but that it encompasses the part of the situation which has by far the greatest potential significance for us. The future of the multinational, even if one includes the mineral extracting enterprises, lies not with the less developed world but within the industrialized capitalist states. The statistics on the quantity of foreign direct investment, its sources and its destinations, clearly show that this is the important stage to watch.

The drama that will be played out on it over the next few years will be a gripping one. The logic of the multinationals, a logic which has been worked out in the course of their rapid recent growth, hinges upon their having free access to diverse markets and resources so that they can combine factors found in different states to make profit for themselves and benefits for those around them. States are always tempted to try to tilt the balance so that they may have more of the benefits for their own, a temptation that was resisted collectively with fair success in the first two post war decades but which is assuming a new attractiveness for governments faced with capital flight, balance of payments weakness and unemployment. The recent tensions between the United States and Canada over the latter's National Energy Policy and the worries in other states about the tendency of the Mitterand government in France to go its own way are seen by some observers as symptoms of a new trend towards autarchy.

In a world where nations let their economic policies drift apart it goes hard for multinationals. Dr. Wallace describes in useful detail some of the past episodes in which national policies have put pressure, subtle or otherwise, upon foreign investors. While they spread out over time from the Fruehauf episode (p.100) to the British government's pressure for renegotiating the deal as to North Sea oil rights (p.238), one does have a sense that the pace may be picking up. Faced with such pressures, the resistive capacity of the multinational proves not to be anywhere near as formidable as once imagined. Its political power in the host state where it is a stranger, and a rich one to boot, is not great. Its economic leverage may have been weakened by the worldwide recession; the time when the president of Ford Motor Company could threaten Great Britain with a transfer of its attentions to another country unless its working conditions were improved seems long ago. The home state is not apt to be willing to incur great risks in order to protect one of its corporate citizens, especially when it has been brought home to viewers that outbound foreign investment may have harmful effects upon the state it is leaving.

All of this centrifugal tendency comes about during times when the basic economic laws of international cooperation hold just as true as ever before. Each gesture of economic nationalism has its costs. If Canada in fact retakes much of its energy business from American oil companies that will draw down on the domestic supply of capital. In the second line, it will discourage other investors from selecting Canada. In the third, it may cause United States moves to hamper Canadian firm's activities south of the border. As multinational firms have caused the originally unilateral outpouring of investment from the United States to be matched by capital flows toward the United States the connections are complex enough that they should give states pause at the thought of hacking away at the structure. It remains to be seen how far governments will, nonetheless, go to safeguard their own short-range national economic interests and their general interest in independence and autonomy. For a perspective from which to view both the national initiatives and the attempts to build and preserve international restraints on such moves we cannot do better than to turn to this magisterial work.

Detlev F. Vagts

ACKNOWLEDGEMENTS

I should like to express my sincere and special thanks to Prof. Derek W. Bowett of Cambridge University, who stood behind me as doctoral Supervisor during the dissertation phase of the present work, and gave me his valuable support.

A particular debt of gratitude goes also to the Max Planck Association in West Germany, which provided me with a fellowship during a large portion of my research, both at their Institute of Private International Law in Hamburg at the kind recommendation of the then sole Director, Prof. Dr. Ulrich Drobnig, and, for a longer period, at their Institute of Comparative Public Law and International Law in Heidelberg, whose then sole Director, Prof. Dr. Rudolf Bernhardt, most generously arranged for extensions of my fellowship as the work expanded into a volume of over 700 pages of typescript (since reduced for this publication). Along with my particular gratitude to Prof. Bernhardt for the opportunity and support he afforded, I am recognizant of the Fellows and other colleagues and staff who helped make my time at the Max Planck Institute both fruitful and enjoyable.

In addition I should like to acknowledge the contribution made by conversations with and/or written comments from the following persons, each of whom read a selected chapter of the work: Prof. Detlev Vagts of Harvard Law School, who also very kindly agreed to write the Foreword; Prof. Oscar Schachter of Columbia University Law School; Frederick M. Rowe, Visiting Lecturer at Yale Law School and past Chairman, Section of Antitrust Law, American Bar Association; Prof. Dr. Karl Doehring of the University of Heidelberg Faculty of Law and co-Director of the Max Planck Institute of Comparative Public Law and International Law, Heidelberg; and Prof. Dr. Ernst-Joachim Mestmäcker, co-Director of the Max Planck Institute of Private International Law, Hamburg; also Professor D.J. Harris of Nottingham University, England, who read the work in its entirety and kindly noted down his useful comments.

Meriting a medal for her intelligent decoding of my manuscript, replete with colour-coded signs and symbols, arrows and insertions, is Rachel Baird, who faithfully typed many hundreds of pages of manuscript, and even saw to it that I sometimes ate, and to her family who participated indirectly by their patience and sacrifices. For typing of many pages of revisions, Margot Lintaller's cheerful willingness and competence was also deeply appreciated, as was that of law students Lisa Granik and Janet Levy for their dedicated assistance during the proofing and indexing phase.

Despite the many persons who lent their wisdom and skills to my efforts, the full and sole responsibility for the content here presented, including any errors of fact, judgment or analysis, remain my own.

Cynthia Day Wallace
Heidelberg
March 1981

TABLE OF CONTENTS

INTRODUCTION

The aim of the present work is to determine the desirability of international controls over multinational business activity. In order to determine the desirability of such controls - proceeding on the initial assuption that multinational enterprises (MNEs) do need some kind of control - we must confront the issue of whether the MNE is at present subject to any form of control, or whether, as is popularly alleged, it runs rough-shod, unfettered and uncontrolled across national boundaries, with no heed to national jurisdictions and no answerability to higher authority. If substantial controls do exist, what aspects of MNE activity do they cover, and are they adequate to control all aspects of such activity that are deemed to need regulating? If they are inadequate, in what areas are they inadequate, and could any such control-deficient areas conceivably be covered satisfactorily by international control measures?

Due to the fact that the largest percentage of MNE activity is currently taking place in the industrialized nations, and that it is consequently in these nations that the most innovative legislation is to be found relating to multinationals, and for other reasons elaborated in the text, it is the highly industrialized economies which will be the focus of the present work, with particular reference to the U.S.A., Canada, Great Britain, France, Germany and Japan. It is hoped that the focus on the industrialized world will not deter those interested in the developing nations from reading the following pages. Although many of the problems of these two economic sectors differ sufficiently to require separate treatment in most respects, the material herein is relevant for all those concerned with regulatory measures surrounding the multinational enterprise, whether in the developed or the developing world, considering that national legislation reasonably accurately reflects the problem areas, and that any truly international controls will, by definition, affect all economic sectors.

While concentrating on the six highly capital-intensive states selected to illustrate the current trends in MNE regulation, the emphasis in the present study is not one of comparative law, but centers rather upon the major legal *techniques* of control, drawing practical examples from the relevant legislation and case law of those industrialized states most active in both inward and outward foreign direct investment, as enumerated above.

The fact that there is no allusion to the 'problem of control' is not accidental. This work addresses itself to the 'issue of control'. Whether or not control is, in fact, a 'Problem' is a debatable and a highly subjective question. It would seem safe to assume, considering the spate of literature in socio-economic and political as well as, more recently, in legal circles, to say nothing of the intense international activity centering around the subject in such bodies as the UN, OECD, ILO, UNCTAD, ICC and other international organizations, that *a* problem exists. Whether or not the problem is one of control of multinationals *per se* is in this writer's opinion a moot point, for which this study may provide some possible insights.

It is this writer's opinion that control of the multinationals, as such, (1) is not really, or (2) has ceased to be, a serious 'Problem'. This in not meant to be expanded to imply that control has ceased to be an *issue*, and an issue, indeed, within which very real problems do arise. The statement is nonetheless a bold one, and requires clarification.

First, one can say that the control of the multinational *per se* (1) is not really a 'Problem', in the sense that the accusations of abuses and excesses often directed at the MNEs - and in some cases substantiated - are also perpetrated by purely national corporate 'giants', to say nothing of other, non-corporate organized groups. This is in no way to excuse the abuses, but merely to point out that the 'Problem' may not be exclusively that of controlling the MNE, as such enterprises are not the sole perpetrators of questionable business practices. In fact, statistics show that in comparison with their national counterparts, MNEs have, on the whole, a better record of service to the community than do national firms. This is no doubt partially due to concessions sometimes exacted by a host state in return for the 'privilege' of direct investment extended to the foreign firm - i.e., certain services to the local community being made conditions of entry by the host government - and partially from the realization on the part of the foreign enterprise itself that it will be under closer scrutiny, as a 'foreigner', and viewed with more suspicion than a domestic firm and that consequently, if it does not make a significant contribution to the community, or at least conduct itself according to the 'rules' of 'good corporate citizenship', it may be asked to leave.

It is obvious, however, that a foreign presence does have some implications which are inapplicable when it comes to domestic enterprises, and this fact will not be overlooked in the present study. It is equally obvious that certain control measures will be primarily directed at those business enterprises whose own control centers are located outside the jurisdiction of the host. It thus becomes clear that it is less the abuses themselves than it is the abuses being committed by a foreign element which has become the issue. The question still remains, however, as to whether the issue, or 'Problem', is one of controlling the MNE *per se*. To this we must respond that even when concentrating on 'foreignness', multinational enterprises are only one vehicle for foreign direct investment. Such investments are also made by individuals, by banks, by insurance companies, by partnerships and by other types of business enterprises which are equally capable of holding a controlling interest in the host concern and influencing internal economics as are the multinationals themselves. The present writer would therefore submit that the real issue in this area is not one of control of the multinational enterprise, but one of control of any form of foreign direct investment involving share ownership to a percentage deemed by the individual host state to carry with it undue foreign control over important sectors of its economy.

The multinational has become the scapegoat for all ills resulting from foreign commercial presence in any form. Yet when examining control legislation, it is virtually impossible to single out the MNE as a distinct target. Very little legislation refers to multinationals as such; the laws tend to be aimed at foreign direct investment in general. From the case law, on the other hand, illustrations can be extracted which deal directly with problems arising out of identifiable MNE activity. Where appropriate, then, throughout the body of the work, 'case law' has been drawn upon in an attempt to separate out the MNE from other forms of foreign direct investment, in this limited area, at least. It is in the case law, and in the legislative framework supporting it, that we can find evidence to support the proposition that, although problems inevitably arise out of MNE activity, as out of all brands of commercial activity, the control of the MNE *per se*, while an 'Issue', is in fact not a 'Problem'. In other words, the individual problems which arise within the larger Issue can be dealt with, for the most part, within the existing legal framework, particularly in the Western systems. (This subject, and an attempt at identifying some of those areas which cannot be adequately dealt with within the existing legal framework, is expanded in the text.) As one writer has expressed it: "There are always potential, sometimes even endemic, disputes between the foreign firm and its hosts, but these do not usually become critical, at least in the industrialized countries."[1] And, in the words of another writer, in the case that

> ...the conflict between the international economy and a given national economy or between the aims and goals of a multinational corporation and a given national economy is not reconcilable, then that economy is not suited to the operations of a multinational corporation, and the latter should go elsewhere in the world for its investments.[2]

1. Brooke and Remmers, eds. *The Strategy of Multinational Enterprise: Organization and Finance* (London: Longmans (1970)), at 614.
2. Rogers, "Multinational Corporations: A European View", in Blake, ed., *The Annals of the*

Secondly, one can say that the control of the multinational (2) has *ceased* to be a problem because "[e]vidence exists in the actions of both the international companies and host governments that the role of foreign direct investment may be diminishing on the international scene..."[3] or, as it has been picturesquely described, the shadow of the multinational enterprise is caused by the setting rather than the rising sun.

One substantial addition may be necessary here; it might be more realistic to say that the shadow cast by the *American* multinational comes from the setting rather than the rising sun. American multinational activity reached its peak in the mid 1960's; and in examining legislation aimed at foreign direct investment, and the surrounding literature, it soon becomes clear that such legislation was initially and primarily an attempt to check the strong current of inflowing *American* investment. There is nothing astonishing about that. The U.S. at that time was indisputably the largest - if not the only significant - source of massive foreign direct investment. The tide, however, has turned. The flow of foreign direct investment in the industrialized world is now stronger in the east-to-west direction and the 'Problem' of control is thus, in part, taking care of itself by virtue of the investment flow seeking and establishing its own equilibrium, largely through protected and strengthened competition from Europe, where economic recovery from World War II was inevitably slower than in the United States, but which caught up surprisingly rapidly, due largely to the boost from American post-war aid programmes.

This turning tide, or more precisely to pursue the image, this 'undertow'[4] (as the outward flow from, for example, Europe is, to a large degree, a result of the inward flow, and very strongly reliant upon it for its own outward pull) was already gathering momentum in the early 1970's, and has only recently been given a mammoth stimulus by the more advantageous exchange on the U.S. dollar, the full implications of which cannot yet be calculated.

Thus, having asserted that the control of the multinational *per se* in the industrialized world: (1) is not, or (2) is no longer, effectively a Problem, but rather an Issue within which identifiable problems can and do arise, presenting a continuous challenge to legislators, government officials and lawyers alike, but, in the main, resolvable through the normal judicial and governmental

---

American Academy of Political and Social Science, Vol. 403, September 1972, at 64-65.

3. Behrman, "The Multinational Enterprise and United States Foreign Economic Policy", 52 *Indiana Law Journal* (1977), at 614.

4. "...the current beneath the surface that sets seaward...when waves are breaking upon the shore" (*Webster's New Collegiate Dictionary* [1977]).

processes, it must nonetheless be conceded that the current movement toward international controls did not originate spontaneously, and cannot be ignored. While the fears which arise within the host society tend to be primarily confined to the affiliated company's direct (or indirect) effects upon the individual host state, and the presumed threat to its sovereignty, even if such a threat is more imaginary than real, in one sense a Problem exists if only from the mere fact that one is seen to exist. Fears are real; and that indeed in itself constitutes a Problem. The fears primarily generated by the reverberations of the earlier explosive expansion in the 1960's have mostly proved groundless, or have since become outdated. And as one author writing in 1972 expressed it:

> When the present dispute between sovereignty and multinationalism subsides, and the dust settles down, a better reciprocal understanding will hopefully emerge, and most of the mistrust, doubts, and fears which have been expressed of late will vanish. This writer firmly believes that there is no case for an irremediable conflict between sovereignty and multinationalism. The alleged tensions between them are neither basic nor permanent, but they are rather the result of psychological reactions to spotty instances.[5]

Fears must be replaced by facts. One of the principal functions of the United Nations Center on Transnational Corporations has been the undertaking of a widespread fact- and information-gathering campaign which will hopefully alleviate apprehensions of the undisclosed. In the present work, an attempt will also be made to replace some of the questions regarding the existence or non-existence of controls by fact. The basic issues of control dealt with herein are approached through a systematic exploration of major legal responses to the fears as well as to actual instances of abuse - i.e. the legal techniques used, nationally and transnationally, to effectively control multinational activities from the moment of the MNE's application for entry into the host economy, through the entire duration of MNE operations within the host jurisdiction, to the moment - if that moment ever arrives - of expulsion (or expropriation) of the foreign enterprise by the host government.

This, then, is the main direction of the present study, namely, whether those existing legal techniques enumerated - or other potential legislation envisaged for application within the national legal framework - are sufficient to control, in practice, the MNE in all its operations, to an extent accepted as reasonable; or whether an international regime is required, in addition, in order to attain

5. Rogers, op cit., *supra* note 2, at 65.

the degree necessary and adequate for ensuring that any excesses or abuses on the part of the MNEs be minimized, while at the same time taking care to safeguard and maximize their recognized benefits to the host economies.

PART ONE: SETTING THE STAGE

Chapter I.

THE NATURE OF THE MULTINATIONAL ENTERPRISE

1. Preliminary Observations

It is widely recognized that one of the most significant changes in international economics and, consequently, international relations and politics in recent decades has been the dramatic growth of the private 'international' or 'multinational' business enterprise. The increasing frequency of trans-boundary operations in private direct investment carried out by such enterprises, and the resultant effects on the international flow of capital, materials, goods and technology, have caused academics as well as political and legal observers to regard this type of corporate entity as falling within the scope of international law and, concurrently, as possessing certain rights and duties under international law. These corporate enterprises, which are largely responsible for the vast expansion of business transactions across political boundaries, are considered juridically to be 'artificial persons,' created by law, and clearly have "that minimum access to legal processes transcending state lines - in the sense that they are authorized to make claims and be subjected to claims - which is the principal import of international legal personality."[1] Their involvement with the governments or governmental business operations of foreign countries may call for the application of international law or general principles of law and for direct recourse by the private corporations involved to international arbitration.

The very fact that the individual corporations which generally constitute a multinational enterprise are of different nationalities and have their assets in a variety of national jurisdictions, contributes to the remarkable strength and much-vaunted flexibility of these enterprises. It at the same time, however, poses legal and managerial problems which a strictly domestic company never encounters. Further compounding the difficulties is, for example, the fact that

1. Feliciano, "Legal Problems of Private International Business Enterprises: An Introduction to the International Law of Private Business Associations and Economic Development," 118 *Receuil des Cours* (1966 III), at 220.

by the Anglo-American rule nationality - for purposes of taxation, jurisdiction, enemy treatment in time of war, etc. - is attributed to a parent or subsidiary company according to its state of incorporation,[2] while by the continental systems, the corporation gains the nationality of the state where its center of management or *siège réèl* is located.[3] (Thus any given multinational can take on different nationalities depending on whether one stresses the place of incorporation of the parent, its *siège réèl,* the domicile or place of incorporation of its subsidiaries, or the nationality of its managers, directors and shareholders.) Some multinationals will clearly retain their national identity while others will have such a diversity of nationalities, through the above factors, as to be truly multi-national[4] by Professor Schmitthoff's definition ("a combination of companies of different nationality connected by means of shareholdings, managerial control or contract and constituting an economic unit"). "The multinational enterprise is," says Schmitthoff, "from the legal point of view, conveniently ambiguous: in many respects its subsidiaries are treated as national companies in the host countries but, as an economic unit, it does not lose its character as pertaining to the home country."[5]

It is perhaps important to note here that, in a strictly legal sense, a multinational enterprise can most simply be characterized as an aggregate of corporate entities, each having its own juridical identity and national origin, but each in some way interconnected by a system of centralized management normally exercising its control from the seat of primary ownership. Hence, although a 'corporation', strictly speaking, is a legal entity, the essence of the multinational enterprise is that it is "a political and economic fact which expresses itself in a bewildering variety of legal forms and devices," yet "has no coherent existence as a legal entity."[6] In other words, the particular legal status attributed to a 'corporation' is not valid for the enterprise as a whole, made up, as it is, of a number of separately incorporated entities.

2. See e.g. *Risdon Iron and Locomotive Works* v. *Furness* 1 K.B. 49[1906] (*re* law of place of incorporation for determining shareholder liability); also *National Bank of Greece and Athens* v. *Metliss* [1958] A.C. 509; also *Adams* v. *National Bank of Greece* S.A. [1961] A.C. 255.

3. See e.g. Stein, *Harmonization of European Company Laws, National Reform and Transnational Coordination* (Indianapolis: Bobbs-Merrill, 1971), at 29. Cf. *Cesena Suplhur Co.* v. *Nicholson* [1876] 1 Ex.D. 428; *De Beers Consolidated* v. *Howe* [1906] A.C. 455; *Egyptian Delta Land etc. Co.* v. *Todd* [1919] A.C.1; *Swedish Central Railway* v. *Thompson* [1925] A.C. 495; *Unit Construction Co.* v. *Bullock* [1960] A.C. 351.

4. See Tindall, *Multinational Enterprise: Legal and Management Structures and Interrelationship with Ownership, Control, Antitrust, Labor, Taxation and Disclosure* (Dobbs Ferry, N.Y.: Oceana, 1975), at 13.

5. Schmitthoff, "Multinational Enterprises," 121 *The New Law Journal* (1971), at 1053.

6. Jessup, *Transnational Law in a Changing Society,* Essays, edited by Friedmann et al. (New York, 1972), at 80.

It is, in fact, as expressed by Judge Jessup, the very "complexity of its legal structures, or rather of the interplay of legal entities and relationships constituting that structure, no less than the size of its resources or the scale of its operations, which makes its power so elusive and so formidable a challenge to the political order and rule of law."[7]

Acknowledging that multinational enterprises have existed here and there for nearly as long as the modern corporation itself and that some of their extraordinary modern powers reach back as far as a hundred years or more, it remains a fact that the global profit-seeking commercial enterprise as we know it has largely been a phenomenon of the mid-twentieth century. In broad terms, private direct investment by companies from the various industrialized countries, through legal corporate transactions in other countries, has grown in overwhelming proportions in the years between 1946 and the present day. The network of the multinational enterprise has taken on global dimensions.

It is precisely due to the legal problems which have arisen out of international business activities, that a body of law directed at such activities is beginning to establish itself. This body of law is still relatively new, and consequently, for the most part, still characterized by uncertainties of interpretation. This fact, coupled with the limitations, inadequacies and incompleteness of available data - where data are, in fact, obtainable at all - as well as the confidentiality which governs most internal records and statistics, contributes to the difficulty of objective studies and research into the legal aspects of control of these activities, and accounts in part for the relatively small, though increasing, body of legal literature on the subject. Recent moves to tighten up on disclosure legislation and regulations, on both the national and the international levels, may improve this situation somewhat.

We have already remarked that the corporate structures and operations of the multinational enterprise are varied and complex. We are aware also that the numerous jurisdictions within which they operate are equally diverse and complex. It is consequently inevitable that the economic power and legal ingenuity of multinational corporate enterprises should, again in the words of Judge Jessup, "sometimes be tempted to take advantage of the complexity of political and legal systems to create a world of their own which must accommodate itself in the conduct of its operations to many legal systems but is not in any real sense subject to any of them."[8] The recognition, in the foregoing statement, that the multinational business enterprise "must accommodate itself in the conduct of its operations to many legal systems" is most important, as the

7. *Idem.*
8. Ibid., at 72.

complexity of doing business simultaneously under a variety of differing legal systems poses its own particular difficulties for the centralized management characteristic of multinational operations, and provides a not insignificant source of control over those operations. The statement that the enterprise is accountable to a number of different national legal systems is, however, immediately countered, in its control inferences, by the remark that it "is not in any real sense subject to any of them." We are thus left with the dominant impression that the existing legal order is inadequate to control multinational business enterprises, and that such enterprises are not, "in any real sense", subject to any legal system. One must, with such statements, guard against being left with the false notion that the multinational enterprise, in its individual corporate activities, suffers no legal constraints. It is, in fact, subject to the laws of each and every state in which it carries on business. It is only the enterprise as a complete unit - that is, in the sum of all its individual corporate parts - which does not come under the control of a single comprehensive international authority. This distinction is most important.

In sum, the conduct of private business which exceeds national boundaries generates, in our present-day world, a myriad of different and complex legal problems. The question should be asked, however, is this a situation unique to foreign operations of multinational business enterprises? Do not domestic firms' operations likewise generate varied and complex legal problems, and are they not equally capable of dubious or illegitimate use of economic pressures and power? This is not to question whether there exists no real problem concerning multinational enterprises. If there were no legal problems, there would be no need for legal solutions.

This is to suggest, however, that legal control problems in 'international business' are not unique to the multinationals. Similarly, not all inter-state tensions over economic and financial relations are directly traceable to the business activities of the multinational enterprise. Many such tensions are political in origin, and would exist independently of the presence or absence of such enterprises.

The question is, then, is an international regime of regulation the ultimate solution, or are the legal problems which invariably arise largely resolvable within the current domestic legal framework and institutions available? Is 'control' (in the sense of 'regulation') in itself a 'problem' which requires an international collective response, or is control of the individual corporate parts of the enterprise, through national legislation, the best method of deriving the benefits of corporate foreign direct investment while guarding against excesses and abuses? Or might there, perhaps, be an essential role for both national and international regulation?

It is to these questions that the present work addresses itself, through an examination of the complexity of legal interrelationships and limitations among governments and international business enterprises, and through a look at the techniques used on the national level to control the power and influence of the multinational concerns, as well as an assessment of the prospects, feasibility and practicability of international controls.

Of course to attempt to deal in comprehensive detail with the many issues involved in a subject so vast and complex, under so many differing legal systems, would be a multi-volumed task. The present work is not meant to be a work of comparative law, although the relevant laws of the six highly capital-intensive states[9] selected to illustrate the current trends in foreign direct investment legislation are drawn upon, and their respective case law cited, where appropriate. Neither does the present study pretend to be an exhaustive treatise on multinational activities, nor can it even presume to be a totally exhaustive treatment of the control of such activities. While recognizing the urgent need for in-depth legal studies aimed at identifying, defining and analyzing each of the many-faceted issues of multinational corporate groups, the present study will be confined to examining the major aspects and techniques of control - actual and prospective (*lex lata* and *de lege ferenda*) - to which these corporate 'giants' are subject at present and by which they may, by intensified domestic regulation or by international consensus, be contained or regulated in the future.

It is hoped that the cumulative result will constitute a modest contribution to a vast and absorbing subject.

2. Limiting the Scope

It is well known that the primary thrust of MNE investment has shifted towards the industrialized markets and consumer-goods production, and away from the extractive industries characteristic of developing country investment.[10] In fact, over two thirds of the estimated 'book value' of foreign direct investment activities is located in the industrialized market countries,[11] facilitated by the relative homogeneity of their social, economic, political and

9. United States, Canada, United Kingdom, France, Germany and Japan.

10. Rosenberg, "Weighing the Power of the Multinationals" [bookreview of A.A. Said & L.R. Simmons, *The New Sovereigns: Multinational Corporations as World Powers* (Englewood Cliffs, N.J.: Prentice-Hall, 1975)], 11 *Stanford Journal of International Studies* (1976), at 209.

11. United Nations, *Multinational Corporations in World Development,* United Nations publication E/5500/Rev. 1; ST/ESA/6, Sales No. E.74.II.A.5, New York, 1974, at 8.

judicial institutions. The most 'modern' forms of investment are foreign production or distribution facilities, licensing of patents and technological know-how, managerial contracts, etc.; and this type of investment occurs predominantly in highly industrialized economies, where there is a ready demand and where the infrastructure (general social, political and economic services) is reliable and instills confidence in the investor.[12] It has, in fact, been reported that the nine EEC member states, together with the United States and Japan, constitute almost the sum total of countries required by the multinationals for their economic expansion,[13] while another author has cited the same states as those where "the most influential economic forces at work are located."[14]

Moreover, in the developed states, where a reasonably stable political structure has existed long enough to give governmental policy and legal solutions sufficient continuity to be of interest in our study, the development of legal means of dealing with the multinational are more easily traceable and more juridically significant than in the developing world where, due to historical forces, such a continuity is often lacking.[15] The additional fact that most of the legal innovations in the area of foreign direct investment emanate from the industrialized nations, and that both the major source and ultimate target of MNE investment, as well as of MNE controls, is primarily the industrialized world, makes the industrialized sector the obvious focus for a study on legal aspects of MNE control.

Hence, due to the fact that only a small percentage of all foreign investment is now carried out in developing countries,[16] that such investment is of a limited nature and that the investment problems of the less developed nations and those of the advanced industrialized states differ substantially in kind - those of the developing nations tending to fall more in the politico-socio-economic sphere, and those of the developed states arising generally in the legal arena - the concentration of this work will center on the legal ramifications of multinational activities in these technically advanced nations, rather than on the wider implications of their presence in the developing world.[17]

12. Fulda and Schwartz, *International Trade and Investment, Regulation of* (1970) (University Casebook Series), (Mineola, N.Y.: The Foundation Press, Inc., 1970), at 570.

13. Reese, "Multinational Companies and the Nation State," 28 *Studia Diplomatica* (1975), at 196.

14. Abraham, *Big Business and Government: The New Disorder* (London: MacMillan, 1974), at 145.

15. *Idem.*

16. Less than one third of MNE investments are situated in the developing world. (See *International Chamber of Commerce Bulletin,* "Multinationals," Vol. 40, No. 6 (July-August 1974), at 1.)

17. For a comprehensive coverage of this aspect see *The Impact of Multinational Corporations on Development and on International Relations,* United Nations publication E/5500/Rev. 1; ST/ESA/6 (New York, 1974).

This orientation, however, is not intended to turn away those legal scholars or policy makers concerned with the developing nations from reading the following pages; to the contrary. It should not be forgotten that the United States itself, now indisputably one of the major capital-exporting states, was once an 'emerging nation', whose rapid growth in economic strength was due in no small part to the impetus supplied by substantial foreign capital and investment. The emerging nations have a vital interest in what there is to be said about direct investment of the major capital-exporting nations and should not divest themselves of their share in the benefits of those investments on account of an understandable but self-defeating overreaction to some well-known, but by no means universal, instances of abuse. It must not be overlooked that, even prior to the more recent exposures, statistics have shown that multinationals often have had a better record of serving the community than have their local counterparts. The very exposure of a variety of abuses, and the concurrent publicity keeping them in the public focus and accelerating the elaboration of codes of conduct, the moves toward international controls, and the burgeoning national regulatory legislation aimed at the MNEs, provide possibly some of the strongest deterrents to future abuses. The present climate will tend to force those enterprises which might otherwise be lax in their public responsibilities to the community - or even delinquent in that regard - the be on their best corporate behavior; and it can only prove detrimental to the continued economic growth of the developing nations to encourage the diversion of an increasing percentage of foreign capital, and the accompanying benefits, to the developed world by enacting over-restrictive legislation or creating an insecure investment climate. It is in the interest of the developing nations to take heed of the turning tide of foreign capital toward the industrialized markets and to assess the effects of that swing upon their own economies before it is too late. For this reason, the following pages are addressed as much to the interests of the emerging nations as to those nations whose laws and policies are actually discussed. Both sectors have something to learn from the experiences of the other.

For example, the approach of the less developed nations has been described as follows:

> To establish a degree of local 'control' over the foreigners, the less-developed countries (LDC's) have often enforced joint-venture or share-participation schemes on investors or assigned specific industries to the limbo of government operation. These schemes have served to create what investors call 'a bad economic climate,' to limit badly needed investment in the LDC's, and to reduce the foreign exchange earnings of LDC's into the bargain.[18]

The industrialized nations, on the other hand, have long since realized that economic self-sufficiency is not compatible with economic growth. Jean-Jacques Servan-Schreiber, writing in 1968, asserted that:

> If Europeans want to control their economic growth - and thereby their destiny - they can no longer afford the luxury of economic nationalism. An important book has shown that the system we call socialism has little chance of achieving its effort to build a modern economy within the narrow framework of the medium-sized European state....If a country insists on getting along on its own national efforts, it either will dissipate its resources with little to show for it, as in the case with France and Britain, or it must concentrate its efforts on a few areas and not compete in others that are crucial to tomorrow's society, as Germany, Italy, and Belgium have done. This is why any attempt at economic self-reliance by the individual European nations would simply mean their abstention from technological progress, and a stagnation that would eventually become intolerable.[19]

The dilemma might be summed up by the conclusions of Raymond Vernon in his article, "Economic Sovereignty at Bay":

> There is a stubborn life and purpose in the system of nation-states, and there is a tenacious capacity on the part of mankind indefinitely to disregard the seemingly inevitable...even when the apparent cost of the identity and control seems all out of proportion to its value.[20]

Hence, the developing nations should take heed. In their great surge of nationalistic enthusiasm, resulting in part from what they see as years of unjust exploitation of their natural resources by foreign investors, many of these nations are putting themselves in jeopardy by turning a blind eye to the economic benefits, technological development, and heightened living standards which are otherwise widely acknowledged to accompany foreign investment.

18. Rolfe and Damm, *The Multinational Corporation in the World Economy; Direct Investment in Perspective* (New York: Praeger, 1972), at 31. Cf. "Der Investor sollte sich willkommen fühlen," *Frankfurter Allgemeine Zeitung,* 22 November 1979, at 13, which reports: "Wer ausländische Investitionen haben will, der soll dafür ein günstiger Klima schaffen, der Investor solle sich willkommen fühlen." ("Anyone who seeks foreign investments should create a more advantageous climate; the investor should feel welcome.")

19. Servan-Schreiber, *The American Challenge* (London: Hamish Hamilton, 1968), at 114.

20. Vernon, "Economic Sovereignty at Bay," *Foreign Affairs,* October 1968, at 120-122.

The fact of the matter is, of course, that the MNE is neither all good nor all bad, and what all nations should be seeking, through international law and other channels, is to increase and consolidate the benefits while decreasing and eliminating the abuses. This should be the primary aim of control. Whether or not this can better be accomplished by national legislation or by some form of international control system, or by a combination of the two, is what we will be primarily considering in Part Five of the present work.

3. Definitional Aspects of the MNE

a. Definition of terms relating to the structure of the MNE

Along with the growth of this complex organism we have been calling the multinational enterprise for the purposes of the discussion thus far, has emerged a plethora of terms to define it and its relations (relations 'by marriage' as well as 'blood' relations) and offspring. Before defining the multinational enterprise itself, it is necessary to define some essential terms used to distinguish the various legal relationships associated with multinational operations. The following terms are those most widely used, and their definitions are here composed from a wide assortment, as no definitions have been universally recognized as authoritative.

A *parent company* is simply a company with ownership and control of foreign direct investment.

A *branch* or *branch office* is a local office of the parent company that operates at home or abroad and has no independent or corporate status. (From a legal point of view, it is no more than a physical extension of the parent company and not a separate juridical entity.)[21]

The *headquarters* or *head office* is the seat of central organization of an enterprise, sometimes established in 'tax havens' or 'profit sanctuaries', such as Liechtenstein, the Bahamas, Panama or Hong Kong where low taxes and other favourable financial incentives attract foreign operations, but normally located in the 'home state' of the parent company.

The *home state* (sometimes referred to as the 'capital-investing state') is the nation of origin of any foreign direct investment of its residents or (parent) companies.

21. Kolde, *International Business Enterprise,* 2nd ed. (Englewood Cliffs, New Jersey: Prentice-Hall, 1973), at 186.

The *host state* (also known as the 'capital-importing state') is the recipient nation of any foreign direct investment (normally represented in some form of 'affiliate' of a foreign parent company). Of course any state can be simultaneously both 'home' and 'host' in its foreign investment activities.

An *affiliate* refers to any daughter or associated company or entity of direct investment abroad, without regard to its legal form (but most commonly a 'subsidiary' or an 'associate'), established under the laws of the host state on an equal footing with the parent company, in terms of their respective national legislations.

A *subsidiary* is an affiliate in which the parent company has a controlling, or 'majority' interest.[22]

An *associate* is an affiliate in which the parent has a non-controlling, or 'minority' interest.[23]

The object of the above definitions is merely to facilitate the defining of the 'multinational enterprise' itself, a task which we will now approach with justifiable caution.

b. Analysis of current usage

In the hundreds of articles and other publications on the subject in recent years, we come across the whole range of references from 'international', 'multinational', 'transnational' or 'global', to 'plurinational', 'supranational', 'anational' or 'cosmocorp', depending on the particular purpose at hand, or on the semantic preferences or legal concepts of the writer. In practice, we might say that a number of these terms refer to an 'ideal' of the future, so we shall ignore those in the context of the present work. We will, however, attempt to establish some distinctions between 'multinational' and 'transnational', the most commonly used terms, normally used in combination with such substantives as 'firm', 'company', 'corporation' and 'enterprise'.

Among the latter, justifying the selection of the term 'enterprise' for the present study is relatively straightforward. As mentioned earlier, the multinational entity is simply not a company (or firm) or corporation in the legal sense, but is, rather, an aggregate group or network of corporate and non-corporate entities, established under the domestic laws of different nations and thereby endowed with different nationalities, and assuming correspondingly different

22/23. "Majority-owned" means that the subsidiary's parent company holds 50-94% of the voting stock; "minority-owned," 5-49%; "wholly-owned," 95% or more. (Vaupel and Curhan, *The Making of Multinational Enterprise* (Boston: Harvard Business School, 1969), ch. 3, cited in Vernon, *Sovereignty at Bay, the Multinational Spread of U.S. Enterprises* (London: Longman, 1971), at 141.)

legal forms. The term 'enterprise' is the most suited for covering all the many and varied forms of corporate and operational interrelationships, while clearly indicating that the entity lies outside the conventional corporate model. It is worth noting that the 'Group of Eminent Persons', engaged by the United Nations to study the impact of "multinational corporations" on development and international relations, registered general agreement that the word "enterprise" should be substituted for the word "corporations", but retained the term "multinational corporation" for the sake of conformity with the wording of the Economic and Social Council resolution 1721 (LIII).[24] Special note is also made in the earlier United Nations report on *Multinational Corporations in World Development*[25] that "corporation" is not used in that context as a legal term, but rather, "in accordance with common usage" as reflected in the above resolution. In a legal discussion then, without the aforementioned constraints, the term 'enterprise' can be taken as the most appropriate, and is the one used in this study wherever referring to the multinational entity as a composite unit.

As regards making appropriate distinctions between the attributives 'multinational' and 'transnational', the primary obstacle is that there is simply no generally accepted term, nor even a general agreement on what nomenclature corresponds to what category of distinctions; moreover, each of the terms is currently applied in quite opposite senses in different quarters. While not absolutely crucial to intelligible discussion, it is useful to be aware of this discrepancy. The two main trends of thought on the use of the terms 'transnational' and 'multinational' are that espoused unilaterally by the United Nations and that representing general usage outside of the U.N. context. These two main - and opposing - trends of thought could be graphically illustrated as follows:

	GENERAL USAGE	UNITED NATIONS
TRANSNATIONAL	Ownership/Control transcending national boundaries (i.e., multiple parenthood)	Operations/Activities across national boundaries (uni-national parent)
MULTINATIONAL	Operations/Activities in more than one nation (uni-national parent)	Ownership/Control by nationals of more than one nation (i.e., multiple parenthood)

Figure 1

24. See United Nations, "Report of the Group of Eminent Persons to Study the Impact of Multinational Corporations on Development and on International Relations," in *The Impact of Multinational Corporations on Development and on International Relations,* United Nations publication E/5500/Rev. 1; ST/ESA/6, Sales no. E.74.II.A.5, N.Y., 1974, note 2, at 25.

25. United Nations, *Multinational Corporations in World Development,* op.cit., *supra* note 11, at 4.

Thus, whereas in general usage 'transnational' is a term descriptive of ownership and/or control, in United Nations parlance it describes the extent of operations or activities. Conversely, in general usage 'multinational' describes the extent of operations, whereas in United Nations parlance it describes ownership and/or control distribution.

While the United Nations' use of 'transnational' to focus concentration on operations rather than on ownership is completely valid and correct conceptually, the implication is that these operations are emanating from a single locus. United Nations experts[26] make it clear that the designation is not meant to exclude enterprises of multinational ownership, and yet the term seems less than adequately flexible to cover the various other forms of commercial co-operation between, for example, free-market countries on the one hand and, on the other, state-planned economies which do not allow for participation in typical transnational relationships characteristically created by private economies.

While acknowledging that the problem of regulation and control, to which we shall be turning, is a legal and not a semantic one, an etymological approach can clarify such juridically important elements as, for example, whether the prime stress rests on operations and activities, or on ownership and (managerial) control. Clearly, for purposes of regulation - and this, after all, is the prime concern from a legal viewpoint - it matters little whether the ownership is uninational or plurinational or whether the direction is voiced in one or in many languages; what matters is the activities to be regulated.

In practice, in fact, there is often little or no attempt on the part of researchers and policy makers to confine themselves to rigid definitions of the multinational. For example, the most exhaustive American study of the economic implications of multinationals recently carried out by the United States Tariff Commission define them as "any U.S. company engaging in foreign direct investment in production facilities"; while the Canadians normally include under the rubric any foreign-owned firm, regardless of size, producing in Canadian territory.[27]

26. Karl Sauvant (U.N. staff member) in a private discussion at the United Nations, New York, December 1974; also Odette Jankowitsch (U.N. consultant) in a lecture given at the Faculty of Laws, University College, London, 20 November 1974.

27. Lea and Webley, *Multinational Corporations in Developed Countries: A Review of Recent Research and Policy Thinking* (Washington, D.C.: British-North American Committee (1973)), at 1-2. In the Canadian Government's report on MNEs, nonetheless, they are defined considerably more narrowly as "the embodiment of foreign direct investment by a single business enterprise which straddles several economies (a minimum of four or five) and divides its global activities between different countries with a view to realizing over-all corporate objectives." (Government of Canada, *Foreign Direct Investment in Canada* ("Gray Report") (Ottawa, 1972), at 51).

The Institut de Droit International, at its 1977 Oslo Session [28] did adopt a resolution on multinational enterprises, which provides, in its paragraph I, a 'legal' definition of the MNE, asserting that:

> Les enterprises formées d'un centre de décision localisé dans un pays de centres d'activité, dotés ou non de personnalité juridique propre, situés dans un ou plusieurs autres pays, devraient être considérées comme constituant, en droit, des entreprises multinationales.[29]

It does not yet appear, however, that this definition has enjoyed wider acceptance as an official legal definition of the MNE.

4. Operational Aspects of the MNE

a. Principal legal and organizational forms and structures

The ambiguities of definition can be compounded by the constant variability of the MNEs' legal form, particularly if such definitions rely in whole or in part on criteria of size or legal or organizational structure. The number of subsidiaries may increase or decrease from month to month; or joint ventures may be formed or dissolved; or 'mergers' or takeovers may occur between different parent companies. Moreover, very few enterprises share the same organizational form, partly because of differences in the corporate laws of the home state governing the parent, and partly due simply to different strategies or operational requirements on the part of the corporate management itself. Since there are no specific rules of international law governing the organization of MNEs,[30] their form, as already observed, tends to be a kind of 'juridical improvisation'.

28. Institut de Droit International, *Annuaire,* Vol. 57, Tome II (Session d'Oslo 1977, Travaux préparatoires (suite); Délibérations de l'Institut en séances plénières), (Basel, Switzerland: S. Karger, 1978).

29. While the French text is the only authoritative text, the Institute provides an English translation as follows:

> Entreprises which consist of a decision-making centre located in one country and of operating centres, with or without legal personality, situated in one or more other countries should, in law, be considered as multinational enterprises.

30. See e.g. *Case Concerning the Barcelona Traction, Light and Power Company, Ltd.,* (Belgium *v.* Spain) [hereinafter cited as *Barcelona Traction* case] (Second Phase), *I.C.J. Reports* 1970, p. 3, at 56 (separate opinion of President Bustamente y Rivero). (On the *Barcelona Traction* case see *infra* Chapter XII: 7.)

The number of possibilities for organizational variations within the MNE structure is augmented by the fact that not only does each individual enterprise have a wide variety of organizational forms available to it as a total enterprise, but each component unit of the enterprise also has a number of forms of legal organization to choose among, according to the municipal and commercial laws of the state of incorporation or domicile under which it is instituted and regulated (e.g., England: partnership, corporation (public or private), limited liability company, joint-stock company, etc.; France: *société à responsabilité limitée, société par action,* etc.; Germany: *Gesellschaft mit beschränkte Haftung* (G.m.b.H.), *Aktiengesellschaft* (A.G.), *Kommanditgesellschaft* (K.G.), *offene Handelsgesellschaft* (O.H.G.), etc.) Other than to point out this additional scope for variation, while acknowledging that not all forms are equally amenable to MNE affiliation, it is not the purpose here to further describe the municipal corporate forms, but to emphasize the numerous combinations available to any given multinational enterprise.

There are, nevertheless, despite the almost infinite range of organizational possibilities, some major organizational forms worth pinpointing.

(1) Parent-affiliate

One of the principal agencies for private foreign direct investment is the 'affiliate' (a 'subsidiary' or 'associate' as opposed to a 'branch', or mere production facilities abroad, for example), which we summarily touched upon in our basic definitions. In either form of affiliation - subsidiary or associate - the key factor in the relationship with the parent is not the actual amount of capital interest (or ownership) as much as the extent of managerial control on the part of the parent company. This notion of reliance on control as a criterion in intra-corporate relationship gains support from the statement in *In Re Investigation of World Arrangements* (*Oil Cartel* case)[31] that:

> If a corporation has power, either directly or indirectly, through another corporation or a series of corporations, to elect a majority of the directors of another corporation, such corporation may be deemed a parent corporation and in control of the corporations whose directors it has the power to elect to office.

31. *In Re Investigation of World Arrangements (Oil Cartel* case), 13 F.R.D. 280, 285 (D.D.C. 1952).

Traditionally, MNE's have had a preference for wholly owned subsidiaries, largely due to the earlier linkage of control with ownership but there has been a notable shift in this tendency, as we shall see later when examining certain aspects and techniques of control. As share ownership is not always - as is now widely recognized - commensurate with the extent of managerial control, this writer would suggest that the operative words in distinguishing the subsidiary from the associate are "effective control" as regards the former and "substantial interest" as regards the latter. As our concern in the present study focuses on control, it is the subsidiary form of affiliation in which our interest will lie.

It should be noted that a company can be an affiliate of another by means of contract as well as stock ownership[32] and management control. This relatively new method of acquiring a controlling interest represents a shift in the system of intra-corporate controls as well as in the legal relationship within the larger intercorporate network, in that conflicts in such cases would fall under the scope of contract rather than company law. This type of nonequity affiliation will be referred to again when we come to examine the various techniques of control involving the MNEs and their relationships with governments. There we shall see that for jurisdictional purposes, the crucial issue is indeed not so much one of ownership as one of control or "substantial link"[33]; ownership and ownership forms are significant only insofar as they represent real and effective managerial control.

It might be worth briefly mentioning here the 'sub-subsidiary' or 'sub-affiliate', which is a corporate entity established by an affiliate of the parent company rather than by the parent itself, as this can lead to very complex legal ramifications in that the semi-autonomous relationships established between the affiliate and sub-affiliate can complicate the control system of the parent company and result in serious legal difficulties (the sub-subsidiary, in effect, treated as it is as a subsidiary of the ultimate holding company[34]).[35]

(2) Joint venture as a form of MNE

Additional to this fundamental form of MNE structure, *viz.*, the aggregate

32. Wilkinson, "International Accounting: Harmony or Disharmony," *Columbia Journal of World Business,* March-April 1969, at 32.

33. See e.g. *Barcelona Traction* case, loc. cit., *supra* note 30, at 9.

34. Schmitthoff, "The Role of the Multinational Enterprise in an Enlarged European Community," in Bathurst, et al., eds., *Legal Problems of an Enlarged European Community* (London: Stevens & Sons, 1972), at 214.

35. The potential legal complications when, for example, trading-with-the enemy legislation is involved, are obvious.

of various types of affiliated corporate entities, is another legal form of association, the 'joint venture'. In the joint venture, the financial interest is sometimes said to be equally divided between two or more companies of different national origins. Such a definition, however, fails to distinguish between equity and nonequity participation, while other definitions which do take into account nonequity or even disproportionate equity participation (e.g., minority positions) may equally distort the true picture by failing to eliminate firms whose shareholders include the general public. Although such an arrangement of partially corporate-owned and partially individual-owned shareholdings could be classified, from a purely legal point of view, as a joint venture, it ignores the concept of true 'partnership', which is the fundamental idea of joint companies. Professor Endel J. Kolde elucidates this distinction when he says that:

> there can be no partnership in the pure sense of the word between a foreign corporate owner and the local or, for that matter, the international stockholders of an enterprise. Although the stockholders are entitled to exercise control over the company's activities, they do not legally share in practice in the management and direction of the firm.[36]

Professor Kolde puts forward what would seem an adequately inclusive definition of the international joint venture when he calls it:

> a business enterprise in which two or more economic entities from different countries participate on a permanent basis. When the partners' rights stem from their equity participation, the enterprise is classified as an equity joint venture; when one or more of the partners have made no equity contribution, the enterprise is a nonequity joint venture.[37]

He continues by pointing out that "from a legal standpoint, the equity joint venture is a creature of company or corporation law, while the nonequity joint venture is based on contract law." We will look more closely at the various types, combinations, modes of participation and operational techniques of joint ventures when we consider the whole aspect of control in later chapters.[38]

36. Kolde, op. cit., *supra* note 21, at 192.
37. *Idem.*
38. See *infra* Chapters IX, X.

b. Relation of legal form to managerial control

One could, here, proceed to an analysis of more complex legal structures, such as those enumerated by Robert Tindall,[39] which include "linkages based purely on contract", "linkages based on cross-shareholders and external non-legal co-ordination devices", "jointly owned holding companies", "jointly owned operating companies", etc.; but while some of these forms will be touched upon in later chapters, the important thing to keep in mind at this juncture is that the real structure of the MNE cannot be ascertained by merely examining its legal form. Since the legal form of the entity varies in any case according to the dictates of the different legal systems, the actual organization of any one unit as a branch, a subsidiary or an associate may in fact be of little consequence. Moreover, the legal structure, basically designed for cash-flow and tax purposes, in accordance with governmental regulations, is not always even an accurate reflection of the true distribution of management and control functions. "In fact," writes one lawyer, "some authorities on the organization of MNE's have concluded that 'legal structure can be ignored'."[40] After all, "it is beneficial rather than legal control which counts....Similarly it is effective control over the appointment of the majority of directors on the subsidiary's board which counts, whatever the legal form through which that control is exercisable."[41]

Although the *de facto* structure of an enterprise, i.e. the actual managerial and control hierarchy among the various affiliates and the parent, may constantly fluctuate - for example, at one stage the parent may wish to deal with a particular subsidiary at 'arm's length' for tax purposes, while at another stage, for purposes of avoiding possible incidents of intra-enterprise conspiracy in contravention of antitrust regulations, the parent may wish to exercise tighter control - foreign subsidiaries "generally retain a considerable amount of tactical discretion and autonomy for routine, detailed, short-term (2-3 year) operations."[42] According to the International Legal Center:

> It is partially the attempt to obtain this delicate balance between autonomy and control which has spawned the wide range of legal and organiza-

39. Tindall, op. cit., *supra* note 4, at 72-73.

40. Griffin, "The Power of Host Countries over the Multinational: Lifting the Veil in the European Economic Community and the United States", 6 *Law and Policy in International Business* (1974), at 380, 381; also Stopford and Wells, *Managing the Multinational Enterprises* (London: Longman, 1972), at 10.

41. Hadden, *Company Law and Capitalism* (London: World University, Weidenfeld and Nicolson (c. 1972)), at 289.

42. Griffin, loc. cit., *supra* note 40.

> tional forms ... but no single organizational form has been able to service the needs of public enterprise over time, and hence the need for maintaining a high degree of organizational flexibility can hardly be overstressed.[43]

The significance of the legal form of the MNE as it relates to managerial control has been summed up well by one legal writer who states:

> The distinction between one or another form may have very important tax or other legal consequences, but, in the sense of the relation between internationalism or foreignness, of ownership or control, and national jurisdiction or sensibilities, it is probably not very relevant. What is important is the fact that in each situation a productive activity is taking place in the jurisdiction of one country (the host) which is to some substantial extent under the control of nationals of another country (the home); and that the nationals of that country in which control resides are themselves subject to the jurisdiction of the state of their nationality.[44]

Hence, once again, the central factor becomes not the actual legal form, but effective control, and the locus from which that control is being exercised.

Despite the almost infinite variety of legal and organizational forms open to the MNE, there is a characteristic common to all, and that is that the separate parts ideally function as one economic unit. The variations of inter-connection constituting the legal structure are of secondary importance, as in each case the legal arrangement which binds the parents and their subsidiaries and their associates will be determined by individual contract or local laws. The unified aim is to achieve consolidation while preserving the corporate individuality of each national member of the greater enterprise.

In order to simplify to the extent that some relevant comments can be made, one can safely say the principal legal form of the multinational enterprise is simply an aggregate of variously organized companies, incorporated, as stated above, under a variety of legal systems, but controlled centrally by a parent company, and thus forming a single economic unit.

It is not fortuitous that the most common form of multinational corporate organization is a cluster of affiliates; the control which a parent company is able to exercise over its locally incorporated foreign subsidiaries is a prime

43. International Legal Center, *Law and Public Enterprise in Asia* (London: Praeger Publishers [c. 1976], at 56.

44. Rubin, "The International Firm and National Jurisdiction," in Kindleberger, ed., *The International Corporation: A Symposium* (Cambridge, Massachusetts: MIT Press [1970]), at 181-182.

reason for the preference of the MNE to operate through these agents as the best means of protecting its corporate assets and valuable technology, while providing maximum flexibility.

Moreover, as we are reminded by Christopher Tugendhat, "subsidiaries are judged not by their individual performance, but by the contribution they make to the group as a whole. Thus a subsidiary which records a loss but whose operations prevent a rival from moving into one of its parent company's more profitable markets may be fulfilling a more valuable task than a subsidiary with a better financial record."[45] In other words, the activities of an affiliate may be less geared to meeting its own commercial objectives than they are to meeting those of the enterprise of which it is a part.[46]

5. Terminology Selection and Definition Formulation for Purposes of the Present Study

While it may seem that an inordinate amount of attention has been devoted to defining the MNE and its legal and organizational structures, it is obvious that, while for certain purposes distinctions among the various terms or forms may be of only limited import, some basic working terminology and definitions are necessary for any discussion on controls, even if for no other reason than that without a working definition on what constitutes a multinational enterprise there is nothing to indicate to just what categories of enterprises any international control guidelines would be applicable.[47] Or, in practical terms, as pointed out by the U.N. Commission on Transnational Corporations, the related Information and Research Centre would surely require a working definition as a basis for gathering information, and "the elaboration of a code of conduct would require a general understanding as to which companies it was intended to cover."[48]

45. Tugendhat, *The Multinationals* (New York: Random House, 1972) at 11. This is reminiscent of the "defensive investment" concept of Alexander Lamfalussy who, with reference to domestic capital formation, observed that some investment is aimed not at gaining profits but at avoiding losses.

46. Dunning, *Economic Analysis and the Multinational Enterprise* (London: Allen & Unwin, 1974), at 364.

47. A similar recognition on the municipal level is evidenced by the statement of Clive M. Schmitthoff that a definition of the MNE should be adopted for purposes of identifying what enterprises fall under the provisions of the British companies regulation. (Schmitthoff, "Multinationals in Court," *Journal of Business Law,* 1972, at 103-111.)

48. United Nations, *"Commission on Transnational Corporations: Report on the First Session,* (March 17-28, 1975)", Economic and Social Council, Official Records: Fifty-Ninth Session, Supp. No. 12, U.N. document E/5655, E./C.10/6, at 12.

Hence, while we cannot here presume to establish any official definition for universal use, it is expedient, for purposes of consistency and clarity, to select the terminology and formulate a definition which will at least adequately serve the purposes of the present work. In the present study, then, the term "multinational enterprise", which in the writer's view lends itself to the broadest spectrum of international corporate direct investment activity, will be used in its wider application to indicate any commercial enterprise, public or private (or combined public/private), of uni-national, bi-national, or multi-national ownership, under any one or combination of legal and organizational forms of association but necessarily having a number of directly-controlled operations in various states, normally performed through affiliated companies established under the national legal systems of each host state and thus under correspondingly varied legal arrangements, yet collectively tending toward a 'global perspective' and functioning as a single economic unit. In other words, juridically speaking, it is simply the extension of ownership or control into many states, by means of international operations, that makes the enterprise multinational; and international law has been using the term as one which has, up to now, proved flexible enough to cover all aspects of "an institution which in many ways is a kind of juridical improvisation."[49]

6. Conclusion

What we ultimately have in the MNE then, is a directly (or indirectly) controlled single enterprise composed of a number of affiliated business establishments, each functioning simultaneously in different countries, and ideally characterized by centralized control and decentralized decision-making, resulting in a kind of 'unity in diversity'.[50] And of all the essential or possible criteria one might mention, the one that is absolutely crucial and common to every form of multinational enterprise - and correlative with the obvious propensity to have a considerable collection of foreign branches and affiliates - is: central direction.

49. Jankowitsch, loc. cit., *supra* note 26. Clive Schmitthoff, writing in *Legal Problems of an Enlarged European Community,* takes the position that "it would be more correct, though cumbersome, to refer to the group as a multinational business organisation." Op. cit., *supra* note 34, at 211.

50. Cf. Behrman, *Some Patterns in the Rise of the Multinational Enterprise* (Chapel Hill: Graduate School of Business Administration, University of North Carolina, 1969), at 62; Kolde, op. cit., *supra* note 21 at 134; also "Multinational Business Enterprises", prepared by A.J.N. Judge, Union of International Associations, Brussels, 1970 for *Yearbook of International Organizations,* 1968-1969.

This "centralization of policy and...integration of key operations among the affiliates"[51] enables a tremendous wealth of human and material resources from different nations, with sometimes 'centrifugal tendencies', to function together in a legal framework as an economic unit. Such centrality of management control has been possible only since the development of modern-day rapid and reliable communication systems and air travel, not to mention computers efficient in handling an endless input of information never before possible on such a scale. One can see, then, that the prime importance of discerning the true seat of control within the MNE economic unit, with a view to external legal controls, is clear: if external controls are not aimed at the nerve center, or at least at the point of policy and decision-making, such controls can only be of negligible effectiveness.

With this in mind, we shall, in the next chapter, take a closer look at the particular relevance to MNE regulation of the relationship of internal to external control systems, from which it will become evident that locating the actual point of decision-making is not always an easy task. In addition to the fact that the internal corporate control structure of each individual enterprise differs according to the numerous variables we have already mentioned, along with others such as the degree of experience and proficiency of the parent, the extent of experience and economic maturity of the subsidiary - which, of course, will itself vary from subsidiary to subsidiary even within the same MNE - there are yet other factors which lend to determining control centers, factors such as general trends to increase centralization or to decentralize managerial control, trends which themselves can be influenced by still other external political, social and economic factors, and which are relatively unpredictable.

The vast scope of activities of an MNE, far from being limited to investment of monetary resources or even of managerial know-how, extends, as we have seen, to the determination and co-ordination of various legal forms of organization and ownership affiliation, and, as we shall see later, to the entire 'functional spectrum' ranging from distribution of products to advanced on-the-spot research and to the physical location and plans of production facilities, and even to relations with foreign governments and peoples. In sum, "multinational enterprise represents the totality of organizing and operating business establishments in an international context."[52] It is hardly surprising that in the course of operations of these 'energetic' enterprises, conflicts of national interest and of jurisdiction will sometimes ensue. The industrialized

51. Behrman, quoted in Eels, *Global Corporations* (New York: Interbook, 1972), at 25.
52. Kolde, op. cit., *supra* note 21, at 136.

nation-state, however, has not proven to be a helpless bystander, and governments have responded with restrictive legislation and counter measures. The situtation is summed up as follows, by consensus of the Jamaican Roundtable:

> The nationstate is not withering away. Instead it will grow in terms of its role in organizing and improving the social standing and entire environment of its people.... By and large, multinational corporations and nationstates have many parallel interests. When tension does occur, accommodation should be accomplished on a case-by-case basis.[53]

At the risk of oversimplifying, one might say that the externalized responses to the internal 'fears' have taken basically two forms: one is non-legal and consists of "meeting the 'enemy' on his own ground", which translates into a challenge for host countries to step up their own foreign investment initiatives (emphatically endorsed by Servan-Schreiber in his *Défi américain*[54]); the other is a legal one, which finds its official expression in bilateral or multilateral treaties and agreements as well as in a plethora of existing and emerging domestic legislation, particularly in areas of disclosure, taxation, investment controls and restrictive business practices.

The fundamental aims of control, then, should be to deal legislatively with any genuine sources of conflict, to allay fears that foreign MNEs infringe upon national sovereignty and ultimate industrial independence, and to curb any abuses or excesses committed by MNEs in such specific areas as tax avoidance, transfer pricing, repatriation of profits, restrictive business practices, or any other practices potentially detrimental to the host state and its national interests. Broadly, as expressed earlier, the primary aim of control should be to increase and consolidate the benefits of MNE activity while decreasing and eliminating the abuses. It is to this interplay of private and governmental policy, and to resultant legislative restrictions, then, that we shall direct our attention in the pages which follow.

53. From discussions of the Roundtable for Chief Executive Officers, organized by Business International, Jamaica, January 6-10, 1971. (See Barnet and Müller, *Global Reach* (London: Jonathan Cape, 1975), at 59-60.)

54. Servan-Schreiber, *Le Défi américain* (Paris: Denoël) 1967. (English edition: *The American Challenge,* op cit., *supra* note 19.)

Chapter II.

IMPORTANT PRELIMINARY DISTINCTIONS *RE* CONTROL AND CONTROL RELATIONSHIPS

1. National *v.* International Control

Having submitted that the aims of control over multinational enterprises, broadly speaking, are to minimize the detrimental effects and maximize the beneficial effects of MNE investment activity, the two obvious general means for effectuating such control are through national legislation and through international regulations or guidelines. It is important to recognize that these two levels of regulation are not mutually exclusive; they both play a part in 'international' control measures. What must be kept in mind is that 'international control' is not necessarily synonymous with a single international regulatory system or agency, nor are 'national controls' confined purely to domestic law. National controls become directly involved in the international law arena through, for example, conflict of laws, extraterritorial extensions of domestic legislation, bilateral and multilateral treaties, conflicts of jurisdiction, and simply conflicts of national interests. Some of these issues belong to the private international law sector, some to the public international law sector, and some to both. Moreover, while certain problems may arise on the international or regional level, most originate, at least, at the national level.

For reasons already reviewed in the previous chapter, we cannot, in the context of a single work, explore control legislation on a global scale.

Hence, in the ensuing pages, we shall consider the national and regional responses of the industrialized nations to the 'fears' and areas of conflict arising out of MNE activity, as expressed in various types of domestic legislation and legal techniques aimed at regulating MNE activity within national jurisdictions. We shall approach this task by first reviewing briefly some basic aspects of intra-company control, as well as the inter-reacting control relationships among home and host governments and multinational enterprises, which must first be understood in order to fully appreciate the complexity of the control issue and of its legal implications, whether on the national or on the international level.

2. Internal *v.* External Control

We have said a good deal in Chapter I about control - in particular that centralized control is the *sine qua non* of the multinational enterprise. In that context, the term 'control' has referred to the internal command hierarchy and organizational structure of the individual enterprise in its intra- and intercompany relationships. But control is not a single clearly defined issue; it is, just as the MNE itself, a many-faceted phenomenon, appearing in many forms and expressing itself in a variety of ways, requiring some distinctions to be drawn.

a. Distinctions: internal *v.* external/*de facto* v. *de jure* control

In juridical terms, internal and external corporate control are quite distinct from one another, primarily in that while the latter relies on the legal requirements of individual municipal law systems, the former asserts itself less through formal legal impositions (although a number of formal internal regulations do exist - often redundant where the parent already wields effective control over affiliates) than through managerial control techniques and such financial control mechanisms as the generally *ad hoc* review and approval of capital projects by headquarters, or the employment by headquarters of remittance policies, which, through a systematic repatriation of foreign earnings, enables the parent, by so holding the purse strings, to exercise a considerable degree of regulatory power over the subsidiary. Under German law, a corporation can gain this financial 'upper hand' contractually, through a *"Gewinnabführungsvertrag,"* or contract-to-transfer-profits, by which one corporation obligates itself to turn over all of its profits (or losses) to another. The obvious benefit to the subsidiary company - as this is, after all, a contractual agreement, which presupposes the mutual consent of the parties - is the assumption of financial responsibility by the controlling parent for any losses which the subsidiary may sustain.[1] So far there is no evidence that this has been applied outside the purely national business organization in Germany, but the law would not appear to preclude a wider application extending to the MNE.

Whatever a company's form of extra-legal internal control mechanism, it is obliged to operate within a framework of legal regulations. The legal (or *de*

1. See §§. 291(1), 302 and 303 of the German Companies Act *(Aktiengesetz)* of 1965, *Bundesgesetzblatt* [BGB1] 1965 I S.1089, amended by Art.1 of the *Gesetz vom 13.12.1978* BGB1 1978 I, S. 1959; last amended 4 July 1980 (BGB1 1980 I S.836). See also *infra* note 13 and text accompanying notes 7 and 23.

jure) form of organization is imposed upon a company by its own official charter, drawn up within the limitations of the respective domestic legal system, as well as by the legal specifications contained in most democratic municipal systems, relating to ownership distribution, numbers of stockholders, qualifications for company officers, and so on. In the British system, for example, a company's charter, or "memorandum," defines the limitation of its powers; and there exists:

> a direct relationship between the conception of the company as a distinct legal entity and the rule that a company may not legally carry out any activity which is not expressly or impliedly authorized by statute or by the list of objects and powers in its own memorandum of association. Any such activity is *ultra vires*,...in that the legal capacity of the company is held to be exhaustively defined by the Companies Acts and its own constitution.[2]

The managerial (or *de facto*) organization, although influenced by the statutory one, is not always coincident with it, but rather, in many cases, bestows the actual control upon persons other than the legally prescribed officers and directors. It becomes necessary, then, in drawing distinctions between internal and external control, to distinguish at the same time between the command or managerial organization and the statutory or juridical form.

A serious dichotomy has arisen where the radically changing managerial structures, which are constantly being altered to meet the ever-changing needs of an evolving and diversifying corporate enterprise, have not been accompanied by a concurrent evolution of the corporate legal structure. A majority of the existing legal provisions, whether these be the statutory provisions or the memorandum or articles of association of the corporation, are not universally designed simply with the criterion of commercial efficiency in mind. Consequently, they rarely lend themselves to the requisite levels of managerial performance or competitive efficacy.

Yet a company cannot ignore the legal requirements simply because they may be ill-suited to the firms's functional objectives; nor can it overlook the necessity, juridically, for a structure of legal stature, which will endow it with the right to operate in any number of different countries for the optimization of benefits to the overall enterprise. Accordingly, a *de jure* structure is set up which satisfies all the requisites of legal existence, based on municipal laws and

2. Hadden, *Company Law and Capitalism* (London: World University, Weidenfeld & Nicolson (c. 1972)), at 47.

regulations. But since, managerially, the need is for an instrument which will lend itself to the necessary centralized co-ordination, planning and evaluation of operations and personnel, it is the *de facto* command or management which, in reality, exercises effective control.[3] In light of this dichotomy, it is not surprising that the tendency is for managment to consider the legal structure, such as it is, as a 'necessary evil' or 'incidental necessity'; nor is one apt to disagree with the writer who suggests that "for purposes of 'internal' and 'external' control the law has not fulfilled the role that it might or should."[4]

For example, some U.S. parents have a strong tendency to surround their subsidiaries with numerous formal restrictions, legally limiting their areas of doing business, etc.,[5] but as long as control is secure, headquarters may well sacrifice the interests of any single wholly owned subsidiary to the strategy of the overall enterprise, with little regard for the restrictions previously imposed.[6] In German law, this right to give to the executive board of an affiliated company directives which may be disadvantageous to it, though favourable to the enterprise as a whole, is given legal sanction under a contract of domination (*Beherrschungsvertrag*) in Section 308(1) of the German Companies Act (*Aktiengesetz*) of 1965; [7] and a similar scheme is being explored by the EEC.[8] Of major significance here is the fact that, while the German *Aktiengesetz* ostensibly gives legal authorization to domination of one company by another, at the same time it provides the subsidiary with protection against abuse by regulating the conditions under which domination may exist and by affording special safeguards for cases of *de facto* though non-contractual domination. In English company law, the Companies Act[9] defines the legal re-

3. Kolde, *International Business Enterprise,* 2nd ed. (Englewood Cliffs, N.J.: Prentice-Hall, [1973]), at 190.

4. Tindall, *Multinational Enterprises: Legal and Management Structures and Interrelationship with Ownership, Control, Antitrust, Labor, Taxation and Disclosure* (Dobbs Ferry, N.Y.: Oceana, 1975), at 154.

5. It is currently under debate as to whether these arrangements, even though carried on within one enterprise, might not be contravening antitrust regulations. This issue, however, does not seem to have been satisfactorily resolved at this time.

6. See Vernon, *Sovereignty at Bay; the Multinational Spread of United States Enterprises* (London: Longman, 1971), at 135 [hereinafter cited as *Sovereignty at Bay*].

7. Loc. cit., *supra* note 1.

8. See Leleux, "France, Belgium, the European Economic Community and the Multinational Enterprise," in Hahlo, ed., *Nationalism and the Multinational Enterprise: Legal, Economic and Managerial Aspects* (Dobbs Ferry, N.Y.: Oceana, 1973), at 134 *et seq.* France, also influenced by the German Act, proposed legislation in August 1974, dealing with groupings of companies whereby under a *contrat d'affiliation,* a dominant company would control the operations of the affiliates under a single centralized management and assume some of their liability.

9. British Companies Act 1980 c.22.

lationship of 'holding' and 'subsidiary' companies not in contractual terms, as in German law, but simply in terms of the control of one company by another;[10] thus it is effective control over the appointment of a majority of directors on the subsidiary's board, rather than actual ownership of shares or voting power which is decisive. The legal form is largely irrelevant.[11] This holding company/subsidiary arrangement has been strongly contributory to the widely recognized separation of control from ownership and is thus partially responsible for the *de facto* separation of the managerial structure from the legal form.

Of course the MNE is not within the terms of reference of the British Companies Act, but British company law has at least taken notice of the existence of the MNE,[12] and as the observations are applicable as well on the multinational scale, they seem worth noting here, particularly in connection with the German *Aktiengesetz* which does make some provision for the multinational group, and because English company lawyers are raising serious questions as to the adequacy of the traditional legal framework, in the face of the modern MNE, to deal with the increase in managerial power which has been steadily and effectively displacing shareholder control.

While readily acknowledging, in contemplating internal *v.* external control, that there is a wide divergence in the provisions of municipal company laws of different nations and in the degree of parent company liability under each system,[13] it is important to take into account that there is also a variation from company to company within a single legal system, and even from subsidiary to subsidiary within a single MNE, depending on such factors (assessed not according to legal norms but by the controlling management of the parent company itself) as the degree of experience, self-sufficiency and proven reliability of the affiliated company;[14] its organizational form (joint venture, wholly or

10. Ibid., § 154.

11. Hadden, op. cit., *supra* note 2, at 289.

12. See e.g. reference to "oversea companies" in Part X of the Companies Act 1948 (§§ 406-423).

13. The law of the parent company governs the extent of liability of the parent for acts and even debts of the subsidiaries, giving rise to an extremely complex problem of private international law. Liability may even be assumed by contractual agreement, as in the *Gewinnabführungsvertrag* of the German Companies Act *(Aktiengesetz)* of 1965, §§ 302, 303 (loc. cit., *supra* note 1). See also text accompanying note 1, *supra*.

14. Research has shown that, at least in the case of U.S. parents, supervision tends to decrease in proportion as the subsidiary gains experience (Vernon, *Sovereignty at Bay,* op. cit., *supra* note 6, at 133). It has also been suggested that the degree of autonomy granted to foreign affiliates is, to some extent, correlated both with environmental and operational peculiarities and simply with their tendency to increase in size (Kolde, *International Business Enterprise,* op. cit., *supra* note 3, at 190).

partially owned subsidiary, etc.); whether it is a state or privately owned enterprise; and other similar criteria. And paradoxical as it may seem, the degree of internal or 'personal' control exercised by a parent over its affiliates is influenced not only by the extent of experience of any individual subsidiary, but also by the degree of experience and proficiency of the parent itself. It is, after all, not unreasonable to expect that "experienced parents with on-going systems for the direction and control of their subsidiaries" will tend to follow one pattern, while "inexperienced parents, uncertain of their ability to direct a foreign subsidiary"[15] will be likely to adopt another. This could explain why, contrary to popular opinion, some of the stronger multinational 'giants' often tend to afford a far greater degree of independence to their subsidiaries than do smaller or younger enterprises still feeling their way in the international arena and still learning to cope with their growing responsibilities.

Similar distinctions can be drawn between "subsidiaries that are to be integrated tightly into a well-articulated global strategy [exemplifying the "reality of the dialectic contradiction between the legal separateness and factual interdependence of affiliated or 'related companies' "[16]] and those that are expected to lead a semi-independent life."[17]

The one element common to all the internal control systems is that delicate matter of striking a proper balance between centralized and decentralized control. While it is recognized that *over*centralized planning and decision-making is often unprofitable, ineffective and self-frustrating - a poor substitute for the judgment of local managers in the field and an impediment to the ideal of international management - it is deemed paramount for the parent to at least set broad policy guidelines and to rationalize operations in such a way as to ensure the capacity to "co-ordinate and guide activities of a large number of far-flung affiliates into a unified whole."[18] For this reason - and given the basic incompatibility of decentralization schemes with the increasing tendency of the courts to hold the parent company accountable for the acts of its subsidiaries[19] - despite the vaunted ideal of decentralization, the most prevalent current trend, as we have seen, is toward centralization. After all, no unified system can function without a nucleus, or base of operations, which not only retains ultimate control but also bears ultimate responsibility.

15. Vernon, *Sovereignty at Bay,* op. cit., *supra* note 6, at 131.

16. Bringezu, "Parent-Subsidiary Relations under German Law," 7 *International Lawyer* (1973), at 140.

17. Vernon, *Sovereignty at Bay,* op. cit., *supra* note 6, at 131.

18. Yoshino, "Toward a Concept of Managerial Control for a World Enterprise," *Michigan Business Review* (March 1966), at 25.

19. See e.g. the *Dyestuffs* case (*Imperial Chemical Industries Ltd.* v. *E.C. Commission,* 2 CCH *Common Market Reporter* [1969]).

When any legal difficulties arise within these internal systems - such as a contractual dispute between parent company and subsidiary, a challenge by shareholders to the powers of the directors with respect to the establishment of a foreign subsidiary, or other such management/shareholders disagreements - a resolution of the conflict is usually achieved internally, based on the council of the company's own legal advisers, occasionally with the aid of external company lawyers. The complexities increase, of course, when the internal managerial control system, concerned essentially with efficiency and geared toward a global perspective, comes into conflict with the external local government legal system, directed toward broader social and political objectives[20] and contained within a prescribed geographical area; or further, when the local government legal system, as a result of a conflict of interest arising from MNE activities, runs headlong into confrontation with an alien legal system, functioning outside those prescribed geographical confines.

Where the external legal problems arise within a single national unit of the enterprise, it is, again, the municipal company lawyer who is called in; while the conflict of laws expert (or private international lawyer) is the best equipped to deal with cases where the wider jurisdictional questions arising from relationships of one or several subsidiaries to each other or their states of incorporation, or to the parent company or its national government, are involved. Here we have clearly entered the domain of international law, since the whole area of the conflict of laws is largely coextensive with that of private international law.

b. Relation to international law

It has been suggested that "jurisdiction in international law has nothing to do with the question of municipal law whether certain State organs have jurisdiction in a given case, whether, for instance, a Court has jurisdiction to entertain certain proceedings, or whether an Inspector of Taxes has jurisdiction to set aside an assessment. These are matters of internal[21] organization in which international law does not ordinarily have an interest."[22] While this is of course indisputable, it is nonetheless true that there not only exists a correlation between the internal control systems of an enterprise and external municipal

20. Whether or not commercial enterprise internal control mechanisms are compatible with a broader role is open to speculation. Some actually predict a return to the historic role where companies were conferred with broad social and quasi-governmental responsibilities. (See e.g. Tindall, op. cit., *supra* note 4, at 171.)

21. 'Internal' here, meaning internal to the state, is not to be confused with the purpose for which it has been used throughout this chapter, to mean internal to the enterprise.

22. Mann, *Studies in International Law* (Oxford: Clarendon Press, 1973), at 2-3.

legal systems, and that each has an influence on the other, but that a similar relationship is evident between each of these systems and international law itself. For example, it is not difficult to recognize as external regulation municipal laws governing registration, audit, disclosure, taxation, and respect for the law in such pertinent areas as restrictive business practices (antitrust), investment codes, balance-of-payments codes, export controls and securities regulations; and preliminary moves for international agreements in just some of these same areas are already being discussed in legal and government circles. Some difficulty is encountered, on the other hand, in drawing such a clear line between external and internal control when it comes to the company charter and laws relating to shareholders, directors, and various other more internal matters. Taking this a step further, parallels could even be drawn, if one wished to pursue the question, between the remittance policies established by a corporation in respect to its foreign subsidiaries, and the formal legislative remittance and balance-of-payments controls of governments.

One prime example of the connection between internal or parent-subsidiary control systems and external or statutory regulation is the provisions contained in Book Three of the aforementioned German Companies Act (*Aktiengesetz*) of 1965[23] (the *sedes materiae* of the fundamental rules governing parent-subsidiary relations in Germany) for six different kinds of *contractual* arrangements (*Unternehmungsverträge*) by which parent-subsidiary relations are made subject to statutory recognition and regulation. The Act expressly recognizes the legal right, by contract of domination (*Beherrschungsvertrag*), of one company to assume control over another within an affiliated group. This contractual agreement links the internal corporate control system with the external municipal control system and lends legal status to a *de facto* position of dominance by transforming it into a *de jure* arrangement.

As regards the interrelationship of the internal corporate control system, as well as the municipal legal system, with international law, an illustration of "the international character of the basic concepts of company law" is furnished by the judgment of an international arbitral tribunal in the *Standard Oil Company* claim, over the issue of the extents and limits of shareholders rights:

> The decisions of principle of the highest courts of most countries continue to hold that neither the shareholders nor their creditors have any right to the corporate assets other than to receive during the existence of

23. See German *Aktiengesetz* of 1965, loc. cit., *supra* note 1, especially §§ 291, 292, 302, 303 and 308; see also Bringezu, op. cit., *supra* note 16, at 114-146; also Coing, "Germany and the Multinational Enterprise," in Hahlo, op. cit., *supra* note 8, at 88-98; also Leleux, in ibid., at 130-135.

> the company a share of the profits, the distribution of which has been decided by a majority of the shareholders, and after its winding up a proportionate share of the assets.[24]

Here, the issue of shareholders' rights, as much a problem of internal controls as of municipal company law, became a matter for judgment by an international tribunal. And the "decisions of the highest courts of most countries" were taken into account in deciding this international claim. The position held in this case was reaffirmed by the International Court of Justice decision in the *Barcelona Traction* case (Second Phase) in 1970, in which the Court also resorted to municipal law, given the fact that there is no corporate legislation for private entities in international law, to determine "the meaning, scope and limitations of the legal concept of 'corporation' (limited liability company, *société anonyme, société de capitaux, Kapitalgesellschaft)* as a...*question préjudicielle* on which depends the international law issues of the case."[25] The International Court, in turning to municipal law, "did not look into a given municipal law system but endeavored to extract a general concept of corporation which can be considered as a common denominator of all national legislation on the subject."[26] International law proceeds, after all, in part, from the general principles of law recognized by civilized nations, and what better evidence of a general principle than its embodiment in the municipal legal systems of a large number of states? Conversely, international law rules are often incorporated into the various municipal systems, which means that the interaction between the two is unquestionably reciprocal.

In addition, there are a great number of governments pursuing and enacting bilateral and multilateral treaties on some of the issues concerning the MNE, notably taxation and antitrust; and as more and more governments come to see the need for harmonization wherever practicable, there is increasing discussion of agreements of international application in some of the same selected areas as those just mentioned. There is, moreover, a move in some countries to bring the public and private sectors into closer association, which will also mean closer relations between business and governments, and hence, between municipal and international law.

24. *Standard Oil Co.* claim, United Nations, R.I.A.A. ii, at 777; 8 *British Yearbook of International Law* (1927), at 156.

25. *Case Concerning the Barcelona Traction, Light and Power Co., Ltd.* (Belgium *v.* Spain) [hereinafter cited as *Barcelona Traction* case], *I.C.J. Reports* 1970, p. 3. For the facts of the case and further discussion see *infra* Chapter XII: 7.

26. *Delagoa Bay Railway Co.* case (Great Britain *v.* Portugal), [1875], *Receuil des Arbitrages Internationaux,* Vol. 3 (1954), 596. See also Strupp-Schlochauer, *Wörterbuch des Völkerrechts,* Vol. 1, at 325; Moore, *International Arbitrations,* Vol. 2, at 1865.

c. Relevance of internal control to external legal controls

As regards internal, or 'personal' control within the enterprise, then, its relevance to the wider issue of external legal controls is directly related to the fact that external controls are virtually ineffective if they are not aimed at the effective control centers within the MNE's 'personal' control system. In other words, in considering any form of external controls, national or international, the legislators will have to bear in mind the locus of the effective internal controls in order for the external ones to have any impact. Any further preoccupation with these internal corporate control systems, for purposes of the present study, is limited to only those instances in which a parent company *loses* its control over a subsidiary through expropriation or some other external factor; or those in which the degree of influence (or 'agency') exercised over the subsidiary by the parent must be established in order to determine the locus of liability or jurisdiction in an international claim;[27] or instances where the degree of internal control exercised by a parent becomes the means of exerting, through one of its subsidiaries, an undue influence on the economic or political stability or security of a host state, thereby threatening the national interests of that state and producing an international incident; or, lastly, in any case where a question relating to the internal system becomes an issue in an international court action, as in the two cases cited above.

In talking of control of the MNE, whether internal or external, managerial or juridical, 'personal', municipal or international, the ultimate issue remains the same: who wields effective control, and how are those controllers to be controlled?

As noted in the preceding pages, international law has not, up to now, developed a system of international controls for business; but the import of the issue cannot be overstated. C. Wilfred Jenks, expressing what he felt te be the "fundamental issue" as "the relationship between the public interest and the economy when the scale of the economy dwarfs the representation of the public interest and the complexity of economic structures escapes the control of any government or legal system," went on to assert that "[t]his is an issue on the same order of importance for the future of international law as the control of force, the peaceful settlement of international disputes, the protection of human rights, [and] the provision of an adequate legal framework for a buoyant and expanding economy...."[28]

27. See e.g. the *Dyestuffs* case *(Imperial Chemical Industries, Ltd.* v. *Commission of the European Communities),* 2 CCH *Common Market Reporter* [1969].

28. Jenks, "Multinational Entities in the Law of Nations," in Jessup, *Transnational Law in a Changing Society;* Essays, Friedman, ed., (New York Columbia University Press, 1972), at 80.

We have set our course to examine more closely the claim that "the complexity of economic structures escapes the control of any government or legal system," by considering, through a look at some examples of domestic policies and regulations touching upon multinational business activities as well as at the evidence of actual cases, some of the techniques used within existing legal systems to assert governmental sovereignty and control over affiliates of foreign multinational enterprises.

3. Host-State Control over Foreign MNE Affiliates: Incentives and Inducements *v.* Unilateral Restrictions

It remains largely undisputed that the multinational enterprise - falling as it does simultaneously under a host of different jurisdictions - *when regarded as a whole,* extends beyond the controlling capacity of individual national company law systems and that it has developed an independence of action which to all appearances is beyond the reach of traditional legal restraints. But the oft-voiced allegation that the MNEs effectively evade national legislation on taxation, labour, etc., where it is in their interest to do so, is rarely, on closer investigation, borne out by fact. Even though the MNEs have expanded their production and marketing facilities around the globe, the fact remains that, ultimately, the individual state 'hosting' these activities is essentially concerned not with the MNE in its entirety as much as with that particular unit of the enterprise which operates within its territory[29] and with that local entity's foreign parent to the degree to which that parent makes decisions which directly or indirectly affect[30] the local affiliate or pose a potential threat to the host's particular national economy. The fears which arise within the host society, then, tend to be primarily confined to the affiliated company's direct (or indirect) effects upon the individual host state, and the presumed threat to its sovereignty.

Hence, while it is true that the multinational enterprise is generally seen to exhibit an extraordinary flexibility and mobility which enables it to manoeuvre adeptly among the many different legal systems to take advantage of the most favourable positions in the allocation of its operations; one still must ask whether it really "escapes the control of any government or legal system". This writer would agree that although "the preponderant portion of the enterprise,

29. Thereby falling subject both to its laws and to its jurisdiction by the simple territorial principle (see the *Lotus* case, [1927] *P.C.I.J. Reports,* ser. A., No. 10).

30. Cf. the 'effects' doctrine as established in the *Alcoa* case *(United States* v. *Aluminum Company of America),* 148 F. 2d 416 (2d Cir. 1945).

including the parent, is usually outside the jurisdiction of any single host government and, therefore, the enterprise is felt to have power over the host government[, t]here are... no entities with such power, and no enterprise is able to achieve this stature among the advanced countries at least.''[31]

The popular view which depicts the MNE as a totally unfettered, almost supernatural entity, above restraint, beyond the reach of law, ignores certain hard realities. More specifically, once production plants have been established in a particular location, it is rarely expedient for headquarters suddenly to uproot such facilities and transplant them elsewhere simply because conditions have become less favourable than they were at the time of entry. ''The vaunted mobility of the multinational is somewhat illusory,'' points out Seymour Rubin: ''certain activities are not movable at discretion. Much of the net worth of multinationals, like that of other large corporations, consists of fixed assets....[T]he image of a headquarters staff issuing orders, shifting resources, and generally acting in an interest which is possibly not that of home or host nation suggests power limited only by a dubious self-restraint. It is doubtful, however, that such power in fact exists...[E]ven the smallest of governments tends to develop a system of administrative controls, permits, and approvals which may substantially restrict mobility.''[32]

Some limitations are the product of the very nature of the MNE - for example, those of self-arresting growth, fixed assets, or co-ordination problems. Other limitations result indeed from legal restrictions imposed by host states - restrictions which normally take the form of total exclusion, exclusion from 'key sectors', 'discretionary' legislation and practice, including screening on a case-by-case basis, or 'conditional' entry, sometimes requiring joint ownership or joint management.[33]

Due to the characteristic lag of the law behind the event, national legal systems have been slow to enact legislation dealing specifically with MNEs or corporate groups[34] which function as a single economic unit; nor was the MNE in its present form foreseen when most of the corporate legal provisions which do exist were being formulated. Harvard's Detlev Vagts, for example, wrote in 1970: ''As the literature about the MNE grows exponentially, the question arises whether the legal profession should not be developing responses

31. Behrman, *National Interests and the Multinationals: Tensions Among the North Atlantic Countries* (Englewood Cliffs, N.J.: Prentice-Hall, Inc., (c. 1970)), at 4.

32. Rubin, ''The Multinational Enterprise at Bay,'' 68 *American Journal of International Law* (1974), at 476, 477.

33. Each of these types of legal restriction is considered in turn in Chapters III and IV *infra*.

34. German legislators were first to complete a system of rules on corporate 'groups' *(Konzerne)*. (See e.g. Leleux, op cit., *supra* note 23 at 134); also *supra* note 13.

to it. As yet it has not; statutory or case law reaction is virtually nonexistent and the secondary coverage is thin."[35]

Since that time, however, not only has a body of case law begun to emerge relating to MNE activity, but such highly developed states as England, Canada, Australia and Germany have begun to enact legislation aimed directly at MNEs (Britain's Industry Act 1975 (Part II),[35a] Canada's Foreign Investment Review Act.[36] Australia's Foreign Take-overs Act[37]), or at least at corporate groups (Germany's *Aktiengesetz*[38]). Moreover, as corporate entities have gradually become endowed by civil and common law systems (more through pragmatic adaption that through foresight) with a "capacity to act [within national legal systems] as legal units, with virtually all the perquisites...initially and normally attributable only to natural persons," and, by exercising such basic rights and accruing additional legal powers and privileges, and have been able to expand beyond their state of incorporation or principal place of business by means of "the cluster of rules which permit companies to own shares in other companies wherever situated, and allow the shares of local companies, created or having their principal place of business in the domiciliary jurisdiction, to be owned by companies and individuals located outside the jurisdiction,"[39] the juridical picture has begun to change. Cognizant of the new legislative and administrative demands resulting from the present-day coalescence of trade and investment activities and the consequent expansion of multinational operations through foreign-controlled affiliates into their own territory, governments are increasingly adapting their national laws to meet the challenge of foreign direct investment and to utilize it for their own national objectives. They should take care, however, not to abuse their power:

> Every legal system as it develops must grapple with the problem of placing an effective restraint upon power and insuring responsibility; this is the essence of the whole concept of due process of law. The forms and types of power which the law seeks and needs to control become more varied and complex, and the standards of responsibility which it seeks and needs to enforce more exacting, as society develops.[40]

35. Vagts, "The Multinational Enterprise: A New Challenge for Transnational Law", 83 *Harvard Law Review (1970),* at 739.

35a. Industry Act 1975. c. 68.

36. Foreign Investment Review Act 1973-74, *Statutes of Canada* 1973-74, c. 46.

37. Companies (Foreign Take-overs) Act 1972 (*Commonwealth Acts: Australia:* No. 134 of 1972).

38. *Aktiengesetz* of 6 September 1965, loc. cit. *supra* note 1, esp. sects. 15, 291, 338.

39. Angelo, "Multinational Enterprise", 125 *Receuil des Cours* (1968.III), at 448-449.

40. Jenks, op. cit., *supra* note 28, at 71.

In 1812, for example, "foreigners" were assured a "general license...to enter the dominion of a friendly power,"[41] according to U.S. Chief Justice Marshall in the *Schooner Exchange* v. *McFaddon;*[42] yet today a state has an unquestioned right to refuse entry to any foreigner or any class of foreigners,[43] a right of refusal which naturally extends to the MNE, as a bonafide 'legal person'. It is of course clear that, despite the possession of many of the basic rights of natural persons, corporations seeking entry into a foreign state encounter more restrictions than do natural persons, goods or capital.[44] Nonetheless, no-one today would dispute the virtually unlimited right of a sovereign state to prevent aliens - natural or legal persons - from entering into its territory; or, alternatively, if the state chose not actually to prohibit the entry of an alien, to prescribe in what cases and under what conditions that alien would be admitted. Sovereign authority equally rests with the state "to prevent the acquisition by aliens of rights, whether respecting property or otherwise in its territory."[45] According to the 'vested rights' theory, a state is under no obligation to confer particular substantive rights upon aliens, especially in the economic field.[46] Even the ultimate right to expel an alien whose presence is deemed to be not in the national interest is unquestionably accepted as residing within the sovereign powers of the nation-state. Such sovereign rights are derived from the municipal law of the host state, but it is international law which guarantees a state the right to decide who should form part of its population; and any attempt to deny a state that right "would be as serious a breach of international law as an attempt to take away the...state's territory or to change its form of government....[47]

Of course, once an alien MNE has gained entry according to whatever host-exacted conditions it has agreed to accept, that enterprise must recognize its subjection to all the legal provisions ordinarily applicable to commercial enterprises under the domestic legal system of the host. The host state, for its part, however, is also bound to certain legal obligations. Namely, once a state has admitted an alien into its territory, or bestowed upon 'him' specific substantive rights, that state has placed itself under certain international law obligations

41. This 'license was understood, of course, not to extend to a military force.

42. *Schooner Exchange* v. *McFaddon,* 11 U.S. (7 Cranch) 116 (1812).

43. Akehurst, "Jurisdiction in International Law," 46 *British Yearbook of International Law* (1972-1973), at 149-150.

44. See e.g. Kolde, op. cit., *supra* note 3, at 185.

45. Arnett, "Canadian Regulation of Foreign Investment: The Legal Parameters," 50 *Canadian Bar Review* (1972), at 234.

46. See Abi-Saab, "The International Law of Multinational Corporations", 2 *Annals of International Studies* (1971), at 108.

47. Akehurst, op. cit., *supra* note 43, at 150.

with respect to those rights, and must provide for their legal protection.[48] As the International Court of Justice pointed out in the *Barcelona Traction* case[49]: "When a state admits into its territory foreign investments or foreign nationals it is...bound to extend to them the protection of the law." This legal 'protection', however, is neither absolute nor unqualified, and whether or not in practice it extends to guarantees against discrimination is an important corollary which will be taken up in a latter chapter.[50]

Let us now turn, then, to the evidence of the trend of various types of domestic legislation and control techniques, and to some key cases, in order to determine whether or not the MNE, as so often alleged, does pose a genuine threat to the sovereignty of nation-states and whether or not the nation-state has, in fact, been reduced to the status of a "helpless observer" *vis-à-vis* the MNE.

1. Incentives and inducements

The legal techniques used by advanced host countries to implement policies dealing with foreign direct investment take two different fundamental orientations:
(1) legal inducements, and (2) legal restrictions. Though clearly, in concentrating on 'control', we shall leave aside the techniques aimed at legal inducements or incentives to investment,[51] it is important not to lose sight of that aspect of the relationship, and not to be left with the impression that all host legal motions are in the direction of restriction. There is hardly an advanced nation today which does not recognize the benefit to itself and to its economic growth of an inflow of foreign capital and foreign direct investment, and which does not compete to some extent for the resources and capabilities available through the multinationals. This, coupled with the fact that the objectives of the nation-state and those of the MNE are, at some points, essentially compatible, notably in the areas of economic growth and stability, lends support to the position that the benefits to the host tend to outweigh the potential risks. This is one reason why legal inducements to foreign investment, such as tax incentives, are not uncommon in industrialized nations.

48. See separate opinion of Judge Morelli, *Barcelona Traction* case, loc. cit., *supra* note 25, at 231-233.

49. Ibid., paras. 33 and 87, at 32 and 46 respectively.

50. See *infra*, Chapter V: 2.

51. E.g. low-cost loans, rents, and utilities; grants and assistance in personnel-training programmes; provision of land and production plants. (See Behrman, *U.S. International Business and Governments* (New York: McGraw-Hill, 1971), at 5.)

This being said, it is equally clear that in addition to acting as a catalyst to economic activity within and among the industrialized states, the multinational has also evoked overt and sometimes highly defensive reactions. Since it is the formulation of those reactions into restrictive legislation, or their instigation of legal 'control'[52] techniques which is our present concern, it is to that aspect of the host MNE relationship that we now turn.

2. Unilateral restrictions

Somehow it has been assumed that "multinationalism (or foreign ownership or control) implies conflict [and] from that assumption it is concluded that in the best interest of the 'host' state the multinational enterprise must be brought under control."[53] "Unfortunately," writes Henry King, Jr., the Chief Corporate International Counsel of TRW, Inc., "in the charged political climate of many countries, economic issues are too frequently presented as confrontations between foreign investors and local interests, whereas, in my view, there is a greater commonality of interest than of conflict."[54] It is obvious that "intelligent control has tremendous advantages over blind struggle,"[55] but as noted earlier, governments will occasionally enact legislation in the 'national interest' which departs from the efficiency criterion and obstructs the normal operations of a corporation, operating internationally, which happens to be efficient.[56] This, of course, ultimately can hardly have other than a deleterious boomerang effect upon the regulating (host) government itself. Clearly:

> The tension in 'host countries' between autonomy and self-sufficiency as opposed to gaining access to the most efficient means of production available through investment by foreigners, underlies the crucial regulatory problem. Here the full range of considerations supporting the necessity for decisive government intervention are encountered.[57]

Somehow a solution must be found which meets the requirements of the na-

52. In the remaining pages the term "control" is used to mean legal control - whether municipal or international - *external* to the 'personal' systems of the enterprises themselves, as distinguished in Section 2 of this chapter.

53. Rubin, "Multinational Enterprise and National Sovereignty; A Skeptic's Analysis," 3 *Law and Policy in International Business* (1971), at 4.

54. King, "Foreign Restrictions on U.S. Investment," 11 *San Diego Law Review* (1975), at 28.

55. Bringezu, op. cit., *supra* note 16, at 139.

56. See Kindleberger, *International Economics* (Homewood, Illinois: Richard D. Irwin, Inc., 1968), at 403.

57. Fulda and Schwartz, *International Trade and Investment, Regulation of* (1970) (Mineola, New York: Foundation Press, 1970), at xv (Preface).

tional interest without nullifying the benefits or obstructing the vital processes of the multinational. Otherwise neither the "commonality of interest" nor the individual and mutually beneficial interests of either party will be served. "The challenge then," writes King, "is for both parties to keep these common interests in focus. [The investor] must try to avoid actions which provoke, or provide an excuse for, such restrictions, and the host country must avoid primitive-type actions which serve no salutory economic or social purpose and work in the long run against its best interests."[58]

The difficulty here is that governments characteristically hold the belief that their national interests are dependent upon a strong indigenous capacity. Canada, particularly sensitive in this area, largely as a result of its unique position *vis-à-vis* its extensive capital-exporting neighbor, has, in three government reports,[59] called specifically for restrictive legislation thought to be in the national interest, aimed at limiting the freedom of the MNEs and at blocking the extraterritorial application of foreign laws, in an obvious effort to maintain domestic control while reducing external 'interference' to a minimum. Yet it is difficult to reconcile this policy with the findings disclosed in one of these reports, that, "it is often the large foreign multinational which has the most up-to-date technology and is able to make a product available at prices which, in the short run at least, are less than the cost of indigenous development."[60] The official Canadian stance is no more easily reconcilable with the statement made by Canadian law professors I.R. Feltham and W. Rauenbusch at an international law conference in 1971 that "foreign investment has been significant, indeed essential, in providing the basis for prosperity in Canada"[61]; nor with the fact that most attempts[62] to implement 'Canadianization' policies have, on the whole, met with little success. In the words of the Gray Report: "some efforts have been made to stimulate Canadian ownership, but to date they do not appear to have any substantial impact on the pattern of ownership in the economy."[63]

58. King, op. cit., *supra* note 54, at 68.

59. (1) *Foreign Ownership and the Structure of Canadian Industry: Report of the Task Force on the Structure of Canadian Industry* (1968) ("Watkins Report"), Ottawa, 1968; (2) *Eleventh Report of the Standing Committee on External Affairs and National Defense* ("Wahn Report"), No. 33, House of Commons, 28th Parl., 2d Sess. 1969-1970; (3) *Foreign Direct Investment in Canada* ("Gray Report"), Ottawa, 1972.

60. Ibid. (Gray Report), at 335.

61. Feltham and Rauenbusch, "Canada and the MNE," in Hahlo, op. cit., *supra* note 8, at 39.

62. For example, the tax legislation (Bill C-259) passed by the House of Commons, Dec. 17, 1971 as An Act to amend the Income Tax Act, *Statutes of Canada* 1970-71-72, c. 63, effective Jan. 1, 1972, as an incentive to further 'Canadianization'.

63. Gray Report, op. cit., *supra* note 59, at 328.

That sums up at least the pre-1972 experience of the Canadian tentative toward national ownership. As Profs. Feltham and Rauenbusch point out: "All of these techniques are part of an over-all policy to counter extra-territoriality which we can call 'countervailing power'."[64]

The extent to which a host-state restricts foreign direct investment substantially reflects the extent of its own fears and is in proportion to the degree to which it sees its national goals and interests threatened. "It is unlikely," writes one English lawyer, "that serious tensions will develop in Europe between the host country and the multinationals and that it will be necessary for the host country to resort to the ultimate weapon of public policy. On the contrary, one may expect the relations between multinationals and their host countries to develop amicably, as this is in their mutual interest."[65]

European states which exhibit, particularly, an 'open' or 'very open' legal climate for investment, with few restrictions, include Britain, Denmark, the Netherlands and West Germany. Notable among other such states outside Europe are Australia and the United States. Even the most liberal regimes, however, utilize certain techniques to regulate inflow when it is deemed necessary to protect particular sectors of the economy, and both the 'intermediate' and advanced industrial societies have felt compelled to review past liberal policies which invited virtually unlimited and uncontrolled entry of foreign investment.[66]

In Australia, for example, the hitherto relatively free-handed investment activity has been curtailed by virtue of the Take-overs Law enacted in late 1972[67] which requires government review and approval of all foreign acquitition of shares - either by merger or direct acquisition - in Australian concerns. Even in traditionally 'open' West Germany, the amendment of the German Competition Law (*Gesetz gegen Wettbewerbsbeschränkungen*) in 1973[68] and again in 1980[69] has affected the freedom of acquisition and merger of the larger firms. Freedom in the financing of foreign-owned operations in West Germany also was threatened when, in the 1973 amendment of the West German *Aussen-*

64. Feltham and Rauenbusch, op. cit., *supra* note 61, at 81.

65. Schmitthoff, "The Multinational Enterprise in the United Kingdom," in Hahlo, op. cit., *supra* note 8, at 37-38.

66. Church, "The Multinational Enterprise" (Foreword), 11 *San Diego Law Review* (1973), at iv.

67. Companies (Foreign Take-overs) Act 1972, loc. cit., *supra* note 37.

68. *Zweites Gesetz zur Änderung des Gesetzes gegen Wettbewerbsbeschränkungen,* BGBl 1973 I S.1363.

69. *Viertes Gesetz zur Änderung des Gesetzes gegen Wettbewerbsbeschränkungen vom 26. april 1980,* BGBl 1980 I S.458; *Gesetz gegen Wettbewerbsbeschränkungen in der Fassung vom 24. september 1980,* BGBl 1980 I S.1761.

wirtschaftsgesetz,[70] section 6a bestowed governmental powers to impose tight exchange controls. Up to the time of writing, however, these new legal powers have not been applied, according to one German legal expert.

As each nation has its own particular historical experience and special peculiarities, each has approached the matter according to its own individual national policies and legal background. Canada's economic policy, for example, has, until relatively recently, been characterized by an essentially 'open' legal framework. Anyone, whether citizen, resident or alien, was free to "establish a branch of a foreign enterprise, incorporate a subsidiary or acquire an existing corporation without concern for exchange controls or controls on direct investment."[71] In fact, earlier in its history, Canada openly encouraged foreign investments, particularly from the United States, as a means of developing its economic strength. However, despite the large Canadian presence maintained in certain industries, resulting from public investment, fears of foreign takeovers have more recently caused restrictions[72] to be applied to foreign investments for the purpose of guarding specified 'key sectors'[73] from foreign control.

This interest in protecting 'key sectors' in the economy from foreign control is evident in the municipal legislation of many of the industrialized states, as we shall see in the following chapter. Where these and other unilateral restrictions do exist, they fall under three broad categories: (1) restrictions on entry and establishment, (2) restrictions on operations once the affiliate is established, and (3) restrictions terminating or leading to the termination of operations; or, more simply, (1) entry, (2) operations, and (3) disinvestment of foreign-controlled enterprises. In the following chapters, each of these categories will be considered individually, in an attempt to assess the effective control capacity, on the national level, at each stage of MNE investment within foreign territory.

70. *Aussenwirtschaftsgesetz* [AWG] *vom 28. April 1961* (BGB1 I S.481) *in der Fassung des 2. ÄndG vom 23. Februar 1973* (BGB1 1973 I S.109) (AWG *Lieferung 8/76 vom 25. August 1976,* at 12.)

71. Feltham & Rauenbusch, op. cit., *supra* note 61, at 53.

72. Notably, the Foreign Investment Review Act, loc. cit., *supra* note 36.

73. See *infra* Chapter III: 2; also Chapter III, note 100.

PART TWO: TECHNIQUES OF RESTRICTIVE HOST-STATE CONTROL OVER FOREIGN MNE AFFILIATES: ENTRY AND ESTABLISHMENT

Chapter III.

EXCLUSIONARY TECHNIQUES AT ENTRY

Restrictions on MNE investment are greatest at the time of entry, when the bargaining position of the host is at its height. It is at this point that the host state can either prohibit entry altogether, or exercise its utmost degree of bargaining power and exploit its capability to influence the location of facilities in economically depressed or otherwise designated areas, and to exact other conditions such as export performance, local equity participation, the presence of nationals on the board of directors, procurement of services, or any other considerations deemed favourable to the host economy. This is the point at which negotiations are strictly between the host government and the parent company, the one offering its conditions and terms of entry and operations, the other deciding if those conditions are acceptable. Of course, the resources of the MNE, in terms of management and technology, are frequently of sufficient value to the host country that the enterprise can negotiate for the establishment of an affiliate on terms that involve little or virtually no local control.[1] This has sometimes been the case with highly technical industries such as IBM. In most cases, however, the bargaining power of the two parties is more equally balanced, the principle of course being that, while the foreign investor has something of value to offer the host, the host also has a valuable asset for the investor - access to its economy and domestic markets. Each state, after all, controls access to its territory, and that access is the 'life-blood' of the multinational.

1. Griffin, "The Power of Host Countries Over the Multinational: Lifting the Veil in the European Community and the United States", 6 *Law and Policy in International Business,* (1974), at 407.

1. Total Exclusion

At the height of the restrictive scale, the fullest utilization of a sovereign state's prohibitive power is outright denial of entry. This denial technique is certainly a lawful exercise of a state's sovereign will, but it could be argued that control by total exclusion is really no control at all. While this technique is not viable in today's economic climate, and is not practised in its extreme form by any industrialized state, Japan can nonetheless be cited as coming the closest to an adherence to this principle in practice.

Japan was one of the earliest and most active proponents and practitioners of the 'total exclusion' approach - not only of MNEs *per se,* but of any form of foreign direct investment. The Japanese government adopted its restrictive policy toward foreign investment in the immediate post-war period and continued to pursue it into the late 1960's. The policy was simply to keep out virtually all foreign direct investment in order to foster national economic growth and exports. The subsequent slight relaxation of Japan's exclusive policy toward foreign investment was only the result of persistent and increasing criticism and pressures from both commercial and political sources, coupled with its desire for membership in the Organization for Economic Cooperation and Development (OECD) which requires acceptance of and adherence to its Code of Liberalisation of Capital Movements[2] - a code which is incompatible with outright or even unreasonable exclusion of foreign investment. Very active in foreign direct investment itself, Japan could no longer afford to compromise its own investment activities by continuing to hold its exclusive position *vis-à-vis* investors seeking entry into its own market. A certain amount of reciprocity had come to be expected from other investing states.

No other state within the focus of our study has practised 'total exclusion' of MNEs or other forms of foreign investment, although virtually all such states have techniques of *selective* exclusion, as we shall see in the following pages.

It would appear, then, that the 'total exclusion' approach is:

> not... a viable alternative to any country unwilling to sever completely its ties with the Western commercial and financial world, and even those countries which have had the most highly developed concerns about the

2. See *infra* note 11. The success of Japan's unique response to foreign investment previous to its liberalization tentative was largely attributable to its aggressive pursuit of advanced foreign technology through active promotion of licensing agreements with industrialized nations. (See Okita and Miki, "Treatment of Foreign Capital: A Case Study of Japan", in Adler, ed., *Capital Movements* (New York: Macmillan, 1967)).

MNE have shrunk back from such a step. Eschewing regulation in its most extreme form - prohibition - host governments have concentrated on developing control mechanisms felt to be most responsive to their individual needs.[3]

2. Exclusion from 'Key Sectors'

A somewhat moderated exclusion technique which is widely used as a control mechanism is the 'key sector' approach, whereby foreign investors are excluded, or severely limited in their allowable aggregate percentage of share acquisition, from certain categories of activities considered particularly vital to the national interest - particularly those relating to national security and defense matters and cultural identity.

Notable among those states which seek to protect closely their key sectors are Sweden, Norway, Switzerland and Japan, which exclude or restrict foreign investment across wide and major segments of their economies, especially in natural resources. Others which have adopted the key-sector-exclusion technique, but less categorically and to a lesser degree, are Italy, Austria, France and the United States.[4] The list clearly includes some states which are accepted generally as possessing quite 'open' economies. Hence, it is safe to assume that the protection at least of vital 'national interest' key sectors is considered to be more an expression of the normal exercise of national sovereignty than a political or judicial policy of economic exclusivity. Some states, however, might be seen to extend their 'key sector' protection well beyond the vital 'national interest' category. Japan, for instance, has indicated twenty-two protected industries, including data processing, real estate, and drugs.[5]

The criteria serving to establish key sectors are often ill-defined, and can obviously vary markedly according to country, relying, as they do, on historical and political factors particular to each state. Japan, with perhaps the broadest of all spectra of protected 'key sector' industries, has divided its industry into

3. Vagts, "The Host Country Faces the Multinational Enterprise", 53 *Boston University Law Review* (1973), at 271.

4. See Canadian Government, *Foreign Direct Investment in Canada* ("Gray Report") (Ottawa: Information Canada, 1972) [hereinafter cited as the Gray Report], at 331.

5. See Andrews, "An Evaluation of the Need for Further Statutory Controls on Foreign Direct Investment in the United States", 8 *Vanderbilt Journal of Transnational Law* (1974), at 164. For a complete list of the twenty-two protected industries see Japanese Ministry of Finance and Foreign Department, International Finance Bureau, Bank of Japan, *Manual of Foreign Investment in Japan* (1974), [hereinafter cited as *Manual of Foreign Investment in Japan*], at 1-2.

"sectors subject to different degrees of liberality as to the degree of foreign participation that would be tolerated."[6] Japan's overall degree of toleration began at a low level, its earliest manifestations occurring in such safe industries as motor-cycles, cotton textiles, sake brewing, barber shops, beauty parlors, parking lots, amusement parks, toys and wigs.[7] Although Japan announced a liberalization programme in 1973,[8] following a succession of earlier government liberalization programmes in this area beginning in 1967,[9] the extent of "liberalization" has continued to be notably limited. The token moves which have been made have only been in response to increasing pressures on both commercial and political fronts-criticism, for example, from the United States for what it has seen as blatant contradictions between Japan's investment statutes and its commitments under the United States/Japan Treaty of Friendship, Commerce and Navigation[10] as well as under the Convention of the Organization of Economic Co-operation and Development (OECD)[11] with its Code of Liberalisation of Capital Movements, applicable to all member nations, and the General Agreement on Tariffs and Trade (GATT)[12] with its Preamble calling for, *inter alia,* "the elimination of discriminatory treatment in international commerce." Since becoming a member of OECD, Japan has of course had to progressively relax, at least officially, some of its severest restrictive policies toward inward direct investment, but it has still retained a high degree of control over a broad spectrum of the economy, with particularly tight control over such sectors as the automotive, electronic, data processing, photographic and oil industries.

France has had, since 1967,[13] a system, similar to Japan's, though appreciably less restrictive, aimed at separating out those foreign investments that are to be excluded,[14] i.e., those that would intrude upon its 'key sectors'. Aeronautics would rank high among France's reserved sectors.

6. Vagts, "The Host Country Faces the Multinational Enterprise", loc. cit., *supra* note 3.

7. See Kindleberger, *The International Corporation: A Symposium* (Cambridge, Mass.: MIT Press [1970]) [hereinafter cited as *Symposium*], at 11.

8. See Cabinet Resolution of April 27, 1973.

9. July 1967, March 1969, September 1970 and May 1973.

10. Treaty of Friendship, Commerce and Navigation Between Japan and the United States, September 15, 1953, 4 U.S.T. 2063, 2082, T.I.A.S. No. 2863.

11. Convention of the Organisation for Economic Co-operation and Development, December 4, 1960, 2 U.S.T. 1728, T.I.A.S. No. 4891.

12. The General Agreement on Tariffs and Trade, October 30, 1947 (Proc. No. 2761A, 12 Fed. Reg. 8863 (1947)).

13. See *décret n° 67-68 du 27 janvier 1967,* [1967] *Journal Officiel* [J.O.] 1073, and the arrêté du 27 janvier 1967, [1967] J.O. 1074, both of which implement an earlier law *(loi n° 66-1008 du 28 décembre 1966 relative aux relations financières avec l'étranger),* [1966] J.O. 11621.

14. Vagts, "The Host Country Faces the Multinational Enterprise", op. cit., *supra* note 3, at 272.

Among those other European states which feature in the present study, while traditionally no specific 'key sector' policies have been elaborated, there are nonetheless sensitive areas which receive particular attention when foreign ownership is being considered. Britain's shipping and shipbuilding concerns, for example, would be among its sensitive areas, along with its recently acquired petroleum assets. West Germany has shown some reaction to foreign ownership in the computer and petroleum industries, but not to the extent of denying some recent important U.S. acquisitions in those sectors.[15] In the EEC generally, the individual sectors considered most vital under current industrial policies are aerospace, aircraft and computers;[16] and several countries would consider their iron and steel industries inappropriate for foreign ownership.

Canada, itself until recently considered to pursue an 'open' investment policy, has been prohibiting or restricting foreign investment in selected 'key' industries since the mid-1950's. These sectors include financial institutions (banks and insurance companies), public communications (broadcasting, newspapers and periodicals), public transportation (railways, domestic airlines and local transport) and certain cultural activities. The Canadian province of Quebec has enumerated its own selection of "vital sectors in which domestic investment will be favoured." These include the cultural and information sectors, natural resources, financial services, and public services such as transport and communications.

Even the United States, despite its long tradition of a very open legal climate regarding foreign investment, has sought for some years to protect certain selected activities, based on essential national security and international practice, from excessive foreign participation. Foreign-owned companies seeking entry into the United States have met federally legislated[17] limitations on, or exclusion from, ownership in such areas as banking, public broadcasting and telecommunications, coastal and internal shipping, internal air traffic, minerals exploitation on public lands, atomic energy and other activities where foreign ownership or control is deemed prejudicial to the national interest. As early as World War II, the United States Government was concerned over the ownership of various American industrial sectors by German and, though to a lesser

15. See Behrman, *National Interests and the Multinational Enterprise* (Englewood Cliffs, N.J.: Prentice-Hall, 1970) [hereinafter cited as *National Interests*], at 39.

16. Behrman, "Industrial Integration and the MNE", in Blake, ed. "The Multinational Corporation," 403 *The Annals of the American Academy of Political and Social Science* (1972), [hereinafter cited as *The Annals*], at 47.

17. Cf., *inter alia,* 46 U.S.C. §§ 289, 808, 865, 883 (1970); 47 U.S.C. §§ 310 (1970); 49 U.S.C. §§ 1301 (13), 1378 (c), 1378 (f), 1401, 1508 (b) (1970); 30 U.S.C. §§. 22, 24, 72, 181, 352 (1970); 43 U.S.C. §§ 3102-3300 (1970); 42 U.S.C. § 2133 (1970). See also Marans et al., eds., *Foreign Investment in the United States 1980: Legal Issues and Techniques* (Washington, D.C.: The District of Columbia Bar [1980], part 2.

extent, Japanese interests. When the United States Alien Property Custodian came to sell companies which it had vested at the onset of the War, it prohibited, or at least limited, foreign acquisition of their shares.[18] Most of the present statutes, while limiting foreign share ownership, do permit a minority percentage of foreign shareholdings.[19]

Although widely used, the key-sector approach is deemed by some[20] to be not particularly efficacious, due, in part, to the current proliferation in the number of exceptions allowed.

3. 'Discretionary' Legislation and Practice

a. Special legislation with discretionary intent

A technique rather more subtle than total or key-sector exclusion can be discerned in the enactment of laws which simply 'inconvenience' certain categories of enterprise. Or the host enforcement authorities may be empowered with broad 'discretion' to determine upon what basis certain types of investment should be 'favoured' or 'discouraged'.

For example, France's *loi n° 66-1008 du 28 décembre 1966 relative aux relations financières avec l'étranger,* sets out regulatory measures which affect only foreign enterprises on French territory. Under Article 3 of this Law, the French Government reserves discretion, "pour assurer la défense des intérêts nationaux", to require the submission "à déclaration, autorisation préalable ou contrôle", *inter alia,* all movements of capital and goods where a foreign element is involved. The process of notification, as described by *décret n° 67-78 du 27 janvier 1967*[21] and the *arrêté* of the same date, and by *décret n° 71-144 du 22 février 1971,*[22] each intended for the implementation of *loi n° 66-1008,* is time consuming and often protracted. Title II, Article 3, of the *arrêté,* for example, provides that: "Dans les vingt jours qui suivent sa réalisation, chaque opération doit faire l'objet d'un compte rendu adressé au ministre de l'écono-

18. Rubin, "The International Firm and National Jurisdiction", in Kindleberger, *Symposium,* op. cit., *supra* note 7, at 197.

19. Cf., e.g., 16 U.S.C. § 797 (e) (1970); 30 U.S.C. §§ 22, 24, 72, 181, 352 (1970); 43 U.S.C. §§ 3102-3300 (1970).

20. See Vagts, "The United States of America and the Multinational Enterprise", in Hahlo, ed., *Nationalism and the Multinational Enterprise: Legal, Economic and Managerial Aspects* (Dobbs Ferry, N.Y.: Oceana, 1973), at 16.

21. Regarding the EC-member-state exception under *décret n° 71-143,* see Chapter VI *infra,* note 3 and accompanying text.

22. Regarding the EC-member-state exception, see *infra* note 96.

mie et des finances...sur une formule spéciale tenue par cette direction à la disposition des intéressés",[23] while Section II, Article 4, of the *décret* stipulates further that: "Pendant les deux mois qui suivent la réception des déclarations, le ministre de l'économie et des finances peut demander l'ajournement des opérations envisagées."[24] Such formalities and delays are not generally compatible with the rapidity and flexibility required for normal day-to-day operations and movements of goods and capital involved in multinational - or any commercial - activity, and they surely serve, in practice, to substantially 'inconvenience' the foreign MNE investor. The MNE investor thus hindered may turn his investment elsewhere, where he finds the climate more agreeable to foreign investment activity. In such a way, France has been able to discourage entry without having had to resort to outright denial with its possible retaliatory repercussions. Furthermore, above and beyond such inconveniences, the broad discretionary powers bestowed upon the enforcement authorities for the implementation of the Act have up to now tended to display a marked selectivity, even in the approval of official requests for prior authorization of incoming MNE investment.[25]

The French are gradually discovering the detrimental effect of these exclusionary tactics, and on June 25, 1980 the French Minister of Economy and Finance announced a limited relaxation of the Government's stringent foreign exchange control regulations. While the softened policy is directed primarily at export and import transactions, some of the new adjustments also relate to foreign direct investment in France. For example, the size of an investment above which it is mandatory for a foreign firm to seek official authorization has been increased from three million to five million French francs.

Complementary to this measured relaxation of exchange control regulations and notification requirements was the publication, soon after, in the French *Journal Officiel* of August 5, 1980, of new rules governing takeovers of French companies by foreign interests. These similarly showed an easing of the earlier restrictive rules regarding prior notification and authorization procedure,[26] but the Government nonetheless reserves the right, for two months after notification, to prohibit the transaction, and retains specific power to block investments or takeovers which it deems prejudicial to the public order, public health or national defense. Moreover, and perhaps more significantly, the new rules

23. *Arrêté du 27 janvier 1967, Titre II,* Art. 3, para. 2.

24. *Décret du 27 janvier 1967, Section II,* Art. 4, para. 1.

25. See Andrews, op. cit., *supra* note 5, at 166. See also Kozyris, "Equal Joint-Venture Corporations in France: Problems of Control and Resolution of Deadlocks", 17 *American Journal of Comparative Law* (1969), note 4 at 504.

26. See *infra* note 96 and accompanying text.

affect only investment/takeover transactions by companies from member states of the European Community, and these must be "genuine" Community takeovers, in the sense that they must not be the vehicles for investments from non-Community sources. Hence, the discretionary nature of the above-mentioned laws and decrees has not been eliminated. One might even raise the question as to their discriminatory nature.

Likewise certain aspects of the Japanese system can be described as 'discretionary'. For example, the discretion exercised by the Japanese authorities under the Law Concerning Foreign Investment[27] evidences a clear priority for domestic control of existing enterprises.[28] This law exhibits its discretionary nature not only in its statement of purpose (Article 1), which includes "limiting the induction of foreign investment to that which will contribute to the self-support and sound development of the Japanese economy and to the improvement of the international balance of payments...", and which could conceivably be interpreted as merely a strong statement of 'national interest', but also in its definitions (Article 3), where "foreign investors" are defined, *inter alia,* as [a]ny judicial person (corporate body, enterprise) established under foreign law, or having its seat or place of administration in foreign countries, [or wholly owned, directly or indirectly,[29] or in fact *controlled* by such a person (corporate body, enterprise)[30]], *except those* designated by the Minister of Finance" [emphasis supplied].[31] Moreover, the 'discretion' to determine upon what basis certain types of investment should be 'favoured' or, discouraged' is evident in other provisions of the Law. For example, Article 7 provides that:

> The Minister of Finance and the Minister of International Trade and Industry shall, in accordance with the Ministry of Finance Ordinance and the Ministry of International Trade and Industry Ordinance, make public a list of the kinds of technologies concerning which technological assistance from foreign investors is desired.[32]

The competent Ministers are also empowered to revise this list periodically.[33]

27. Law Concerning Foreign Investment (Law No. 163, May 10, 1950), *EHS Law Bulletin Series: Japan,* Vol. V (1976), at DA 1 *et seq.* This Law supplements the prior-existing Foreign Exchange and Foreign Trade Control Law governing all foreign exchange and trade. (See ibid., note 87 at 164. See also *infra* text accompanying notes 102-103.)
28. See e.g. Andrews, op. cit., *supra* note 5, at 164.
29. Law Concerning Foreign Investment, loc. cit., *supra* note 27, Art. 3, para. (1)c.
30. Ibid., Art. 3, para. (1)d.
31. Ibid., Art. 3, para. (1)b.
32. Ibid., Art. 7, para. 1.
33. Ibid., Art. 7, para. 2.

Further, Article 8 stipulates that the responsible Minister shall apply enumerated standards on validating contracts prescribed in the Law, and that the priority will be accorded those which will "most speedily and effectively contribute to an improvement of the international balance of payment."[34] Article 8 also enumerates categories of contracts which should *not* be validated by the competent Minister.[35] These enumerations notwithstanding, Article 8 ends by crowning its discretionary powers by stating that "[t]he provisions of the preceding two paragraphs shall be applied *mutatis mutandis*" at the discretion of the Minister of Finance or the Foreign Investment Council, pursuant to the provisions of the Law.[36] And similarly, Article 3[37] states that:

> In case of doubt as to whether or not a juridical person (corporate body, enterprise) comes under a juridical person stipulated in item (1) c. or d. of the preceding paragraph,[38] it shall be determined by the Minister of Finance.

The foreign MNE is faced with the difficulty that Japan has no judicial review or reliable specified standards against which it can assess its position.[39]

Discretionary legislation toward foreign enterprise appears also among some of the state statutes of the United States, but the relevant case law there[40] is increasingly revealing a tendency to invalidate such statutes on grounds of unconstitutionality, with the argument, *inter alia,* that they deny "equal protection",[41] a highly guarded right extended to resident aliens by the U.S. Constitution, even in time of national conflict. In addition to the constitutionality of equal protection, under the U.S. Constitution any U.S. state statute, particularly one which limits the freedom of aliens, is valid only to the extent to which it remains consistent with United States treaties.[42]

34. Ibid., Art. 8, para. 1.
35. Ibid., Art. 8, para. 2.
36. Ibid., Art. 8, para. 3.
37. Ibid., Art. 3, para. 2.
38. See *supra,* text accompanying notes 29 and 30.
39. Vagts, "The Host Country Faces the Multinational Enterprise", loc. cit., *supra* note 3.
40. Cf. e.g. *Purdy and Fitzpatrick* v. *State,* 456 P.2d. 645 (Calif. 1969); *Takahashi* v. *Fish and Game Commission,* 334 U.S. 410 (1948).
41. Vagts, "The United States of America and the Multinational Enterprise", op. cit., *supra* note 20, at 16.
42.
> [A]ll Treaties made, or which shall be made, under the authority of the United States, shall be the supreme Law of the Land; and the Judges in every State shall be bound thereby, anything in the Constitution or Laws of any State to the contrary notwithstanding.

(United States Constitution, Art. VI, para. 2) This has been well established in U.S. case law since such early cases as *Ware* v. *Hylton,* 3 U.S. (3 Dall.)199 (1796) and *Chirac* v. *Chirac,* 15 U.S. (2 Wheat.) 259 (1817).

It is worth noting in this regard that, in recent years, a substantial number of treaties of friendship, commerce and navigation (FCN treaties) have been made between the United States and its major world trading partners.[43] The major emphasis of these treaties is on freedom of entry and establishment, and while the earlier commercial treaties of the 1920's and 1930's did not go very far in bestowing rights specifically on companies, the post-1945 FCN treaties did.[44] The near-complete investment freedom accorded under such treaties is manifest, for example, in Article VII, paragraph 1 of the FCN treaty between the United States and the Federal Republic of Germany, which is typical of the bilateral FCN treaties concluded by the United States with many other states:

> Nationals and companies of either Party shall be accorded, within the territories of the other Party, national treatment, with respect to engaging in all types of commercial, industrial, financial and other activity for gain, whether in a dependent or an independent capacity, and whether directly or by agent or through the medium of any form of lawful juridical entity. Accordingly, such nationals and companies shall be permitted within such territories: (a) to establish and maintain branches, agencies, offices, factories and other establishments appropriate to the conduct of their business; (b) to organize companies under the general company laws of such other Party, and *to acquire majority interests* in companies of such other Party; and (c) *to control and manage* enterprises which they have established or acquired. Moreover, enterprises which they control, whether in the form of individual proprietorships, companies or otherwise, shall in all that relates to the conduct of the activities thereof, be accorded treatment no less favorable than that accorded like enterprises controlled by nationals or companies of such other Party [emphasis supplied].[45]

Here we see that foreign majority interests and even foreign control and management of an enterprise established or acquired by a foreign investor in the United States is assured.

43. Cf. e.g. Treaty of Friendship, Commerce and Navigation with the Federal Republic of Germany, October 29, 1954, 2 U.S.T. 1839, T.I.A.S. No. 3593; Treaty of Friendship, Establishment and Navigation with Luxembourg, February 23, 1962, 1 U.S.T. 251, T.I.A.S. No. 5306; Treaty of Friendship, Commerce and Navigation with Japan, September 15, 1953, 4 U.S.T. 2063, 2082, T.I.A.S. No. 2863. See also Walker, "Modern Treaties of Friendship, Commerce and Navigation", 42 *Minnesota Law Review* (1958), at 805-824.

44. See Wilson, "A Decade of New Commercial Treaties" (Editorial Comment), 50 *American Journal of International Law* (1956), at 928-929.

45. Treaty of Friendship, Commerce and Navigation Between the United States of America and the Federal Republic of Germany, loc. cit., *supra* note 43, Art. VII, para. 1.

On the basis of the 'self-executing treaty doctrine'[46] in U.S. law, established by Chief Justice Marshall a century and a half ago in the landmark *Foster & Elam* v. *Neilson*[47] case, and subsequently upheld and repeatedly confirmed as established precedent,[48] the constitutional provision mentioned above[49] - establishing the supremacy of treaty law over state statutes - is largely operative in the case of FCN treaties, as the U.S. courts generally consider treaties concerned with foreign commerce to be self-executing[50] and therefore to supersede

46. This is the doctrine that establishes that only self-executing treaties are recognized as the "supreme Law of the Land." (See e.g. Friederich, "Criteria for Self-Executing Treaties", (Comment), *University of Illinois Law Forum* (1968), at 238-248. See also Schweitzer, "The United Nations as a Source of Domestic Law: Can Security Council Resolutions Be Enforced in American Courts?", 4 *Yale Studies in World Public Order* (1978), esp. pp. 216-224). The 'self-executing treaty doctrine' is embodied in the historic opinion of Chief Justice Marshall, as follows:

> Our constitution declares a treaty to be the law of the land. It is, consequently, to be regarded in courts of justice as equivalent to an act of the legislature, whenever it operates of itself without the aid of any legislative provision. But when the terms of the stipulation import a contract, when either of the parties engages to perform a particular act, the treaty addresses itself to the political, not the judicial department; and the legislature must execute the contract before it can become a rule for the Court (*Foster & Elam* v. *Neilson,* 27 U.S. (2 Pet.) 253, 314 (1829)).

47. *Foster & Elam* v. *Neilson,* 27 U.S. (2 Pet.) 253 (1829). The central question in *Foster & Elam* revolved around whether a treaty provision should be given effect in U.S. courts without subsequent implementing legislation. See also Chief Justice Marshall's opinion, *supra* note 46.

48. This is so despite the fact that *Foster & Elam* was later reversed by *United States* v. *Arredondo,* 31 U.S. (6 Pet.) 691, 741 (1832) and *United States* v. *Percheman,* 32 U.S. (7 Pet.) 51, 87-88 (1833), on other grounds. (See e.g. Schweitzer, op. cit., *supra* note 46, note 47 at 176, 215; Friederich, op. cit., *supra* note 46, note 6 at 239.) See, also *Clark* v. *Allen,* 331 U.S. 503, (1947); *Bacardi Corp.* v. *Domenech,* 311 U.S. 150, 158 (1940); *Bill Co.* v. *United States,* (C.C.P.A. 1939) 104F. (2d) 67 at 70-71; *Santovincenzo* v. *Egan,* 284 U.S. 30, *(1931):Asakura* v. *Seattle,* 265 U.S. 332 (1924); *Dainese* v. *Hale,* 91 U.S. 13 (1875); see also Gordon, "Tests for Determining the Status of a Treaty Provision as Domestic Law" (Comment), 48 *Michigan Law Review* (1950), at 854-855, 857.

49. See *supra*, note 42.

50. In practice, distinguishing self-executing from executory treaty provisions is not always easy, as no single criterion is decisive. See also e.g. Evans, "Self-Executing Treaties in the United States of America", *British Yearbook of International Law* 1953; Hackworth, 5 *Digest of International Law* (1943), sect. 488: "Self-Executing Treaties", at 177-185; Bishop, *International Law: Cases and Materials* (Boston: Little, Brown & Co., 1962), esp. pp. 141-149; Walker, loc. cit., *supra* note 43; Wilson, *The International Law Standard in Treaties of the United States* (Cambridge, Mass.: Harvard University Press, 1953), esp. pp. 87-105. Out of court proceedings themselves comes the assessment that: "The self-execution question is perhaps one of the most confounding in treaty law" (*United States* v. *Postal,* 589 F.2d 862, 876 (5th Cir. 1979)); or that: "it is difficult to extract any clear principle for judicial guidance from the cases discussing the subject" (*Aerovias Interamericanas De Panama, S.A.* v. *Board of County Comm'rs,* 197 F. Supp. 230, 245 (S.D. Fla. 1961)). Nonetheless, FCN and other commercial treaties have been fairly consistently held to be

conflicting state statute provisions. In any case, unconditional most-favored-nation clauses, as well as provisions against discrimination, in U.S. treaty language are typically self-executing, as borne out by a number of cases in which such clauses were considered to be self-executing without question[51] and hence, again, to possess the authority to override discriminatory or discretionary state legislation.[52] The same could safely be said of national-treatment provisions, since a strong implication that national-treatment clauses are equally self-executing can be derived from the most-favored-nation and anti-discrimination position, coupled with the fact that treaties granting equal rights or treatment to aliens are normally deemed self-executing, no legislation being required to implement the grant of equality.[53]

We shall return to the subject of FCN treaties when we come to consider 'national treatment' in Chapter V. Mention is made here simply to underline the fact that, in the United States, only if a state statute does not contravene a standing treaty (or if a particular restriction therein does not violate the equal protection provision of the Constitution) can it legally and effectively restrict investment from abroad.[54] Accordingly, in the United States, the very existence of only a limited number of statutes inhibiting foreign direct investment, the current trend of American case law, and the growing number of federal treaties of friendship, commerce and navigation by which national treatment is ensured in all but those areas of national security enumerated earlier, [55] combine to illustrate the continuing U.S. policy to accord to foreign corporate entities an equal footing with American enterprises of like nature

---

self-executing by U.S. courts. See e.g. *Clark* v. *Allen,* 331 U.S. 503 (1947); *O'Donnell* v. *Great Lakes Dredge & Dock Co.,* 318 U.S. 36 (1943); *Bacardi Corp. of America* v. *Domenech,* 311 U.S. 150 (1940); *Asakura* v. *Seattle,* 265 U.S. 332 (1924). See also Schweitzer, op. cit., *supra* note 46, at 221; Friederich, op. cit., *supra* note 46, at 248.

51. See e.g. *Santovincenzo* v. *Egan,* 284 U.S. 30 (1931); *Dainese* v. *Hale,* 91 U.S. 13 (1875). See also Schweitzer, op. cit., *supra* note 46, note 229 at 223; Wilson, *United States Commercial Treaties and International Law* (New Orleans, La.: Hauser Press, (c. 1960)), at 12; Gordon, op. cit., *supra* note 48, at 855.

52. See also *infra* Chapter V, text accompanying notes 35-38.

53. See *Bacardi Corp.* v. *Domenech,* 311 U.S. 150 (1940); *Asakura* v. *Seattle,* 265 U.S. 332 (1924); *Maiorano* v. *Baltimore & Ohio Railroad,* 213 U.S. 268 (1909); *United Shoe Mach. Co.* v. *Duplessis Shoe Mach. Co.,* 148 Fed. 31 (D. Mass. 1906). See also Friederich, op. cit., *supra* note 46, at 240; Schweitzer, op. cit., *supra* note 46, note 229 at 223.

54. Barnes, "State Regulation of Foreign Investment", 9 *Cornell International Law Journal* (1975), at 91, 99.

55. See *supra,* text accompanying note 17. For definitions of 'national treatment' in international law generally, and in FCN treaties in particular, see *infra* Chapter V, text accompanying notes 28 and 32, respectively.

and size. In sum, with a few reservations regarding entitlement to certain benefits, the foreign enterprise in the United States enjoys much the same "equal treatment" guaranteed to American-established corporations by the Constitution.[56]

b. General legislation with fortuitous deterrent effect and discretionary potential

It is appropriate to add here that sometimes domestic regulatory legislation of general applicability, such as restrictions on financing, antitrust regulation, tax obligations and registration requirements, while not aimed at impeding foreign entry, can act to deter prospective foreign investors from establishing bases in a given host country. Registration in itself, for example, though not intentionally aimed at barring foreign investment, constitutes in practice a *de facto* control point, in that in some countries "no foreign investment carries with it full rights (and obligations) until it has, in fact, been registered by the foreign government.[57]

In the United States, no company, foreign or domestic - other than in certain regulated industries[58] – is required to register with the government, other than registering any securities offered to the public. Such securities are nonetheless required to be registered with the Securities and Exchange Commission (SEC) whose rigorous disclosure requirements prompt many would-be foreign entrants to look elsewhere for their investment opportunities. Other deterrents in this line of generally applied domestic controls likewise affecting the foreign firm investing in the United States - though, again, without discriminatory intent - are the requirement of government approval for acquisitions and 'mergers' in many economic sectors, and the potential injunctive action by the Federal Trade Commission (FTC) for alleged unfair trade practices.[59] The SEC and the FTC are among the so-called "independent regulatory agencies". The FTC, for example, has important supervisory and enforcement powers and is endowed - as are the SEC and other U.S. regulatory agencies - with the author-

56. Compare *Kukatush Mining Corporation* v. *SEC,* 309 F. 2d 647 (D.C. Cir. 1962), in which it was ruled that a non-resident alien has no standing to sue, with *Russian Volunteer Fleet* v. *United States,* 282 U.S. 48 (1931) in which it was held that property of alien corporations is protected by the Fifth Amendment. (Vagts, "The United States of America and the Multinational Enterprise", op. cit., *supra* note 20, at 15.)

57. King, "Foreign Restrictions on U.S. Investment", 11 *San Diego Law Review* (1973), at 37.

58. See *supra* Chapter III, text accompanying note 17.

59. Cf. e.g. 16 U.S.C. § 824 (1970); 46 U.S.C. § 808 (1970); 49 U.S.C. § 5(a) (1970); 46 U.S.C. § 1378 (a) (4) (1970); see also Andrews, op. cit., *supra* note 5, at 160-161.

ity to issue administrative orders and decisions having the force of law. The Commissioners are appointed by the President (with and by the advice and consent of the Senate) for specified terms of office but remain independent of all three branches of government in their functions, subject to the provisions of the statutes which created them, to constitutional and general law, and to judicial review of their orders and decisions.[60] In the exercise of their functions, most importantly, no discrimination is directed against foreign firms.

Similarly, in West Germany MNEs may find themselves considerably limited by the Competition Law (*Gesetz gegen Wettbewerbsbeschränkungen*),[61] last amended in 1980, which, since the significant amendment of 1973, has substantially strengthened merger and monopoly controls. Under the amended law, it is size and market share standards which determine the necessity of prior approval of entry, along with certain other considerations such as amount of total turnover in Deutsche mark, number of employees, market share percentage, proportion of acquisition of assets, creation or strengthening of a dominant position, and exchange control criteria. As in the United States, however, these controls apply to all business entities, foreign and domestic alike, operating within the national territory, and are likewise not discriminatory in nature. As regards the degree of control exercised in general by West Germany over the entry of foreign capital, it is at a minimum, reflecting the German receptivity to foreign direct investment. Although MNEs must report their German activities to the Government, no prior approval is required for investments under a stipulated size and scope;[62] and any which exceed those limits are subject only to the same restrictions as those affecting comparable domestic firms.

In British law as well - though here again, direct investment over a stipulated value, or those in industries where the relevant market shares exceed a certain percentage, are subject to review by the Department of Trade and Industry and possible referral to the Monopolies Commission[63] - foreign investors have been accorded the same treatment as that enjoyed by domestic firms. With the October 1979 removal of essentially all remaining foreign exchange controls[64]

60. See Securities Exchange Act of 1934, 15 U.S.C.A. § 78d; Federal Trade Commission Act, 15 U.S.C.A. § 41.

61. *Viertes Gesetz zur Änderung des Gesetzes gegen Wettbewerbsbeschränkungen,* of 26 April 1980, *Bundesgesetzblatt* [BGB1] 1980 I S. 458. See also *infra* Chapter IX, text accompanying notes 92-95.

62. See *supra* Chapter II; text accompanying notes 66-70.

63. King, op. cit., *supra* note 57, at 33.

64. See Exchange Control Orders 1979 (Nos. 1331-1339), operative as of October 24, 1979 (S.I. 1979/1331-1339), set in motion by the budget speech of 12 June 1979 (see *Keesing's Contemporary Archives,* Vol. XXV (1979), at 29821, 29823, 29825 (text of speech)). See also *infra* Chapter VI, text accompanying notes 9-14.

existing under the Exchange Control Act 1947[65] which required prior approval of any investment transaction between residents and non-residents of the United Kingdom and regulated the establishment both of new firms or affiliates and of buy-ins by foreign investors and the subsequent management of their financial transactions in Britain - there now remains virtually no statutory discrimination against foreign companies or enterprises, even those engaged in banking, insurance, or property holding, some of the key areas most carefully guarded under exclusive or discretionary legislation in many other states. Even the relevant provisions of the Companies Act 1948[66] exhibit an attempt to treat the "oversea company" as nearly like its domestic counterpart as possible, with no legal requirements of prior government approval for entry and no administrative obstacles to establishment; and this lack of discrimination has been preserved in the 1980 Companies Act. Moreover, the "Steuer Report", the most authoritative of a number of British assessment studies on inward foreign direct investment, suggested no further governmental regulation of foreign investment, except to place a general overall limit on the total amount of foreign direct investment in Britain.

Of course investment in all EEC member states is affected by the EEC Directive requiring prior notice for acquisitions and mergers involving companies with sales volume levels over a designated amount. The jurisdiction of the EEC in this area is of course in addition to the enterprise's answerability to the domestic legal provisions of each individual member state, such as those of the U.K. or West Germany mentioned above. An increasing number of other states have likewise imposed restrictions on financing of an acquisition. These restrictions vary from country to country, and from year to year, depending on the state of the domestic economy and the international monetary situation.

The above glimpse into American, German, British and general EEC practice is meant to illustrate how domestic regulation of general applicability, while not aimed at excluding foreign MNE investment, still has a regulatory effect which may deter entry. The most significant of the regulations of this nature are those regarding merger and acquisition activities with monopoly or antitrust implications, and while such review could be seen as a possible vehicle for host-state (or EEC) exercise of indirect discretionary measures against foreign (or non-EEC member-state) entrants, it is clear that the rationale behind such measures was not to exclude foreign investment.

65. The Exchange Control Act 1947, 10&11 Geo. 6 c. 14. (See esp. § 1, 2, 5(c), 6, 8, 9 and 30(2).)

66. Companies Act 1948, 11&12 Geo. 6 c.38, Part X §§ 406-423.

c. Non-statutory discretionary practice

Having submitted that is is clear that legislation of general applicability in the areas of merger and monopolies control was not enacted to exclude or deter corporate investment from abroad, it must be conceded that it is slightly less clear that such measures are not sometimes utilized to that end. More specifically, when a government enacts and enforces legislation restricting mergers and similar activities by enterprises with monopolistic, oligopolistic or dominant positions in a given field, such rules "may or may not bear even-handedly on foreign and domestic enterprises that achieve such positions, and it may be difficult to convince foreigners that such is the intent."[67]

The inference has been made, for instance, that the inquiry by the U.S. Federal Trade Commission (FTC) into the 1970 acquisition of majority control in Libby, McNeil & Libby by the giant Swiss firm, Nestle Alimentana S.A., and into Nestle's outright purchase of Stouffer Corporation in March 1973, was an instance of discriminatory treatment on the part of the FTC against foreign investment, and warnings were sounded of possible retaliation from foreign sources.[68] The feeling has also been expressed that there may have been an American bias displayed in the proceedings of *Bayer*[69] or in those of *BP,*[70] or, on the other hand, a European retaliation in the *Continental Can* case,[71] the EEC's "pioneer attempt to vitalize Article 86 of the Treaty of Rome."[72] Such inferences of discretionary treatment could of course raise questions of international law relating to the principles of 'non-discrimination' and 'national treatment',[73] which is an obvious Achilles heel of discretionary legislation.

It was also remarked above that statutory limitations on foreign MNEs are virtually nil in the United Kingdom, yet the British Government nonetheless holds out some non-statutory "discretionary criteria of acceptability", gener-

67. Vagts, "The Host Country Faces the Multinational Enterprise", op. cit., *supra* note 3, at 273.

68. See *Wall Street Journal,* March 19, 1974, at 18, column 2, and March 25, 1974, at 1, column 5. See also Andrews, op. cit., *supra* note 5, at 160-161.

69. *United States* v. *Monsanto Company,* 1967 CCH Trade Cases, ¶ 72,001 (W.D. Pa. Mar. 20, 1967).

70. *United States* v. *The Standard Oil Company et. al.,* 1970 CCH Trade Cases, ¶ 72, 988 (N.D. Ohio, 1970) [consent decree].

71. *Europemballage Corp. & Continental Can Co., Inc.* v. *EC Commission,* 12 *Common Market Law Reports* 199 (1973).

72. Vagts, "The Host Country Faces the Multinational Enterprise", op. cit., *supra* note 3, note 55 at 273.

73. For a definition of the international law principle of 'national treatment', see *infra* Chapter V, text accompanying note 28.

ally relying on a *quid pro quo* proposition, weighing "the effect of a proposed inward direct investment on foreign exchange reserves, its broader political and economic implications, and other non-statutory and discretionary considerations."[74]

Another discretionary tactic, also a non-statutory one, used by a number of governments is that of simply delaying action indefinitely on an application for investment which they do not favour, in order to avoid possibly compromising political or economic relations with the enterprise's home government or failing to meet existing treaty provisions. The MNE, for its part, based on the same economic and political considerations, will seldom force its 'right' through government intervention, for fear of generating possible host-government reprisals which could only jeopardize future investment attempts. Furthermore, the time and expense involved in an MNE trying to satisfy the administrating agency of its suitability for entry when the agency is not so disposed, can amount to a more significant restraint on entry than the substantive requirements of the law.[75]

Two Canadian lawyers have publicly expressed the view that erecting a protective wall of any sort implies a state of underdevelopment both of a country's economy and of its distinctive culture, and that such measures are hardly conductive to the development of either. "Creation of any barrier," they assert, "implies a weakened condition that cannot stand competition and potential influence from outside. What we need is more positive strength and not more generalized protection. Protection may be justified in selected cases, the traditional 'infant industry' policy being an example. But, how long must protection be maintained to achieve desired goals? For, protection implies some inefficiency, at least in the short run, as far as industry is concerned, and protection implies something less than the best so far as cultural development is concerned."[76]

Reflecting this attitude is a less negative discretionary technique used as an alternative to discouraging investment from abroad, while achieving similar ends of favouring the home market; that is the enactment of special legislation aimed at stimulating national industries and national ownership, and can be achieved by legislated tax incentives, government loans and subsidies, or other types of government-legislated support in favour of its own industries. For

74. Andrews, op. cit., *supra* note 5, at 170.

75. Schwartz, *Free Enterprise and Economic Organization,* 3rd ed. (1966): I. *Concentration and Restrictive Practices,* II. *Regulation of Entry, Rules and Discrimination* (Mineola, N.Y.: Foundation Press, Inc., 1966), at 313.

76. Feltham and Rauenbusch, "Canada and the Multinational Enterprise," in Hahlo, op. cit., *supra* note 20, at 50-51.

example, in Canada, several measures were introduced under the amended Income Tax Act[77] aimed at providing an incentive for Canadian ownership, though these have not in fact proved to be of much effect.[78] The establishment in 1971 of the Canadian Development Corporation (CDC), with the power to make loans to Canadian industry, and to attempt to regain control of 'Canadian' companies from American shareholders,[79] is another reflection of this technique in practice. The intent was to increase opportunities for Canadians to invest and to participate in Canadian economic development, and to help establish and maintain strong enterprises managed and controlled by Canadians. Special attention was to be given by the CDC to industries considered to have the greatest importance and potential for the future economic development of Canada. Like the tax law, however, the CDC did not fulfill initial expectations. There is still insufficient evidence as to whether this technique is even economically viable, or whether the results - apparently meager given the Canadian experience to date - justify the drain on public funds and the substantial costs of establishing "none-too-efficient giants".[80]

Such legislated 'vitalization' programmes may not always be necessary to discourage investment from abroad. In some cases, established national enterprises can pose their own non-statutory entry barriers to the would-be MNE investor - barriers which would appear superficially to be non-legal, such as "product differentiation" (achieved by massive advertising) which disadvantages an aspiring entrant, "absolute cost advantage" over a potential entrant, and "economies of scale" advantages over a smaller aspirant for entry into the local market. Legal ramifications may well arise, however - at least within the EEC member states - from these ostensibly non-legal entry barriers if the established corporation posing such barriers is deemed, under Article 86 of the Rome Treaty, thus to be abusing a dominant position.[81] It has been suggested that both 'unfair competition' by major companies and 'artificial product differentiation' are under the purview of Article 86 of the Rome Treaty, and further, that this conclusion has considerable support both in the text of Article 86 itself and in the case law of the European Commission and the Court of Justice.[82]

77. R.S.C. 1952, c. 148, as partially repealed by 1970-71-72, c. 63, s.1, and as otherwise amended. See also the Gray Report, op. cit., *supra* note 4, at 326. See also *infra* Chapter XII, note 14 and accompanying text.

78. See *infra* Chapter XII, note 14 and accompanying text.

79. See Rubin, "The Multinational Enterprise at Bay", 68 *American Journal of International Law* 1974), at 481-482.

80. Vagts, "The Host Country Faces the Multinational Enterprise", op. cit., *supra* note 3, at 275.

81. See Vogelenzang, "Abuse of a Dominant Position in Article 86; The Problem of Causality and Some Applications", 13 *Common Market Law Review* (1976), at 74.

82. Ibid., at 61.

Such unofficial and ill-defined discretionary practices impeding the entry of foreign MNE investment leave much to be desired in the way of an integrated consistent system of controls on the part of the host and foster an atmosphere of uncertainty generally counter-productive to effective international business relations. Discretionary techniques are not always left in such an unformulated state, however, and, when formalized, can constitute one of the most effective controls over entry of foreign direct investment practised in the industrialized world today, as we shall see below.

d. Systematic case-by-case screening

A closely-associated form of discretionary legislation, if not simply a more outright or formalized expression of some of the techniques outlined above, is systematic screening on a case-by-case basis. This is simply the procedure of considering each potential foreign investment as a special case. Apart from blanket key-sector exclusions, the 'screening' process is perhaps the most widely-used approach to controlling the entry of foreign MNE investment in current practice.

The case-by-case approach, whereby each proposal for foreign investment is reviewed and dealt with on its own merits, was initially practised by countries whose semi-developed conditions led them to do so. The majority of them retained that approach, however, even when the original reasons for it no longer pertained. Due to the ever-increasing volume of enterprises seeking entry by direct investment since the early days of isolated petitions when the government could handle them easily enough within the existing administrative framework, a number of advanced states are enacting laws which empower specially set-up governmental agencies with the responsibility solely of screening and restricting foreign investment generally deemed deleterious to the host economy. (The term "investments" is of course meant to encompass acquisitions and takeovers - or even merely substantial buy-ins - as well as new facilities.)

The most comprehensive example of such legislation is Canada's Foreign Investment Review Act,[83] which delegates its reviewing activities to the Foreign Investment Review Agency (FIRA), a special screening agency created to super-

83. Canadian Government's Bill C-132, adopted December 12, 1973 as Foreign Investment Review Act, *Statutes of Canada* 1973-74, c. 46. The Bill, labelled "Foreign Takeover Review Bill", was announced simultaneously with the publication of the Gray Report *(Foreign Direct Investment in Canada,* op. cit., *supra* note 4) which concluded that government machinery should be established with wide power to regulate foreign investment.

vise the regulatory process, which, while welcoming foreign investment, assures that the control rests in Canadian hands. While the Act became law on December 12, 1973, the takeover provisions (Phase I) first came into effect on April 9, 1974, and the provisions relating to new businesses (Phase II) were first operative as of October 15, 1975.

Phase I applies to takeovers of existing Canadian firms by foreign-owned enterprises. Existing Canadian firms, within the meaning of the Act, clearly include Canadian-incorporated subsidiaries of foreign enterprises; such firms too, then, come within the purview of the Act's relevant provisions.[84]

Phase II of the Act has two aspects: first, foreign investors establishing new businesses in Canada must submit their proposed investments to review of the FIRA; secondly, existing foreign-controlled firms which wish to diversify into new and unrelated businesses must likewise submit their plans to the Agency. Only the first aspect of Phase II is relevant to a discussion on screening at entry. We shall therefore return to the second aspect when considering controls over MNE operations, in the following chapter. Under those provisions relating to initial entry - whether by takeover or by establishment of a new business - the Agency refers all applications to the Minister of Industry, Trade and Commerce, who considers them and then takes a recommendation to the Cabinet if he feels the investment will be "of significant benefit to Canada."[85] The final decision is the responsibility of the Cabinet.[86]

During the initial two years of the Act's enforcement, the FIRA approved around eighty per cent of all proposed takeovers which came under review. Within the first nine months of the operation of Phase II of the Act, the Agency recommended approval for all but one out of forty-five proposed new business investments, five requests having been withdrawn.[87] In view of the very high acceptance rate of entry applications since the Act took effect, it would appear that the screening mechanism, to date, has been used relatively liberally. The significant fact is that such a mechanism exists, has a statutory base, and can be applied in whatever degree of severity the Government deems to be in the national interest under any given set of economic or political cir-

84. See e.g. Hayden and Burns, "Canadian Foreign Investment Review Act", 21 *Practical Lawyer* (1975), at 58-59.

85. Foreign Investment Review Act (FIRA), op. cit., *supra* note 83, §§ 10, 12.

86. Hayden and Burns, op. cit., *supra* note 84, at 61. There has been some criticism in Canadian circles that the Act does not go far enough, in that it does not restrict expansion of already-existing foreign enterprises into "related industries", the substance of the term "related industries" itself being difficult to circumscribe.

87. Rugman, "The Regulation of Foreign Investment in Canada", 11 *Journal of World Trade Law* (1977), at 323.

cumstances. The current liberal enforcement of the Act ought not to elicit cursory dismissals of its effectiveness. Two additional facts should not be overlooked: first, that MNEs seeking entry may be taking more pains, before even submitting an application for entry, to ensure that some benefit will accrue to Canada through their proposed investment, in order to avoid refusal under the new Act; and secondly, that various provisions of the Act continue to be operative after the enterprise has gained initial acceptance for entry. In consideration of these two facts, further mention of the FIRA will be made in the context of "conditional entry" and in that of control over operations of MNEs after entry and establishment.[88]

In drafting The Foreign Investment Review Act, the Canadian Government had reference to the then newly-enacted Australian Companies (Foreign-Take-Overs) Act of 1972,[89] which created a special Committee on Foreign Take-overs to review any direct share acquisition in an Australian company which had gained the prior approval of the Reserve Bank in accordance with the Banking (Foreign Exchange) Regulations Act. While the "Foreign Take-overs" Act does not explicitly require investors to obtain approval, it does provide the government with a legal means of seeking a divestment order, should the foreign ownership be deemed to be contrary to the national interest. ("National interest" is not defined in the Act.)[90]

The earliest significant example of this type of governmental delegation of the screening process is to be found in the present French regime of controls on inward foreign investment, which first took effect in December 1966. The principal statutory instruments of this regime are the *loi n° 66-1008 du 28 décembre 1966 relative aux relations financières avec l'étranger*[91] and the 1967 *décret n° 67-78* and accompanying *arrêté,*[92] along with the 1971 *décrets n° 71-143* and *71-144,* all of which implement the 1966 law and which were mentioned earlier in the context of 'discretionary' legislation. French foreign exchange controls in some form or another have existed since 1939, but the 1966/1967 French legislation establishing a comprehensive system of regulation and control of foreign direct investments, supplemented by the 1971 *décret* explicitly aimed at the control of capital movements, specifically endowed special enforcement authorities with wide discretionary powers for its implementation; and the official announcements in 1980 of a limited relaxation of some of the stringent

88. See, respectively, *infra* Chapter IV, text accompanying notes 7-9, and *infra* Chapter V, text accompanying notes 9-15.

89. Since rewritten to broaden its application.

90. See King, op. cit., *supra* note 57, at 59.

91. *Loi n° 66-1008 du 28 décembre 1966* [1966] Journal Officiel [J.O.] 11621.

92. *Arrêté du 27 janvier 1967,* [1967] J.O. 1073 & 1074.

foreign exchange controls did not compromise the discretionary power of the French enforcement authorities. One problem encountered by would-be investors in France is deciphering just what constitutes a "direct investment",[93] and what is thus subject to prior government approval. For example, mere loans from foreign parents to local subsidiaries are generally classed in France as foreign investment and are thus subject to French Government approval.[94] The Minister of Economy and Finance in his 1980 announcement made it clear that the liberalization would not extend to such loans, which would continue to be examined on a case-by-case basis. Licensing agreements between a French affiliate and a foreign parent, while requiring no prior approval, must be disclosed to the Ministry of Industrial Development and Scientific Research within one month of the conclusion of the agreement;[95] and while it is quite clear to the foreign investor in France[96] that acquisition of 20 per cent or more of a French company, establishment of a new operation, or expansion of a company already under foreign control must go through the government approval process of the Ministry of Economy and Finance,[97] it is not so clear to the investor how he is to regard a purchase of less than 20 per cent, since the French Government has indicated that clearance ought also to be sought from the Ministry in certain cases where a less-than-20 per cent purchase would appear to carry with it the capacity for effective control, regardless of whether that capacity is in fact ever to be exercised or was ever indeed intended in the first place.[98] The importance of potential effective control - even if only latent -is thus apparent in French legislation on foreign direct investment, but introduces a note of vagueness for the investor in determining what is included within that term, and thus which investments require submission for government approval before entry.

An additional problem which has been raised with the French regulations in this area - though the problem, while particularly manifest in France, is hardly exclusively a French one - is that, although some patterns have been identified in the administration of these rules, there is a tendency for the rigour of their

93. For a complex, if not to say perplexing, definition of what is meant by "direct investment" under the French Law, see 3 CCH *Common Market Reporter,* ¶ 22, 655 [1964].

94. See *Circulaire du 21 mars 1969,* [1969] J.O. 3067.

95. See *See décret du 20 mai 1970,* [1970] J.O. 441.

96. With the exception of companies from member states of the European Community which will, following the new rules of August 5, 1980, simply have to notify the Government of any "genuine" investment/takeover moves. If the Government raises no objections within two months of notification, such company may proceed unhindered.

97. *Décret du 24 novembre 1968,* [1968] J.O. 1021, as modified by *décret du 22 février 1971,* [1971] J.O. 144.

98. See King, op. cit., *supra* note 57, at 43-44.

application to shift with each change of the Ministry.[99] Characteristically, however, as remarked earlier, the Ministry utilizes broad discretionary powers and is very selective in its approval.

The particular attraction of the case-by-case approach is that it provides the government with a degree of flexibility far less rigid than that afforded by the explicit laws specifically regulating foreign investment in certain designated industries.[100] Moreover, there is no legal accountability on the part of a government to justify a refusal of entry under the legally established screening mechanism. A case in point was the refusal of France to admit ITT and several other large firms seeking investment opportunities, while at the same time allowing access to a large number of smaller companies.[101] No justification for the discriminatory selection was offered, nor was any required.

Another case is that again of Japan, where the creation of a serious problem affecting the national economy is considered sufficient grounds for justifying the rejection of an investment.[102] In Japan, the fact that official decisions in this area are communicated verbally rather than in writing, coupled with the practice of not publicizing the internal ministerial rules and regulations, known as "Naiki", which govern official procedures relating to foreign investment, only enhances the discretionary powers exercised by the authorities. This discretionary power accorded the Japanese Government under the Law Concerning Foreign Investment[103] is utilized liberally and demonstrates the rigour of the case-by-case screening process in action. Japan, even under this Law, has not actually legislated for the creation of special governmental agencies for review and screening of foreign investments in the way that France, Canada (and Australia) have done, but Japan figures among those states which simply utilize governmental machinery already functioning to achieve similar ends. The

99. Torem and Craig, "Developments in the Control of Foreign Investment in France", 70 *Michigan Law Review* (1971), at 322-334.

100. Cf. e.g. Canadian legislation in banking (The Bank Act, R.S.C. 1970, c. B-1 §§ 10(4), 18(3) & (4), 20(2) (b), 52(1), 53-56); in broadcasting (The Broadcasting Act, R.S.C. 1970, c. B-11, §§ 22(1) (iii), 27 with its specific restrictions on foreign ownership and control of private broadcasting stations); in insurance (Canadian and British Insurance Companies Act, R.S.C. 1970, c. 1-15, as amended by R.S.C. 1970, c. 19 (1st supp.) *inter alia.* For similar U.S. legislation, see *supra* note 17.

101. Torem and Craig, op. cit., *supra* note 99, at 314, 316-317, 324-334.

102. See Japan's Law Concerning Foreign Investment (*supra* note 27) esp. Article 8, para. 2(3):

> The competent Minister shall apply the following standards on validating contracts prescribed in this Law, and the priority shall be given to those which will most speedily and effectively contribute to an improvement of the international balance of payment.

See also Article 1; also *supra,* text accompanying notes 27-38. See also Andrews, op. cit., *supra* note 5, at 164.

103. See *supra* note 27.

difference is, however, that Japan's screening is systematic, hence aligning it more with those states mentioned above which have legislated a screening process than with those states which utilize discretionary legislation, but without the specific statutory base characteristic of, say, Canada's Foreign Investment Review Agency.

Under Japan's traditionally tight restrictive policies there has really been no need for a screening agency as such, since, as early as 1950, the Japanese Law Concerning Foreign Investment referred to above endowed "competent ministers" with the authority to review and approve or reject virtually all long-term foreign equity investment,[104] whether on a buy-in basis or upon the establishment of a new company. In the case of a buy-in of an existing company which does not figure in the twenty-two protected industries mentioned earlier, there exists an "automatic validation" feature, without limitation as to the extent of ownership, provided the consent of the company being acquired is obtained from the management.[105] Where such consent is lacking, automatic validation is accorded only where the individual shareholdings and the aggregate number of all foreign-held shares do not exceed certain specified percentages. These percentages vary from industry to industry. In cases where automatic validation on either grounds is absent, the investor is subject to thorough screening, and consequently, government approval is less likely. In all but minor cases, the review and approval process must be carried out in consultation with the Foreign Investment Council, appointed by the Minister of Finance.[106]

The United States has no special screening mechanism. There, the entire question of foreign direct investment has only in recent years aroused sufficient official interest to warrant its undergoing governmental review. Such review gained statutory sanction through a Congressional Bill passed in 1974 as the Foreign Investment Study Act,[107] which directed the executive branch to undertake a comprehensive analysis of foreign investment in the United States. To date, the Act has resulted in no stronger measures than simply "monitoring" the amount of foreign investment and its impact on the American economy,[108] by means of periodic surveys. The benchmark survey proceeding from the Act recommended that the present unrestrictive American policy

104. For a definition of what is meant by "foreign investors" under this Law, see *Manual of Foreign Investment in Japan,* op. cit., *supra* note 5, note 1 at 1; for a definition of what is included as "direct investment", see *Manual,* at 6, 8, 14.

105. Cf. Cabinet Order No. 221 of July 1, 1952, and Cabinet Resolution of April 27, 1973; see also King, op. cit., *supra* note 57, at 56, and Andrews, op. cit., *supra* note 5, at 165.

106. *Manual of Foreign Investment in Japan,* op. cit., *supra* note 5, at 4.

107. Foreign Investment Study Act, Pub.L. 93-479, 88 Stat. 1450.

108. Ibid., at 1.

toward inward direct investment should be continued without the imposition of restraints. The subsequent and closely related International Investment Survey Act of 1976,[109] while heightening Presidential powers to conduct surveys of foreign investment in the United States, still went no farther than to ordain periodic surveys and a feasibility study on the establishment of a monitoring system. It looks highly unlikely, then, that anything in the nature of a screening system will appear on the American investment scene in the foreseeable future.

The picture would be incomplete if it were not mentioned here that, for the MNE itself, as well as for the host state, the legal aspects of establishment can only realistically be dealt with on a case-by-case basis.[110] Given the fact that the organization of the foreign entities of a company is basically a matter of law, and that an enterprise can gain entry into a state's territory only if it complies with all the laws and conditions to which it is subject under that government, and since the laws and conditions differ in each host state where the enterprise seeks to establish a base, the MNE itself must approach each government as a special case, as well as vice-versa, when it comes to the legal aspects of establishment.

It must not be forgotten that the element of uncertainty - that element largely responsible for much of the restrictive measures imposed on MNEs by host governments - exists not only on the part of the host, but also on the part of the MNE. While the host's uneasiness derives from the uncertainty generated by external decision-making of the foreign parent, the MNE is uneasy about investing in countries where political and/or economic instability holds the tenure of its investment constantly in the balance. The inherent diversity of the different legal systems and jurisprudence encountered by the MNE across the range of prospective host states is plainly exacerbated by the fact that the degrees of state intervention are no less diversified; and, furthermore, as foreign governments change and public pressures shift, so do government policies on foreign investment. Consequently, foreign investment restrictions, rules and regulations are constantly undergoing changes brought about by new legislation, decree, or simply administrative practice. For this reason, the technique of governmental review and approval, which, in fact, has normally been an implicit, if not explicit, feature of registration in the company laws of many states for some years, "can have an affirmative value to the foreign investor as evidence of the government's knowledge of, and acquiescence in, the investment, possibly important for future reference purposes."[111]

109. Pub. L. No. 94-472, 90 Stat. 2059 (codified at 22 U.S.C. § 3101 (1976)).

110. Kolde, *International Business Enterprise,* 2nd ed. (Englewood Cliffs, N.J.: Prentice-Hall (1973)), at 185.

111. King, op. cit., *supra* note 57, at 36; cf. also ibid., at 43, 44.

Chapter IV.

CONDITIONAL ENTRY

1. Negotiation for Maximum Benefits to the Host State

Should, ultimately, the prospective foreign investor actually succeed in meeting initial requisites for entry and be allowed access in principle, he may next discover that he is up against certain constraints limiting the area of choice open to him within the host economy which he has just penetrated, or that certain specified conditions must be met or assured before an agreement is actually concluded. In other words, his 'right' of entry may be made conditional.

The "conditional entry" technique was initially only widely practised by the developing countries, but by the 1960's, the tendency to apply special conditions of entry for foreign-owned enterprises was in evidence not only in the developing world but in many of the more advanced nations as well.[1] The aims of the advanced nations in applying this technique were similar to those of the less developed states, but more subtly achieved. While the governments of developing states generally insisted on local production as a condition of entry, or imposed such high tariffs that a local plant became the only viable means of entry, the governments of the industrialized nations might require purchasers under their direct influence - such as their own departments, public utilities, public services or the armed forces - to agree to purchase their equipment only from companies with local plants, thus discouraging pure imports, licensing, or assembly facilities, and encouraging local production. Or the government might simply make it clear that if the enterprise wanted governmental favour it had better help the balance-of-payments by local production, or assume certain responsibilities in such areas as finance, depressed industries, research and development, worker and management training, and local participation in equities and direction of the local company.[2]

1. See Vernon, "Future of the Multinational Enterprise", in Kindleberger, ed., *The International Corporation: A Symposium* (Cambridge, Mass.: MIT Press, [1970]) [hereinafter cited as *Symposium*], *at 390, 391.*

2. See Tugendhat, *The Multinationals* (New York: Random House, 1972), at 34.

The Canadian Province of Quebec, for example, claims a "favourable" reception to foreign investments, "but," qualifies the Quebec Minister of Financial Institutions, Companies and Cooperatives, "it must meet our conditions." Quebec's conditions, according to the Finance Minister are as follows:

> (1) We do not favor outright takeovers...
> (2) We require that foreign investors obey our laws and conduct themselves as proper corporate citizens...
> (3) We expect companies, both domestic and foreign, to pay a fair share of taxes...
> (4) We ask foreign investors to employ citizens of Quebec *throughout* the organization, not only at the lower echelons, but right at the top...
> (5) We ask foreign corporations to respect our languages and to use them...
> (6) We expect reciprocity...
> (7) A fair share of the total research conducted by the corporation must be done in Quebec. Further to this point, an equitable amount of the activity generated by what we call "new finds" resulting from these Quebec-based research activities must be conducted in Quebec...
> (8) We insist that an ever-increasing amount of transformation be carried out in the province...
> (9) Our citizens must be able to participate actively in new economic activity; they must be able to become directors and shareholders of new business enterprises....[3]

The Finance Minister summarized Quebec's conditional entry approach by saying that "proposed foreign investments will be considered in terms of the extent of their integration into [the Quebec] economy."[4]

Or as we have seen in the case of Japan, even the "automatic validation" accorded to "liberalized" industries by the Japanese Government is dependent upon certain conditions set down by the responsible authorities.

In the context of the EEC, conditional entry is also preferred as a technique over that of outright denial of non-member foreign direct investment. Negative measures directed against non-member states are in any case deemed unfeasible, as denial by one country will simply cause the prospective entrant to apply elsewhere and subsequently most likely penetrate the market of the

3. "Should Investment Capital Stay Home? A Canadian-U.S. Dialogue", *Proceedings of the Sixty-eighth Annual Meeting,* American Society of International Law (Washington, D.C., 1974), [hereinafter cited as *Proceedings* (1974)], at 25-26.

4. Ibid., at 26.

original refusing state through exports or through affiliates gaining entry under the right of establishment. In other words, because of the right of establishment in the EEC, no single state can successfully exclude a foreign (i.e. non-member-state's) corporation or affiliate, since that corporation, if it gains entry in one EEC member state, where it is then registered, and provided it is genuinely doing business there and not simply using that state for purposes of a 'name-plate' of convenience, can in no way be excluded from also establishing an affiliate in another EEC member state,[5] even in that state which originally denied it entry.

The parent company may, however, choose not to penetrate the market of the state initially refusing it entry, and the refusing state may consequently be confronted with increased competition from an enterprise doing business within the Common Market, but over which it has no direct or even indirect local control.

France, for example, even though it tends to favour bargaining, over outright rejection of investments,[6] lost a valuable American investment by imposing excessive restrictions, at the time of application, as conditions of entry. French officials were somewhat dismayed when the enterprise subsequently gained entry in Belgium.

The Canadian Foreign Investment Review Act[7] mentioned earlier has as one of its functions the role of bargaining agent with would-be foreign investors. The very essence of the administration of the Act appears to be the determination to negotiate greater benefits for Canadians than would normally accrue under the pre-existing arrangements. The argument for relying on the Act to increase the benefits to Canada of proposed takeovers and new foreign direct investments has been advanced by the Ontario Economic Council (1976) as follows:

> In practice, and as intended by the Government, FIRA has not operated merely as a screening agency. It has taken part in a bargaining process with the objective of increasing the benefits to Canada, while reducing the costs. It has apparently withheld approval until more jobs, investment and exports have been promised by the firm in question.[8]

5. See Lipstein, *The Law of the European Economic Community* (London: Butterworth, 1974), Chapter 6.

6. See Canadian Government, *Foreign Direct Investment in Canada* ("Gray Report") (Ottawa: Information Canada, 1972) [hereinafter cited as the Gray Report], at 332.

7. See *supra* Chapter III, note 83.

8. Cited in Rugman, "The Regulation of Foreign Investment in Canada", 11 *Journal of World Trade Law* (1977), at 324.

The high success rate of investor applicants could be seen to reflect the FIRA's prowess in negotiating benefits for Canada on an individual basis.[9]

Host-state/parent-company negotiations are sometimes formalized in explicit agreements; the 'assurances' or benefits therefrom are, once again, not all one-directional. The foreign MNE investor is often desirous of an explicit agreement to lend legal enforceability to the assurances on the part of the host government that guarantee the investor the control he needs to ensure efficiency of operations. Moreover, it removes some of the vagueness and uncertainties at the outset by defining the terms of the investment and establishing a certain degree of responsibility, on the part of the host government, implicit in the host's recognition of the investment. Explicit agreements are particularly desirable in states where the foreign investment regulations are not always clearly visible or are prone to subtle nuances of government and public interpretation which are not always predictable, as is particularly the case - in addition, of course, to much of the developing world - in, for example, Japan and France.[10]

Even in Britain - despite its long tradition of liberal policies toward capital movements for non-residents and the sweeping abolition in 1979 of virtually all remaining foreign exchange controls - while no formal set of investment conditions has been set out, government representatives have gone along "quietly negotiating with major foreign investors over the terms of entry."[11] To cite a classic example, in 1964 when the British Government was allocating licenses for North Sea oil and natural gas exploration, the international oil companies were actively competing for the coveted rights. The British Government astutely exploited its bargaining position and offered preference to those companies which would most contribute to Britain's fuel economy. This resulted in assurances from several hopeful applicant companies that they would build their own refineries to handle crude oil, and thus cut down on imports of more expensive products refined elsewhere.[12]

Another British example can be seen in the acquisition of majority control of British Rootes, Ltd. by Chrysler. Among the conditions sought from Chrysler by the British negotiations were the retention of a majority of British directors on the Rootes board, assurances of a progressive increase in exports, the nomination of a British Rootes director both to the board of Simca (French Chrysler) and to that of Chrysler International, plus the retention of 15 per cent

9. Ibid., at 324-325.
10. See King, "Foreign Restrictions on U.S. Investment", 11 *San Diego Law Review*, at 43, 66.
11. Vernon, "Future of the Multinational Enterprise", op. cit., *supra* note 1, at 392.
12. See Tugendhat, op. cit., *supra* note 2, at 34.

of the equity of Rootes by non-Chrysler shareholders. Though the British Government possesses no instruments for the enforcement of these conditions, most foreign investors have cooperated readily.[13]

The 'conditional' entry technique further assures that there is no control gap between restrictions on entry and those over operations. Thus it is that, in addition to the usual entry prerequisites relating to financial (balance-of-payments) considerations and stipulations regarding location, selected industries, etc., conditions regarding future operations of the affiliate are also exacted at the moment of entry in an effort on the part of the host to guarantee that the initial infusion of up-to-date technology and management skills will be followed by a continuous input[14] of technological and managerial know-how, perpetually enhancing its international monetary and economic position.

2. Guarantees of Continuing Flows of Technology

One means of attaining this continuing contribution is for the host government to require assurances regarding future import and export policies on the part of the affiliate. In France, for example, an affiliate of Libby was required to give assurances that any semi-finished products which it imported would be turned into processed food products for export. Britain's improvement in foreign subsidiary export performance since World War II may well be attributable to her application of the test of whether a foreign investment would increase U.K. exports by substituting for imports.[15]

The means which appears to be most widely favoured by host states of securing such a continuing contribution - other than the requirement of locally established research and development facilities, and training and promotion opportunities for local management - is to stipulate that entry of the foreign affiliate will be allowed only on condition of joint ownership or joint managment, ensuring thereby a degree of local control through substantial local participation. Hence, before leaving the subject of entry controls behind, although we are already crossing the threshold into the domain of operations, let us consider two final entry conditions: joint ownership and joint management.

13. United Kingdom, *The Impact of Foreign Direct Investment of the United Kingdom* ("Steuer Report"), prepared by M.D. Steuer, et al., (HMSO: London), 1973 [hereinafter cited as Steuer Report], at 9:18-19.

14. This is one strong argument for direct investment as opposed to licensing.

15. See Behrman, *National Interests and the Multinational Enterprise* (Englewood Cliffs, N.J.: Prentice-Hall, 1970) [hereinafter cited as *National Interests]*, at 25.

a. Joint ownership

Looking first at joint ownership, it may seem somewhat surprising to find that even in some of the more advanced states there appears still to be an emphasis on substantial ownership, despite the fact that it has been widely recognized for some time that the critical issue is not one of ownership but one of control, and that control is not inevitably bound up with ownership. Ownership implications, as we have seen, have been greatly exaggerated; and the popular notion that power necessarily accompanies ownership is largely a myth, outside the possible exception of wholly owned subsidiaries. But short of 100 per cent ownership of an affiliate, shareholding percentages are widely acknowledged to have little significance as regards control implications.

In spite of this fact, nearly all but the most liberal of host government tend to favour investments with opportunities for domestic equity ownership, and many make outright requirements of joint ownership as a prerequisite to entry. Even in Canada, the 'magical' 25-10 formula, under which no more than 25 per cent ownership of a corporation could be held by foreigners and no more than 10 per cent by any one individual and his associates, continued to be "unimaginatively" applied[16] up until very recently.[17] In a number of other industrialized states (notably Sweden, Finland and Switzerland), alien ownership similarly faces statutory limitations.[18]

MNEs, aware that there are means of retaining control other than through majority or full ownership, are not reluctant to share ownership, and often do so - in states which require substantial local or government equity participation - by entering into joint-venture or other partial-ownership agreements. Many U.S. enterprises, for example, are willing to sell up to around 30 per cent of an affiliate's shares to the public, or to enter into some joint-venture (fifty-fifty or even minority) agreement, if internal company arrangements assure that full control is retained by the parent company.[19] The object in a minority position is to discover what means of control are legally exercisable, under the laws of the host state, for ensuring sufficient effective participation of the minority parent in the decision-making and managerial control of the joint venture, taking care not to obstruct thereby the proper functioning of the enterprise.[20]

16. See Feltham and Rauenbusch, "Canada and the Multinational Enterprise", in Hahlo, ed. *Nationalism and the Multinational Enterprise* (Dobbs Ferry, N.Y.: Oceana, 1973), at 52.

17. For a shift in this policy, see *infra* Chapter V, text accompanying note 14.

18. See e.g. Vagts, "The United States of America and the Multinational Enterprise", in Hahlo, ed., op. cit., *supra* note 16, at 26.

19. See Behrman, *U.S. International Business and Governments* (New York: McGraw-Hill, 1971), at 113.

20. See King, op. cit., *supra* note 10, at 42.

A case in point is Japan. A substantial proportion of Japanese MNE affiliates are minority-owned joint ventures, but the methods of control, coupled with the industrial and geographical distribution of their foreign investment, are designed to ensure adequate retention of domestic (Japanese) control.[21]

The joint venture can even have certain advantages for the MNE by minimizing the effects of host restrictions on - or discrimination against - it as a foreign investor, or by deflecting the sometimes unfavourable reception awaiting the entry of a wholly foreign-owned multinational affiliate, and by providing the foreign enterprise with a more local character and identity. The distribution of ownership in the larger enterprises is in any case becoming increasingly dispersed as ownership becomes ever more widely separated from control and management responsibility. Companies are devising ways, such as the introduction of forms of non-voting shares, of spreading ownership among foreign shareholders, to a certain measure, without diminishing national control of the parent in any way.[22] (This is particularly true of such countries as Switzerland and Sweden.) Thus, for these states, it is the *functions* of ownership (i.e. control) rather than titles of ownership that are carefully guarded.

There are, in addition, situations where, regardless of ownership distribution, control of critical patents or a new technological breakthrough by one partner - even a minority one - may give that partner overall effective control.[23] For example, the fact that General Motors of Canada is technologically dependent on its U.S. parent means that even were it to become 100 per cent-owned by Canadian interests, it would still be dependent on the parent to provide the technical assistance necessary for its survival. Again, the stock ownership in such cases has little relevance as a controlling influence, the real control residing at the source of the vital technical assistance.

Why, then, is the interest of the host state so great in this area of joint ownership, when such ownership often has so little to do with effective control? There are several reasons. For one thing, the joint venture is seen by some as a sort of "international middle ground", a "common cure" for strained relations between host states and foreign parents, and as a means of accommodating the interests of both parties.

In addition, many companies enter into joint ventures abroad for which the relationship was never intended to be a permanent one, but was envisaged merely as the best means of entering an unknown and highly competitive mar-

21. United Nations, *Multinational Corporations in World Development,* U.N. publication ST/ECA/190, sales No. E.73.II. A.11 (New York, 1973), at 13.

22. Phatak, *Evolution of World Enterprise,* (New York: American Management Association, 1971), at 102.

23. See Ibid., at 165.

ket which would otherwise be too awesome to the first-time investor. In such cases, which are particularly common for European companies investing in the United States, the joint venture arrangement is regarded as a "temporary expedient", or transition mechanism, in preparation for assuming full control once the concern has become sufficiently established.

Such means of entering a foreign market are not always as "expedient" as they might appear. Dissolution of a joint venture can confront the uninitiated investor with unforeseen host restrictions on the return of his capital, patents, and other aspects of his investment. "Unfortunately", comments one business executive, "the institutional framework of business ownership is not of the type to encourage smooth transitions of equity participation, and considerable foresight and international legal skill are often necessary to safely navigate this contingent danger."[24] It is therefore of utmost importance that foreign firms considering the joint venture merely as a means of entry, be well aware at the outset, *before* they are fully engaged in operations, of the intricacies of the future control transfer, and that they be fully familiar with the relevant legal procedures of the host state involved in such a transfer.[25]

Thirdly, the joint venture has become a major symbol of sovereignty and control.[26] In this regard, it is significant to note that host countries are sometimes more concerned with who appears to have control than they are with who actually exercises effective control.[27] For these states, it is the *evidence* of control (i.e. ownership), more than the *exercise* of control, which counts. An indication of this is seen in the tacit acceptance by some host governments of provisions made by certain MNEs which, while publicly proclaiming their adherence to the host government's call for a joint venture, in practice restrict the authority and management responsibilities of the domestic partner.[28] Some host governments have even gone so far as to back down entirely on their requirements in order to secure the benefits of a foreign firm's local presence. This has been the case on at least two occasions involving IBM, according to Business International which reported that IBM "convinced both the Indian

24. Clausen, "The International Corporation: An Executive's View", in Blake, ed., "The Multinational Corporations", 403 *The Annals of the American Academy of Political and Social Science* (1972) [hereinafter cited as *The Annals*], at 16.

25. See King, op. cit., *supra* note 10, at 43.

26. See Stopford and Wells, *Managing the Multinational Enterprises* (London: Longman, 1972), at 168.

27. See Tindall, *Multinational Enterprises: Legal and Management Structures and Interrelationship with Ownership, Control, Antitrust, Labor, Taxation and Disclosure,* (Dobbs Ferry, N.Y.: Oceana, 1975), at 146.

28. See Behrman, *U.S. International Business and Governments,* op. cit., *supra* note 19, at 114.

and Japanese governments that it is better to have IBM on its own terms than not at all."[29]

The host's tolerance of such arrangements would imply that, just as the enterprise is often willing to make certain concessions regarding local foreign ownership when it does not entail the loss of managerial control, so is the host government at times willing to overlook management control in the hands of the foreign partner, or even occasionally full ownership by the foreign parent, particularly when the requisite skills or technology are lacking locally, as long as the *appearance* of control (i.e. ownership, or at least a formal screening prerogative) is maintained and in public evidence. After all, management contracts - which are becoming increasingly frequently relied on - vest management responsibilities in foreign hands in any case, the domestic firm thereby voluntarily relinquishing full management control. Most governments do not regard this as a potential threat, being perfectly aware that ultimate control over multinationals' activities inside their borders lies within their sovereign powers, and is not ultimately dependent upon local management any more than it is upon local ownership.

Hence, it is partly to satisfy the need to assert their sovereignty, but perhaps more to satisfy the heightened nationalistic sensitivities of the domestic population, that many governments continue to seek joint ownership, which can be counted, in terms of shares, and which affords at least ostensible tangible evidence of local participation. "Probably," postulate Messrs. Stopford and Wells, "governments will continue to pay an economic price to acquire the feelings of increased influence over their own destiny that come with some local ownership of foreign subsidiaries",[30] even if that source of "influence" is in appearance only, and has little or nothing to do with effective control.

Fourthly, in addition to desires for a "middle ground", for a "temporary expedient", or for the maintenance of an appearance of local autonomy, most advanced states have begun to recognize the wider implications of joint ownership going beyond mere share percentages. They have begun to realize that the really significant economic resources today are technology and management, and, as these are both continuing requirements, that it is clearly they that have become the effective controlling influence where the MNEs are concerned.[31] Those advanced states favouring joint ownership see it as a means of benefiting from technological innovations and managerial ingenuity, as well as a way of introducing their own innovations into the distribution channels of a foreign

29. Business International, "Pros and Cons of Joint Ventures Abroad", *Management Monographs,* No. 18 (N.Y., 1964), at 4.

30. Stopford and Wells, loc. cit., *supra* note 26.

31. See Ross, "An Attempted Summing Up", in Hahlo, op. cit., *supra* note 16, at 337.

market environment which is alien to them but which is native and easily accessible to the foreign partner.[32]

Some less technically advanced states have seen joint ventures as a way of tapping these same technological and managerial resources without expending vast sums of research capital. They have seen also the obvious advantages of increasing control over the operations of the local MNE affiliate and of sharing in its profits. Furthermore, joint-venture arrangements foster the international transfer of technology without demolishing the state's sense of local autonomy. This may also partially explain why joint ventures are being increasingly permitted by governments of state-run economies, hitherto closed to foreign equity participation. And as joint ventures are at present the only channel open to these countries for such participation, the trend, begun in 1967 by Yugoslavia, and most recently reaffirmed by a new Chinese law on joint ventures,[33] will undoubtedly continue to accelerate.[34]

In sum, from the point of view of either investment partner in any joint-venture relationship, the key aspects of the venture are participation in, and/or influence over, the activities of the concern, even where the extent of the control is no more than a negative one, through the exercise of the right of veto.[35]

The *Summary of United Nations Hearings* on the multinational enterprise, following its assertion that: "[t]he fundamental issue in the relationship of the multinational enterprise to Government is control", goes on to say that "[t]he issue of ownership forms (i.e. joint ventures) is a false issue. If the problem is symbolic and ownership is a symbol of control, then ownership may be important. But Governments have many ways of exercising control other than ownership."[36] This has been demonstrated.

32. This has been true both of U.S. enterprises investing in Europe and European firms investing in the United States, the relative proportion of each being remarkably similar, and the major benefits to each appearing to be equally similar. (See Brooke and Remmers, *The Multinational Company in Europe; Some Key Problems* (London: Longman, 1972), at 66.)

33. The Law of the People's Republic of China on Joint Ventures Using Chinese and Foreign Investment (adopted by the Second Session of the Fifth National People's Congress on 1 July 1979), 18 *International Legal Materials* (1979), at 1163 *et seq.*

34. Specific joint-venture legislation has been enacted not only in Yugoslavia but also in Rumania and Hungary, with Poland showing signs of following. This legislation clearly limits the foreign participation to a minority position with an explicit separation of ownership and control or management, at least in form, and any rights of the foreign partner derive solely from contractual provisions; but the joint venture has provided the vehicle necessary to allow these countries a means of participating to a small degree in the free enterprise system, without their sensing a compromise of their autonomy. (See Tindall, op. cit., *supra* note 27, at 158-159; see also King, op. cit., *supra* note 10, at 29.)

35. See King, op. cit., *supra* note 10, at 30-31.

36. United Nations, *Summary of the Hearings Before the Group of Eminent Persons to Study*

b. Joint management

Many governments, aware of the inadequacies of pure joint-ownership requirements, have made entry stipulations that all or a percentage of managers and directors be local residents or nationals. This is true of Switzerland and all the Scandinavian countries, *inter alia,* though the government has discretion to dispense with this requirement in special cases.[37] Supplemental to this requirement of local management are host-government restrictions on the employment of "expatriate" personnel - in other words, managers from the home country working abroad. Compliance with these requirements and restrictions results, as noted earlier,[38] in a statutory or *de facto* administration which is generally considered unsuitable for the actual management of the affiliate, and is accordingly countered by charter provisions of the company which limit the functions of these statutory local executives.

While considering management requirements, it should not go unmentioned that many MNEs have taken their own initiative in extending management opportunities to local personnel. E.J. Kolde reports that: "...in the last decade multinational companies have initiated training and executive development programs for local nationals and have begun to emphasize the use of local talent to a much greater degree than previously. Where such programs have been in existence for some time, the results are most encouraging.[39]

Some large MNEs are advancing recruitment policies whereby management positions are opened up "on equal terms to nationals of all countries." Unilever, for example, as a matter of company policy, now aims at locally recruiting 90 per cent of the senior management staff in each host country. In addition, its policy is to maintain, in the parent companies in both Britain and the Netherlands, a staff comprised of employees from every nation.[40]

Local management, whether fostered by the enterprise or exacted by the host government, inevitably means some degree of control diminution on the part of the parent. Perhaps it is the theory of the MNE that the loss of control will

---

the Impact of Multinational Corporations on Development and on International Relations, United Nations publication ST/ESA/15, N.Y., 1974, at 4.

37. See Schmitthoff, "The Multinational Enterprise in the United Kingdom", in Hahlo, op. cit., *supra* note 16, at 26.

38. See Kolde, *International Business Enterprise,* 2nd ed. (Englewood Cliffs, N.J.: Prentice-Hall (1973)), at 187, 271-272.

39. Kolde, "The Administrative Structure of International Business with Special Reference to Foreign-Based Affiliates", 22 *University of Washington Business Review,* (1963), at 38-50.

40. Modelski, "The Corporation in World Society", 22 *Yearbook of World Affairs,* 1968, at 77.

be minimized if the local management initiatives come from the enterprise itself, rather than from a governmental directive.

Even the initiative originating with the enterprise rather than with the government, however, is no guarantee or retention of parent-company control. Sighting a headline in the *International Herald Tribune* of October 9-10, 1976[41] which read: "Saudis Expected to Take All of Aramco", the present writer was reminded of an interview with Arnold Toynbee by a *Forbes* correspondent, two and a half years earlier, in which Toynbee recalled: "In 1957 Aramco invited me to visit the American oil cities in Saudi Arabia. It was most interesting. The senior staff was American, but there were up-and-coming Arabs - coming straight from growing date palms in the oasis or pasturing flocks. They were being put into technical jobs."[42] Only nineteen years after Toynbee's visit we read that the Arab Government will take over control of the entire Aramco operation, not just the oil-producing assets: "It now appears", reads the article, "that the Saudis will take over all of the Aramco operations, including Aramco Overseas Co. at the Hague, which supplies logistic and technical assistance, and Aramco Services Co. in Houston, which provides service and engineering support to the Arabian operation." It must not be forgotten that the discovery of oil in the Arabian subsoil was made by the American company, and that the opportunity of rising up the technological ladder was given to the Arabs by the American company long before such stipulations were government-initiated, and even more than ten years before the first outcries against multinationals were evoked by Servan-Schreiber's widely publicized book, *The American Challenge.*[43] Yet here is an example of how loss of control can be total, even when local management opportunities are initiated by the enterprise itself.

Having separated, for the sake of convenience of the foregoing discussion, joint ownership (ownership joint ventures) from joint management (managerial joint ventures) in considering them as conditions of entry, it should be emphasized that the most characteristic joint-venture relationship is a combination of the two. Joint ventures, however, have not proved to be the most effective means of transferring technology or enhancing operations. Studies have demonstrated that the weaker communication and control systems inherent in the joint venture mean a loss in efficiency, effectiveness and "global optimiza-

41. See *International Herald Tribune* (Paris), October 9-10, 1976, at 11.

42. "Arnold Toynbee: Are Businessmen Creating A New Pax Romana?" *Forbes,* April 15, 1974, at 70.

43. Jean-Jacques Servan-Schreiber, *The American Challenge* (London: Hamish Hamilton, 1968) [translation of *Le Défi américain*].

tion potential'' of the enterprise. In the words of one writer, ''the presence of mixed ownership makes it difficult to accomplish the adjustment of unified global logistics systems which rational economics would require'',[44] since a uniform company policy is difficult to maintain in a jointly owned subsidiary where the local partners are apt to be influenced by domestic political pressures.[45] It is possible that a ''strong international management corps'', as recommended by Messrs. Brooke and Remmers,[46] with ''international staffing and promotion schemes'' to aid in running an otherwise decentralized system, would alleviate some of the complexities; but such a concept is still a long way from realization, and would not be without its own difficulties. Meanwhile, there continues to be a very high 'divorce rate' among joint-venture partners; and even the 'divorce proceedings' themselves can often lead to unforeseen legal complications.

We have already been perambulating in the ill-defined borderland between entry and operations since the point at which we took up guarantees of continuing technology inflow and joint ownership and management. The real legal difficulties often arise as a result of the failure of most legal systems still to fully recognize and act upon the control implications of the separation of ownership and management in the course of operations.

In order to look at some of those legal difficulties which have arisen in practice from the compounding of the ownership/management implications, we must pass from the realm of pure entry restrictions into that of operations, actual court cases arising as they do not out of initial denial of, or conditions placed upon, entry, but rather out of irregularities or conflicts of interest resulting from actual corporate practice. In the following chapter, then, we shall examine some cases which emphasize the importance to future operations of the initial entry requirements relating to joint ownership and joint management. Before leaving the subject of entry restrictions *per se,* however, it would seem useful to sum up the objectives of the host in exercising such restrictions.

Conclusion

In sum, the obvious aim of the host state in its use of any of the entry control techniques reviewed in this chapter is to maximize the foreign contribution in

44. Fayerweather, ''The Internationalization of Business'', in Blake, ed. *The Annals,* op. cit., *supra* note 24, at 9.

45. See Clausen, loc. cit., *supra* note 24.

46. Brooke and Remmers, *The Multinational Company in Europe,* op. cit., *supra* note 32, at 169.

the pursuit and furtherance of its own national objectives. Common objectives of the developed nations in setting entry restrictions or conditions are basically, then, the protection of the 'national interest' and the strengthening of the balance of payments, the use of these and other indirect means to discourage certain forms of foreign investment or to channel it into host-government-selected industries, and the encouragement of other selected areas of foreign investment and investment forms to provide for local equity and management participation and technology transfer, to the benefit of the host economy.

Even the smallest of governments can use the apparatus available to it -either to restrict or to bargain, or both - in negotiating for the best possible conditions for its own economic requirements and for commitments which will provide ongoing benefits; and the case-by-case approach, with the review and screening mechanism which it implies, is perhaps the single most effective and widely-used regulatory technique employed by industrialized nations to control, from the moment of initial application for entry, all multinational activity passing into its territory.

PART THREE: TECHNIQUES OF RESTRICTIVE HOST-STATE CONTROL OVER FOREIGN MNE AFFILIATES: OPERATIONS

Chapter V.

GENERAL POLICY AND PRACTICE

We have now looked at the main techniques by which the host state exercises control over MNE activity within its borders at the moment of entry, and how some of the entry requirements and conditions are specifically aimed at securing maximum control over future operations. Due to this close integration of control over entry with regulation of future operations, a clear-cut line cannot easily be drawn between the two, in that, to some extent, future operations of an enterprise have become subject to regulation even before they are actually set in motion in the host territory. It is clear that there is no challenge to the host state's control over MNEs at the moment of entry, and that the host, as far as possible, seeks to ensure that there is no break in continuity in the control exercised at entry, and that extending over the MNE's ongoing activities.

But one may well question to what extent the host state is capable of actually controling activities and operations of foreign affiliates already established within its borders prior to the enactment of entry restrictions and elaborate screening practices, or of even screened affiliates whose activities unforeseeably become detrimental to the host economy in course of time, or which only latterly come into conflict with the host's national interests.

1. Legal Power of Host over Established Foreign Affiliates

a. General legislation and practice

In the first place, of course, it is clear that once the MNE has established itself in the host state, regardless of the presence or absence of initial entry requirements, it automatically becomes subject to all the relevant laws of that state. Even mere branch offices are entirely answerable to the laws of the host. It is no more possible for a multinational enterprise to ignore the relevant laws of the state in which it carries on business than it is for the enterprise to force its entry into that state in the first place. This constitutes one obvious control over operations.

Secondly, it seems hardly necessary to reiterate that, as far as the state's legal capacity to control is concerned - subject of course to its treating a foreign corporation in conformity with international law - its sovereignty within its own territory is indisputable and supreme; and the territorial sovereignty of governments carries with it full juridical control over all persons - natural or artificial - located within its territory.[1] No multinational enterprise, however large or whatever its calculated GNP, has the power or authority to overrule governments, nor would it be in the enterprise's best interests to do so if it could. The very term "host state", as applied to the recipient of the foreign investment, reflects the notion that the enterprise has accepted the hospitality of the national government, and is welcome only as long as its behaviour conforms to the 'rules of the house'. We have, of course, remarked on the bargaining strength of the MNE, but bargaining strength is not to be confused with legal capacity or 'sovereignty' over state governments. Moreover, the relative bargaining positions of MNE and government often shift over time, as we shall discuss later in this chapter. Legally, the state's sovereignty and competence to control in a given situation can only be surrendered with the full consent of its government, and cannot be undermined with impunity from any outside force, be it political or commercial.[2]

In short, ultimate powers of control over operations, as well as over entry, reside with the governments; and should the enterprise's activities cease to serve the public interest in course of time, or overstep the limits of good corporate citizenship or the bounds of legality, the government's ultimate control weapon, for which it has ample legal authority, is its sovereign power to compel the enterprise to conform to its wishes or to leave, through expropriation procedures or simply by expulsion. The record of nationalizations and expropriations of foreign-controlled business are witness enough to the exercise of this capacity.

1. See *Case of the S.S. "Lotus"* [the *Lotus* case] (France *v.* Turkey), [1927] P.C.I.J., ser.A, No. 10.

2. See Behrman, *National Interests and the Multinational Enterprise: Tensions Among the North Atlantic Countries* (Englewood Cliffs, N.J.: Prentice-Hall 1970), [hereinafter cited as *National Interests*], at 136.

Although such governmental action clearly indicates that where the host wishes to exercise its legal power over the operations of foreign investors its will prevails, this capacity is not always exercised. Most governments of industrialized societies have little desire to regulate closely the many facets of the MNE's day-to-day business operations, which would involve regulating – along with initial capital inflows, local borrowing, and remittances of dividends, etc. – such internal concerns as intercorporate debts, capital transfers among affiliates, increases in equity, intercompany charges, intercompany pricing, profit allocations and similar activities.[3] Not only would such controls pose problems of application, and tend to increase disagreements and tensions between the host and the MNE, but they would most likely engender reprisals affecting the host's own MNEs operating abroad, not to mention generating fears on the part of domestic companies that similar controls could well be extended to their own operations.

The tendency, then, is for the government to control the larger-scale movements and operations of the foreign enterprise, within the state's jurisdiction, which could have a direct effect upon its domestic economy. Or, as Jack Behrman has written regarding the United States economic policy of non-discrimination toward foreign investments, "the United States Government has formulated policies toward the international companies based on functional activities rather than on the results of overall operations in support of major policy objectives such as international integration."[4]

3. This is not to ignore certain *illegal* incursions on the state's competence to control, such as bribery and other illicit business practices, though some governments, unhappily, actually foster such practices as a profitable way of doing business. Up to the present, on the national level, only the United States has enacted legislation making bribery and other corrupt business practices a criminal offense. (See United States' Foreign Corrupt Practices Act of 1977,Pub. L. No. 95-123, 95th Cong. (Dec. 19, 1977)). The fact that no other nation has enacted such legislation puts the United States at an obvious competitive disadvantage on the world market. An international guideline, such as that being worked on by the U.N. *Ad Hoc* Intergovernmental Working Group on the Problem of Corrupt Practices (see United Nations, "Report of the *Ad Hoc* Intergovernmental Working Group on the Problem of Corrupt Practices on Its First, Second, Third and Resumed Third Sessions", U.N. document E/6006 (July 5, 1977), reprinted in 16 *International Legal Materials* [I.L.M.] (1977), at 1236), or that being drafted by the International Chamber of Commerce (see International Chamber of Commerce, Commission on Ethical Practices, "Draft Report on Ethical Practices in Commercial Transactions," ICC Document No. 192/36, March 14, 1977, reprinted in 16 I.L.M. (1977), at 686) may help to alleviate some of the discrepancies. Unless there is adequate and effective machinery for enforcement, however, such guidelines may do little to alter the present situation.

4. Behrman, "The Multinational Enterprise and United States Foreign Economic Policy", 52 *Indiana Law Journal* (1977), at 618.

Hence, the extent to which legal control over MNE operations is exercised depends largely on the degree of importance attributed by the host to the desired productive or commercial activity,[5] or yet on the degree to which such action could create a commercial or political backlash more detrimental to the host than the activity it wishes to curtail. Government attempts to alter foreign corporate behaviour are, therefore, normally reserved for extreme cases,[6] the customary exercise of control by industrialized states taking the form of oral communication or persuasion, means which appear to be preferred over the imposition of regulatory controls that could lead to official discrimination against the foreign investor.[7]

There are, of course, exceptions, and even the governmental attitude of the majority of industrialized states, as just described, is subject to vacillation. "It is conceivable," speculates one writer, "that, at some point, host governments will decide [to] seriously restrict [the MNE's] entry and operations as Spain has done, and Japan before her. But such restriction is at a cost in terms of economic growth."[8]

Whether resorting to legal or extra-legal means, for legal or extra-legal reasons, the state has open to its use all the techniques and devices developed to control direct investment activities, just as was the case with initial entry. For example, the host might encourage or discourage operations by imposing quotas on exports or imports, by limiting the exportation or repatriation of capital, by offering various incentives to investors - who were not placed under such obligations as a condition of entry - to channel any investment expansion, or relocation of investment, into specified depressed areas, through low-cost loans, tax advantages, donation of plant sites, government subsidies and the like, or by regulating foreign or local borrowing, imposing profit-sharing obligations or resorting to similar incentives and disincentives geared to influencing MNE operations.

This in no wise means that legal restrictions are not imposed, but it points up the current tendency of most industrialized states to treat the foreign firm on a par, legally speaking, with domestic companies, and to refrain from imposing special legislation aimed solely at the foreign investor. Some deviations from

5. *See* Rubin, "The International Firm and the National Jurisdiction", in Kindleberger, ed., *The International Corporation: A Symposium* (Cambridge, Mass.: MIT Press, [1970]), [hereinafter cited as *Symposium*], at 198.

6. See Behrman, *National Interests, supra* note 2, at 137. See also, e.g., the *Fruehauf-France* case, *infra* note 61 and text following.

7. See Behrman, *U.S. International Business and Governments* (New York: McGraw-Hill, 1971), at 56.

8. Ibid., at 28.

this trend, however, as regards operations, are to be found in those same states which most systematically and closely screen foreign entry, notably Canada, France and Japan.

b. Special legislation

Canada's Foreign Investment Review Act,[9] which we discussed in connection with screening for entry,[10] reserves powers over certain aspects of operations as well, under those provisions in Phase II of the Act[11] which deal with existing foreign-controlled firms diversifying into new and unrelated industries within Canada. It does leave unhindered, however, the expansion of already-established enterprises into "related" businesses,[12] as well as the establishment of new enterprises, provided they are related to a business already operating in Canada as a foreign investment. Outside of these two exceptions to review, the Act undisguisedly discriminates between the Canadian company and the foreign-controlled company. A foreign investor ("non-eligible person"[13]) is deemed to have acquired control of a Canadian corporation for the purposes of the Act, if it purchases 5 per cent of its voting shares in the case of a public corporation, or 20 per cent of its voting shares in the case of a private corporation. Only if, in either case, the share purchases have clearly not led to control, is the purchaser exempt form review and the obligation to apply for Agency approval. Any investments not made in compliance with the Act may be nullified by the court, which can also suspend the voting rights of any shares, order the purchaser to dispose of any shares or property, or, if the holder of the shares or property resides outside Canada, vest the shares or property in a trustee authorized to dispose of them and turn the proceeds over to the dispossessed "noneligible person". Any purchaser of more than 50 per cent of the voting shares of a corporation operating in Canada is deemed automatically and absolutely to have acquired control, necessitating Agency review and approval, unless *de facto* control was deemed already to have existed prior to the additional share purchase. In other words, since one of the objects of the Act is specifically to review and regulate the transfer or

9. Foreign Investment Review Act, *Statutes of Canada* 1973 - 74, c.46.

10. See *supra* Chapters III and IV, text accompanying notes 83-88 and 7-9 respectively.

11. Proclaimed effective 15 October 1975.

12. A detailed set of guidelines has been published by the Foreign Investment Review Agency for determining what constitutes a "related business".

13. Certain enumerated categories of corporations are referred to as "non-eligible persons" under the terms of the Act. (See, Hayden and Burns, "Canadian Foreign Investment Review Act", 21 *Practical Lawyer* (1975)).

acquisition of *control,* if it can be demonstrated that control was already secured before the additional share purchase, presumably the controlling shareholder can increase his ownership percentage in whatever degree he likes without submitting to review procedures, subject to the provisions relating to step transactions referred to in Section 3(8) of the Act.[14]

The Act has not, in practice, been administered in a restrictive manner so as to curtail substantially the expansion of foreign investments in Canada, any more than it has substantially curtailed new entries, if we can take as an indication the high percentage of successful applicants in both categories. What those percentage statistics do not indicate, as was remarked in the case of entry figures, is the number of investors who were discouraged from applying for expansion of operations because of the new restrictions. On all available evidence, however, it would appear that, despite the detailed provisions of the Act, Canada still favours foreign direct investment for the benefits which accrue to her domestic economy,[15] and is therefore unlikely to interfere to too great a degree with the expansion requirements of foreign corporations operatting on Canadian territory. Still the machinery supplied by the Act is in place, and the severity of application potentially exercisable through it will be largely dependent on those responsible for its administration, and is therefore susceptible to modification with any change of government or of governmental policy.

In France, as in Canada, expansion of already existing investment is statutorily subject to review in the same way as initial entry by a new or acquired enterprise. It is interesting to note that, under the French laws governing foreign direct investments,[16] just as in the Canadian legislation, even the understanding of what constitutes a direct investment is governed by the notion of control. Direct investments under the French laws are described as all operations...

> ...lorsque, seule ou à plusieurs, concomitantes ou successives, elles ont *pour effet* de permettre à une ou plusieur es personnes *de prendre ou d'accroître le contrôle* d'une société exerçant une activité industrielle, agricole, commerciale, financière ou immobilière, quelle qu'en soi la

14. See Bonney, "Foreign Investment Review Act", 13 *Alberta Law Review* (1975), at 84.

15. See e.g. Rugman, "The Reglation of Foreign Investment in Canada", *Journal of World Trade Law* (July-August 1977), at 328, 332.

16. Notably the *loi du 28 décembre 1966* and the *décrets* for its application, *décret 67-78 du 27 janvier 1967* and *décret 68-1021 du 24 novembre 1968; l'arrêté du 9 août 1973;* see also the *Circulaire du 26 juillet 1974, Journal Officiel* [J.O.] of 17 Aug. 1974, on the notion of "*contrôle*".

forme, ou d'assurer l'extension d'une telle société déjà sous leur contrôle. [Emphasis supplied.][17]

Hence, even investments are affected where the mere *effect* of operations results in an assumption or increase of control over an enterprise, or in an expansion of its 'controlled' activities.

According to the regulations under the *loi du 28 décembre 1966* and its related *décrets,* the notion of "contrôle" is not even limited to the normal concept of control as effective decision-making power over the enterprise and its management; to be deemed to have gained control, under these regulations, the foreign MNE has only to exercise a "direct *or indirect* influence on the management of the company" ("influence directe *ou indirect* sur la gestion de la société") [emphasis supplied]. It does not even matter how the direct investment is made: whether by share purchase, licensing contract, or any of the other means of entrance into the market. All that matters is that there has been an "assumption of control" "prise de contrôle", and even that, under the strict interpretation of control described above, which equates "control" with "influence", even when that influence is only indirect.

Control, under the French law, maintains nonetheless a certain relationship with ownership. For example, for the purposes of the law, it is 20 per cent ownership of a publicly traded company which marks the threshold requiring, of a foreign investor, prior approval for a new acquisition or for expansion or increase of control of an existing enterprise.[18] The French legislation has not, however, formally recognized or made allowance for the absence-of-control exception as perceptively applied by the Canadians. Some similarity with the Canadian law reappears, however, in the stipulation that nonobservance of the special reporting provisions and prior approval required by the Minister of Economy and Finance under Article 3 of the law (*loi n° 66-1008*) will result in legal action. The penalties under the French law are more severe than those of the Canadian legislation; in addition to fines, the offender may find himself faced with imprisonment and possible confiscation of the acquired equity (Article 5-1). By such policies and legislative provisions, as elaborated in *décret*

17. *Décret n° 67-78 du 27 janvier 1967, Titre* II, Art. 2 (3°) (b). (English translation: "...where, individually or collectively, simultaneously or successively, their *effect* is to allow one or several persons *to assume or increase control* of a company *(société)* performing an industial, agricultural, commercial, financial or real estate activity, in any form whatsoever, or to assure the expansion of such a company already under their control. [Emphasis supplied.]")

18. *Loi n° 66-1008 du 28 décembre 1966; décret 67-78 du 27 janvier 1967* [1967] *Journal Officiel* [J.O.] of 29 January 1967. Since the new rules announced by the Minister of Economy and Finance published in the *Journal Officiel* of 5 August 1980, member states of the European Community are no longer subject to the 20 percent threshold rule. See *supra* Chapter III, note 96. The rule still holds, however, for companies from outside the Community.

67-78 and other legislation referred to above, the French authorities have an extremely effective system for maintaining control over foreign direct investments already operating within their territory.[19]

The French legislation of the late 1960's was not the first signal of France's intention to exercise control over the activities of foreign investors within its economy. Foreign-owned oil companies in France were having limitations imposed upon their refining and distribution activities for close to twenty years prior to the enactment of the more recent laws.

Japan's traditional hostility to foreign direct investment needs little elaboration. Due to the fact that the gradual relaxation of the government's highly restrictive inward investment policies[20] - initiated in the 1960's - has only been assessable within the last couple of years, some clarity is still lacking as regards restrictions on operations of foreign enterprises subsequent to initial entry. Clarification may indeed develop slowly, since Japan's Foreign Investment Law[21] and other official regulations governing foreign business investment within her territory are intentionally left unspecific and undefined in order to allow the greatest possible discretion in their administration.[22] These broad discretionary powers are undoubtedly seen by the Japanese government as a necessary counterfoil to Japan's new regulation which, in theory, opened up, in 1976, most Japanese industries to possibilities of 100 per cent foreign ownership.[23]

This new policy has not signalled the demise of case-by-case screening for entry,[24] and, as in Canada and France, approval must be sought for any changes in product lines or other expansion of foreign enterprises operating within the country. Unaccountability for decisions made under the liberalized laws is assured by Japan's practice of not publicizing the internal ministerial rules and regulations ("Naiki") which govern official procedures relating to

19. See Schmidt, "La protection des entreprises nationales contre les prises de contrôle par des sociétés multinationales étrangères", 21 *Revista della società* (1976), at 623-625.

20. Such a policy change was necessary for admittance to the Organisation for Economic Co-operation and Development (OECD), of which Japan became a member in 1964, thereby accepting adherence to the OECD Code of Liberalisation of Capital Movements.

21. Law Concerning Foreign Investment (Law No. 163, May 10, 1950), 5 *EHS Law Bulletin Series: Japan* (1976), at DAl *et seq.:* see also *supra* Chapter III, note 27.

22. See Ozawa, "Technology Imports and Direct Investments in Japan", 7 *Journal of World Trade Law* (1973), at 675.

23. Exceptions include mining, retail chains, agriculture, petroleum, and the leather industry (Lenrow, "Foreign Direct Investment in the United States: Possible Restrictions at Home and a New Climate for American Investment Abroad", 26 *American University Law Review* (1976), at 126).

24. See *supra* Chapter III, text accompanying note 103.

foreign investment, and of communicating the official decisions verbally rather than in writing. This frequently forces the foreign investor to consult the officials in person on questions of investment activities, giving the officials yet another administrative advantage.[25]

Japan's Fair Trade Commission is also beginning to assume investment monitoring functions. The Commission has recently taken on a 'watchdog' role over foreign enterprises operating in the Japanese market, to guard against any foreign investment activity which would result in a competitive advantage over the domestic counterpart. This new "mission of policing foreign companies or foreign-Japanese joint ventures to prevent them from disrupting existing oligopolistic control of markets", observes one Western critic, "is a far cry from the original one which was to guard the consumer against unfair monopolistic practices of business and industry."[26] The Fair Trade Commission has even taken the initiative, in keeping with the Japanese government practice of making and publishing periodic surveys on the activities of foreign-affiliated enterprises in Japan, to conduct its own study of potential problem areas caused by foreign-based multinationals in the Japanese economy.[27]

All indications point to a continued hypersensitivity and apprehension on the part of the Japanese Government toward the inflow of foreign investment capital into the country; the Government's legal authority to regulate such inflow has not been challenged.

2. 'National Treatment' Principle in Practice

One might be inclined to ask: Where does the principle of 'national treatment', as advocated under international law, come into all this discriminatory legislation as it pertains to international commercial transactions?

In the context of MNE activities, 'national treatment' means that host states should accord to foreign-controled enterprises "treatment under their laws, regulations and administrative practices, consistent with international law and no less favourable than that accorded in like situations to domestic enterprises."[28] From what we have seen of the discriminatory legislation against

25. See Ozawa, op. cit., *supra* note 22, at 675.

26. Glazer, *The International Businessman in Japan* (Rutland, Vermont & Tokyo: C.E. Tuttle Co., 1968), at 18, extracted by the present writer from a longer citation in Ozawa, op. cit., *supra* note 22, at 676.

27. See Ozawa, op. cit., *supra* note 22, at 677.

28. Organisation for Economic Co-operation and Development, *Declaration on International Investment and Multinational Enterprises by the Governments of OECD Member Countries* (21st June 1976), OECD Publications, Paris, 1976,[hereinafter cited as OECD *Declaration*], at Section II:1.

foreign 'legal persons' doing business in Canada, France and Japan, some serious questions could be raised as to the legality, under international law, of such practices.

a. National practice

The question could be raised, for instance, as to whether certain provisions of the Canadian Foreign Investments Review Act, such as those limiting foreign shareholdings, transgress the national treatment principle of international law. As yet, however, no serious objections appear to have been advanced from international sources. Moreover, if objections were raised, the implications would needs be extended to such states as Sweden and Finland, where alien ownership is likewise statutorily limited, not to mention France and Japan, where certain aspects of the investment control systems could hardly be described as other than discriminatory.

This whole area of national treatment as it relates to commercial activities is inconsistently applied by the various states - certainly internationally, but even within the context of the largely free-enterprise industrialized nations. For example, in contrast to those states mentioned above which legislate against foreign shareholders, the company laws of Great Britain, the Republic of Ireland, France, Belgium, the Netherlands, West Germany, Austria and Israel prohibit any company quoted on the stock exchange from discriminating against foreign shareholders.[29] Similarly, in striking contrast to Canadian discriminatory legislation against foreign investors are the policies of Canada's sole contiguous neighbor, the United States, perhaps the most ardent advocate of national treatment - even in commercial matters - to be found anywhere.[30] Other than in essential national security and related industries, the United States accords national treatment to all foreign investors, putting them on an equal footing with their domestic counterparts. One of the chief legal instruments used in the extension of such treatment is the U.S. treaty of friendship, commerce and navigation (FCN treaty) which the Government has concluded with many of its investment partners in recent years.[31] These treaties contain a reciprocal guarantee of national treatment by each signatory state.

29. Vagts, "The United States of America and the Multinational Enterprise", in Hahlo, ed., *Nationalism and the Multinational Enterprise: Legal, Economic and Managerial Aspects* (Dobbs Ferry, N.Y.: Oceana, 1973), at 26.

30. See e.g. Sections 404-405 of the 1974 U.S. Trade Act (signed into law, January 3, 1975) relating to non-discrimination in commercial agreements.

31. See *supra* Chapter III, note 43 and text accompanying notes 44-53.

"National treatment", as used in these treaties, means that an alien contracting party must receive no less favourable treatment than that "accorded therein, in like situations, to nationals, companies, products, vessels or other objects, as the case may be..."[32] of the contracting national.

In practice, the unreserved application of national treatment equally by both parties is sometimes sidestepped by general exceptions and restrictions contained in protocols appended to the treaty. In a protocol to the U.S. FCN treaty with Luxembourg, for example, Luxembourg reserves to itself the privilege of rejecting (U.S.) aliens seeking gainful employment within the country, unless the "appropriate authorizations for access to and exercise of such activities have been granted."[33] This type of qualification, which demands of the alien an authorization not required by the state's own citizens, constitutes a significant curtailment, if not a *de facto* denial, of the principle which the treaty has otherwise sought to achieve and by which each party has mutually pledged to refrain from imposing upon nationals of the other signatory any restrictions more severe than those it imposes upon its own citizens. In the view of the present writer, only if the reservation is interpreted as referring to initial entry of the alien, in keeping with the normal sovereign power of a state over the entry of aliens into its territory, could it be construed as not compromising the letter or the spirit of the treaty. In any case, as the Protocol does not represent a unilateral act by Luxembourg, but rather was agreed to by both parties, a certain degree of inequality in the equality of treatment has clearly been allowed.

By the same FCN treaty, the United States has, for its part, specifically assured national treatment to Luxembourg nationals, and has elaborated the assurances as regards the commercial activities of the foreign party within the U.S. in terms of explicit permission granted both to companies and to nationals of the other party to establish branches and production facilities within the United States, to set up companies on U.S. territory and to "control and manage enterprises which they have established or acquired" in the U.S.[34] It is noteworthy that control and management have been given specific reference, in express recognition of the importance of these aspects of investment, and so as to leave no ambiguity as to the unrestrictive nature of the U.S. policy of national treatment. Such a treaty, in effect:

32. Treaty of Friendship, Establishment and Navigation with Luxembourg, Feb. 23, 1962, Art.XV, para.1, [1963] 1 U.S.T. 251, T.I.A.S. No. 5306.

33. Ibid., Protocol, para. 4.

34. Ibid., Art. VII, para. 1. Cf. *supra,* Chapter III, citation accompanying note 45.

> affords citizens of the party nation the same rights a citizen of Texas would have if he were to attempt to invest in California. There is almost no limit to the type of commercial activity they can engage in: they can organize or create new industry or an industrial plant, and can purchase or hold real estate as easily as any American citizen, regardless of state statutory language to the contrary. There is no numerical limitation as to percentage of control or absolute acreage to limit their holding. The investment freedom is almost complete.[35]

The question might be posed as to how this official U.S. Government policy to treat foreign capital essentially the same as domestic investment works out in practice. One indication can be derived from reports of the Düsseldorf Conference on Multinational Corporatons in 1973,[36] where a number of European investors long engaged in the U.S. market attested to their satisfaction and success with their investment experience in that country.[37] The Record of the Conference also affirmed that "once these [foreign] companies undertake U.S. operations, they are treated without discrimination under the same laws that apply to U.S. companies."[38]

It is unlikely that the United States will reverse its traditional policy of welcoming inward private foreign direct investment or of including such foreign commercial enterprise within the purview of its exercise of national treatment. Even the Government's most recent legislation on the subject of multinational enterprises, the Foreign Investment Study Act of 1974[39] and the International Investment Survey Act of 1976,[40] requires no more than the conducting of periodic surveys on the extent of foreign inward direct investment in the U.S. To date, such surveys have resulted in little which would alter the present policy, other than the proposal for monitoring foreign investment of over 5 per cent stock acquisition[41] in certain specified areas, no system having hitherto

35. "State Regulation of Foreign Investment", 9 *Cornell International Law Journal* (1975), at 92.

36. The conference papers were edited by Don Wallace and published under the title, *International Control of Investment: The Düsseldorf Conference on Multinational Corporations* (New York: Praeger, 1974).

37. Ibid., at 115.

38. Ibid., at 116.

39. Pub. L. No. 93-479, 88 Stat. 1450; approved Oct. 26, 1974.

40. Publ. L. No. 94-472, 90 Stat. 2059 (codified at 22 U.S.C. § 3101 (1976)).

41. See Simmonds, "Foreign Investment, The International Law Standard, and the Multinational Corporation, An Overview", in Simmonds, ed., *Legal Problems of Multinational Corporations,* British Institute of International and Comparative Law (Dobbs Ferry, N.Y.: Oceana, 1977), [hereinafter cited as *Legal Problems*], at 9.

existed in the United States for monitoring the amount of foreign investment in the country or for assessing its impact on the domestic economy. In fact, the Study resulting from the 1974 Act, while recommmending continual assessment of trends and of significant developments in inward investment, as well as the undertaking of special studies where needed, concluded that the current unrestrictive policy toward inward direct investment should continue without imposition of new restraints.[42] Hence, while acknowledging the right of other governments to place constraints upon entry and operations of foreign companies, the U.S. Government holds the view - which it encourages other governments to share[43] - that in accordance with the national treatment principle, such constraints should be commensurate with those same governments' constraints on their own domestic industries and nationals.

b. EEC and international practice

It has been suggested that the more developed a nation's economy, the less justified is any discrimination between foreign and domestic capital.[44] This would tend to imply that discrimination under certain conditions is indeed justifiable. The opinion has been more overtly expressed by one writer who, while advocating corrective action against any industrial practice - whether of foreign or domestic origin - that goes against the national interest, nonetheless asserts that "influencing the behavior of foreign-owned firms or segments of multinational enterprise requires policies that differ from those required for purely national firms."[45]

A rational approach would seem to require that, in order to warrant differential treatment between foreign and domestic enterprises, there must first be convincing evidence that the two are essentially different from one another. In addition to the United States, both the Organisation for Economic Co-operation and Development (OECD) and the European Economic Community (EEC) appear to have decided that the two - foreign and domestic firms - do not essentially differ. The OECD has evidenced this by its Code of Liberali-

42. United States, Department of Commerce, *Foreign Direct Investment in the United States* (1976), at 240-241.

43. See Behrman, "The Multinational Enterprise and United States Foreign Economic Policy", op. cit., *supra* note 4, at 620.

44. See "Freedom for Capital Movements," *ICC Information,* Vol. 40, No. 8 (December 1974), Paris.

45. Simmonds, "Is the World Going More Multinational?", Internationalization of Business, Paper read at the Society of Business Economists Conference at Churchill College, Cambridge, 1971, at 7.

sation of Capital Movements[46] providing for non-discrimination between foreign and domestic investors within a country, and for the freedom of establishment (with the normal security exceptions) and of transfer of funds. The EC Commission has similarly demonstrated its advocacy of the equal-treatment position by its recent proposals to undertake measures that would not "impede the development of a phenomenon with recognized economic and social advantages, but...merely aim at guarding the Community against its harmful effects with the help of a suitable legal framework" - a framework which would "contain *no discriminatory aspect* and...[would] apply alike to individuals and to undertakings, whether of national, international, Community or extra-Community foundations." [Emphasis supplied.][47] Virtually all those measures proposed by the Commission with regard to MNEs relate to problems which are just as likely to arise in national enterprises or in undertakings by private individuals as they are to arise from MNE operations.[48]

In practice within the EEC, the *Continental Can* case[49] has been frequently cited as an example of an extra-Community corporation, the treatment of which most likely deviated from the current policy on mergers of companies within the Community, i.e. deviated from the supposed non-discriminatory position of the EEC *vis-à-vis* extra-Community undertakings. We shall go into this case in considerable detail when considering the question of MNE control through merger legislation later in this chapter.

It is true of many countries, though to a far lesser degree in the developed than in the less-developed nations, that while national treatment *vis-à-vis* foreign enterprises is professed in principle, in practice it is not granted without substantial qualifications.[50] The thought was expressed at the 1974 Annual Meeting of the American Society of International Law (A.S.I.L.) that "the national treatment formula is too simplistic, that the implied equality does not

46. May 1962.

47. Squartini, "The EEC and the Multinational Enterprise", paper read at the International Conference on Legal Problems of Multinational Enterprises, the British Institute of International and Comparative Law, London, September 1976; subsequently published in Simmonds, *Legal Problems,* op. cit., *supra* note 41.

48. *Idem.*

49. *Re Continental Can Co.,* 15 E.C.J.O. L7/25 (1972), CCH *Common Market Reporter,* [1970-1972 Transfer Binder] ¶ 9481, 11 *Common Market Law Reports* (1972), D27; *Continental Can Co.* v. *E.C. Commission,* 2 CCH *Common Market Reporter* ¶ 8171, 12 *Common Market Law Reports* 216 (E.C.J. 1973).

50. See Vernon, "Future of the Multinational Enterprise", in Kindleberger, ed., *Symposium,* op. cit., *supra* note 5, at 389-390.

correspond to the real feelings of people and governments."[51] Certainly in such areas as balance-of-payments regulations, it is inevitable that distinctions between foreign and domestic capital be made. But that distinction is inherent in the very nature of the regulation. There is due cause to question the extension of the distinction to the extent suggested by Siqueiros in his report to the UNIDROIT Conference in Rome, in September of 1976. Siqueiros stated the opinion that "equality of treatment" should never mean equal treatment with nationals of the host state, his idea being that aliens, multinationals in particular, should enjoy a less privileged status than nationals, but that all aliens should be treated alike. By Siqueiros' view, "equality of treatment" is clearly distinguished from "national treatment" in the sense intended under the international law principle. His stance is also in direct conflict with that embodied in the OECD Guidelines for Multinational Enterprises[52] in which "equality of treatment" is expressly held to mean equality of treatment with the nationals of the home state,[53] i.e. national treatment. Siqueiros' view would seem to correspond rather with the most-favoured-nation (MFN) clause in commercial treaties, by which a government agrees to grant to the contracting state trading or investment terms no less favourable than those granted by it to any third state dealing in a like commodity. Though the most-favoured-nation clause was originally characteristically a feature of trading agreements rather than investment agreements, the modern commercial treaties, dealing specifically with corporate investment, have readily incorporated MFN standards, and, further, increasingly tend to juxtapose MFN and national treatment in the treaty clauses. In addition to the obvious example of the FCN treaties in force between numerous nations world-wide, another interesting example is to be found in an exchange of letters constituting an Agreement between the Governments of Denmark and Malawi regarding private investment in the latter by the former.[54] In the Danish letter, most-favoured-nation provisions have been very closely associated, if not all but equated,[55] with national treatment:

51. "Should Investment Capital Stay Home? A Canadian-U.S. Dialogue" *Proceedings of the 68th Annual Meeting, American Society of International Law,* April 25- 27, 1974, Washington, D.C. [hereinafter cited as *Xroceedings*], at 30.

52. OECD Guidelines for Multinational Enterprises, Press/A(76)20 of 21 June 1976, 15 (1976) *International Legal Materials,* at 969 *et seq.*

53. See e.g. Seidl-Hohenfeldern, "The United Nations and Transnational Corporations", in Simmonds, ed., *Legal Problems,* op. cit., *supra* note 41, at 54.

54. Exchange of Letters constituting an Agreement between the Governments of Denmark and Malawi, 1 Aug. 1966, Copenhagen, as supplements to a Loan Agreement of the same date, 586 U.N.T.S. 3.

55. Compare paras. 4 and 6 with para. 5 (supplied in text *supra*).

(4) Such investments of Danish Investors in Malawi shall not be accorded a treatment less favourable than the Government of Malawi accords to *any other similar investments in its territory belonging to its own Nationals or Companies or to National or Companies of third countries.*

(5) The Government of Malawi shall not subject the activities of Danish Investors in connection with their investments guaranteed by the Danish Government to conditions less favourable than it imposes on activities in connection with *any other similar investments in its territory.*

(6) Such investments by Danish Investors should be accorded no less degree of protection than the Government of Malawi accords to *any other similar investments in its territory belonging to its own Nationals or Companies or to Nationals or Companies of third countries.* [Emphasis supplied.][56]

The notable difference between Siqueiros' position and that set out in the above Agreement is that while both seek to establish a certain alignment of most-favoured-nation with equal treatment, Siqueiros, in effect, reduces national treatment to most-favoured-nation status, while the Agreement, on the other hand, tends to elevate most-favoured-nation status to a point where it is all but incorporated into national treatment.

One participant in the Annual Meeting of the A.S.I.L.[57] proposed what seems to the present writer to be a realistic concept "somewhere between MFN and national treatment. The new concept would recognize that national treatment for the foreign-owned enterprise is too much to ask for from either the investor's country [for purposes of regulatory jurisdiction over export controls, balance-of-payments, taxation, etc.] or the host country, but it would establish some guidelines (i) to define the link; (ii) to define the areas in which distinctions can legitimately be drawn in economic regulation by virtue of this link; and (iii) to define the areas in which distinctions should not be drawn by virtue of the link - i.e. where the distinctions become discrimination if imposed by the country of investment and over-reaching if imposed by the country of the source of the investment." Although the author of this observation admits that he has not yet worked out the concept, he expresses his willingness to do so, and goes so far as to offer a tentative suggestion toward this end.[58] The concept appears to be based on practical and realistic observations, worthy of

56. Loc. cit., *supra* note 54.

57. Andreas F. Lowenfeld of the New York University School of Law.

58. See *Proceedings,* op. cit., *supra* note 51, note 10 at 31.

development, and represents a possible workable compromise between the principle of national treatment in theory and in practice, *viz.*, a policy advocating the avoidance of any discrimination on the part of the host which is inconsistent with a reasonable exercise of national sovereignty.

3. Application of Law and Policy

We have now had a look at some of the major legislation, techniques and policies governing operations of MNEs once they are established in the host state. Theories or techniques of control over operations are, however, of little use as long as they remain theoretical; and there can be no application until the operations are in motion. In theory, as long as host regulations over operations are adhered to by the foreign enterprise, there should be little room for conflict. Experience shows, however, that conflicts do arise. What, then, is the chief source of tension, and how are conflicts over operations most often generated?

Perhaps first and foremost, the uncertainties and fears generated by foreign decision-making are a prime source of tensions between host and MNE. These fears, in addition to initiating the type of regulatory legislation which we have been looking at in Chapter III, contribute to inconsistencies in the application of the national treatment principle, as just reviewed. Actual conflicts can of course only arise in the course of operations.

On the part of the MNE, the source of contention is most likely to originate in flagrant host-state transgressions of national treatment, or over other more subtle means of discrimination, such as discriminatory taxation[59] and other policies or laws which unreasonably inhibit the normal profitability or effective functioning of the enterprise. The MNE, in its capacity as 'guest', is in a difficult position to seek, much less, obtain, redress of its grievances, as the enterprise can simply be forced out of business, or be required to relinquish its local control, if it does not conform to the terms of the host.[60]

On the part of the host, the source of the conflict is usually not so much an outright violation of the law by the MNE as some action on the part of the enterprise which would result in an unacceptable loss of control by the host government, or in some other apparent threat to the domestic market or national interest. A legal or extra-legal remedy is then pursued to rectify the alleged imbalance.

59. See *infra* Chapter XII: 5.
60. See generally *infra* Chapters XI-XII.

The role of operations, then, obviously does not stop at a clinical look at techniques geared to their control, but pervades every area of business-government relationships, once the enterprise has gained entrance into foreign territory. What we are concerned about now is the actual consequences of these controls and conflicts, having at last arrived at the stage where conflicts are generated, namely: operations.

a. Fruehauf-France

The classic case demonstrating the extent of host state control over the activities of the local foreign affiliate is the *Fruehauf-France* case,[61] which is an illustration *par excellence* of the practical significance of that ever-central theme: the ownership/control, or ownership/management balance.

While the ownership/management question in the context of *entrance* requirements, as we saw in the preceding chapter, revolved around host requirements that both ownership and management be characterized by substantial local - even joint - participation, in the context of MNE *operations* one becomes aware that, whatever the source of the managers and directors, 'expatriate' or local, the fact remains that "[t]he law holds the management to certain standards of conduct", and it is this standard of conduct which is "the legal link between ownership and management."[62] This link, and its relation to effective control, is a delicate one, as the law has only recently begun to cope with the fact of the separation of ownership and management, though it has developed rapidly in that regard. The present legislation in this area "has to be considered rather as a framework to be filled in than as a set of settled rules....It is more likely that the law will deal, blunderingly, with each situation as it comes up on its individual merits; and most likely of all, the transactions by the 'control', lying outside the technical sphere of corporation action, will remain outside the normal cognizance of the law."[63]

Something of this "legal link" can nonetheless be aptly illustrated by the *Fruehauf-France* case, one of the most striking examples of the importance, in practice, of management control in the delicate ownership/management balance, and the role of the law in maintaining it. In *Fruehauf-France,* involving U.S. trading-with-the-enemy legislation, largely due to the less than

61. *Société Freuhauf* v. *Massardy,* [1968] D.S. Jur.147, [1965] J.C.P. II 14, 274 *bis* (Cour d'Appel, Paris).

62. Berle and Means, *The Modern Corporation and Private Property,* revised ed. (New York: Harcourt, Brace and World [c. 1968], at 196.

63. Ibid., at 207, 218.

full ownership position of the U.S. parent, a French management manoeuvre was possible, based upon the French legal concept of *abus de droit,* which enabled the French subsidiary to prevail over the U.S. denial policy regarding trade with the People's Republic of China.

The relevant facts of the case are as follows: Fruehauf-France, S.A., a two-thirds American-owned subsidiary of the American-based multinational Fruehauf International, contracted to supply Automobiles Berliet, S.A. (Berliet) with truck assemblies which Berliet would then incorporate into trucks it was exporting to the People's Republic of China. Before the obligations of the contract were fulfilled, however, the U.S. parent received orders from the United States Treasury Department to cancel the order, in accordance with the provisions of the Trading-with-the-Enemy Act.[64] Berliet refused to accept termination of the contract, and threatened to sue Fruehauf-France for close to one million dollars.

The French directors[65] next filed suit in the Commercial Court of Corbeil, claiming, under the French legal principle of *abus de droit,* that cancellation of the contract was illegal, as its sole motivation was the desire on the part of the American directors to avoid liability under the Trading-with-the-Enemy Act, and such motivation was extraneous, if not contrary, to the corporate interest. The principle of *abus de droit* authorizes the French courts to overrule the management and directors of a French corporation, even when the decision is arrived at by normal corporate procedures, if that decision is found to be incompatible with the company interest.[66]

Fruehauf-France accordingly sought and was granted by the Commercial Court the appointment of a temporary administrator to perform the contractual obligation entered into with Berliet. This decision was affirmed by the Court of Appeals of Paris which held that the appointment of an outside administrator could be made by the Court when the normal functioning of the corporation was in jeopardy and thus threatened with ruin. The Court felt this to be the case in the instance of Freuhauf, when assessing the potential liability and damage to Freuhauf's credit standing if performance were withheld. Even the French Government interceded on behalf of the French directors, arguing for the interests of the corporation and society in protecting the French economy, over those of the "private interests" of the American directors.

64. Foreign Assets Control Regulations, 50 U.S.C. App. § 5 (b) (1) (1964).

65. Five of the eight directors of Fruehauf-France had been designated by the parent company.

66. See Skol and Peterson, "Export Control Laws and Multinational Enterprises", 11 *International Lawyer* (1977), at 31-32, relying generally on Craig, "Application of the Trading with the Enemy Act To Foreign Corporations Owned by Americans: Reflections of Fruehauf v. Massardy", 83 *Harvard Law Review* (1970), at 579, 589.

"Private interests", in this case, referred to the American directors' desire to avoid liability under the U.S. legislation, seen by the French Court as a pursuit of personal financial gain.

It would appear that the ruling in *Fruehauf* was subsequently strengthened by, if not directly responsible for, some additional French legislation assuring the protection of national enterprises against the exercise of control by foreign MNEs. The *loi n° 66-537 du 24 juillet 1966,*[67] in addition to stipulating various provisions regarding voting rights of different categories of shareholders, with the aim of limiting the power of majority shareholders and protecting the interests of minority holders, instituted the theory of *abus de majorité,* in which one sees reflected the very elements of the Fruehauf ruling. Under the concept of *abus de majorité,* it is possible for minority shareholders to nullify "les déliberations collectives contraires aux intérêts de la société par lesquelles les majoritaires s'avantagent sans contrepartie au profit des minoritaires".[68] Similarly, minority shareholders may institute such repressive sanctions as those found in Article 437-3° of the *loi n° 66-537* which penalizes directors who "de mauvaise foi auront fait, des biens ou du crédit de la société, un usage qu'ils savaient contraire à l'intérêt de celle-ci, à des fins personelles ou pour favoriser une autre société ou entreprise dans laquelle ils étaient intéressés directement ou indirectements." These provisions can of course have a wider application than simply to circumstances such as those in *Fruehauf-France,* but an additional provision appears to derive directly from the *Fruehauf* ruling, *viz.*: "les minoritaires pourront demander, par voie de référé, la nomination d'un administrateur provisoire de la société, lorsque la politique suivie par les majoritaires et les dirigeants en fonction des intérêts de la société multinationale qu'ils représentent fera courir à la société sous contrôle de graves périls ou des risques de ruine".[69]

It would hence appear that, contrary to an assertion by Messrs. Brooke and Remmers[70] that the local manager of a foreign-controlled subsidiary must "set aside any nationalistic attitudes and appreciate that in the last resort his loyalty must be to the shareholders of the parent company, and he must protect their interests even if it might appear that it is not perhaps in the national interests of the country in which he is operating", in France, at least, such is not the case. The French laws favour the general duty of the corporation to the local minority shareholders, to the (host) state, and to the (host) society, and endow the

67. *Loi n° 66-537 du 24 juillet 1966 sur les sociétés commerciales,* J.O., (1966 juillet), at 6402.

68. Schmidt, op. cit., *supra* note 19, at 627.

69. *Idem.*

70. Brooke and Remmers, *The Strategy of the Multinational Enterprise: Organization and Finance* (London: Longman [1970]) [hereinafter cited as *Strategy*], at 8.

minority shareholders with the legal power to ensure those interests. Any other state, regardless of size, has the prerogative to do the same.

b. 'Serving two masters'

The *Fruehauf-France* case, in addition to its being a classic example of the practical significance of the ownership/management "legal link", and of the ultimate power of the sovereign state over the foreign MNE affiliate, also highlights another source of tension leading to conflict, namely, the fact that the MNE affiliate is essentially answerable to two masters: the parent company and the host government. This can result in divided loyalties on the part of the affiliate, as well as confused and overlapping jurisdictions, and can, in the course of operations, easily lead to conflict and legal difficulties.

The potential for conflict in this area has led to the appearance in several countries of "Guidelines for Good Corporate Citizenship", directed at foreign investors. Such guidelines are to be found in Canada and Japan, for example, and are an expression of the anxiety on the part of the host that when an enterprise faces divided loyalties it is more inclined to adhere to the policies of the parent or the parent's government than to those of the host.[71]

This anxiety is not always borne out in case law, however, as demonstrated by *Fruehauf-France*[72] and such other well-known cases as *British Nylon Spinners*[73] and *Swiss Watchmakers*.[74]

One rather less-known case which addresses the question of divided corporate loyalties, and which should also serve to counter the anxiety that the parent-company's government will necessarily prevail over that of the host when loyalties are divided, is *Texasgulf, Inc.* v. *Canada Development Corporation*.[75] The Canada Development Corporation (CDC) was created as the result of Canadian legislation[76] aimed at increasing Canadian participation in

71. See e.g. "Some Guiding Principles of Good Corporate Behaviour for Subsidiaries in Canada of Foreign Companies", *Trade and Commerce* (1967), at 40-41; see also Litvak and Maule, "The Multinational Corporation: Some Economic and Political-Legal Implications," 5 *Journal of World Trade Law* (1971), at 637-638.

72. Loc. cit., *supra* note 61.

73. *United States* v. *Imperial Chemical Industries Ltd.* 100 F. Supp. 504 (S.D.N.Y. 1951), 105 F. Supp. 215 (S.D.N.Y. 1952); *British Nylon Spinners Ltd.* v. *Imperial Chemical Industries Ltd.*, 2 All E.R. 780 (1952), *final judgment*, [1954] 3 All E.R. 88 (Ch).

74. *United States* v. *The Watchmakers of Switzerland Information Center*, [1963] CCH Trade Cases ¶ 70,600 and [1965] CCH Trade Cases ¶ 71,352.

75. *Texasgulf, Inc.* v. *Canada Development Corporation*, 366 F. Supp. 374 (S.D. Tex. 1973).

76. Canada Corporation Development Act, *Statutes of Canada*, 1970-71-72, c. 49.

the economic interests and development of Canada, largely through encouraging an increase in domestic shareholdings in foreign enterprises operating in Canada. In the instant case, the CDC, wholly owned by the Canadian Government, made a cash tender offer to purchase ten million additional[77] shares of the common stock outstanding of Texasgulf, Inc. Texasgulf responded by seeking from a U.S. court a permanent injunction against the acquisition which would carry with it a shift in effective control, contending, *inter alia,* that the transaction would create a conflict of interest between the statutory objectives of the acquirer (CDC) and the latter's duties to Texasgulf and its non-Canadian shareholders.[78] The court denied a preliminary injunction, despite its finding that a future conflict of interest between the two parties was indeed a genuine possibility, on the basis that, if such a conflict proved injurious to the shareholders, there were already-established adequate legal remedies in municipal company law available to Texasgulf to rectify any injustices.

The court, while astutely applying the separation-of-powers doctrine which precludes the courts from establishing political and economic policies,[79] deferring such matters to the Executive and Legislative branches of the Government, which are most competent to decide questions of U.S. foreign policy and national interest, nonetheless went on to pronounce, citing no previous authority for its ruling, that this particular transaction was not contrary to United States public policy nor to its national interest. U.S. case law, while establishing the power of the courts to interpret and apply policy decisions incorporated in statutes, does not extend this power to the actual determination of national interest and public policy, particularly with regard to questions of a complex international economic and political nature for which the courts lack the adequate authority and expertise.[80]

The *Texasgulf* case is of particular significance to our discussion, in that it marks the first instance of a U.S. court dealing with the problem of divided corporate loyalties and conflicts of interest resulting directly from control implications of stock acquisition. Of significance too is the U.S. court's finding that:

77. CDC already owned an insignificant percentage of Texasgulf stock.

78. Outside of Canada, Texasgulf had substantial assets and operations in a number of other states, including the United States, Mexico and Australia.

79. *Timken Roller Bearing Co.* v. *United States,* 341 U.S. 593 at 605 (Justice Frankfurter dissenting); also later in *National City Bank of New York* v. *Republic of China,* 348 U.S. 356, 370-71 (1955) (Justice Reed dissenting).

80. Parker, "Foreign Relations Law," (Recent Decisions), 8 *Vanderbilt Journal of Transnational Law* (1974), 226, 228-229.

> Acquisition of control of [a] domestic multinational corporation by a wholly owned foreign Governmental Corporation does not *per se* create an unreasonable conflict of interest between the objectives of the acquirer and its duties to the domestic corporation and its shareholders.[81]

It is especially noteworthy here that it was the court of the parent company's home state which ruled in favour of the *foreign* corporation's acquisition of control.

The MNE's answerability to two masters is clearly recognized in German company law. In the case of German multinationals, the controlling power of the parent over the subsidiary abroad can be secured by the legal device of inserting a clause in the contract drawn up with the subsidiary, requiring its directors to obey not only the laws of the state of its incorporation, and its own bylaws, but also the rules and directives of the German parent.[82] Although this device may well clarify the private law of the enterprise in question, it would seem to this author to do nothing to avert potential conflicts of interest between the policies of the parent corporation and those of the host government when these diverge.

Of course the problem is compounded by the fact that the multinational enterprise as a whole, operating simultaneously in more than one jurisdiction external to the home country, is often subject to multiple conflicting efforts to control its activities on the part of each state where it does business. As no two nations have identical laws or policies governing all aspects of MNE activities, the multinational can get caught up in a web of powerful and often contradictory forces, through an assortment of national policies dictated by varying local conditions and economic forces. This existence of a variety of national jurisdictions is popularly viewed as a means by which the MNE is able to maximize its profits by moving to the most advantageous jurisdiction, or of somehow avoiding *all* legal controls and jurisdictions by dint of being answerable to so many and consequently subject to none. The logic of the latter paradoxical suggestion is not, as far as the present writer can judge, readily ascertainable. The possibility is rarely considered that this same position could amount to the MNE "getting the worst of all possible worlds by being penalized everywhere."[83]

81. *Texasgulf, Inc.* v. *Canada Development Corp.,* 366 F. Supp. 374 (S.D. Tex. 1973). Finding, as paraphrased in ibid., at 223.

82. See Coing, "Germany and the Multinational Enterprise," in Hahlo, ed., op. cit., *supra* note 29, at 97.

83. Kindleberger, *International Economics,* 4th ed. (Homewood, Ill.: Richard D. Irwin, 1968), at 404.

A case decided in the Supreme Court of Hong Kong, Appellate Jurisdiction, gives an idea of the dilemma of the MNE caught in the middle of conflicting jurisdictions. The case in question is *American President Lines, Ltd.* v. *China Mutual Trading Company, Ltd. and the Hong Kong & Kowloon Wharf and Godown Company, Ltd.,*[84] in which the American company (A.P.L.), appealed an award of damages for its failure to deliver goods purchased by the Chinese company (C.M.T.C.).

The goods had been transported by an A.P.L. cargo vessel, and unloaded for deposit with a Hong Kong storage company which held the cargo for the account of C.M.T.C. While the cargo was in transit from the United States to Hong Kong, however, two sets of regulations were issued by the U.S. Government which directly affected any transport, discharge or transfer of goods destined for the People's Republic of China. One set of regulations, issued under the Defense Production Act, required the procurement of a license by all United States flagships transporting or discharging goods for re-export to the People's Republic of China; the other set, the Foreign Assets Control Regulations, required specific approval for all transfers of property from, or under the jurisdiction of, the United States to certain specified states, including the People's Republic of China. When the American company refused to endorse the bill of lading which would release the goods to the Chinese company, the latter instituted legal proceedings, supported by the Hong Kong storage company to which C.M.T.C. owed storage charges.

Subsequent to C.M.T.C.'s filing suit, A.P.L. was notified by letter from the head of Foreign Assets Control in the United States Treasury Department that it was prohibited from delivering the cargo without a permit, and that the issuance of such a permit would be contrary to U.S. government policy. In addition, a telegram from the U.S. Secretary of State to the United States Consul in Hong Kong, in response to the trial court's request for interpretation of the Regulations, confirmed that A.P.L. would be in violation of both the Defense and Foreign Assets Regulations, and hence subject to American penal sanctions, if it were to release the cargo to the plaintiff.

The American company was thus caught between liability for damages sought by one jurisdiction and the threat of penal sanctions by another to which it was equally subject.

The court of first instance, disregarding both specific contractual wording

84. *American President Lines, Ltd.* v. *China Mutual Trading Company, Ltd. and the Hong Kong & Kowloon Wharf and Godown Company, Ltd.,* 1953 American Maritime Cases 1510 (Appellate Court opinion). The case is commented upon in Skol and Peterson, op. cit., *supra* note 66, at 32-34, from which the following facts of the case are derived. The analysis, however, is the present writer's own.

and express provisions in the U.S. Regulations, or so construing them as to alter their obvious intent, held that the sanctions applied solely to the actual voyage and not to the goods after they were discharged at the "owner's final destination." Once the cargo had been discharged to the Hong Kong storage company, the lower court held, it ceased to be subject to United States jurisdiction. In addition to ignoring specific references to "delivery", "surrender" and "disposition" in the contractual language, and declaring (in an *obiter dictum*) that "United States law applied only to carriage", the court seems similarly to have ignored the fact that it was not the final destination of the *owner* that was pertinent under the terms of the relevant regulations but rather the final destination of the "*goods*" or "*property*"; and if Hong Kong had been the final destination of the *goods*, neither set of regulations in question would have been applicable, and no proceedings necessary.

Regardless of the above facts, the lower court's decision was affirmed by the appellate court, though on rather different grounds. Acknowledging that the U.S. law did indeed apply to delivery as well as to carriage of the cargo, it held simply that the cargo was no longer within the jurisdiction of that law, and hence not under the control of the United States.

Although the instant case is really a matter of the control - or lack of control - of the home country over its own enterprises, rather than one of host control over the MNE affiliate, it is cited here to illustrate the way in which the enterprise can be the victim trapped between opposing or contradictory commercial and governmental forces.

The case of *First National City Bank* v. *IRS* (*Citibank*)[85] provides another interesting example of "a possible double and conflicting allegiance" on the part of a commercial entity[86] caught between two conflicting legal systems. In *Citibank* the question was one of disclosure of documents for purposes of assessing tax liability of a Panamanian corporation with offices in New York City and Panama. The relevant documents were located in Citibank's Panama branch, where, the bank argued, production of the documents would contravene both the Constitution and laws of the host government, as well as established international principles of comity. Without further investigation of the factual substance of the case, as we shall be returning to the subject of disclosure later on in this chapter, it suffices in the present context to note the opinion stated in the *Citibank* case that:

85. *First National City Bank* v. *IRS*, 271 F.2d 616 (2d Cir. 1959), *rev'9* 166 F. Supp. 21 (S.D.N.Y. 1958).

86. See Onkelinx, "Conflict of International Jurisdiction: Ordering the Production of Documents in Violation of the Law of the Situs", 64 *Northwestern University Law Review*, at 514.

> If the Bank cannot, as it were, serve two masters and comply with the lawful requirements both of the United States and of Panama, perhaps it should surrender to one sovereign or the other the privileges received therefrom.[87]

Such a statement would still seem a long way from providing a viable solution to the problem, no further elaboration being offered.

Citibank was looked to in a similar but more recent case, that of *United States* v. *First National City Bank,*[88] where again, the question was one of extraterritorial disclosure, this time requiring Citibank in New York to produce documents located, *inter alia,* in its Frankfurt branch, in connection with certain alleged antitrust violations. Citibank was left in the position that compliance with the U.S. court subpoena could subject it to liability under German contract or tort law, while noncompliance would put it in legal jeopardy under U.S. antitrust law. Unlike *Fruehauf-France, British Nylon Spinners* and *American Presidential Lines,* in the two *Citibank* cases the home rather than the host law prevailed. This may partially be attributed to the fact that the foreign element in question, in each case, was a branch and not a full-fledged separate entity incorporated under the laws of the host state. Nonetheless, in *United States* v. *First National City Bank,* relying on the "balancing-of-interest approach", as suggested by the American Law Institute in Sections 39 and 40 of the *Restatement (Second) of the Foreign Relations Law of the United States,*[89] the U.S. court did undertake to balance the respective national interests of both the United States and Germany, and the relative hardship which Citibank might eventually suffer. In so doing, the Court applied, for the first time, this approach recommended in the *Restatement.*[90] Even so, for the MNE caught in the middle, whether the home or the host law prevails, it cannot avoid the kafkaesque dilemma that whichever way it turns, it is penalized.

Although the MNE, in locating, does naturally seek a favourable legal environment for its investment, with possible tax, foreign-exchange or other advantages, this situation of being caught in the middle can arise even in the unlikely areas of taxation, capital repatriation, and research and development, as well as in the more obvious areas of antitrust, balance-of-payments and ownership rights. And since several states may be exercising concurrent

87. *First National City Bank* v. *IRS,* 271 F.2d 616, 620 (2d Cir. 1959).

88. *United States* v. *First National City Bank,* 396 F. 2d 897 (2d Cir. 1968).

89. American Law Institute, *Restatement of the Law (Second): Foreign Relations Law of the United States* (St. Paul, Minn.: American Law Institute Publishers, 1965) [hereinafter referred to and cited as *Restatement*], at 111 *et seq.*

90. See Onkelinx, op. cit., *supra* note 86, at 525-527.

jurisdiction over one or another aspect of an MNE's operations, and since it is not unknown for an act to be forbidden by the laws of one jurisdiction and permitted or even required by the laws of another, the 'legal package' which the parent must handle is indeed a formidable one.

The complexity of the MNE's position has been ably summed up as follows:

> The picture then is a complex one, for the multinational company typically finds itself subject to multiple political and economic systems, each with its attendant controls and risks, advantages and disadvantages, opportunities and dangers. These grow with the number of countries in which it operates.[91]

Of course what must always be kept in mind is that the MNE parent not only is faced with a myriad of differing foreign laws and policies, but it does not even have an entirely free hand in dealing with those various states hosting its operations, the parent itself being additionally subject to the laws and jurisdiction of the home state, i.e., its state of incorporation or *siège*. Take, for example the *Ford* and *B.F. Goodrich* cases between the United States and Canada, in 1957/8 and 1958/9 respectively. In each case the question arose from the export, through the Canadian subsidiary, of American products to Communist China. The American parents, being subject to the U.S. Treasury Department's Foreign Assets Control Regulations (trading-with-the-enemy legislation[92]), under which trade with Communist China was forbidden, instructed their subsidiaries to refrain from carrying through the export order. Canada has no such restrictions on trade with China; therefore the refusal of subsidiaries incorporated in Canada to carry on trade which was perfectly legal under Canadian law created serious tensions between the Canadian Government and the MNE. The MNE, however, was not the genuine source of the conflict. The MNE subsidiary, in each case, acted under instructions from the American parent which, in turn, was acting according to the dictates of the U.S. Treasury Department - i.e., the dictates of the home state.

These cases, surely for diplomatic reasons, never entered the courts; but the resultant tensions made their way up through the control hierarchy, leading ultimately to instances of confrontation between the U.S. and Canadian governments,[93] and certainly having an effect on future MNE/host state

91. Brooke and Remmers, *Strategy,* op. cit., *supra* note 70, at 9.

92. Loc. cit., *supra* note 64.

93. Culminating, in the first instance, in the Eisenhower-Diefenbaker Agreement of July 11, 1958.

relations in Canada. A similar interaction was evident in the case of *Fruehauf-France,*[94] discussed above, which did find its ultimate resolution in the courts, and resulted in victory for host-state control over the foreign affiliate and, consequently, over the affiliate's home government policy regarding its trading-with-the-enemy legislation.

By such a control chain, it is clear that what may start off as a host/subsidiary disagreement may end up, via the foreign parent and the home laws to which it is responsive, in a confrontation between the host and home governments, and then 'return to roost' on the subsidiary itself, in aggravated relations with the host state. Here is a practical display of the complex interactions of home-state, MNE and host-state powers of influence and control. As we have seen, through looking into some instances of the application of host control techniques over local affiliates of foreign MNEs, all these relationships are closely bound together by the very fact that, in reality, if indirectly, the affiliate, while subject to all the laws of the host state, can also be subject to the laws of the home state of its parent when that affiliate is controlled by the parent which is itself subject to those laws.

Hence, while each MNE affiliate is answerable to essentially two masters: the host government and the parent company, the MNE parent is answerable to a multitude of masters: it's own home government, and each individual host government where it operates through a subsidiary or through any other form of affiliated company.

c. 'Lifting the veil'

We have seen that control, as concerns the MNE, can come from all sides. The picture would be distorted, however, if it were not also pointed out that the intra-enterprise exercise of control can pose jurisdictional difficulties of its own. Intra-enterprise relationships are not always what they appear to be.

In most legal cases arising out of MNE activities abroad - most often resulting, as per the examples just reviewed, from confrontations with restrictive business practices (antitrust), related discovery orders (disclosure)[95] or trading-with-the-enemy legislation - implications of effective control are often ignored in favour of more obvious ownership criteria. This remains true despite the use (and abuse) of the technique of 'lifting the veil'[96] in an apparent attempt to

94. For case reference and facts of the case, see *supra* note 61 and text following.

95. See generally *infra* Chapter VIII.

96. This is to be distinguished from 'piercing the veil' due to fraud or other illegality, as per Griffin's distinction. See Griffin, "The Power of Host Countries over the Multinational: Lifting

assess more accurately the responsibility in a corporate claim, or to set aside the 'legal fiction' of separate personality of parent and affiliate, based upon separate incorporation, when in reality the two are acting as a single entity. Neither governments nor courts are ignorant of the distinction between the legal form and the actual or *de facto* status of the corporate relationships.[97] Nonetheless, the record of court decisions does not bear witness to a particularly consistent policy in this regard, nor does it appear, for the most part, even to fully take this distinction into account.

In the *Commercial Solvents* case,[98] for example, an American parent company holding 51 per cent of the share capital of an Italian subsidiary and supplying 50 per cent of the board and executive committee of the subsidiary, was held by the EC Commission to "in fact [exercise] the resultant dominant policy control" and to thus be seen, for purposes of application of Article 86 of the Rome Treaty, "as forming only one single and identical undertaking or economic entity."[99]

The main issue in the Decision was the abuse of a dominant position by the American parent, Commercial Solvents Corp. of New York (Commercial Solvents) and its Italian subsidiary, Instituto Chemioterapico Italiano (IC), collectively through 'their' refusal to supply essential raw materials to a third drug manufacturer, the Italian Laboratorio Chimico Farmaceutico Giorgio Zoja SpA (Zoja).

IC had previously negotiated with Zoja regarding a merger, but without success, and subsequently Zoja definitively cancelled - with the agreement of IC, after discussions - a large order of supplies, contractually agreed to during the merger negotiations, on grounds that it had found a more advantageous source of supply elsewhere.

Eventually, all other sources dried up, and Zoja, turning once again to IC, was informed that its supplier, Commercial Solvents, had ceased to make available the products in question. Zoja then submitted a request to the Commission for initiation of proceedings for a finding that Commercial Solvents and a number of its distributors had violated Articles 85 and 86 of the EEC Treaty. The Commission, relying on the fact of 51 per cent share owner-

---

the Veil in the European Economic Community and the United States, 6 *Law and Policy in International Business* (1974) [hereinafter cited as "Power of Host Countries"], note 44 at 383-384.

97. Ibid., at 382-385.

98. Decision of the Commission of the European Communities (73/457/EEC), December 14, 1972 [*Commercial Solvents* case], 15 E.C.J.O. L299/51, [1973] 12 *Common Market Law Reports*, D50.

99. Ibid. at D50.

ship of Commercial Solvents in IC, the composition of the executive boards, the mention in an annual report by Commercial Solvents of IC as its subsidiary, the definition in Article 2359 of the Italian Civil Code of "controlled companies" (*società controllate*), and the "attempted takeover" of Zoja by IC, "concluded" that Commercial Solvents "holds the power of control over Instituto Chemioterapico and exercises it in fact, at least as it regards its relations with Zoja....Therefore the companies Commercial Solvents Corp. and Instituto Chemiterapico Italiano should be treated as forming, in their relations with Zoja and for the purposes of application of Article 86, only one single and identical undertaking or economic entity...."[100]

The Commission proceeded to impose a fine "jointly and severally" upon both companies for withdrawal of supplies of a basic pharmaceutical ingredient for which Commercial Solvents was the sole manufacturer, ordered the companies to make supplies available and to submit a scheme to that effect, and imposed daily penalties for each day's failure to comply with the order.

Since only the American firm, Commercial Solvents, produced the ingredient in question, it could be argued that the Court used the CSC-IC group tactic solely as a means of obtaining extraterritorial jurisdiction over the non-Community American company. The factors relied upon to determine where the control was centered in the attempted takeover of Zoja by IC were particularly unpersuasive. Such vagueries as the "unlikelihood" that Commercial Solvents "refrained from in fact exercising its power of control" over IC, or the unlikelihood that the attempted takeover would have taken place without the control of IC by Commercial Solvents, along with the "presumption" that Commercial Solvents controlled IC's activities concerning Zoja merely because the former owned 51 per cent of the stock and because of the composition of the executive boards, would seem to fall well short of affording proof that Commercial Solvents did, in fact, control IC's transactions with Zoja, or of providing sufficient grounds for the ultimate imposition of a fine on Commercial Solvents and IC together, as a single entity. Even if financial, managerial or general control is felt to be established, beyond a reasonable doubt, of one member of an enterprise over another, the fact of whether that control is actually exercised in a given instance should also be determined with a reasonable degree of certainty, based on more than likelihoods and presumptions. In the case of *Commercial Solvents,* the Commission, having "concluded" that the ultimate authority rested with the parent, though lacking evidence of any instructions to IC on the part of Commercial Solvents, made no attempt to analyze the true structure of the relationship between IC and Zoja nor to

100. Ibid., at D56-57.

determine the genuine relationship between IC and Commercial Solvents for the particular activity in question.

A similar approach can be seen in the *Continental Can* case,[101] where Continental Can was held responsible for a merger transaction on the part of its subsidiary, Europemballage, solely on the basis of shareholdings (i.e. ownership) and financial considerations. Continental Can contended that the action complained of was that of Europemballage and not that of Continental Can. The Commission, nonetheless, "imputed" to Continental Can the conduct of Europemballage, and ruled that the acquisition by Europemballage was an abuse of a dominant position, for which both Continental Can and Europemballage were held responsible. Here, as in *Commercial Solvents,* the finding was based upon "assumptions". The Commission held "...that it must be assumed...that Europemballage did not display any autonomous behavior and did not have any economic independence at the relevant time...."[102]

While, in *Continental Can,* the imputation of the subsidiary's (Europemballage's) actions to the parent (Continental Can) gained some support from the fact, as expressed by the Court's Advocate General, "that the funds for the acquisition of the shares in Thomassen had been made available to Europemballage by Continental Can and that, at the date when Continental Can caused Europemballage to make an offer to buy, the latter company was still not fully organized,"[103] it has been suggested[104] that severe shortcomings of analysis may have resulted from the failure to ask such questions as: "On what terms did Europemballage receive the funds from Continental Can? What evidence supports the statement that Continental Can 'caused' Europemballage to make the offer? Which executives actually administered the acquisition of Thomassen shares? What was Europemballage's relationship to other members of the Continental Can group?", and that the omission of such an analysis is illustrative of the all-too-common application of the 'two-as-one' assumption applied to wholly owned subsidiaries.

The same sort of reasoning can be observed in the *Dyestuffs* case,[105] in which

101. *Re Continental Can Co.,* 15 E.C.J.O. L7/25 (1972), CCH *Common Market Reporter* [1970-1972 Transfer Binder], ¶ 9481; 11 *Common Market Law Reports* D27 (1972); *Europemballage Corp. and Continental Can Co.* v. *Commission of the European Communities,* 12 *Common Market Law Reports* (1973), 199 [hereinafter cited as *Continental Can Co.* v. *E.C. Commission*].

102. *Continental Can Co.* v. *E.C. Commission,* 2 CCH *Common Market Reporter,* ¶ 8171, 8312; 12 *Common Market Law Reports* 216, 217 (E.C.J. 1973), at.

103. *Idem.*

104. Griffin, op. cit., *supra* note 96, at 395.

105. Commission Decision of 24 July 1969 [Dyestuffs Decision (Commission)], 12 E.C.J.O. L195/11 CCH *Common Market Reporter* [1965-1969 Transfer Binder] ¶ 9314; 8 *Common Market Law Reports* D23. There were nine separate appeals against the Dyestuffs Decision (e.g. *Imperial Chemical Industries Ltd.* v. *E.C. Commission, Receuil de la Jurisprudence de la Cour* 619 (Cour de Justice de la Communauté européene 1972); 2 CCH *Common Market Reporter* ¶¶.

Imperial Chemical Industries, Ltd. (ICI) was fined by the EC Commission for illegal concerted practices under Article 85 of the Treaty of Rome[106] on the basis of price rises effected by its subsidiaries within the EEC.[107] The Court's holding that ICI and its subsidiaries acted as one entity, thus making ICI liable through its subsidiaries, relied on ICI's *capability* to direct the affairs of its subsidiaries due to their wholly or majority-owned status. ICI contended that the pricing policy was that of the subsidiaries and should not be imputed to itself. But the Court rejected this contention on the basis of the ownership criteria which afforded ICI the capability to control, and on the strength of telex messages from the parent to the subsidiaries relating to the first only of three price increases and phrased in a binding manner. On the strength of these first messages relating to the initial price increase, which messages are not reprinted anywhere,[108] the Court *assumed* any subsequent instructions regarding pricing (without indicating whether any such subsequent instructions actually existed) to be equally mandatory. Many of the details of the case are left ill-defined, and the apparently inadequate handling of *Dyestuffs* has prompted the remark that "[t]he reasoning put forward by the Court falls below the standard that is required and has in the past been observed in national courts."[109]

Of the various strong criticisms of the Court in the *Dyestuffs* case, perhaps the most significant is that, regarding the Court's treatment of the parent-subsidiary issue ('enterprise entity'), the *capability* of control, based solely on ownership, was equated with the actual *exercise* of control. "The most important question", observes one commentator, "was who, in fact, exercised how much control and when, over the pricing of dyestuffs within the Common Market."[110] The mere fact that a subsidiary company is wholly owned should not be sufficient in itself to establish the liability of the parent for the abuses of its subsidiaries.

8161-69 [1972]; *Common Market Law Reports* 557 (1972), as commented on in Griffin, op. cit., *supra* note 96, at 402-404.

106. Treaty Establishing the European Economic Community (with annexes and Protocol). Done at Rome, on 25 March 1957; reprinted in 295 U.N.T.S. 23, [hereinafter cited as the Treaty of Rome]. English translation in 298 U.N.T.S. 3 (1958).

107. I.C.I. was an English company, and Britain had not yet entered into membership in the EEC.

108. See Griffin, op. cit., *supra* note 96, at 403-404.

109. Mann, "The Dyestuffs Case in the Court of Justice of the European Communities", 22 *International and Comparative Law Quarterly* (1973), at 35, 48, as cited in Griffin, op. cit., *supra* note 96, at 404.

110. Ibid. (Griffin), at 403.

Clive Schmitthoff, speaking at a London Conference on the Legal Problems of Multinational Corporations in 1976,[111] made a recommendation which, although in the context of parent liability for the debts and obligations of its subsidiaries, merits consideration in the present context. His suggestion was that the courts develop, in the case of a wholly owned subsidiary, a "strong presumption" that the subsidiary is being used as an agent of the parent, but that in appropriate cases the parent should reserve the right to rebut this presumption, if it can show that it neither expressly nor impliedly authorized the transaction in question or was privy to it. This would seem to the present writer to be a more equitable approach than to conclusively presume as self-evident that ownership *per se* automatically indicates legal responsibility of a parent for the acts of its subsidiary.

Other examples[112]could be given which reflect the court's reluctance to probe too deeply into the real control relationships of the MNEs, such as *Frummer* v. *Hilton Hotels International,*[113]or *Delagi* v. *Volkswagenwerk A.G.*[114] The former involved a tort claim by a U.S. citizen, injured in the London Hilton Hotel while on vacation, who subsequently filed suit in a New York State court against Hilton Hotels, Ltd. (Hilton U.K.), a British corporation, Hilton Hotels International, Inc., a Delaware corporation with large shareholdings in Hilton U.K. and Hilton Hotels Corp., a Delaware corporation with some stock ownership in Hilton International, Inc. New York jurisdiction revolved around the question of agency, and whether Hilton U.K. had a presence in New York. The New York Court of Appeals, in holding that such a presence did exist, relied on the ownership implications embodied in the fact that Hilton International and Hilton Hotels Corp. jointly owned Hilton Credit Corp., one branch of which was the Hilton Reservation Service which operated in New York with the purpose of generating business for Hilton U.K. and was thus an 'agent' of Hilton U.K.. Little attention was given to the actual authority and control structures relating the different members of the Hilton complex. Here, apparently for the sake of convenience, the agency of the Hilton Reservation Service was imputed not to the parent, but to a sister company, Hilton U.K. The court held that since both Hilton Reservation Service and Hilton U.K. were jointly owned by Hilton International and Hilton Hotels

111. Schmitthoff's paper, entitled "Group Liability of Multinationals", published in Simmonds, *Legal Problems* op. cit., *supra* note 41, at 79.

112. Examples given in Griffin, op. cit., *supra* note 96, at 395-397.

113. *Frummer* v. *Hilton Hotels International,* 19 N.Y.2d 533, 227 N.E.2d 851, 281 N.Y.S.2d 41, cert. denied, 389 U.S. 923 (1967).

114. *Delagi* v. *Volkswagenwerk A.G.,* 29 N.Y.2d 426, 278 N.E.2d 895, 328 N.Y.S.2d 653 (1972).

Corp., this constituted "a valid inference as to the broad scope of the agency in the absence of an express agency agreement...."[115] Thus, once again, a court decision was based upon an ownership "inference", in this case utilized to determine presence, through agency, for purposes of establishing jurisdiction.

In *Delgai* v. *Volkswagenwerk A.G.*,[116] the same court again glossed over the effective control relationship between a foreign car manufacturer (Volkswagen) and a local franchise distributor (whose entire distributing and servicing business was solely with Volkswagen), in favour of the legal form, but this time with a different outcome. Relying on the existence of "truly separate corporate entities, not commonly owned",[117] the court ruled that a valid inference of agency could not be sustained.[118] As the legal form (or perhaps legal fiction) in this case was separate ownership rather than a parent-subsidiary relationship, the 'inference-of-agency' rationale was swept aside, and, without inquiry into the nature or source of control regarding the two entities, or into the practical franchisee-supplier relationship, the court made its distinction solely on the basis of ownership.

The court might have done well to consider the type of reasoning embodied in Section 3(6) (h) of Canada's Foreign Investment Review Act[119] which provides a more realistic approach:

> (h) a business carried on by a corporation that is controlled in any manner that results in *control in fact,* whether directly through the ownership of shares or indirectly through a trust, a contract, the ownership of shares of any other corporation or otherwise, by another corporation shall be deemed to be carried on by the controlling corporation as well as by the corporation by which the business is in fact carried on. [Emphasis supplied.]

Or the court might have gained some insight from the definition of control as applied under the U.S. tax laws[120] which includes "any kind of control, direct or indirect, whether legally enforceable, and however exercisable or exercised. It is the *reality of the control* that is decisive, not its form or the mode of its

115. *Frummer* v. *Hilton Hotels International,* 19 N.Y.2d at 538. 227 N.E.2d at 854, 281 N.Y.S.2d at 45.

116. *Delagi* v. *Volkswagenwerk A.G.,* loc cit., *supra* note 114.

117. *Idem.*

118. *Idem.*

119. Foreign Investment Review Act, loc. cit., *supra* note 9.

120. U.S. Internal Revenue Code of 1954, § 482.

exercise." [Emphasis supplied.][121] The "control in fact", or the "reality of the control", should be established through more than mere assumptions or inferences.

All this being said about the insufficiency of "likelihoods", "assumptions", "presumptions" and "inferences", it must be conceded that material proof of the source of control is not always easily obtainable; yet if the court were to rely on statements such as that in *Cannon Manufacturing Co.* v. *Cudahy Packing Co.*,[122] in which a U.S. district court held that "a parent's complete commercial and financial domination of its subsidiary did not bring the parent within the jurisdiction as long as the formal separation was scrupulously maintained", the legal corporate form could easily hide a host of abuses.

The same could be said about the English court decision in *Salomon* v. *Salomon*[123] which established the theory in English law of legal separation. This decision has understandably come under increasing criticism by both courts and writers. Lord Denning M.R., in a more recent case, [124] summed up the *Salomon* position, as he saw it, as follows:

> The decision in Salomon v. Salomon & Co. Ltd. has to be watched carefully. It has often been supposed to cast a veil over the personality of a limited company through which the courts cannot see. But that is not true. The courts can, and often do, pull off the mask. They look to see what really lies behind. The legislature has shown the way with group accounts and the rest. And the courts should follow suit.

Two broad qualifications to the rule in *Salomon* v. *Salomon* have been admitted by the English courts. The rule is held not to apply if it can be established, to the satisfaction of the court, (1) that the controlled company was employed solely as an agent of the parent (incorporator), or (2) that there has been an abuse of the corporate form. The mere fact of 100 per cent ownership, however, is not deemed to constitute an abuse of the corporate form. This point, at least, was clearly established in the *Salomon* case which, in that regard, is still law.[125] Wholly owned subsidiaries are normally expected to submit key

121. U.S. Treasury Regulations § 1.482-1(a) (3) (1968), as cited in Griffin, op. cit., *supra* note 96, note 89 at 394.

122. *Cannon Manufacturing Co.* v. *Cudahy Packing Co.*, 267 U.S. 333, 337 (1925), cited thirty years later in *United States* v. *Watchmakers of Switzerland Information Center,* 133 F. Supp. 40 (S.D.N.Y. 1955), at 45.

123. *Salomon* v. *Salomon & Co., Ltd.* [1897] A.C. 22.

124. *Littlewoods Mail Order Stores Ltd.* v. *I.R.C.* [1969] 1 W.L.R. 1241, 1254, as cited in Schmitthoff, "Group Liability of Multinationals", op. cit., *supra* note 111, at 73-74.

125. Ibid. (Schmitthoff), at 74. See also *Berkey* v. *Third Ave. Railway Co.* 244 N.Y. 84, 95, 155 N.E. 58, 61, 50 A.L.R. 599 (1926).

management questions to the parent for approval, but the proposal may well be initiated at the subsidiary level, influenced by local conditions. To actually establish abuse the English courts require, additionally, as affirmed in *Jones* v. *Lipman,*[126] evidence confirming that the controlled company was nothing more than a "device and sham, a mask - which he [the incorporator] holds before his face."

Moreover, in the United States courts as well, despite the 1925 *Cannon* v. *Cudahy* holding cited above, it is now commonly recognized, if not always acted upon, that if the corporate form is largely a 'paper arrangement' which does not reflect the business realities, as was the case in, for example, *National Labor Relations Board* v. *Deena Artware, Inc.*[127], the court has the power actually to reconstruct the enterprise, recognizing its true corporate entity, relying on the economic realities. In this way, one corporation may be shown to be a mere 'instrumentality' of another, and the operations of the two (or more) units of the enterprise shown to be so intermingled as to make any realistic separation of the units, or any identification of corporate boundaries, indistinguishable.[128]

Hence, as with the English *Salomon* decision of 1897, the 1925 U.S. *Cannon* v. *Cudahy* holding, now viewable as naive, is eclipsed by more recent decisions expressing views such as that of Justice Stone in *In re Clarke's Will,*[129] who stated that:

> Many cases present avowed disregard of corporate entity [citation omitted]. But they all come to just this - courts simply will not let interposition of corporate entity or action prevent a judgment otherwise required. Corporate presence and action no more than those of an individual will bar a remedy demanded by law in application to facts. Hence, the process is not accurately termed one of disregarding corporate entity. It is rather and only a refusal to permit its presence and action to divert the judicial course of applying law to ascertained facts. The method neither pierces any veil nor goes behind any obstruction, save for its refusal to let one fact bar the judgment which the whole sum of facts requires.[130]

126. *Jones* v. *Lipman* [1962] 1 W.L.R. 832, 836, as cited in *Idem.*

127. *National Labor Relations Board* v. *Deena Artware, Inc.,* 361 U.S. 398 (1960).

128. See Cary and Eisenberg, *Cases and Materials on Corporations* (5th ed. unab'd. 1980), (University Casebook Series), Mineola, N.Y.: Foundation Press, 1980), text and note 5 at 81.

129. *In re Clarke's Will,* 204 Minn. 574, 284 N.W. 876 (1939).

130. *In re Clarke's Will,* 204 Minn. 578-79, 284 N.W. at 878.

"What the formula comes down to, once shorn of verbiage about control, instrumentality, agency and corporate entity," offers one writer, "is that liability is imposed to reach an equitable result."[131] One would hope this will increasingly be the case, since although a general resort to equity does carry with it the risk of considerable uncertainty for those planning the corporate activity of an enterprise, a just resolution of a case cannot always be obtained from merely the ostensible factual data.

More specifically, in the application of ownership and control criteria for a just resolution of commercial disputes involving foreign elements, it would seem expedient that a more consistent approach be adopted by the courts, with the legal liability of a parent for its subsidiaries, and the corresponding questions of jurisdiction, relying not on obvious ownership percentages, but on genuine control affiliations, as far as these are ascertainable. Jurisdiction based on presence is legally quite straightforward, but when implications of agency are involved for purposes of jurisdiction, responsibility relationships are key, and if these relationships are based on assumptions of responsibility relying on ownership criteria, ignoring the fact of the clear separation of ownership and control in most of today's enterprises, just resolutions can hardly be expected to result. Methods or tests for ascertaining control should, ideally, be worked out to at least offer a basic standard of guidance for achieving greater consistency in establishing jurisdiction through agency, or other links of liability, without the temptation to resort to ownership inferences. In general, as regards 'lifting the veil', it is said that corporate personality will be disregarded in all cases where it is "used to defeat public convenience, justify wrong, protect fraud, or defend crime."[132]

At the level of the International Court of Justice, there has, up to now, only been one request for lifting the veil, and that was in the case of *Barcelona Traction.*[133] The Court, however, refused to comply, relying on a narrow interpretation of the concept of nationality.[134] We cannot therefore look to the ICJ to furnish us with precedent or international policy as regards this technique of ascertaining control relationships. Nonetheless, nearly all veil-lifting cases decided in national courts have referred to the broader principles of jurisdiction recognized under international law for their interpretation.[135]

131. Latty, *Subsidiaries and Affiliated Corporations* (1936), as cited in ibid., at 110.

132. Stevens, Corporations (1949), § 18, at 95, as cited in ibid., at 109.

133. *Case Concerning the Barcelona Traction, Light and Power Company, Ltd.* (Belgium *v.* Spain), *I.C.J. Reports* 1970, p. 3, at 9. For facts of the case and discussion of certain aspect, see *infra* Chapter XII: 7.

134. See Griffin, op. cit., *supra* note 96, at 386.

135. *Idem.*

It is clear that the ownership/management issue never ceases to be of central importance; and, from the cases cited above, and from other similar examples,[136] it is evident that while management may be more important than ownership - both to the MNE and to the host government - for purposes of exercising effective control over the operations of an enterprise, ownership has nonetheless played an important role for purposes of jurisdiction and other aspects of legal actions and will undoubtedly continue to do so, in some cases, until a more consistently control-oriented approach is generally adopted.

136. Cf. *inter alia, Swiss Watchmakers* case, loc. cit. *supra* note 79; Commission Decision of June 18, 1969 [*Re Christiana & Nielsen N.V.*] 12 E.C.J.O. L165/12; CCH *Common Market Reporter* 9308[1965-1969 Transfer Binder] ; 8 Common Market Law Reports, D36.

Chapter VI.

CONTROL OVER CAPITAL MOVEMENTS

Among other areas in which the host state asserts control over the foreign MNE affiliate are capital movements (repatriation of earnings and capital, and other remittance and capital transfer policies affecting balance of payments), taxation (including transfer pricing[1]), and disclosure. These are areas in which the issues are rarely pressed into court action, and case law is correspondingly slim, but we have already indicated that they are areas in which the MNE can find itself caught between the dictates of 'two masters', and consequently caught up in legal complications of some complexity. Of course the host, for its part, is just as likely to discover abuses on the part of the MNE in these same areas, and may respond by enacting additional legislation and by entering into an increasing number of inter-governmental treaties and agreements. It is therefore worth commenting briefly on these aspects of multinational activity as host control techniques.

1. Host-State Law and Policy

In considering control over capital movements it is significant, for example, that the French government has used the very device of capital movement regulation to accomplish ends which were, in another form, incompatible with the spirit of the Treaty of Rome as regards freedom of establishment. Specifically, the requirement for prior announcement of intentions (*obligation de déclaration préalable*) by a foreign investor, as stipulated by the *décret 67-78 du 27 janvier 1967,* is effectively a requirement for prior authorization (*condition d'authorization préalable*) of any projected operations by the foreign enterprise, and is recognized as such by the *décret 68-1021 du 24 novembre 1968.*[2] Such restrictions on the freedom of establishment placed the French

1. For a definition of transfer pricing, see *infra*, text accompanying notes 2, 3.
2. See *infra*, text accompanying note 18.

Government under the condemnation of the Court of Justice of the European Communities on grounds of incompatibility with the spirit of the Rome Treaty. Rather than face being brought before the Court, the French Government issued a *décret (n° 71-143 du 22 février 1971)* which released from the obligations of *décret 67-78* all nationals of member states of the EEC (though still discriminating against non-EEC members), hence ostensibly according them freedom of both establishment and dissolution of direct investment in France. On the very same day, however, another *décret (n° 71-144)* was issued which submitted to prior notification and authorization procedures the same operations under a different title, that of control of capital movements (*contrôle des mouvements de capitaux*), effectively reversing the exemption for nationals of EEC member states from *décret 67-78* by requiring the same nationals to obtain authorization for direct investments in France when such investments are "susceptibles d'entraîner un mouvement de capital"; and what foreign direct investment can operate without capital movements? Moreover, the Ministry of Economy and Finance is not bound to a predetermined time period for rendering its decision, nor is it required to give any grounds for why it has granted or refused requests for prior authorizations in any given case.[3]

Thus, by *décret n° 71-144,* the technique of control of capital movements enabled the French Government to extend its control over foreign investments even into areas which otherwise would have infringed upon the law of the European Economic Community; and despite the existence of the OECD Code of Liberalisation of Capital Movements to which France theoretically adheres, it was not until June 25, 1980 that a limited relaxation of the stringent foreign exchange regulations was announced by the French Minister of Economy and Finance.[4] This relaxation was part of a general move to liberalize business conditions and encourage investment, and was motivated also, in some degree, by the success of the virtually total removal of exchange controls by Great Britain in 1979,[5] which the French Government observed with great interest and some awe. Whether this latest French policy actually represents a reliable trend in practice, or is only a reflection of the present mood of the Government, will only become clear over the course of time.

In Britain, according to findings by Professor John Dunning[6] published as

3. See CHH *Common Market Reporter: Doing Business in Europe,* ¶ 22,674, at 22,654 [1976].

4. See *infra* Chapter III, text accompanying note 26.

5. See below and *supra* Chapter III, notes 64, 65 and accompanying text.

6. Professor of economics at Britain's Reading University and specialist in matters relating to the multinational firm.

early as 1958,[7] the potential drain on the host state of large earning dividends flowing to the home country was, at the time Dunning was writing, one of the prime concerns in the financial area of British policy. We also saw in 1974, to name just one concrete example as reported in *Business Week,*[8] that the large Swiss multinational, F. Hoffman-Laroche was at that time in serious dispute with the British Parliament over the transfer of enormous profits out of Britain. This trend continued until the 1979 suspension of foreign exchange restrictions in Britain after some forty years of controls.[9] Other than the minor relaxations in the exchange control law, harbingered at the time of the June 12, 1979 Budget Speech by Britain's Chancellor of the Exchequer, Sir Geoffrey Howe,[10] in which Howe announced his plan for a step-by-step "progressive dismantling of exchange control" - which subsequently took the form of orders made operative on 13 June, 13 July and 2 October[11] - the remaining controls were, in fact, removed with 'one stroke', with effect from midnight, October 24, 1979.[12] Insufficient time has passed to allow formation of a perspective view or objective assessment of the effect on foreign MNEs of the new capital movements policy which has given Britain greater freedom from exchange control than almost any other nation in the world. Two observations can nonetheless be made: The fact that the French have subsequently begun to ease their traditionally stringent exchange control laws is some attestation to the initial positive results observable in the wake of the British move; on the other hand, the fact that the removal of the exchange controls eliminated the 10 per cent limitation on foreign companies' holdings in U.K. companies, in the absence of specific Bank of England provision, has led to mounting pressure in Britain for statutory controls over foreign enterprises. Pressures are

7. Dunning, *American Investment in British Manufacturing Industry* (London: Allen and Unwin (1958), at 304.)

8. *Business Week,* July 6, 1974, at 73.

9. See *supra* Chapter III, notes 64, 65 and accompanying text.

10. See *Keesing's Contemporary Archives,* Vol. XXV, 1979 [hereinafter cited as *Keesing*], at 29823, 29285.

11. Exchange Control (Import and Export) (Amendment) Order 1979 (No. 647), (S.I. 1979/647), operative on 13 June, 1979; Exchange Control (Gold Coins Exemption) Order 1979 (No. 648), (S.I. 1979/648), operative on 13 June, 1979; Exchange Control (Authorised Dealers and Depositaries) (Amendment) (No. 2) Order 1979 (No. 740), (S.I. 1979/740), operative on 13 July 1979; Exchange Control (Authorised Dealers and Depositaries) (Amendment) (No.3) Order 1979 (No. 1194), (S.I. 1979/1194), operative on 2 October 1979.

12. See Exchange Control Orders 1979, Nos. 1331-1339, S.I. 1979/1331-1339. See also e.g. "Ende britischer Kapitalverkehrskontrollen", *Neue Züricher Zeitung,* 25 October, 1979, at 11; "La Grande-Bretagne abolit tous les contrôles", *Le Monde,* 25 October 1979, at 42; "England jetzt ohne Devisenkontrollen", *Frankfurter Allgemeine Zeitung,* 24 October 1979, at 13; "U.K. Removes Foreign Exchange Curbs", *International Herald Tribune,* 24 October 1979, at 1.

also mounting for the London Stock Exchange to strengthen is regulatory system. Hence, early observations would seem to indicate that the absence of exchange controls have been beneficial for the host state, but may mean the imposition of additional statutory controls for the MNE. While there is an obvious immediate impact on British investment overseas, there is far less of a direct impact on foreign investments in Britain. Further measures are being envisioned to lure additional foreign direct investments into Britain to offset the anticipated acceleration of British corporate investment abroad, but according to one recent economic review[13] on the subject, the removal of exchange controls should automatically bolster the relative profitability of investment in Britain. In any case, all would agree that the removal of the British controls responds positively to Britain's international responsibilities *vis-à-vis* the EEC and OECD policies of liberalization of capital movements.[14]

Another example of control over capital movements, which has since been rescinded, was the United States Foreign Direct Investment Controls Act of 1 January 1968. Despite the fact that these controls are no longer operative, they deserve mention here as an illustation of the way in which requirements for repatriation of earnings can easily collide head-on with legislation in the host state restricting remittance of dividends. For example, U.S. policy under these regulations required an American subsidiary to repatriate dividends to the United States, while that subsidiary, if located in, say, France, by doing so would have been acting contrary to the French government policy of retention of dividends within France. Here again is an echo of the difficulties, on the part of the subsidiary, of being subject to 'two masters', and the frustration on the part of the host at finding its own policies sometimes thwarted by policies determined elsewhere. It should be remarked in passing, however, concerning these U.S. controls, that the French Minister of Economy and Finance, Michel Debré, while mildly protesting, did accept the U.S. balance-of-payments regulations, though it has been suggested by Kindleberger[15] that this French acceptance of the U.S. controls was influenced by the gravity of the then U.S. balance-of-payments deficit which, he suggests, gave the French a certain amount of *Schadenfreude,* and that that outweighed the legal issue.

The fact remains that, in general, on the European scene, the introduction of the mandatory U.S. direct investment control program instilled heightened

13. See "Nat West predicts a boost for investors", *The Guardian,* 5 November 1979, at 21.

14. See e.g. "Ende britischer Kapitalverkehrskontrollen", loc. cit., *supra* note 12; *Keesing,* op. cit., *supra* note 10, at 29825.

15. Kindleberger, ed., *The International Corporation: A Symposium* (Cambridge, Mass.: MIT Press, [1970] [hereinafter cited as *Symposium*], at 6.

confidence in the U.S. economy, and any apprehensions on the part of host states that it might instigate greatly augmented repatriation of profits to the United States, accompanied by a proportionately sharp drop in desired inward investment or by a credit shortage for native firms, were soon dispelled.[16]

In fact, despite the germ for jurisdictional conflict in this area of capital movements in general, significant difficulties surprisingly rarely arise, and when they do, practice seems to prove them resolvable.[17] Of course, the subsequent retraction of the U.S. Foreign Direct Investment Controls has also solved many potentialities for conflict, particularly between the United States and Canada, although, characteristically, Canada had early sought and gained exemptions from the controls.

France, for her part, soon afterwards had balance-of-payments difficulties of her own, notably subsequent to the May-June 1968 disturbances, which resulted in a temporary emergency system of tight exchange controls embodied in *décret 68-1021* already mentioned above. This subjected to regulation all payments between residents and non-residents, while a general authorization was issued for remittances abroad for royalties, interest and dividends.[18] This legislation, while not affecting *entry* of foreign direct investment, decidedly had its effect on foreign *operations*. The non-remission of earnings to the home country, ironically enough, is not always the solution to host anxieties over balance of payments, since without remission there results a build-up of foreign corporate ownership with no accompanying inflow of foreign currency, a situation that only adds to the tensions between MNE and host.[19]

Not all states have systematic capital movements restrictions. In Germany, for example, there exist no foreign exchange controls on foreign investments, regardless of the form of the investment, though in order to discourage the inflow of speculative money, the Federal Government is authorized to require from residents borrowing abroad the deposit of a certain percentage of the total loan, without benefit of interest, in a special account with the *Deutsche Bundesbank* (the so-called *Depotpflicht*), as set out in Section 6a of the *Aussenwirtschaftsrecht* (Foreign Trade Law).[20]

16. See Willey, "Direct Investment Controls and the Balance of Payments", in ibid., at 115.

17. Kindleberger, ed., *Symposium,* loc. cit., *supra* note 15.

18. Article 2(i) and (n) of the *arrêté du 24 novembre 1968,* [1968] *Journal Officiel [J.O.]* 11082; Cf. Kozyris, "Equal Joint-Venture Corporations in France: Problems of Control and Resolution of Deadlocks", 17 *The American Journal of Comparative Law* (1969).

19. Behrman, *National Interests and the Multinational Enterprise: Tensions Among the North Atlantic Countries* (Englewood Cliffs, N.J.: Prentice-Hall, 1970), at 78.

20. See *Aussenwirtschaftsgesetz vom 28. April 1961 Bundesgesetzblatt* [BGBl.] I S. 481 (*in der Fassung des 3. AndG vom 29 März 1976,* BGBl. I. S. 869), at 12; see also CCH *Common Market Reporter: Doing Business in Europe,* ¶ 23,154 [1977].

2. MNE Practice

The MNE, aware that the capital repatriation laws of certain host states may prevent its subsidiaries from conforming to its corporate strategy, anticipate such host regulations even where they do not yet exist, and often employ such techniques as instituting and maintaining regular and consistent payments from subsidiary to parent, even if the funds must later be returned, in order to establish a pattern of acceptance of the policy on the part of the host, as assurance that the practice will be allowed to continue unhampered.[21] Needless to say, such is not the only motive for a company's internal remittance policies. These policies are also governed by anxieties over potential losses from foreign exchange fluctuations, by the desire to maintain control over the subsidiary by holding the purse strings, and by other such considerations; but in large measure, internal corporate policies are dictated to a reasonably significant degree by external factors, primarily the legal restrictions on repatriation or remission of earnings or capital issued by both home and host governments to improve their balance-of-payments position and protect their monetary reserves.[22]

21. Brooke and Remmers, *The Multinational Company in Europe; Some Key Problems* (London: Longman, 1972), at 23.

22. Ibid., at 25.

Chapter VII.

CONTROL THROUGH TAX LEGISLATION

The repatriation of profits in the form of dividends, where permitted, or the payment of royalties by the affiliate to the foreign parent, is often controlled by levies imposed by the host, the object of course being to preserve the funds as retained earnings for reinvestment in the host economy.[1] Where such profits or royalties are subjected to a higher tax rate than those which remain within the country, the relevant tax legislation is generally being used by the host government as a means of control over foreign enterprises. If the restrictions are severe or taxes excessively high, the multinational firm will attempt to reduce its profits in the highly restrictive states by means of transfer pricing.

1. Transfer Pricing

Transfer pricing is that practice whereby the MNE, in its intra-enterprise transactions, can sometimes effectively modify the tax base on which its entities are assessed, or possibly avoid exchange controls, by 'doing business' within the MNE corporate structure itself, so as to reallocate costs and revenues in such a way that its profits are realized where the tax and exchange environment is most favourable.[2] It has been commented by Hans Schaffner, one of the members of the "Group of Eminent Persons" in a United Nations study on

1. See Kolde, *International Business Enterprise*, 2nd ed. (Englewood Cliffs, N.J.: Prentice-Hall, [1973]), at 242.

2. United Nations, Commission on Transnational Corporations, Intergovernmental Working Group on the Formulation of a Code of Conduct, "Transnational Corporations: Code of Conduct; Formulations by the Chairman", U.N. document E/C.10/AC. 2/8 (December 13, 1978), para. 29, at 7; see also Organisation for Economic Co-operation and Development, "Guidelines for Multinational Enterprises": Taxation, para. 2. (Annex to OECD *Declaration on International Investment and Multinational Enterprises by the Governments of OECD Member Countries* (21st June 1976), OECD Publications, Paris, 1976. See also Linde, "Regulation of Transfer Pricing in Multinational Corporations: An International Perspective", 10 *Journal of International Law and Politics* (1977), pp. 67-123.

MNEs,[3] that the term "transfer pricing" applies indiscriminately to all pricing for the transfer of goods within one corporate group or enterprise, and that the term itself is strictly neutral, though usually used in a pejorative sense denoting artificially manipulated intra-enterprise pricing. Legislation has hence grown up to curb any artificial pricing and to prevent gross inequities and tax avoidance resulting from such practices.[4]

Schaffner feels that, in the majority of instances, transfer pricing is not really a problem since identifiable 'arms-length' prices[5] exist against which to measure the genuineness of the transfer prices. He comments further that even where an MNE has clear tax incentives for contemplating artificial pricing, the practical opportunities for manipulation are very limited, since such practices are under intense and continuous scrutiny by a number of different local authorities who would be quick to discern any unjustifiable fluctuations or deviations from a proper transfer price.

It is pointed out in Schaffner's comment that comprehensive and refined machinery for the control of transfer pricing is already available and used with remarkable efficiency, eliminating the need for any new international machinery to duplicate this function, and that if governments were to strive to harmonize the existing tax rates, any incentive to manipulate transfer prices would immediately disappear. Moreover, no firm, regardless of the strength of its position on a given market, wishes to provoke a court battle with a government.

The French, in their *Code général des impôts,*[6] have anticipated transfer-pricing manoeuvres by Article 57 which refers to "bénéfices indirectement transférés:

> Pour l'établissement de l'impôt sur le revenue dû par les entreprises qui sont sous la dépendance ou qui possèdent le contrôle d'entreprises situées hors de France, les bénéfices indirectement transférés à ces

3. United Nations, *The Impact of Multinational Corporations on Development and on International Relations,* U.N. publication E/5500/Rev. 1; ST/ESA/6., sales no.E.74.II.A.5 (New York, 1974) [hereinafter cited as *Impact*].

4. For the most common current methods of assessing reasonable and fair market values in an attempt to eliminate transfer pricing abuses, see "National Legislation and Regulations Relating to Transnational Corporations, U.N. Commission on Transnational Corporations, 2nd sess., Lima, 1-12 March 1976". U.N. doc. no. E/C.10/8. See also Farnsworth, "Tax Loophole for Multinationals", *The New York Times,* August 21, 1977. sect. 3, at 1.

5. The 'arms-length' price is the open market price, i.e. the proper price which is or would be charged by an independent seller to an independent buyer. (See United Nations, *Impact*, op. cit., *supra* note 3, at 89).

6. General Tax Code.

dernières, soit par voie de majoration our de diminution des prix d'achat ou de vente, soit par tout autre moyen, sont incorporés aux résultats accusés par les comptabilités. Il est procédé de même à l'égard des entreprises qui sont sous la dépendance d'une entreprise ou d'un groupe possédant également le contrôle d'entreprises situées hors de France. [Translation below.][7]

It is of interest that in Article 57 the reference is to the dependent relationship of one enterprise *vis-à-vis* another, whether it be one situated outside of France or whether it be one located within France but exercising control over an enterprise outside of French territory. Share percentages and other ownership criteria are not even mentioned, the operative words governing the applicability of the transfer-pricing provisions being, rather, "dépendance" and "contrôle". This regulation is supplemented by other provisions in the *Code,* notably Article 238(A) which provides that, for the imposition of corporate taxes:

> [Certain intérêts, des redevances, etc.] ou les rénumérations de services, payés ou dus par une personne physique ou morale domiciliée ou établie en France à des personnes physiques ou morales qui sont domiciliées our établies dans un État étranger ou un territoire situé hors de France et y sont soumises à un régime fiscal privilégié, ne sont admis comme charges déductibles pour l'établissement de l'impôt que si le débiteur apporte la preuve que les dépenses correspondent à des *opérations réelles* et qu'elles ne présentent pas un caractère anormal ou exagéré. [Emphasis supplied. Translation below.][8]

It would seem safe to assume that prior to specific legislation controlling the manipulation of transfer pricing, such abuses were becoming widespread;

7. Translation: To establish the income tax due from those enterprises which are subject to or which control enterprises located outside France, the profits indirectly transferred to the latter, whether by way of an increase or a decrease in the purchase or the selling price, or by any other means, are included in the income statement. The same procedure applies to those enterprises which are subject to an enterprise or group likewise controlling enterprises located outside France.

8. Translation: [Certain interest payments, fees] or payments for services, paid by or due from a natural or legal person domiciled or established in France to natural or legal persons domiciled or established in a foreign country or territory located outside France, and entitled there to a tax preference, are not deductible charges in establishing tax liability unless the debtor furnishes proof that the expenses relate to *actual operations* and that they are not irregular or overstated. [Emphasis supplied.]

otherwise no such legislation would have been deemed necessary. As mentioned earlier, legal measures rarely precede the perpetration of the abuses they purport to curtail. Hence, if a serious problem no longer exists in this area, except perhaps in isolated cases which can be dealt with adequately in the local courts, transfer-pricing legislation can surely be seen to constitute an effective means of exercising control over MNE operations by the host state, particularly as such controls have no meaning within a strictly national context.

Tax legislation, in general, however, can hardly be regarded as a major control technique, as the primary aims of tax laws are simply to appropriate for the host government a share of the revenues from the firm's operations, to facilitate foreign trade and investment, and even to offer inducement to foreign investors. These aims are accomplished not only through legislation affecting transfer pricing and other tax avoidance schemes, but also through such measures as legislated tax incentives and tax relief schemes, foreign tax credits and double taxation treaties and agreements. The differences in national taxing systems, rates, and methods of assessment, and the dependence upon the widely varying contents of the numerous bilateral tax treaties and agreements, only add to the complexity of the subject and to the difficulties encountered by corporate tax lawyers.[9]

2. Tax Treaties

To cite a few examples in this area, we might begin by looking at a tax treaty between the United States and the United Kingdom which came into force on April 20, 1980. The controversial convention had been signed as early as December 31, 1975, but did not benefit from the advice and consent of the United States Senate until June 28, 1978, nor from the ratification of the British House of Commons until February 18, 1980. The U.S. Senate made a reservation which rendered inapplicable to any political subdivision or local authority of the United States the treaty provision of Article 9(4) which limits the states' capacity to tax foreign corporations investing in the United States. This issue revolved around the fact that several American states apply a unitary tax system whereby a company's state tax liability is determined on the basis of its world-wide activity rather than on its local earnings. This system is seen as a

9. For a more detailed look at MNE taxation in the U.S., France, Britain, Germany and Japan, see Carroll, "Taxation of U.S.-Based Transnational Corporations", 27 *Mercer Law Review* (1976) at 441-468; also United Nations, *The Impact of Multinational Corporations on Development and on International Relations: Technical Papers: Taxation,* United Nations, New York, 1974 (ST/ESA/11).

way of counteracting any attempts at tax avoidance through artificial transfer-pricing techniques transacted within multinational corporate groups. Application of this unitary system was precluded under the original wording of the treaty; however, as a result of the ensuing controversy and subsequent renegotiation, the final version of the treaty text did not prohibit the unitary tax being applied by those states which have adopted that system. The decision not to incorporate a waiver of unitary tax liability into the treaty had even farther-reaching implications than it might at first appear, in that an inclusion of the waiver would have surely led to the necessity of revising other currently applicable treaties which the United States has with foreign states such as France, West Germany and Japan.

Several other features of the U.S.-U.K. tax treaty are worth noting here. Of interest, for example, is that the treaty is patterned closely after the Model Convention established by the Organisation for Economic Co-operation and Development. Of interest as well is the fact that, for tax purposes, the treaty provides that the British continental shelf comprises part of the United Kingdom,[10] making any North Sea operations by United States resident companies subject to British taxation - although this tax can, under double-taxation provisions of the treaty,[11] be set off against U.S. tax liability. Perhaps of greatest significance in the particular context of the present work is that the treaty provisions decidedly favour the establishment of subsidiaries over branch offices by those U.S. enterprises investing in Britain: the tax applicable to subsidiaries operating in the United Kingdom is appreciably below that applicable to branch offices. Here, then, is a built-in incentive for foreign direct investment as a means of entry into the British market on the part of an MNE. The French also have tax treaties with many other nations, including each of those industrialized states which fall within the focus of the present study. Additionally, France's company tax laws[12] extend to all foreign companies that maintain a "permanent establishment" in France. Normally companies incorporated in France are not taxed on their operations outside French territory when those operations are of an independent and autonomous character and are permanently related to an establishment located outside of France. As this means that losses from such operations are, by the same token, not allowed to be set off against profits derived from operations within France, French companies may, if they so desire, request from the Ministry of Economy and Finance authorization for the company tax to be applied to either a system of world-wide profits and losses or a system of "consolidated profits" (and

10. Art. 3 (1) (h), (i).
11. U.S.-U.K. Double Tax Treaty, Art. 2(2) (b), 23.
12. *Code général des impôts* (General Tax Code).

losses) which includes the calculation of world-wide profits and losses plus the result of French or foreign subsidiaries' operations calculated proportionately to the parent company's ownership percentage. Generally a subsidiary is exluded from a system of "consolidated profits" where the parent participates - directly or indirectly - in less than 50 per cent of the subsidiary's voting shares.

Of particular interest too is the provision in the Tax Code (*Code général des impôts*) mentioned earlier[13]that authorizes the French tax authorities to adjust reported gross operating profits and allowable deductions to reflect what they deem to be reasonable figures for such profits and deductions. This is of particular relevance to parent-subsidiary transactions where one of the companies is a foreign enterprise, and is obviously a safeguard against such devices as artificial transfer pricing, as we have noted.

3. Relevant National Tax Laws and Policy

For the most part, and in keeping with France's recent moves at liberalization in the investment area, the French Ministry of Economy and Finance is using tax schemes as incentives to investment. One major scheme of tax relief is aimed at encouraging enterprises to relocate their facilities from the Paris area into less industrialized parts of the country.[14]Another tax-incentive scheme to encourage private investment is seen in a law under which stock companies incorporated in France between January 1, 1977 and December 31, 1981, or companies increasing their existing capital investments, between those dates, may make certain deductions from their taxable profits.[15] This deduction is applicable to all corporations listed on the French stock exchange or admitted to official quotation on the exchange within a three-year period from the date of incorporation or of increase of capital.

Additional tax and related incentives were introduced by the 1978 Budget Law for the creation of small and middle-sized industrial enterprises.[16] The Budget Law of 1979 enlarged upon this with yet another tax exemption relating to profits realized in the first and subsequent two years of establishment of new industrial enterprises.[17] Significant here is that the 1979 exemption was made

13. See *supra,* text following note 6.

14. See *Code général des impôts,* Art. 39 *quinquies* D; Art. 1473 *bis.* Annex 3, Art. 265; *Arrêté du 3 mai 1976; inter alia.*

15. *Loi de finances 1977, n° 76-1232 du 29 décembre 1976,* Art. 60, as amended by *loi n° 78-741 du 13 juillet 1978,* Art. 9.

16. *Loi n° 77-1467 du 30 décembre 1977, [1977] Journal Officiel* [J.O.] at 6316.

17. *Loi n° 78-1239 du 29 décembre 1978,* esp. Art. 19, [1978] J.O., 4339.

conditional, and applied only to those enterprises which undertook to retain the profits for their further operations. The exemption was reduced in proportion to that amount which was not retained for such purpose. In this way, the Ministry managed to employ tax measures to influence capital movements.

An additional law enacted to stimulate industrial investment, passed on July 3, 1979,[18] offered to the private investor in France further tax incentives, the most significant of which - for the corporation assessing its tax liability - was the 10 per cent deduction for increased investment available to all companies subject to corporation tax. The French Government has since taken this a giant step further in the continuing trend to stimulate private investment - particularly in the export-oriented sector - and in its 1981 budgetary proposals included a provision that companies would be allowed the deduction of a certain percentage of their investment spending from their taxable profits. The novelty here, as distinct from the 1979 and 1980 incentives of this type, is that the earlier incentives were available only to such enterprises as could demonstrate that they had increased their investment capital, whereas under the new rules, beginning in 1981 the incentives were made applicable to *all* investment expenditures, even when no increase can be shown.

One last item of interest under French corporate taxation policy is that certain tax advantages exist for corporate mergers and that these advantages have been extended to partial mergers in addition to full mergers. We shall return to the subject of 'mergers' in a later chapter, at which point it will become clear that in encouraging such combinations France stands in a rather isolated position amongst other industrialized states.

What must be kept in mind all the while is that although French company tax laws extend to all foreign enterprises that maintain a "permanent establishment" in France, and hence the above-discussed incentives are as applicable to foreign MNE subsidiaries as they are to domestic firms, this does not alter the discriminatory nature of the laws which screen the initial entry of foreign firms. For these incentives to apply to MNE subsidiaries, then, such subsidiaries must have already succeeded in gaining entry and establishment within French territory; and, as we have seen, this is not always easy for companies outside the European Community, not to discount the difficulties of Community members themselves.

To include a brief mention of the situation in Germany, there is a similar interest in providing incentives for relocation of business concerns to stimulate economic activities in certain geographic regions, particularly West Berlin and along the borders with East Germany and Czechoslovakia. As in France these incentives largely take the form of tax favours. There are also, as in France, tax advantages for small and middle-sized business. While a foreign subsidiary is

18. *Loi n° 79-525 du 3 juillet 1979, [1979]* J.O. 1607.

not perforce a large company simply because it is one part of a multinational group of companies which together form a presumably large corporate group, it is not clear whether such a subsidiary, if falling withing the range otherwise qualifying it for the available small-company tax advantages, would be considered in its own right or only as a part of the larger corporate whole operating outside German territory. The same question could be raised regarding the French rules for small and medium-size companies. In each case, it would no doubt be determined more as an issue of policy than of law.

The most significant aspect of German taxation policy for purposes of this study is the fact that, under a new tax system introduced in 1979,[19] parent companies established outside Germany and owning or controlling subsidiaries inside Germany have become subject to a substantially higher tax liability than German domestic parent companies. This is not a direct statutory discrimination, but results rather from the fact that the foreign company does not have a right to claim a credit for corporation tax paid by its subsidiary; this produces a *de facto* discriminatory practice. The new system created further dissatisfaction among U.S. multinationals with subsidiaries in Germany in that on top of the extra tax burden shared with other foreign subsidiaries, U.S. parent companies lost the special arrangements agreed to under Article VI of the German-American tax treaty whereby the amount of tax that Germany was permitted to levy on dividends paid by a German subsidiary to its U.S. parent was limited to 15 per cent, as opposed to the 25 per cent required of German companies or subsidiaries owned or controlled by non-American foreign companies. German and American tax officials subsequently negotiated to bring about an amendment to the German-U.S. tax treaty with the aim of resolving the discrepancies.

As the main thrust of tax legislation, as noted above, is in the direction of inducements to both inward and outward foreign direct investment, rather than in the direction of restrictions, a more detailed investigation of the complex tax legislation, practices and problems connected with the functioning of MNEs, aside from being impracticable within the confines of this study, would stray from the work's primary emphasis. This being said, however, it would be unrealistic to dismiss the subject of taxation without acknowledging, with a few specific examples, the influence which tax legislation has upon MNE operations, where that influence is systematic, and calculated with a control-oriented objective in view.

In Canada, for example, a systematic programme was instituted aimed at influencing foreign enterprises to share ownership of their Canadian sub-

19. See CCH *Common Market Reporter: Doing Business in Europe,* ¶ 23,344. (1979).

sidiaries with local investors. The incentive offered was a lower tax on dividends for subsidiaries with at least 25 per cent Canadian ownership.[20]

In the United States, the Interest Equalization Tax, introduced in September 1964,[21] was a measure instituted to discourage the purchase of foreign-source shares from non-residents. The non-resident selling shares to an American purchaser was required to effectively pay a capital tax from which a U.S. resident selling foreign-source shares was exempt. Due to the discriminatory nature of this tax, however, inconsistent as it was with the general policy of U.S. tax laws and bilateral tax treaties aimed at avoiding either privileged or discriminatory treatment of foreign investment income,[22] the U.S. government soon expressed its intention to reduce and eventually to remove it. The Canadians, meanwhile, as is their usual practice, immediately sought, and gained, their customary exemption.

In addition to systematic schemes like those just mentioned, the foreign subsidiary's operations are, in normal practice, limited by the local income tax and customs authorities and by existing tax codes in force in the host states and, in some cases, by those in force in the home state as well. This can sometimes be more of a deterrent to foreign MNE investment than one might at first suppose. For example, the United States ranks tenth out of twelve major nations in the amount of personal income tax it requires of its nationals, but the additional U.S. taxes payable by Americans working abroad - and their employers - over and above those taxes they must pay to the host government, has made taxes "the most important factor in U.S. firms' employment costs overseas."[23] The deterrent power of the inevitable cuts into the profitability of the foreign enterprise in such a position is not insignificant.

Many of the taxation laws growing up around multinational operations are of an entirely new character to those which have traditionally served, and, as in a large proportion of legislation developing around the MNEs, most have developed in a rather *ad hoc* fashion, as problems arise. This process will no

20. See Safarian, "Country of Ownership and Performance of the Firm", 44 *Economic Record* (1968), at 83.

21. Interest Equalization Tax Act, Pub. L. No. 88-563; 78 Stat. 809, §§ 4911, 4918; 1 U.S.C., 88th Cong., 2d Sess. (1964) §§ 923, 949. See also Clausen, "The Internationalized Corporation: An Executive's View", in Blake, ed., "The Multinational Corporation", *403 Annals of the American Academy of Political and Social Science,* (1972), at 16.

22. See e.g. the U.S. Foreign Investment Tax Act of 1966, which provides specifically that net income derived by foreign enterprises from their U.S. operations will be subject to the same rate of taxation as their domestic (U.S.) counterparts. (See Don Wallace, ed., *International Control of Investment: The Düsseldorf Conference on Multinational Corporations)* New York: Praeger, 1974, at 128.

23. "Tax a Deterrent for U.S. Firms", *International Herald Tribune,* October 3, 1978, at 9.

doubt continue, as the problems which result from international operations are constantly changing as well as growing in complexity.[24]

4. Evaluation

On the whole, the multinationals have proved to be good taxpayers, if for no better reason than that, under ever-present scrutiny, they cannot afford not to be. Where, however, taxes can legally be avoided,[25] firms will utilize every feasible means to do so. This is as true of purely national enterprises as it is of multinational ones, however, and is a part of al normal business's preoccupation. As Britain's E.B. Mortcliffe pointed out at the 1974 International Chamber of Commerce Commission on Taxation,[26] "it is neither legally nor morally wrong for any company to adopt the course of action involving the lowest tax burden." When the 'prudence' is carried too far, or a façade is created to mask tax evasion, the courts will step in.

In *De Beers Consolidated Mines Ltd.* v. *Howe*[27] the court looked behind the corporate façade to determine, for tax purposes, that a company's place of incorporation will not perforce be accepted as its place of business. It was consequently held in *In re F.G. Films Ltd.*[28] that a firm could not evade regulations imposed on foreign enterprises by merely establishing a formal subsidiary in Britain. In *F.G. Films,* an American film company set up a subsidiary in Britain which formally contracted to make and market a film for the American parent. The British subsidiary, however, was no more than a façade, with no staff and no place of business other than its registered office. The Board of Trade declined to register the film as a British production; this contention was upheld by the court; and the film was ultimately produced by the American company.[29]

In *Kraus* v. *Commissioner,*[30] an American parent company, wishing to gain a tax advantage with regard to its 'controlled foreign corporation' in Liechtenstein, 'decontrolled' the subsidiary. But the tax court, insisting upon the principle of 'actual control', ruled that the 'decontrol' could not be recognized

24. See Brooke and Remmers, *The Strategy of the Multinational Enterprise: Organization and Finance* (London: Longman [1970], at 174.

25. Avoidance is to be distinguished from evasion or other illegalities.

26. I.C.C. doc. 180/136, 30.I. 1974.

27. *De Beers Consolidated Mines Ltd.* v. *Howe,* [1906] A.C. 455.

28. *In re F.G. Films Ltd.* [1953] 1 W.L.R. 483.

29. See Hadden, *Company Law and Capitalism* (London: World University, Weidenfeld & Nicolson (c. 1972)), at 146-147.

30. *Kraus* v. *Commissioner,* 490 F.2d 898 (2d Cir. 1974), *aff'g* 59 T.C. 681 (1973).

for tax purposes. It was found that there had occurred no "meaningful transfer of 50 per cent of voting power"[31] and that there was not even evidence of a shift in managerial participation.[32]

As expressed earlier, the role of tax legislation is not primarily that of controlling MNE operations; and, while tax problems are not to be minimized, they are, for the most part, technical problems, reserved for the municipal tax lawyer. The major legislative direction of control legislation, then, as it regards taxation of multinationals, is simply against tax evasion and transfer pricing abuses, with perhaps one notable exception, namely, unreasonable taxation discriminatorily applied by the host government with the aim of forcing a foreign enterprise out of business without the obligation, on the part of the host, to pay the compensation which would normally be expected to accompany an expropriatory act. This technique clearly does qualify as a means of controlling MNE activity through taxation, but will be discussed in the context of "creeping expropriation" when considering disinvestment, in the following chapter.

31. Ibid., 59 T.C., at 693.

32. Liebman, "Taxation of Foreign Source of Income", 17 *Harvard International Law Journal* (1976), at 339-340.

Chapter VIII.

CONTROL THROUGH DISCLOSURE LEGISLATION

Disclosure, an area which until recently would have attracted little serious attention as a host control mechanism over activities of multinational enterprises, assumed increasing prominence in the wake of the exposures in the late 1970's of bribery, pay-offs and other illicit payments involved in certain international business transactions, as well as through strong official reactions against extraterritorial discovery orders emanating largely from U.S. courts seeking to enforce their government's stringent antitrust laws. The intent here is not to go into the problem of illegal payments but rather to focus upon disclosure itself in its control capacity, particularly in those areas where differing attitudes and approaches between the United States and other industrialized nations toward disclosure have begun to generate international tensions, often owing to the extraterritorial reach of jurisdiction in court discovery orders.

As the heightened activity in disclosure regulation is still relatively recent, whatever case law might in fact be relevant in the area of extraterritorial discovery orders (most frequently in the area of antitrust) fails to adequately provide a reliable basis for resolving the fundamental policy conflict between *lex fori* and international comity, or, more specifically, the frequent incompatibility between domestic court discovery orders and foreign nondisclosure laws. Nonetheless, significant case law is emerging, and the subject itself, with its implications as regards extraterritorial jurisdiction, merits due consideration.

There are various types of corporate disclosure: for example, that by a corporation to the relevant market, that by a corporation to an organ of its government or other administrative authority, and that by a corporation under a court discovery order. Our primary interest in the present context resides in those aspects of disclosure which serve as a means of control by the host state - and its judicial organs - over foreign enterprises. Among such aspects are the normal expectation of compliance by any foreign corporation with those disclosure requirements of the host to which the domestic corporation is also routinely subject; and as regards the judicial-control aspect, jurisdictional conflicts between states are bound to arise when documents located abroad are sought by court order and the production of those documents would contravene the laws of the state in which the documents are located.

1. Generally Applicable Host-state Disclosure Requirements

a. National approaches

The United Nations Commission on Transnational Corporations was made acutely aware of the general paucity of national legislation in this whole area of disclosure, in the initial efforts on the part of its Information and Research Center to collect data for a "comprehensive information system"[1] across an international spectrum. It is hardly surprising that little legislation has existed requiring disclosure by subsidiaries of foreign enterprises when, at least in Europe (with the notable exception of Britain[2]), the standards of disclosure have historically been extremely low for domestic firms themselves, as regards either their domestic or their foreign operations. For one thing, European states other than Britain have traditionally been very reticent to reveal just how international their enterprises really are,[3] and in addition, business managers in Europe have feared that extensive disclosure of data will be used to their disadvantage by (particularly foreign) competitors. In the United States, on the other hand, as we are told by two American business lawyers:

> similar anxieties [were expressed] during the debates over the passage of the disclosure legislation of the 1930's but [Americans] have since become reconciled to their operation. In any event, since the federal securities laws cover all major concerns in the entire United States, an American firm knows that its competitors are bound to equal disclosure requirements. The less integrated European markets raise different

1. See United Nations, Economic and Social Council, Commission on Transnational Corporations, Report on the Second Session (March 1-12, 1976), New York, May 1976, U.N. ECOSOC Document No. E/5782, E/C10/16.

2. See e.g. The British Companies Act 1967 c. 81, §§ 3-5; also the Companies Act 1976 (c. 69) and 1980 (c. 22); Restrictive Trade Practices Acts 1956 (c. 68), 1968 (c. 66), 1976 (c. 34) and 1977 (c. 19); Fair Trading Act 1973 c. 41.

3. See "The Continental Challenge", *The Economist* February 4, 1978, at 78. It is of interest, in this context, that Norway in 1978 passed a law (No. 66 of 16 June 1978) amending her 1950 Currency Control Law to facilitate the obtaining or seizure of documents in cases where breaches of the foreign currency exchange regulations are suspected.

problems. A corporation in, say, Germany may be reluctant to reveal information that its competitors in Italy can conceal.[4]

Consequently, in contrast to Europe, the United States' domestic disclosure requirements have been characteristically far more rigorous. In this connection it must not be overlooked that a national disclosure system relies not only upon strictly legal requirements, but also on stock-market listing standards, availability of trained market analysts and domestic business tradition. This is perhaps most true in the United States where, for example, the sophisticated, continually evolving disclosure system is the result not only of governmental legislation, as embodied in the federal securities laws supervised by the Securities and Exchange Commission (SEC).[5] but also of the New York Stock Exchange's disclosure regulations. The latter are, nonetheless, neither as stringent nor as comprehensive as those imposed by the Federal Government, which are significantly more developed than those of perhaps any other nation-state today.

Keeping in mind that this type of disclosure was designed to protect and to aid the investing public in making informed investment decisions and *not* to function as a control mechanism, the stringency of the requirements may nonetheless be regarded by an established enterprise as a burdensome inconvenience or even as an incursion on business confidentiality. On the other hand, the reporting requirements serve to provide the would-be investing firm itself with a rich source of information regarding companies with which it may wish to enter into some kind of business arrangement. Hence, the requirements can actually benefit the foreign enterprise considering entry through acquisition or 'merger' by supplying it with the date necessary to formulate a sound judgment.[6]

In addition to those requirements of the SEC regulations adopted pursuant to the Securities Act of 1933[7] and the Securities Exchange Act of 1934,[8] a valuable source of data should also be provided by the later Domestic and Foreign Investment Disclosure Act of 1977[9] which further tightened the

4. Steiner and Vagts, *Transnational Legal Problems,* 2nd ed. (Mineola, N.Y.: Foundation Press, 1976), at 1048-1049.

5. See e.g. the Securities Act of 1933, the so-called "Truth in Securities" law (48 Stat. 74 (1933)), as amended, 15 U.S.C.A. §§ 77a *et. seq.*); the Securities Exchange Act of 1934, 48 Stat. 881 (1934), as amended, 15 U.S.C.A. §§ 78a, *et seq,* and Rule 10b-5, 17 C.F.R. § 240. 10b-5.

6. Some hold the view that the SEC is no longer adequately fulfilling its statutory purpose. (For a discussion of this view see Kripke, *The SEC and Corporate Disclosure: Regulation in Search of a Purpose* (New York: Law and Business, Inc./Harcourt Brace Jovanovitch, 1979), reviewed in 78 *Michigan Law Review* (1980), pp. 819-824.

7. See *supra* note 5.

8. *Idem.*

9. Pub. L. No. 95-213, 95th Congr. (Dec. 19, 1977), Title I.

government's own disclosure requirements, with deference to "the public interest" and "the protection of investors", and about which we shall say more in the following pages.

Even the SEC regulations are not limited to strictly legal requirements. In addition to proposing specific legislation, the Commission has reacted with a number of measures which include some extra-legal elements for confronting the problem of illicit payments: (1) the Enforcement Program, (2) the Voluntary Disclosure Program, and (3) the Advisory Committee on Corporate Disclosure.[10]

The Enforcement Program is concerned with violations of the reporting and proxy provisions of the Securities Exchange Act. The Commission has attempted to avoid the enactment of regulations that would strictly define requirements for the disclosure of payments, as this would necessitate a quantified determination of materiality, either in amount or impact upon the corporation's business, whereas the Commission is of the opinion that the determination of materiality depends on "the relative economic implications of the payment to the company as a whole or to a significant line of the [company]."[11] The Enforcement Program is more in the nature of a 'policing' mechanism or adjudicatory program than a legal instrument, allowing "an examination of the facts and circumstances of each case". It is also geared to preclude a continuance of illegal payment practices which could unintentionally result from a strictly legal regulation declaring unlawful such payments or nondisclosure of payments as exceeded a specified monetary sum.

The Voluntary Disclosure Program is meant to supplement the Enforcement Program, and is based on corporate self-investigation and reporting to the Commission. The Advisory Committee on Corporate Disclosure was established to study the function and purpose of the Commission's corporate disclosure system and its revised objectives as compared with the then-existing system, and to formulate recommendations for improving that system. One of its first moves was to solicit position statements from all interested parties on a proposed revision of the securities laws.

None of these measures, nor the strictly legal ones, are generally regarded by the foreign investor as restrictive control measures; in fact they are normally welcomed by both foreign and domestic investors for the security and protection they afford the investor. The reporting requirements of the New York

10. See Carroll, "Securities and Exchange Commission", in "Administrative Survey: October 1975 to September 1976: IV. Investment Regulation", 9 *Law and Policy in International Business (1977)* at 234-237, from which the following factual material is derived.

11. Senate Committee on Banking, Housing, and Urban Affairs, Report to the Securities and Exchange Commission on Questionable and Illegal Corporate Payments and Practices, 94th Congr., 2d Sess., 3-5 (1976) (views of Commissioner Loomis), as cited in ibid., at 235.

Stock Exchange as well as the wider-reaching regulations and measures of the U.S. Securities and Exchange Commission are of interest to potential foreign investors for the protection they offer against misrepresentation, manipulation and other fraudulent practices, too often characterizing security transactions. The Commission itself does not in any way regulate access to the capital markets and consequently poses no effective barrier to foreign multinationals or to any other form of foreign investment in the United States. The major disclosure regulation of the SEC is the stipulation that share ownership of more than a certain percentage of a U.S. corporation (by foreign or domestic investors) requires disclosure. As little as 5 per cent ownership delimits the amount above which disclosure is required for certain classes of equity security ownership - direct or indirect - under the U.S. Domestic and Foreign Investment Disclosure Act of 1977[12] amending the Securities Exchange Act of 1934.[13] The stipulations of the 1977 Act are not regarded as major control mechanisms any more than the SEC regulations, since the disclosure thus required is aimed at supplying information to investors and not to prospective regulators.[14]

In the case of the 1977 Act, however, the addition of "the public interest" along with each mention of "the protection of investors" would seem to imply a broader function of the disclosure requirements than solely investor information, an inference strengthened by the type of information requested, including residence and citizenship[15] of the purchaser,[16] or whether the purpose of the purchases or prospective purchases is to acquire control,[17] etc.

The Act of 1977, then, takes the SEC regulations a step further, surely as a direct result of the earlier U.S. Foreign Investment Study Act of 1974[18]

12. Pub. L. 95-213, 95th Congr. (Dec. 19, 1977), Title I.

13. 15 U.S.C. § 78m. Under the Securities Exchange Act of 1934, problems have arisen from the fact that the Act applies to some foreign corporations that have never listed their securities in the United States, but that have five hundred shareholders, do business in interstate commerce, and generally participate in the American commercial process without having established a 'presence' in the form of a subsidiary.

14. See Domestic and Foreign Investment Disclosure Act of 1977, op. cit., *supra* note 9, sect. 202(d)(1), sect. 203 (2), (5), (6), sect. 204.

15. Ibid., sect. 202(d) (1) (A), (d), sect. 203(g) (1) (A).

16. Note the following definition of "person" for the purposes of this section ofthe Act, legal persons: "When two or more persons act as a partnership, limited partnership, syndicate, or other group for the purpose of acquiring, holding, or disposing of securities of an issuer, such syndicate or group shall be deemed a 'person' for the purposes of this subsection". (Ibid., sect. 203(g)(3)).

17. Ibid., sect. 202(d) (1) (C).

18. Pub. L. No. 93-479, 88 Stat. 1450; approved 26 Oct., 1974; see *supra* Chapter V, text accompanying notes 39, 40.

and International Survey Act of 1976[19] proposing the monitoring of foreign investment of over 5 per cent stock acquisition. This is still not to be confused with actual control regulations, nor does it necessarily presuppose the same.

While the securities regulations and other disclosure requirements in the United States are basically aimed at the regulation and control of American MNEs and domestically operating firms, with no differentiation as regards locally incorporated affiliates of foreign MNEs,[20] there is one U.S. law which is directed solely at "foreign persons" for disclosure purposes, and that is the Agricultural Foreign Investment Disclosure Act of 1978.[21] This law requires:

> foreign persons who acquire, transfer, or hold interest in agricultural land to report such transactions and holdings to the Secretary of Agriculture and to direct the Secretary to analyze information contained in such reports and determine the effects such transactions and holdings have, particularly on family farms and rural communities, and for other purposes.[22]

The rigour of the United States' domestic disclosure requirements as compared with those of Europe, together with the general practice outside the United States of segregating companies into two general categories for legislative purposes (and in France and Germany, for example, into even additional subdivisions) virtually exempting private limited liability or similar types of companies from disclosure requirements,[23] has made comparisons between European and American MNE operations extremely difficult and lends support to the suggestion that the "American challenge"[24] itself was partly the result of the stringent disclosure requirements and the consequent availability of American statistics.

The European scene has begun to change in this regard.[25] Both France and

19. S. 2839, 94th Congr., 2d Sess. (1976); see text accompanying notes 39, 40, Chapter V *supra*.

20. See e.g. Borton and Goss, "Control of Multinational Corporations' Foreign Activities", 15 *Washburn Law Journal*, (1976), at 441-444.

21. Pub. L. 95-460; 95th Congr. (October 14, 1978); 7 U.S.C. § 3501.

22. Ibid., preamble.

23. Vagts, "Law and Accounting in Business Associations", in *International Encyclopedia of Comparative Law*, Vol. XIII: "Business and Private Organizations" (Dobbs Ferry, N.Y.: Oceana, 1972), at 12.

24. See Servan-Schreiber, *The American Challenge* (London: Hamish Hamilton, 1968), which emphasized the magnitude of the American industrial presence in Europe, largely based on statistics made available by America's strict disclosure regulations.

25. Steiner and Vagts, op. cit., *supra* note 4, at 1054.

Belgium, in the tradition of the American SEC, have recently begun to base their control of the issue of securities on the "disclosure philosophy", aimed, as traditionally in the United States, solely at the protection of shareholders and investors.[26] And in Great Britain, since the 1979 abolition of exchange controls lifted the limitation on allowable shareholding percentages for foreign firms in British companies, there has been increasing pressure there as well to strengthen the regularory system of the Stock Exchange in addition to the heightened statutory disclosure requirements of the U.K. Companies Law 1980[27] to which we shall return below. In West Germany there has also been a definite move toward more comprehensive reporting on investments. There, the purpose has been to gain an overall picture of the total volume of investments by non-residents in Germany as well as by German corporations and nationals abroad, and this has been accomplished largely through an amendment to the *Aussenwirtschaftsgesetz* (Foreign Trade Law)[28] that has broadened the statutory basis for investment reporting, and through a provision of the *Abgabenordnung* (Fiscal Code)[29] which requires resident taxpayers to report to the local tax authorities the establishment or acquisition of businesses abroad, investment in foreign partnerships, and acquisition of interests in foreign entities where direct holdings of at least 10 per cent, or indirect holdings of at least 25 per cent, are involved. In addition, the Federal Government has increased its regulatory powers to compel residents (*Gebietsansässiger*) to disclose both the volume and specific items of assets located abroad; this of course applies as well to non-residents (*Gebietsfremder*) with assets in West Germany. The West German Government, in amending its laws in this area, was responding to the fact that "while other countries have extensive rules on investment reporting, the Federal Republic has no rules as yet that would provide accurate data on the volume, type and regional location of German investments abroad and foreign investments in Germany."[30] The German disclosure rules are now in closer alignment with the relevant EEC recommendations. Moreover, many German firms disclose substantially more than the required minimum, as evidenced by any recent VW or BASF annual report.

26. See Leleux, "France, Belgium, European Community and the Multinational Enterprise", in Hahlo, ed., *Nationalism and the Multinational Enterprise* (Dobbs Ferry, New York: Oceana, 1973) at 120.

27. Companies Law 1980 c. 22.

28. *Entwurf eines Dritten Gesetzes zur Änderung des Aussenwirtschaftsgesetzes, Drucksache* 543/75, September 5, 1975; see, *Aussenwirtschaftsgesetz vom 28.4.1961* BGB. 1961 I, s.481, 495, 1555) *in der Fassung des 3. Anderungsgesetzes vom 29.3.1976* (BGBl 1976 I, 869), esp. sect. 26.

29. *Abgabenordnung*/sect. 138(2), BGBl 1976 I, S. 613.

30. CCH *Comm. Mkt. Rep.*: *Doing Business in Europe,* para. 30,820, [New Developments 1978].

There is, moreover, an arrangement between West Germany and the United States[31] calling for co-operation in various commercial matters and some information exchange, though care was taken to maintain certain safeguards for confidentiality. As this is generally with respect to antitrust issues, we shall defer further discussion of the agreement until the following chapter.

To return to the U.K. for another example of the general tightening of European disclosure standards, having already acknowledged that Great Britain has a longer tradition of disclosure regulations in general than have other European nations, the British Fair Trading Act 1973[32] vests express power to require the disclosure of relevant documents in investigating a reference under the 1973 Act in an advisory body (the Commission),[33] and any alteration, destruction, falsification or suppression of any documents so required is punishable by fine and/or imprisonment.[34] By the terms of the Act a party is nonetheless protected from compulsion to give evidence or produce any document or provide any informational evidence which he would not be required to give, produce or provide in normal civil proceedings.[35] And while there appears to be an additional protection for the party engaged in business, in that no information on any aspect of that business obtained under the provision (other than Part II) of the 1973 Act may, so long as the business continues to operate, be disclosed without the consent of the party in question, this provision does not apply in cases where the disclosure is made "(a) for the purpose of facilitating the performance of any functions of the Director [General of Fair Trading], the [Monopolies and Mergers] Commission, the Secretary of State or any other Minister..., or (b) in pursuance of a Community obligation within the meaning of the European Communities Act 1972", except in cases of proceedings before the Restrictive Practices Court or of any other legal proceedings under the 1973 Act, or under the Restrictive Trade Practices Act of 1956 and 1968.[36]

31. Agreement between the Government of the United States of America and the Government of the Federal Republic of Germany Relating to Mutual Cooperation Regarding Restrictive Business Practices, BGB1 1976 II S.1711; CCH *Common Market Reporter Doing Business in Europe,* ¶ 23,529, [1976]; 27 U.S.T. 1956, T.I.A.S. No. 8291; [1978] 5 CCH *Trade Regulations Reports,* para. 50,283.

Further, some very narrow bilateral agreements about cooperation in illicit payments issues have been concluded between the United States and Japan; and there is a treaty which binds the United States and Switzerland to mutual assistance in obtaining data in certain criminal investigations, but not in the subject of Interhandel, (see *infra* note 66 and accompanying text, *et. seq.*).

32. Fair Trading Act 1973 c. 41.

33. Ibid., sect. 85(1) (b), (c).

34. Ibid., sect. 85(5) and (6).

35. Ibid., sect. 85(3).

36. Ibid., sect. 133 (1), (2), (3). Currently in force are also the Restrictive Trade Practices Act

More recently, under the British Competition Act 1980,[37] the investigatory powers of the Office of Fair Trading established under the terms of the 1973 Fair Trading Act have been increased to enable it - along with its role in monitoring mergers and monopolies policy - to investigate anti-competitive conduct on the part of individual companies rather than being limited to investigations on an industry-wide or product-category basis, as was the case prior to the 1980 Act.

Additional significant changes in British law relating to disclosure are observable in the latest Companies Act (1980)[38] in which, largely as a result of the U.K. Department of Trade's report published on August 5, 1980 and its consultative document released six days later,[39] the stringency of the notification provisions in British Companies Acts, as well as of the disclosure provisions in U.K. company law generally, were appreciably strengthened; the Act also provides severe penalties for any breach of disclosure provisions. Those disclosure provisions relating to share acquisitions reflect the mounting pressure which arose in the wake of an important market manipulation in 1980[40] which showed up certain weaknesses in U.K. company law relating to share acquisition. In this connection, as mentioned above, the abolition of all exchange controls in the United Kingdom and the consequent lifting of limitations on shareholding percentages allowed to foreign enterprises in U.K. companies have made disclosure rules and Stock Exchange regulations even more important than in the past, and have led to pressures for statutory controls over foreign companies. This is reflected in the rigid statutory penalties to be imposed under the 1980 Companies Act on investing enterprises which do not make reasonable efforts at ascertaining whether an acquisition involves "notifiable" interests, or on "groups" of investors which do not disclose their formal links.

The overriding consideration in all such provisions, according to the Department of Trade, is to ensure the prompt disclosure to shareholders and the public when a significant holding in a company's voting shares is acquired,

---

1976 and 1977 (c.19) (see esp. sect. 41); but while the 1976/1977 Act amends and/or repeals certain sections of the Acts of 1956 (c.68) and 1968 (c. 66), as well as of the Fair Trading Act 1973 (c. 41) and the European Communities Act 1972 (c. 68), the above remains unaffected.

37. Competition Act 1980 c.21.

38. Companies Act 1980 c.22 (see esp. Part IV).

39. *Disclosure of Interests in Shares: A Consultative Document,* U.K. Department of Trade, London, August 11, 1980.

40. The February 1980 "dawn raid" engineered by the De Beers mining group of South Africa on the shares of Consolidated Gold Fields (see CCH *Common Market Reporter: Doing Business in Europe,* ¶ 40,067 [New Developments 1980]).

regardless of whether the acquisition is to be used to influence policy or to lead to a subsequent acquisition of a controlling interest.

Other noteworthy provisions of the Companies Act 1980 relate to the potential legal questions that could arise in instances where a foreign company or corporate group might express a readiness to co-operate in an investigation but plead the inability to perform owing to legal requirements in its country of origin. We shall look at these provisions more closely in the consideration of jurisdictional conflicts in the following section.

In remarking on recent developments in U.K. disclosure law and policy, one should perhaps also mention the new accounting standard, SSAP 17, announced by the British Accounting Standards Committee, which makes specific provision for the disclosure of "window dressing" in company accounts. "Window dressing" is not to be confused with fraudulent falsification of accounts, but is rather a "lawful arrangement" of a company's affairs which nonetheless has the effect of giving an appearance which alters the impression one otherwise would have had. SSAP 17 stipulates that accountants must disclose instances of "window dressing", under certain specified circumstances, in their accounts.

b. Regional approaches

On the regional level, it was proposed some years ago in the context of the EEC that the practice of disclosure be applied increasingly strictly to MNEs in general, and that, accordingly, the British Companies Act 1967,[41] in which a greater emphasis on disclosure requirements was one of the primary innovations (since amended, as we have noted, by the Companies Act 1976[42] which maintained this emphasis, and that of 1980[43] elaborating even further the disclosure provisions), should serve as a blueprint for all EEC member states as a first step in the regulation of MNEs. There have been continued efforts on the part of the EEC to harmonize national legislation in the area of disclosure regulations; in addition to proposing directives to this end, a specific effort at harmonization was apparent in a response to a Written Question[44] submitted by a British member of the European Parliament to the EC Commission in

41. Loc. cit., *supra* note 2.

42. U.K. Companies Act 1976 c. 69.

43. U.K. Companies Act 1980 c.22 (see esp. Part IV).

44. Written Question No.23/77, submitted by Sir Derek Walker-Smith, Member of the European Parliament, to the Commission of the European Communities, Official Journal No. C289, December 1, 1977, at 1.

1977, with regard to U.K. company rules on the registration of directors in light of the Commission's disclosure Directive of March 9, 1968. The Commission expressed its view that British law - despite its apparent relative stringency - was, at that time, insufficient to give full effect to Article 2(1) (d) of the EEC disclosure Directive (relative to obligatory disclosure on the part of companies for certain "acts and specifications"), and the Commission put itself "in contact with the United Kingdom Government with regard to the necessary adjustments to be made to the laws of that member State"[45] to bring them into conformity with the EEC position. This pronouncement would tend to indicate that, in some respects, the EC Commission at one stage actually overtook the U.K. in the comprehensiveness of its emerging disclosure measures, or at least in particular provisions thereof. The U.K. Companies Act 1980 mentioned above, however, has completed Britain's restoration to conformity with the Community position and, in a number of provisions, has gone beyond it.

c. International approaches

On the international plane, what has been said concerning the U.S. SEC position and the new directions in France and Belgium, has also been said by one writer[46] concerning the disclosure provisions of the 1975 OECD "Guidelines for Multinational Enterprises" ("Guidelines"),[47] *viz.*, that it is made clear therein that disclosure is considered a matter of information for investors rather than for prospective regulators. This assessment of the OECD position on disclosure seems to the present writer, however, to rather misread the stated aim of the Guidelines, which is not, as with the SEC, solely to protect the investor, but rather to (a) "encourage the positive contributions which multinational enterprises can make to economic and social progress and to minimize and resolve the difficulties to which their various operations may give rise", and to (b) "contribute to improving the foreign investment climate."[48] While these somewhat broadly-stated aims could conceivably, taken on their own, be interpreted as geared toward investor protection, they can only be properly

45. *Idem,* as reported in CCH *Common Market Reporter: Doing Business in Europe,* ¶ 30,989 [New Developments, 1978].

46. Lichtenstein, "Current Proposals for Marshalling Data on and Disclosure by Multinationals", 11 *International Lawyer (1977),* at 63.

47. "Guidelines for Multinational Enterprises", Annex to the Declaration of 21st June 1976 by Governments of OECD Member Countries on International Investment and Multinational Enterprises, published in: *International Investment and Multinational Enterprises,* OECD Publications, Paris, 1976 [hereinafter cited as OECD Guidelines], at 11-17.

48. Ibid., para. 2, at 11.

assessed within the wider context of the Guidelines as a whole which would seem, according to the above-stated aims, to have a different objective in view. The expositor of the investor-protection interpretation of the Guidelines, to support her position, cites the OECD proposal that "enterprises 'should, having due regard to their nature and relative size in the economic context of their operations and to requirements of business confidentiality and to cost, publish in a form suited to improve public understanding...' "; but that writer fails to complete the citation which goes on to say that the information so published, "on the structure, activities and policies of the enterprise as a whole" should appear "as a *supplement*...to information to be disclosed under the national law of the individual countries in which they operate." [Emphasis supplied].[49] This, along with the particular types of information recommended for disclosure in the Guidelines,[50] as well as the statement under General Policies that "[e]nterprises should, while observing their legal obligations concerning information, supply their entities with supplementary information the latter may need in order to meet requests by the authorities of the countries in which those entities are located for information relevant to the activities of those entities, taking into account legitimate requirements of business confidentiality"[51], would seem to the present writer to be aimed more at satisfying government administrators and legislators, and at quelling the fears of the host society and its authorities by providing factual information, in an awareness that fears of the unknown generate restrictive legislation, than to be aimed purely at informing the private individual or corporate investor. It is clear that fears are best dispelled when speculation is replaced by fact. Hence, better disclosure of corporate operations, including financial data, geographical distribution, enterprise structure, ownership percentages, principal activities, employee figures and other areas listed as desirable for disclosure in the OECD Guidelines, by better revealing a company's current activities and policies, its degree of involvement in the national economy and its long-range goals, should primarily serve to allay fears that otherwise tend to lead to tighter regulation. This would appear to the present writer to be the main aim of the OECD proposals of supplementary disclosure as expressed in the Guidelines, and to better explain what is implied therein by "improving the foreign investment climate" than solely investor protection.

49. Ibid., at 14.

50. The types of information recommended for disclosure include, *inter alia,* structure of the enterprise, ownership percentages, geographical distribution, principal activities, and research and development policies (ibid., at 14-15).

51. Ibid., para. 3, at 13.

The argument could perhaps benefit here from a brief reversion to the U.S. Domestic and Foreign Investment Disclosure Act of 1977.[52] In this Act, the dual function of disclosure is clearly stated in its directive to owners of over 5 per cent of the relevant equity securities to file "such additional information as the Commission *may*, by rules and regulations, prescribe as necessary or appropriate *in the public interest or for the protection of investors.*" [Emphasis supplied.] This dual function probably expresses more-or-less accurately a similar duality of intent, on a wider scale, present in the Guidelines, although in the Guidelines the emphasis appears to be more on the public interest than on the protection of investors.

The OECD Declaration on International Investment and Multinational Enterprises to which the Guidelines is appended makes no specific legislatire proposals on disclosure. Of course host states are by implication exhorted, under the Declaration, to practice disclosure measures even-handedly on domestic and foreign firms alike, simply on the strength of the general provision of Section II.1 which stipulates that: "Member countries should... accord to enterprises operating in their territories and owned or controlled directly by nationals of another Member country...treatment under their laws, regulations and administrative practices, consistent with international law and no less favourable than that accorded in like situations to domestic enterprises..." - i.e., national treatment, which, according to Section II.2 should be considered also in respect of non-member countries. Specific treatment of disclosure by the OECD is not, however, confined to the Guidelines with their special subdivision on the subject, to which the above remarks refer; it extends also to an OECD Council Recommendation adopted in July 1978 regarding measures against restrictive business practices and to a study currently being carried out by an OECD Committee of Government Experts regarding disclosure of information sought by foreign antitrust authorities and fact-finding methods employed in antitrust suits and proceedings. The Council Recommendation stressed the necessity of conformity with international law and due regard for international comity when developing any laws aimed at facilitating extraterritorial investigation and disclosure, and emphasized the importance of regard for the law and established policies and national interests of the country where the documents are situated.

Also on the international level, some attempts have been made at dealing with the issue by the International Chamber of Commerce (ICC) which, consistent with the OECD position, has formulated the suggestion that "no more extensive standards of public disclosure should be imposed on MNEs than are

52. Loc. cit., *supra* note 9.

imposed on major national companies."[53] Such a statement, while perfectly valid, is effectively void of much practical impact when one considers the minimal disclosure standards of some governments, and is equally deficient as an international norm when taking into account the vast range of national disclosure standards across the spectrum of the various states. The ICC statement would appear in any case to be, in effect, again no more than a restatement of the national treatment principle. The ICC has not stopped there, however, and has included disclosure provisions among those national measures recommended to Governments in its 1977 Report on Extortion and Bribery in Business Transactions.[54] The report itself was researched and produced by an *ad hoc* Commission specially set up by the ICC in December 1975 - composed of members from both developed and developing countries - to investigate "the extent to which individual countries have enacted legislation to prohibit corrupt practices.[55] The results of the initial survey, however, have been less than encouraging. They demonstrate that even where such laws exist, as they do in most countries, "the effectiveness of their enforcement varies considerably."[56] It is to be remarked that the emphasis here is still placed upon national legislation, rather than on general international agreements or other international legal solutions.

The inclination toward national solutions on the part of international bodies is also evident in the 1977 Report of the Ad Hoc Intergovernmental Working Group on the Problem of Corrupt Practices in International Commercial Transactions of the United Nations Economic and Social Council[57] which, while primarily aiming at the ultimate conclusion of an international agreement, nonetheless devotes an entire section to action at the national level, proposing that reporting and disclosure requirements be governed "by law or regulation" of "Each [Contracting] State."[58] In addition, the United Nations

53. International Chamber of Commerce, Special Committee on Multinational Enterprises: "Multinational Enterprises and their Role in Economic Development", ICC Document No. 191/81 or., at 36.

54. International Chamber of Commerce: Commission on Ethical Practices, "Recommendations to Combat Extortion and Bribery in Business Transactions", ICC Publication No. 315 (Report adopted 29 November 1977.)

55. International Chamber of Commerce: Commission on Ethical Practices, "Draft Report on Ethical Practices in Commercial Transactions", ICC Document No. 192/36, March 14, 1977.

56. *Idem*

57. United Nations Economic and Social Council, *Report of the Ad Hoc Intergovernmental Working Group on the Problem of Corrupt Practices in International Commercial Transactions,* Sixty-third Session, Agenda item 17: Transnational corporations, U.N. document E/6006, 5 July 1977, Part A, III.

58. Ibid., Part A, III.3(i).

Commission on Transnational Corporations, in its work related to the formation of a code of conduct,[59] recommends disclosure provisions "to complement information required under national law". This, of course, also echoes the OECD Guidelines recommendation that the information to be published should supplement information to be disclosed under the respective national laws.[60]

Again in the context of the United Nations - but reflecting concerns notably similar to those of the OECD Council Recommendation regarding action against restrictive business practices - the United Nations Conference on Trade and Development (UNCTAD) issued in 1980,[61] in response to an earlier U.N. General Assembly resolution,[62] a "Set of Multilaterally Agreed Equitable Principles and Rules for the Control of Restrictive Business Practices".[63] In the UNCTAD draft resolution, since adopted without vote in its entirety by the thirty-fifth U.N. General Assembly,[64] are included some provisions regarding disclosure as it relates to control of restrictive business practices. Section D(2) of the resolution recommends that enterprises should provide to competent national authorities information required for the purpose of controlling restrictive business practices, "including that [information] which may be located in foreign countries to the extent that in the latter event such production or disclosure is not prevented by applicable law or established public policy." And in Section E(5) it is recommended that where a state obtains such information from enterprises acting upon this directive which contain legitimate business secrets, that state "should accord such information reasonable safeguards normally applicable in this field, particularly to protect its confidentiality." The following paragraph (6) goes on to admonish states to improve or institute procedures for procuring information from enterprises (expressly including MNEs). Here again, and throughout Section E, the individual states are directed to take national (and regional and subregional) measures to implement the international guidelines.

It is not necessarily to be expected, however, that governments will "accept the contention that they are under an obligation to disclose or permit disclosure

59. United Nations Intergovernmental Working Group Report on the Formulation of a Code of Conduct, Commission on Transnational Corporations, Third Session, New York, 25 April - 6 May 1977, Agenda item 5, U.N. document No. E/C.10/30, May 4, 1977.

60. OECD Guidelines, op. cit., *supra* note 47, at 14; see also *supra,* text accompanying note 49.

61. The draft was prepared by the United Nations Conference on Restrictive Business Practices, under the auspices of UNCTAD.

62. U.N. General Assembly resolution 33/153 of 20 December 1978.

63. UNCTAD document TD/RBP/CONF/10, Annex; U.N. document A/C.2/35/6, October 23, 1980, Annex.

64. U.N. document A/RES/35/63, December 16, 1980.

of detailed information in their possession or jurisdiction to foreign courts'',[65] whatever safeguards there may theoretically be for confidentiality.

The difficulties inherent in international solutions must not be underestimated, and the lack of an international consensus among the various states even as to when a fact has sufficient materiality to warrant disclosure, or as to what degree of compulsory revelation of data is appropriate, desirable or even acceptable within a given system in order to remain consistent with other laws and traditions concerning business confidentiality, secrecy of information, etc., only further complicates the issue and discourages well-meaning efforts at international solutions. Nonetheless, the U.N., ICC and OECD efforts, while only partial measures at present, demonstrate a wider concern and represent emerging efforts toward international stanards and co-operation in this area.

2. Problem of Concurrent and Conflicting Jurisdictions

a. National trends

In order to attempt again to translate theory into practice, we must look for evidence of any significant altercations between enterprise and host involving disclosure. In so doing, we see that any serious controversy in this area revolves around extraterritorial discovery orders, i.e., attempts of domestic courts to procure the disclosure of documents located abroad, in an effort to determine facts upon which the outcome of a case may depend for its proper adjudication.

This aspect of disclosure rests not on legislation tightening national disclosure requirements for domestic and foreign firms, but rather on the extraterritorial issue as it relates to disclosure; and it often leads to the enactment of domestic legislation against disclosure measures from abroad.

The key case marking the first major turning point in the recognition of the power of a court to issue a discovery order on foreign documents, even when those documents are located in a country which prohibits their disclosure or removal, is the *Interhandel* case.[66] In *Interhandel,* a suit was brought, under the

65. Stanford, "The Application of the Sherman Act to Conduct Outside the United States: A View from Abroad", 11 *Cornell International Law Journal* (1978), at 211.

66. *Société Internationale Pour Participations Industrielles et Commerciales, S.A.* [*Interhandel*] v. *Rogers,* 357 U.S. 197 (1958) [hereinafter cited as *Interhandel* v. *Rogers*)]. See also *International Case* (Switzerland *v*. United States of America) *I.C.J. Reports* 1959, p.6.

U.S. Trading with the Enemy Act,[67] by a Swiss holding company seeking to recover certain assets seized as enemy property by the U.S. Government during the Second World War. A discovery order was issued by the U.S. court[68] under Government request, as part of its defense, requiring Interhandel to produce for inspection and duplication a considerable number of relevant banking records. These records, however, were in the possession of Interhandel's Swiss banker, enabling Interhandel to take refuge behind the Swiss laws on secrecy of banking records and economic espionage[69] in refusing to produce the documents, over which, Interhandel contended, it did not have effective control. Before the district court had time to rule on this contention, a Swiss federal attorney constructively took possession of the records in question. Interhandel's suit was thereupon dismissed by the U.S. court with prejudice for failure to comply with the discovery order.[70] The Supreme Court subsequently upheld the district court's right to issue the discovery order, regardless of any Swiss laws forbidding such disclosure. At the same time, however, as the withholding of the documents was due to inability on the part of Interhandel, rather than due to willful non-compliance or bad faith, the Court held that the dismissal was not mandatory and remanded the case to the lower court for possible alternative procedures - for example, coming up with other means of securing the documents, or simply conducting the trial without them.

Thus the *Interhandel* case, while establishing the rule that (U.S.) courts could order production of documents regardless of foreign laws to the contrary, modified the rule by permitting judicial discretion to make allowances when a conscientious endeavor can be shown, on the part of the defendant, to evince a significant measure of compliance from its government, or to otherwise endeavor in some way to complete the discovery order.

Notable among other cases[71] since *Interhandel* involving protests against the

67. Trading with the Enemy Act, sect. 9(a), 40 Stat. 415 (1979), as amended, 50 U.S.C.App. sect. 9(a) (1964), as further amended, Pub. L. No. 95-223, 95th Cong. (Dec. 28, 1977) [H.R. 7738], Title I.

68. *Société Internationale Pour Participations Industrielles et Commerciales, S.A.* [*Interhandel*] v. *Clark,* 9 F.R.D. 263, 265 (C.D.C.1949).

69. See Law of November 8, 1934 [1934] *Bereinigte Sammlung der Bundesgesetze und Verordnungen* 337 (Switz.) as amended, Law of March 11, 1971 [1971] *Amtliche Sammlung der Bundesgesetze und Verordnungen* 808 (Switz.). See also *Interhandel* v. *Rogers,* loc. cit., *supra* note 66, at 200.

70. *Société Internationale Pour Participations Industrielles et Commerciales, S.A.* [*Interhandel*] v. *McGranery,* 111 F. Supp. 435, 445-48 (D.D.C. 1953).

71. See e.g. *Ings* v. *Ferguson,* 282 F.2d 149 (2d Cir. 1960), *modifying In re Equitable Plan Co.*, 185 F. Supp. 57 (S.D.N.Y. 1960); *United States* v. *Standard Oil Co.* (New Jersey), 23 F.R.D. 1, 4-5 (S.D.N.Y. 1958); *In re Grand Jury Investigation of the Shipping Industry,* 186 F.Supp. 298

disclosure of documents located abroad are the *In re Ampicillin Antitrust Litigation* (*Beecham*),[72] *United States* v. *First National City Bank* (*Citibank*),[73] and *In re Westinghouse Electric Corporation Uranium Contracts Litigation* (*Westinghouse*).[74]

The *In re Ampicillin Antitrust Litigation* (*Beecham* case) involved an antitrust suit filed against three affiliated Beecham companies by the United States Department of Justice. In this case the U.S. Government alleged that Bristol-Myers Co., Beecham, Inc. (both U.S. companies) and Beecham Group Ltd. (Beecham U.K.), holding 90 per cent ownership of Beecham, Inc., combined and conspired to restrain and monopolize trade in ampicillin and other semi-synthetic penicillin drugs by fraudulent manipulation of patent rights and trade names. By a discovery order of the U.S. court, Beecham U.K. was required to produce information relating to its acquisition of the American patent and to its negotiation of certain agreements with Bristol-Myers. Beecham U.K., under the directive of the U.K. Department of Trade and Industry (D.T.I.), relying on Section 2 of the 1964 British Shipping Contracts and Commercial Documents Act,[75] refused compliance, at least so far as the order related to documents held in the United Kingdom or to any information derivable from such documents, contending that the order "would constitute an infringement of the jurisdiction which, under international law, belongs to the United Kingdom."[76]

The United States Department of Justice cited the *Interhandel* case in asserting that: "even where compliance with a production or discovery order would involve, of necessity, a violation of the criminal or civil law of a foreign country or jurisdiction in which the documents or records are located - the courts of this country are not thereby deprived of jurisdiction to issue such a discovery order."[77] The U.S. court agreed and issued an order, pursuant to

---

(D.D.C. 1960); *Montship Lines Ltd.* v. *Federal Maritime Board,* 295 F.2d 147 (D.C. Cir. 1961); *In re Application of Chase Manhattan Bank,* 297 F.2d 611 (2d Cir. 1962), *aff'g* 192 F. Supp. 817, *modifying 191 F. Supp. 206 (S.D.N.Y. 1961); and American Indus. Contracting, Inc.* v. *Johns Manville Corp.,* 326 F. Supp. 879 (W.D. Pa. 1971).

72. *In re Ampicillin Antitrust Litigation,* Civil No. 822-70 (D.D.C., filed March 19, 1970).

73. *United States* v. *First National City Bank,* 396 F.2d 897 (2d Cir. 1968).

74. *In re Westinghouse Elec. Corp. Uranium Contracts Litigation,* 563 F.2d 992 (10th Cir. 1977). (See also *infra* notes 87, 89.)

75. Shipping Contracts and Commercial Documents Act 1964 c. 87. This Act has been superceded and repealed by the Protection of Trading Interests Act 1980 c. 11.

76. Ibid., para. 1.

77. Memorandum of Points and Authorities of the United States in Support of an Order Granting against Beecham Group Limited the Relief Provided in the Order to Show Cause Entered

Federal Rule of Civil Procedure 37(b), that those factual issues withheld from the proceedings as a result of Beecham U.K.'s non-compliance with the discovery order would be resolved against Beecham U.K. which would also be precluded from introducing evidence in the proceedings to oppose those claims.

D.T.I. then, at the request of Beecham U.K., issued a new order modifying the original one barring compliance. Along with the new order, a letter was sent from D.T.I. to Beecham U.K. assuring "all possible help to the Court in this matter consistent with the maintenance of U.K. jurisdiction." Under the new order, only those documents or related information involving dealings between the British Government - or any public authority in the U.K. - and Beecham were restricted from disclosure. Beecham accordingly filed as many interrogatory answers as it felt it could in compliance with D.T.I.'s order, and the U.S. district court, on the grounds that Beecham U.K. had made a "conscientious endeavor" to complete discovery, rescinded its order to resolve the factual issues against Beecham U.K.

The settlement of the disclosure aspects of the *Beecham* case represents the kind of compromise which has not infrequently, since *Interhandel*, characterized transnational intercourse in this area of difficulties of multiple jurisdictions. Moreover it strengthened the rule established in *Interhandel* more than ten years earlier that once a (U.S.) court has established adjudicatory jurisdiction, it may require the production or disclosure of documents or other relevant evidence, irrespective of their location, even where compliance with the order would violate foreign law, though, with reference to the latter, the court may use its discretion to modify its demands in deference to international comity.

This rule was formalized in the American *Restatement (Second) of the Foreign Relations Law of the United States*,[78] in Section 37 relating to the right of a state, when - and this is an important limitation - prescriptive or enforcement jurisdiction has been established, to exercise that jurisdiction notwithstanding concurrent jurisdiction of another state (subject also to those limitations enumerated in Sections 40[79] and 46-62 of the *Restatement*). The rule has likewise been incorporated into Section 53 of the U.S. *Restatement (Second) of Conflict of Laws* of 1971 which eliminates the foreign illegality limitation

---

Jan. 19, 1973, at 2 (filed January 26, 1973), *United States* v. *Bristol-Myers Co.*, Civil No. 822-70 (D.D.C., filed March 19, 1970).

78. See American Law Institute, *Restatement of the Law (Second): Foreign Relations Law of the United States* (St. Paul, Minn.: American Law Institute Publishers, 1965) § 37 at 104.

79. See *infra* note 85.

found in the first *Restatement of Conflict of Laws* of 1934.[80]

The principle in practice was clearly supported even prior to *Beecham* by the statement in *United States* v. *First National City Bank* (*Citibank*)[81] that: "It is no longer open to doubt that a federal court has the power to require the production of documents located in foreign countries if the court has *in personam* jurisdiction over the person in possession or control of the material." Note the words "possession *or control*". While the defendant may advance the argument that he is not in possession of the required documents, or that they are located outside the forum, the decisive test is control rather than location, and the resolution of the issue hence revolves around the question of control.

Of course, establishing where control actually is vested, in each instance, is no simple matter. Some guidelines have been established through case law such as that proceeding from *In re Investigation of World Arrangements* (*Oil Cartel* case)[82] where the control necessary to procure the required documents - that is, control of the parent over a subsidiary - was linked to the power of that parent to elect, directly or indirectly, a majority of the directors of the other (thus deemed subsidiary) corporation. This case introduces additional issues such as that of sovereign immunity, but it is of particular interest within the context of the present work in that the concept of control here duly took into consideration the practical and actual managerial aspects of control rather than relying on the strictly formal and legal aspects such as ownership percentages and share distribution. Basically, once appropriate jurisdiction has been established -through lifting the veil or any other legitimate means - the primary consideration should be who is in control of the enterprise's documents, not where they are located - temporarily or otherwise. Theoretically, this should pose little problem in the case of the MNE, as, once the veil is lifted, the host-state entity is deemed to have control over the corporate records, regardless of which particular entity has actual possession of them at the time.[83] This is based on the premise that if the corporation on which the subpeona is served has control

80. Compare *Restatement* (*Second*) *of Conflict of Laws* § 53 (1971) with *Restatement of Conflict of Laws* § 94 (1934); see generally, Onkelinx, "Conflict of International Jurisdiction: Ordering the Production of Documents in Violation of the Law of Situs", 64 *Northwestern University Law Review* (1969), pp. 487 *et seg., [hereinafter cited as Restatement*], esp. at 500-501.

81. *United States* v. *First National City Bank,* 396 F.2d 897, 900-01 (2d Cir. 1968).

82. *In re Investigation of World Arrangements* (*Oil Cartel* case), 13 F.R.D. 280, 285 (D.D.C. 1952).

83. See Griffin, "The Power of Host Countries over the Multinational: Lifting the Veil in the European Economic Community and the United States", 6 *Law and Policy in International Business* (1974), at 408.

over the corporation in possession of the documents "the courts will look through the corporate entity."[84]

The *Citibank* case is not directly relevant to the present context in that in *Citibank,* while the issue was indeed one of extraterritorial disclosure and conflict of jurisdiction, the subpoenaed documents in question were located in the New York bank's Frankfurt branch, and a branch does not constitute MNE foreign direct investment by definition. Thus without going into the detailed facts of the case, it is nonetheless of interest in the present context that the balance-of-interest approach to extraterritorial jurisdiction, as set out in Section 40 of the American *Restatement (Second) of the Foreign Relations Law of the United States*[85] was applied by a court for the first time. This approach represents an attempt to weigh the respective national interests of the two states involved and also the relative hardship of the party vulnerable to liability under two jurisdictions simultaneously requiring of him inconsistent conduct. In the case of *Citibank,* the court decided that the U.S. national interest was of greater weight in the particular circumstances; the U.S. courts applying the balance-of-interests doctrine have not, however, always decided in favour of American national interests.[86] In one part of the *Westinghouse* litigation[87] involving Canada, for example, the U.S. Court of Appeals for the Tenth Circuit, in balancing the interests of the Canadian with the American Government, concluded that Canada's national interest - involving as it did the national control of atomic energy - should prevail over that of the United States. In thus reversing the district court's decision, the Court of Appeals relied on

84. *Oil Cartel* case, loc. cit., *supra* note 82. See also Onkelinx, "Conflict of International Jurisdiction: Ordering the Production of Documents in Violation of the Law of the Situs", 64 *Northwestern University Law Review* (1969-1970), at 504.

85. *Restatement,* op. cit., *supra* note 78, § 40. Section 40, on the "Limitations on Exercise of Enforcement Jurisdiction", requires that exercise of enforcement jurisdiction be moderated in the light of such factors as "(a) vital national interests of each of the states, (b) the extent and the nature of the hardship that inconsistent enforcement actions would impose upon the person, (c) the extent to which the required conduct is to take place in the territory of the other state, (d) the nationality of the person, and, (e) the extent to which enforcement by action of either state can reasonably be expected to achieve compliance with the rule prescribed by that state."

86. See e.g. *Timberlane Lumber Co.* v. *Bank of America,* 549 F. 2d 597 (9th Cir. 1976), in which, in addition to the jurisdictional tests of actual or intended effect on American commerce and substantiality of effect, was added a third test considering factors of international comity, and only if all three tests were satisfactorily met was subject-matter jurisdiction deemed to exist; and *Mannington Mills, Inc.* v. *Congoleum Corp.,* 595 F.2d 1287 (3d Cir. 1979), in which it was ruled that even when subject-matter jurisdiction was found to exist, factors of international comity had to be weighed to determine whether that jurisdiction should be exercised.

87. *In re Westinghouse Elec. Corp. Uranium Contracts Litigation,* 563 F.2d 992 (10th Cir. 1977). See also *Re Westinghouse Elec. Corp. and Duquesne Light Co.,* 78 D.L.R. 3d (Ont. 1977).

Interhandel, contending that the American Rio Algam Corporation which had failed to procure the requested evidence from a Canadian corporate office had made diligent attempts at compliance and, further, that *Interhandel* had advocated an *ad hoc* balance-of-interests approach accommodating the principles of the law of the forum with the legitimate national interests of the foreign state, with the presumed result that foreign illegality, while not precluding the discovery order, might act to prevent the U.S. court from imposing sanctions for non-compliance.

As in *Citibank,* the extraterritorial disclosure issue in *Westinghouse* did not involve the normal parent-foreign subsidiary jurisdictional conflict which is the focus of the present study; but rather, in *Westinghouse* it was a question of pre-trial investigation into the existence of an international cartel of which Westinghouse was not itself a member but whose sudden change in pricing and supply policies had vitally affected the capability of Westinghouse to perform its contractual obligations to supply a number of American foreign utility companies with uranium. The evidence sought was for the purpose of substantiating the existence of the cartel for the defense of the American Westinghouse Corporation, and as such exceeded the normal range of extraterritorial discovery orders for directly applicable in-trial evidence, or even pre-trial evidence in certain cases where jurisdiction is established.

Canada was not the only country involved in the 'Westinghouse saga'. This large-scale and many-pronged litigation also involved, *inter alia,* France, Australia, South Africa and the United Kingdom. Without going into the further details of the case itself[88] owing to its limited relevance contextually, it is nonetheless worth mention here in that those laws which obstructed disclosure, relating to possible restrictive business practices in a number of countries allegedly involved in the cartel - laws designed to prevent the production of documents in response to U.S. court orders, are the same laws which can be applied in extraterritorial disclosure attempts relating to MNEs. And the point is that the 'blocking statutes' - of what would amount to the 'host state' in an MNE context - prevailed.

Of those countries enumerated above, only the United Kingdom possessed

88. For detailed facts and analysis of the case, see Comment, "The International Uranium Cartel: Litigation and Legal Implications", 14 *Texas International Law Journal* (1979), pp. 59-124. See also Meng, "Neuere Entwicklungen im Streit um die Jurisdiktionshoheit der Staaten im Bereich der Wettbewerbsbeschränkungen", 41 *Zeitschrift für ausländisches öffentliches Recht und Völkerrecht* (1981), at 476-486. (See entire article for a comprehensive description of recent developments in the extraterritorial application of antitrust laws, the problem of extraterritorial reach in national antitrust and disclosure legislation and practice, and an assessment of state practice in the light of international law.)

no general blocking statutes against U.S. discovery of uranium documents; and for this reason England became a key forum in this litigation. The House of Lords decision in the British *Westinghouse* case,[89] successfully blocking Westinghouse's attempts to procure evidence in Britain, is of interest even in the present context for the fact that it doubtlessly led directly to the elaboration of the Protection of Trading Interests Act 1980[90] which was enacted to "provide protection from requirements, prohibitions and judgments imposed or given under the laws of countries outside the United Kingdom and affecting the trading or other interests of persons in the United Kingdom." Under the Act, the British Secretary of State is empowered not only generally to counter measures taken or proposed under laws of a foreign state for regulating or controlling international trade, but also specifically to prohibit compliance with discovery orders for commercial documents from a foreign court, tribunal or authority, in certain circumstances (Section 2). It also provides specifically, in Section 4, that in proceedings under the Evidence (Proceedings in other Jurisdictions) Act 1975,[91] British courts are not to comply with foreign court requests when the Secretary of State has certified that such a request encroaches upon U.K. jurisdiction or is otherwise prejudicial to the United Kingdom; Section 5 restricts the enforcement of overseas judgments. Such provisions, which appear simply to be a codification of the House of Lords decision in *Westinghouse,* will in its statutory form have far-reaching consequences on foreign - and certainly MNE-related - disclosure attempts. There are already conventions planned between the U.K. and other governments to ensure that the 1980 Act can be enforced against the assets of U.S. corporations located outside Britain.

It is interesting that the earlier Evidence (Proceedings in Other Jurisdictions) Act 1975 specifically anticipated its application in pre-trial procedure by stating, in Section 1(b), that evidence may be requested "for the purpose of civil proceedings which either have been instituted before the requesting court or whose institution before that court is contemplated."[92] All prior British legislation on the subject referred to proceedings that were "pending". In the British *Westinghouse* case, the English Court of Appeal accordingly, within the terms of the 1975 Act, declared that there would be no obstruction to pre-trial dis-

89. *In re Westinghouse Elec. Corp. Uranium Contract Litigation,* [1977] 3 W.L.R. 430 (C.A.); [1978] 2 W.L.R. 81 (H.L. 1977); see also *Rio Tinto Zinc Corp.* v. *Westinghouse Electric Corp.* [1978] 1 All E.R. 434 (H.L.).

90. Protection of Trading Interests Act 1980 c. 11.

91. Evidence (Proceedings in other Jurisdictions) Act 1975 c.34

92. Sect. 9(1) of the Act (*Idem*) defines "civil proceedings" as "proceedings in any civil or commercial matter."

covery.[93] It was the Lords who opposed this view.; this is reflected in the subsequent Protection of Trading Interests Act 1980 discussed above.

Among other legislation arising out of the *Westinghouse* episode, and similar to the British Protection of Trading Interests Act, is the French blocking statute of the same year, *loi n° 80-538 du 16 juillet 1980*[94] forbidding French companies and their representatives to produce documents or furnish information to foreign authorities or courts where the sovereignty, security, public interests or important economic interests of the country would thereby be endangered. Within a week prior to the enactment of the French law, a Bill was introduced before the Canadian Parliament, the Foreign Proceedings and Judgments Bill,[95] which likewise would forbid the production of documents and giving of evidence where this would be prejudicial to the national interest. At the time of writing, the Canadian Bill has not yet had a second reading; hence its future is still uncertain, but the pattern is clear.

Clearly the frustration is not all on the side of the foreign recipient of the discovery order; as expressed by U.S. Attorney General Bell addressing the American Bar Association in Chicago in 1977:

> We owe deference to other nations when their vital national interests are at stake and the conflicting United States interest carries a lesser weight. But other nations owe us, in turn, deference at least to the extent of working toward a compromise arrangement if our fundamental national interests are directly affected.[96]

There is understandably a certain amount of political resentment and frustration in the United States when even evidence indispensable to an investigation of a possible law violation is obstructed.[97] The public interest of the requesting state should certainly also be a consideration taken into account by the state desirous of blocking the disclosure. There should perhaps be a more general resort outside the United States, if not to the U.S. formula, at least to the

93. *In re Westinghouse Elec. Corp. Uranium Contract Litigation,* [1977] 3 W.L.R. 430, 436-437, 442-443.

94. *Loi n°80-538 du 16 juillet 1980, 1980 Journal Officiel [*J.O.] at 1799.

95. Canadian Government Bill C41.

96. Address by Griffin B. Bell, U.S. Attorney General, before the American Bar Association, Chicago, August 8, 1977, as cited in Stanford, op.cit., *supra* note 65, at 207-208.

97. See Baker, "Antitrust Conflicts Between Friends: Canada and the United States in the Mid-1970s, at 187; also Wood and Carrera, "The International Uranium Cartel: Litigation and Legal Implications", 14 *Texas International Law Journal* (1979), at 98.

British balancing test as enunciated in *Conway* v. *Rimmer*[98] whereby disclosure is prohibited only when compliance with the disclosure request would cause greater injury to the public interest than that resulting from the withholding of evidence. The difficulty here, of course, as with the U.S. balance-of-interest approach, is that, when applied intergovernmentally, the "public interest" of two different states is involved, and instances are bound to arise in which each will feel its own "injury" to be the greatest. As Lord Wilberforce remarked in *Westinghouse,* "[i]t is axiomatic that in anti-trust matters the policy of one state may be to defend what it is the policy of another state to attack".[99] Moreover, it is not to be forgotten that the British attitude toward "public interest" is markedly different from and far more restrictive than, that prevalent in the United States.[100]

In citing the *Westinghouse* litigation, one must be careful to distinguish it from other foreign discovery proceedings where there indeed are signs of co-operation and sensitivity to international comity. In the uranium litigation two important factors worked against co-operation on the part of the blocking states: One is the fact that here the disclosure was sought in pre-trial investigations; and the other is that the disclosure could have led to criminal liability in the EEC and in national jurisdictions for those firms which were allegedly members of the cartel, had that membership and the related illegal activities been exposed.

The important thing here to point out is that one needn't view *Westinghouse* as a major reversal in the efforts at co-operation; one must distinguish it on other grounds and avoid the tendency to regard it as a severe setback in the direction of inter-governmental attempts at co-operation and compromise. This does not alter the fact, however, that the MNE doing business internationally and served with a subpoena to produce documents situated abroad runs into a myriad of legislation reflecting statutorily the jurisdictional conflict regarding disclosure. Still to be reckoned with are the nondisclosure provisions of such legislation as West Germany's Law of May 24, 1965 (last amended in 1980)[101] authorizing the Minister of Transport to prohibit the production of maritime documents to foreign authorities; or the related order

98. *Conway* v. *Rimmer,* [1969] A.C. 910, 940, 950-951.

99. *In re Westinghouse Elec. Corp. Uranium Contract Litigation,* [1978] 2 W.L.R. 81, 94 (H.L. 1977).

100. See Note, "Discovery in Great Britain: The Evidence (Proceedings in other Jurisdictions) Act", 11 *Cornell International Law Journal,* (1978), at 338.

101. *Gesetz über die Aufgaben des Bundes auf dem Gebiet der Seeschiffahrt vom 24. Mai 1965, in der Fassung der Bekanntmachung vom 30. Juni 1977* (BGB1 I S.1314), § 11, last amended by Art. 2 of the *Gesetz zum Übereinkommen Nr.147 der Internationalen Arbeitsorganization vom 29. Oktober 1976 über Mindesnormen auf Handelsschiffen vom 28.4.1980* (BGB1 II S.606).

concerning the disclosure of shipping company documents to foreign sources of December 14, 1966;[102] or the above-mentioned British Protection of Trading Interests Act 1980,[103] replacing the Shipping Contracts and Commercial Documents Act 1964[104] mentioned in connection with the *Beecham* case cited earlier[105] and authorizing Ministers of the Crown to prohibit the disclosure of any commercial documents falling outside the jurisdiction of the investigating nation; or Ontario's Business Records Protection Act[106]and Quebec's Business Concerns Records Act[107] prohibiting the disclosure of business records or documents in response to the order of any legislative, administrative or judicial authority outside their own jurisdiction; or Canada's Uranium Information Security Regulations[108] which served to successfully block the production of business documents in the U.S.-Canadian *Westinghouse* litigation;[109] or a number of other such laws designed to counteract the extraterritorial reach of foreign discovery orders, more of which will be mentioned in the pages following.

While the legal attempts in the area of disclosure, then, whether a court discovery order or a blocking statute, may at times prove to be little more than 'paper tigers' in practice, the ultimate test of the limitations of jurisdiction under international law is, in the end, the presence or absence of diplomatic protest,[110] and it should be acknowledged that diplomatic protests in this area have not been without some success. The Canadian Government, for example, notified the United States Government in a note of November 1978 that it had refused a number of urgent pleas from various parties to civil actions in U.S. courts who were desirous of complying with discovery orders, for waivers from the Uranium Information Security Regulations or their amendments, etc., and that its justification for refusing to allow production of the documents in each case was that their release would be detrimental to the Canadian national

102. *Verordnung über die übermittlung schiffahrtgeschäftlicher Unterlagen an ausländische Stellen vom 14.12.1966* (BGB1 II S.1542).

103. Protection of Trading Interests Act 1980 c.11.

104. Shipping Contracts and Commercial Documents Act 1964 c. 87, § 2.

105. See *supra* note 72 and accompanying text, *et seq.*

106. Business Records Protection Act, 1 Ont. Rev. Stat. c. 44, § 1 (1960).

107. Business Concerns Records Act, 4 Que. Rev. Stat. c. 287, § 2 (1964).

108. Uranium Information Security Regulations, Stat. O. & R. 77-836, 111 Can. Gaz., pt.II 4619 (1977), implementing the Atomic Energy Control Act, R.S.C. 1970, c. A-19, § 9, and replacing Uranium Information Secutity Regulations, Stat. O. & R. 76-644, 110 Can. Gaz., pt.II, at 2747 (1976).

109. See *supra* note 74 and text accompanying note 87.

110. See Akehurst, "Jurisdiction in International Law", in 46 *British Yearbook of International Law* (1972-1973), at 176.

interest.[111] The Government of Canada went on, in its note, to raise "serious objection" to the consequent imposition of sanctions by U.S. courts. It was diplomatic protest on the part of the Canadian Government also which led to the eventual withdrawal of a subpoena requiring Canadian paper companies doing business in New York to produce documents situated in Canada in *In re Grand Jury Subpoenas Duces Tecum* (*International Paper* case),[112] though the incident nonetheless prompted the enactment of the Canadian Business Records Protection Act mentioned above.

Another successful diplomatic intervention can be seen in *In re Investigation of World Arrangements* (*Oil Cartel* case),[113] in which orders from the British, Dutch, French and Italian governments prohibited the production of documents of non-American oil companies subpoenaed by a United States district court. On recommendation of the U.S. National Security Council, the subpoenas were vacated and the investigatory proceedings terminated.[114] Again, although the diplomatic protests achieved their immediate objective, the incident nonetheless gave rise, at least in the Netherlands, to directly attributable blocking legislation.[115]

The 1980 *FTC* v. *Compagnie de Saint-Gobain-Pont-à-Mousson* case[116] provides a further example of the effectiveness of diplomatic intervention, this time on the part of France. The case, involving the service of compulsory process by the U.S. Federal Trade Commission in the course of a nonpublic antitrust investigation, had an extraterritorial aspect in the fact that one of the defendants was Saint-Gobain, a French holding company which, while basing a general delegate in New York, is headquartered in Paris. The fact that a subpoena *duces tecum,* directing the defendant company to produce specified classes of documents of relevance to the investigation, was transmitted directly to the defendant's headquarters in Paris by registered mail (simultaneously with three identical subpoenas served locallly) elicited a note from the French

111. One could also mention here the Fulton-Rogers and Basford-Mitchell "understandings" between the United States and Canada, of 1959 and 1969 respectively, providing, *inter alia,* for exchange of information and notification and consultation procedures in antitrust cases affecting national interests. (See e.g. Stanford, op. cit., *supra* note 65, at 207.)

112. *In re Grand Jury Subpoenas Duces Tecum Addressed to Canadian International Paper Co.*, 72 F.Supp. 1013 (S.D.N.Y. 1947).

113. *In re Investigation of World Arrangements,* 13 F.R.D. 280 (D.D.C. 1952).

114. See *In re Investigation of World Arrangements,* 1952-1953 Trade Cases, ¶ 67,480 (D.D.C. 1953).

115. Economic Competition Act, June 28, 1956, Art. 39, Stb. 401, as amended by Act of July 16, 1958, Stb. 413.

116. *F.T.C.* v. *Compagnie de Saint-Gobain-Pont-à-Mousson,* 636 F.2d 1300 (D.C. Cir. 1980).

Embassy to the U.S. State Department to the effect that such a mode of service "is inconsistent with the general principles of international law and constitutes a failure to recognize French sovereignty." Reiterating moreover its reservations regarding the application in France of the principle of pre-trial discovery "characteristic of common law countries", the French note went on to point out the fact that were the defendant to respond to certain of the discovery requests, its directors would be subjected to civil and criminal liability and hence exposed to municipal judicial proceedings.

While this note did not change the opinion of the U.S. district court, which proceeded to issue a second order reiterating its initial enforcement of the subpoena, it may well have been influential in the decision of the Court of Appeals for the D.C. Circuit which vacated both orders on grounds of both the mode of service and "established and fundamental principles of international law." The French note cannot claim sole responsibility for the vacating of the discovery orders, since, as the appeals court pointed out, two separate conferences of the International Law Association had previously taken up the question and had reached the same conclusion presented by the court. This fact does not, however, discredit the role of the French diplomatic intervention.

It is of interest that the French note as well as the earlier Canadian note give some attention to the plight of the party who is caught in the middle. The fact that some official thought is being translated into official terms for the alleviation of the predicament of the party (usually the enterprise) subject to concurrent and contradictory demands shows, in this author's view, a positive step forward, as long as this does not become a shroud to obscure unjustified avoidance of disclosure by the state exercising the 'protection'. And what constitutes policy under one government may indeed be law under another, as illustrated by the Australian Foreign Antitrust Judgment (Restriction of Enforcement) Act 1979. This Act supplements an earlier law[117] which already sufficed to prevent the production of Australian-based evidence in response to U.S. court orders but did not deal with the consequences of resulting default judgments where jurisdictional objections to the proceedings against Australian defendants prevented their entering appearance. The new statute seems to attempt to do by law what the Canadian and French notes tried to accomplish through diplomacy.

The point remains that the fact that the documents may be situated in a state where the government or the laws forbid extraterritorial discovery is on its own, no defense in international law. The dangers of the alternative position are obvious. Any corporation wishing to carry on questionable business

117. Foreign Proceedings (Prohibition of Certain Evidence) Act 1976, Act No. 121 of 1976.

practices with impunity would have only to locate its business records in a state which prohibited discovery in order to escape all attempts by authorities or courts to investigate its activities.

At the same time, while a court does not contravene international law by issuing the discovery order even when the documents sought are located in a jurisdiction prohibiting their disclosure, that court is not thereby necessarily empowered to enforce its order within the foreign territory,[118] although the legality of the order can enable the court to impose sanctions or enter a default judgment when the order is not fulfilled by the party. Here the party served the subpoena can be the real loser; and while that element of the balance-of-interests approach which applies to the party, as distinct from that applying to the 'public interest' or national interest, has meant some relief, if there is a further conflict between the national interest and that of the party in question, it is more than likely that the 'national interests' will receive priority.

As a result, then, of diplomatic expressions, and cognizant of the renewed legislatorial resistance abroad to its extraterritorial reach as regards disclosure and other antitrust and securities-related measures, the U.S. has been making greater efforts to be more sensitive to foreign interests. Attesting to this are: the increasing number of court cases, some of which have been mentioned, in which subpoenas have been modified or vacated so as to avoid inducing conduct which would be illegal under the laws of the foreign state;[119] the statement in the U.S. Department of Justice's 1977 *Antitrust Guide for International Operations*[120] that extraterritorial application of U.S. antitrust laws "should avoid unnecessary interference with the sovereign interests of foreign nations"; the codification of the balance-of-interests approach in Section 40 of the American *Restatement* in the interest of an increasing resort to the principles of international comity and the promotion of this 'comity-balanc-

118. See e.g. *F.T.C.* v. *Compagnie de Saint-Gobain-Pont-à-Mousson,* 636 F.2d 1300 (D.C. Cir. 1980), in which compulsory service served by the Federal Trade Commission on a foreign party on foreign soil was held to be an exercise of enforcement jurisdiction contrary to international law.

119. See e.g. *In re Grand Jury Subpoena Duces Tecum* (*International Paper* case), 72 F. Supp. 1013 (S.D.N.Y. 1947); *In re Investigation of World Arrangements* (*Oil Cartel* case), 13 F.R.D. 280, 285 (D.D.C. 1952); cf. *In re Grand Jury Investigation of the Shipping Industry*, 186 F. Supp. 298 (D.D.C. 1960); *Montship Lines, Ltd.* v. *Federal Maritime Bd.*, 295 F. 2d 147, 154 (D.C. Cir. 1961). For discussion of this point see Onkelinx, op.cit., note 84, at 507, 513, 518, 519, 532.

120. Antitrust Division, United States Department of Justice, *Antitrust Guide for International Operations* (revised March 1, 1977), (reprinted in Antitrust and Trade Reg. Rep. (ENA) No. 799, at E-1 (1977) and CCH *Trade Regulations* No. 266, pt.II (1977)), at 6.

ing' test not only in written policy but also in practice;[121] and the U.S. Antitrust Division's pledge to make every effort to keep at a minimum any requests for documentary evidence located outside the territory and to take care that those requests which are made are restricted to reasonable and responsible standards of relevancy and take into account special difficulties of any party affected; to name some concrete examples.

These U.S. responses to foreign reactions against its attempts at extraterritorial discovery, and those instances where the Justice Department has declined to prosecute, have been more a result of diplomatic protests than of the enactment of new blocking statutes abroad, though the latter also obviously represent a form of protest which could not go unnoticed by the executive and judicial branches of the U.S. Government.

It is not only the protests which are being made on the diplomatic level, but even the efforts at solving the issues are often made on the diplomatic rather than the strictly legal level. As Joel Davidow, Director of the Office of Policy Planning of the U.S. Department of Justice Antitrust Division, stated at a conference held at the University of North Carolina School of Law in late 1979: "greater efforts are being made to solve these issues diplomatically by informing relevant governments early, employing voluntary requests when possible, and clarifying safeguards for ensuring the confidentiality of sensitive material which is produced."[122] In fact the increasing resort to diplomatic solutions has led one writer to suggest that:

> Having created a tradition for itself of vigorous and independent enforcement of the antitrust laws, the Justice Department now is apt to be accused of bowing to political pressures even if it does no more than to yield to...the trend of recent judicial pronouncements and the dictates of global economic interdependence.[123]

Another legal writer goes so far as to assert that in fact "the current differences over the extraterritorial application of antitrust law must be recognized as policy issues rather than as legal issues and dealt with accordingly."[124]

121. See e.g. *Timberlane Lumber Co.* v. *Bank of America* and *Mannington Mills, Inc.* v. *Congoleum Corp.*, loc. cit., *supra note 86.*

122. Davidow, "U.S. Antitrust and Doing Business Abroad: Recent Trends and Developments", paper delivered at Conference on Antitrust Aspects of International Terrorism, Chapel Hill, North Carolina, September 28, 1979, at 8, as cited in Gordon, "Extraterritorial Application of United States Economic Laws: Britain Draws the Line", 14 *International Lawyer* (1980), at 160.

123. Ibid. (Gordon), at 164.

124. Stanford, op. cit., *supra* note 65, at 214.

Whether the issues are political or legal, the fact remains that the conflict of jurisdiction in the area of foreign discovery, in practice, is far from resolved, and while considerable efforts at co-operation are indeed discernable, the spate of national legislation directed against extraterritorial disclosure, in an apparent renewed effort to limit the long reach of the extraterritorial legal arm, continues.

To return, then, to the principle that "a State which has jurisdiction to order the production of documents is not prevented from exercising this jurisdiction by the fact that the State in which the documents are located prohibits their disclosure",[125] it cannot easily be disputed that this principle is defensible under international law, as there exists no international law rule precluding a state from exercising its jurisdiction simply because another state has concurrent jurisdiction with contradictory demands. Moreover, the principle has come to be accepted by courts other than merely those of the United States.

b. Regional trends

Within the EEC, for example, there is some indication of this trend, although there have been no significant cases clarifying the Community's position on extraterritorial discovery, other than possibly *Commercial Solvents*,[126] in which the Commission made an abortive attempt to obtain information from Commercial Solvents in New York. Although in this case the Commission made no further attempts at disclosure, adequate information being available from other sources to pursue the case, the initial tentative would indicate that the EEC's evolving attitude to the extraterritoriality issue as regards disclosure is not dissimilar to that of the United States. In line with the U.S. position also is the EC Commission's indication, in its Third General Report, that the violation-of-foreign-law defense will not be acceptable if all other discovery criteria are met;[127] and a further indication of the EEC's emerging attitude is the suggestion by one of the Commission's legal advisors that the mere presence of a subsidiary within the Community establishes the right of the Commission to order the production of documents held outside the EEC by the foreign parent, apparently independent of the veil-lifting process.[128]

125. Onkelinx, op. cit., *supra* note 84, at 500.

126. Commission Decision of December 14, 1972 [*Commercial Solvents* case,], 15 E.C.J.O. L299/51, 12 *Common Market Law Reports,* D50.

127. *Commission of the European Communities, Third General Report on the Activities of the Community* (1960), at 110.

128. Thiesing, "Antitrust and International Law as Viewed from the United States and the

c. International trends

On the international plane, in addition to the statements of the ICC, OECD and UNCTAD noted earlier, we could add that of the International Law Association: "Where a non-resident alien chooses to appear as claimant [and this is an important limitation] he must submit to the procedure of the court in which he applies, including its procedures of discovery ...."[129] In the wake of *Interhandel* (and its emerging EEC application already reflected in the *Commerical Solvents* case and the Commission's Third General Report), this is likely to mean that the 'procedures of discovery' may well involve extraterritorial implications to the extent that, should any relevant documents be located outside the forum, a discovery order for their disclosure will fall within the competence of the court's normal *in personam* jurisdiction.

Despite the fact that, up to now, all the veil-lifting cases in which extraterritorial disclosure was an issue have been resolved by the judicial machinery of the forum,[130] broad assertions of extraterritorial discovery power have nonetheless brought diplomatic protests on the argument that such assertions contravene the traditional rule established in the *Lotus*[131] case that: "the first and foremost restriction imposed by international law upon a State is that - failing the existence of a permissive rule to the contrary - it may not exercise its power in any form in the territory of another State."[132] Some such protests contend that the use of the machinery of the forum to execute extraterritorial discovery orders is merely a pretext to achieve indirectly what would be against international law if attempted directly;[133] others stress simply the point that international law prohibits a state from ordering foreigners to produce documents situated abroad;[134] and still others maintain that such extraterritorial discovery orders contravene international law for the reason that no right existed for the

European Common Market", 25 *Record N.Y.C.B. Association* 206, 207-208 (1970); as cited in Griffin, op. cit., *supra* note 83, at 412, to whom the present author is indebted for much of the factual material contained above.

129. *Report of the 52nd Conference of the International Law Association* (1966) at 112.

130. See Griffin, op. cit., *supra* note 83, at 415.

131. *Case of the S.S. "Lotus"* (France *v.* Turkey), [1927] P.C.I.J., Ser. A., No. 10.

132. Ibid., at 18.

133. See e.g. Riedwig, "The Extraterritorial Application of Restrictive Trade Legislation - Jurisdiction and International Law", in Report on the 51st ILA Conference (1965), at 403, as cited in Griffin, op. cit., *supra* note 83, at 415. See also *F.T.C.* v. *Compagnie de Saint-Gobain-Pont-à-Mousson,* loc. cit., *supra* note 116.

134. International Law Association (1964), at 403-405, 580-581; 33 *International Law Reports,* at 159-161, as cited in Akehurst, op.cit., *supra* note 110, at 177.

initiation of proceedings in the first place.[135] Some protests rely on combinations or variations of these arguments.

All these arguments are somewhat spurious. The *Lotus* argument is, for example, inappropriate in that an act by one state in the territory of another is contrary to international law only where there is a usurpation of the sovereign powers of the one state by the other.[136] And when jurisdiction has been established in a case with a foreign element, a discovery order by the court of the forum - in, for example, a veil-lifting case - involves no violation of the sovereign powers of the foreign state, and hence no violation of international law, because "it is an inquiry into conduct that the forum has the power to regulate."[137]

The same reasoning negates the other arguments as well. Any argument is misconceived which disregards the widening application of the 'effects' doctrine, the veil-lifting technique and other current trends, concepts and theories of jurisdiction which are evolving in state practice as a result of the increasing internationalization of business, for which the old theories and concepts are often proving inadequate. The 'effects' doctrine and veil-lifting processes are gaining ever-wider application in disclosure as well as in other areas, to the extent that the exercise of adjudicatory jurisdiction has already ceased to rely in every case, *a priori*, on the establishment of legislative jurisdiction. The trend would appear to be heading even toward a gradual separation - in some cases - of the traditional dependence of enforcement jurisdiction upon legislative jurisdiction. It appears that this dependence will no longer perforce be a *sine qua non*. In addition to the accepted fact that adjudicatory jurisdiction can already be legitimately obtained by the host country, through its local subsidiary, over a foreign parent by the veil-lifting process, even legislative jurisdiction, carrying with it the normal enforcement powers, can be asserted - under the objective territorial and protective principles - over certain foreign conduct.[138] And while it cannot be contested that "a State may legislate for cases which fall beyond the jurisdiction of its courts",[139] and that discovery orders can legitimately extend into foreign territory to the measure of legislative jurisdiction, current practice is showing signs of extending even enforcement jurisdiction beyond the traditional limits, when it is considered that the service of subpoenas requiring the production of documents can, when

135. International Law Association (1964), at 404, 579-581, 590, etc., as cited in Ibid. (Akehurst), at 177-178.

136. Ibid. (Akehurst), at 146.

137. Griffin, op. cit., *supra* note 83, at 415

138. Ibid., at 434. Compare, however, Onkelinx, op. cit., *supra* note 84, at 496.

139. Akehurst, op. cit., *supra* note 110, at 179.

properly served, constitute the exercise of enforcement jurisdiction.[140]

While there is, as we have seen, increasing criticism from some quarters, notably Canada and parts of Europe, concerning attempts at extraterritorial judicial enforcement of discovery orders, particularly by U.S. courts, the EEC itself, as mentioned earlier, appears to be moving toward a presumption that jurisdiction over a parent company is justified on the basis of the mere presence of a subsidiary of that parent within the Community, without the necessity of any proof of effective control relationships between the two entities.[141] This presumption, whether it were to be acted upon by either the EEC or by a court of any single state, seems to the present author to stretch extraterritorial jurisdiction to dangerous extremes which could be difficult to justify, as it makes no provision for an absence-of-effective-control defense on the part of the parent, and hence ignores the crucial issue of actual control and consequent responsibility in the parent-subsidiary relationship. It would appear, however, that this presumption has not yet been put to the test, and when it is, in this writers's opinion, it will prove fertile ground for conflict.

Additional evidence of the trend away from the reliance of enforcement jurisdiction upon the measure of legislative jurisdiction - on rather more realistic grounds - can be seen in the reasoning put forward in the Reporter's Note of the *Restatement (Second) of the Foreign Relations Law of the United States*[142] regarding the *Lotus* case,[143] in which it is recalled that in order to exercise the (criminal) enforcement jurisdiction deemed by the Turkish court to be justified, legislative jurisdiction had to be established, and ultimately was - on rather more tenuous grounds - solely in order to validate the desired enforcement jurisdiction. The case was, in fact, argued and determined on this very issue. If Turkey had not been found competent to exert legislative jurisdiction in the case in question, its exercise of enforcement jurisdiction would have violated international law.

Since the time of the *Lotus* ruling, the grounds upon which the legislative jurisdiction was justified, namely the attribution of territorial status to the Turkish vessel, would no longer suffice to assure Turkey's enforcement jurisdiction, owing to the coming into effect of the 1958 Convention on the High

140. See e.g. Onkelinx, op. cit., *supra* note 84, at 495. The mode of service must nonetheless be a proper one; otherwise such service may indeed be in violation of international law (see *F.T.C.* v. *Compagnie de Saint-Gobain-Pont-à-Mousson*), loc. cit., *supra* note 116).

141. See *Commission of the European Communities, Third General Report on the Activities of the Community* (1960), at 110. See also text accompanying note 127 *supra.*

142. Reporter's Note, *Restatement,* op. cit., *supra* note 78, § 7, at 23.

143. Case of the *"S.S. Lotus",* [1927] P.C.I.J., ser. A, No. 10.

Seas,[144] Article 11 of which provides, *inter alia,* that in situations similar to that presented by the *Lotus* case, the flag state or national state of the offender has exclusive jurisdiction. The *Lotus* case points up, then, the somewhat arbitrary nature of the linkage of enforcement with legislative jurisdiction. Moreover, the impracticalities of having to establish such a link, in some cases, become obvious; and it is not far removed to reason consequently that, just as a state having jurisdiction to prescribe a rule of law does not necessarily have jurisdiction to enforce it in all cases,[145] the enforcement of a rule, where jurisdiction is established (through, for example, veil-lifting) ought not perhaps to have to rely in all cases solely on the power to prescribe a rule of law within the foreign territory in question.

It will be interesting to witness the development of the concepts and trends in this area and the direction of state practice as it deals with these issues. For the present, the key to answering each of the contentions mentioned above is whether the court of the forum has, in fact, through legitimate processes, established adjudicartory jurisdiction. If such jurisdiction is present, it has been adequately established that international law does not restrict a state from exercising its normal powers of jurisdiction merely on the grounds that to do so would cause a violation of a foreign law.[146] In other words, when a court has established jurisdiction over a case, it must also be empowered to compel the production of documents which are relevant to its investigation; it must, in a word, have those implied enforcement powers necessary to render the express jurisdictional powers effective.[147]

Where an objection to this principle might be valid is in the case of documents being required for the purposes of *preliminary* investigation, which, as submitted by Professor Jennings, "ranges outside the permissible limits of extraterritorial jurisdiction."[148] But once the court has established jurisdiction,

144. Convention on the High Seas, April 29, 1958. See also *Restatement,* op. cit., *supra* note 78, § 30, at 89.

145. Ibid. (*Restatement*), § 7(1).

146. See Mann, "The Doctrine of Jurisdiction in International Law", 111 *Receuil des Cours* (1964), at 156.

147. See Ibid., at 154-158. This right has been recognized in a number of bilateral and multilateral treaties, notable among which is the Hague Convention on Taking Evidence Abroad in Civil or Commercial Matters of 1970 (opened for signature at the Hague on March 18, 1970, (T.I.A.S. No. 7444 [1972], U.S.T. 2555)), replacing Arts. 8-16 of the Conventions of 1905 and 1954. The 1970 Convention was signed by, *inter alia,* France, the United Kingdom and the United States, and has since been implemented by various national laws, such as the U.K. Evidence (Proceedings in Other Jurisdictions) Act 1975 c.34.

148. See Jennings, "Extraterritorial Jurisdiction and the United States Anti-trust Laws," 33 *British Yearbook of International Law* (1957), at 171. See also Onkelinx, op. cit., *supra* note 84, at

there is, according to Jennings, "no reason in general principle why [it] should not order an alien, subject to its jurisdiction *in personam,* to produce documents relevant to a case in which he is a party, no matter where he may choose to keep those documents."[149]

3. Evaluation

On the whole, then, one could say that protective national legislation against discovery orders from abroad - which has been spreading increasingly in recent years among states which feel themselves threatened by this expression of extraterritoriality - is being applied increasingly forcefully, along with the political protests, the latter, moreover, having been far more numerous - undoubtedly for the very reasons enumerated above, *viz.* that specific municipal legislation against extraterritorial disclosure does not alone hinder the right, under international law, of a foreign court to require disclosure when its jurisdiction over a case has been established.[150] Accordingly, both the courts and the Department of Justice of the United States, and the Commission of the EC, continue to assert a measured prerogative to compel disclosure of documents situated abroad, and, when the accepted legal prerequisites are met, thus do so in accordance with international law.

This notwithstanding, government protests against foreign discovery orders have often resulted in the modification of such orders. Yet while there is evidence of attempts at compromise and co-operation between parties where good faith and 'conscientious endeavors' at compliance have been shown, the effectiveness of actual anti-disclosure legislation, enacted by a host state normally to countermand the exactions of the forum of the parent company, when strictly applied by a host government can, in practice, be considerable as a host control technique.

The present state of international law is inadequate to deal with disputes of this nature or to provide international judicial or alternative dispute settlement procedures.[151] But at least as regards disclosure that is systematic, routine and

---

498-499. The *Westinghouse* litigations (see *supra* notes 87, 89,) fall into this category. The 1970 Hague Convention (see note 147 *supra* and accompanying text) also distinguishes pre-trial disclosure in Art. 23 which allows a contracting state to renounce the execution of Letters of Request for evidence to be issued for the purpose of pre-trial production of documents.

149. Idem. (Jennings).

150. See e.g. Onkelinx, op. cit., *supra* note 84 at 500.

151. See Stanford, op. cit., *supra* note 65, at 214.

general, it will be increasingly difficult for a state that has pledged to respect the OECD Guidelines, for example, to resist international attempts to obtain disclosure; one has conceded its international character. And as regards disclosure that arises out of litigation and is *ad hoc*, adversarial and potentially injurious to the enterprise, further reference to the OECD, in its 1978 Council Recommendation mentioned earlier which stressed regard for international law and comity and for the law and established policies and national interests of the country in which the documents are located, would seem to vindicate the enactment of blocking statutes such as those we have looked at, where they are genuinely aimed at protecting the national interest and security. This position gains support also from the UNCTAD Principles and Rules which, like the OECD Guidelines, promote foreign disclosure in the 'systematic and general' sense, including the normal 'safeguards', but make an exception where such disclosure is "prevented by applicable law or established public policy."[152]

At the same time, in the context of the MNE, it should not be overlooked that the legitimacy under international law of a foreign discovery order, when jurisdiction has been established, can actually work in favour of the host state, whose own extraterritorial reach, through the subsidiary to (a controlling) parent[153] - in cases where a substantial control relationship in regard to the relevant commercial practices has been shown to exist between the two entities - constitutes in itself a host technique of not inconsiderable consequence.

152. UNCTAD, "Set of Multilaterally Agreed Equitable Principles and Rules for the Control of Restrictive Business Practices", op. cit., *supra* note 63, Sect. D(2).

153. The present author likes to term this type of jurisdictional reach: "reverse extraterritoriality", for purpose of distinguishing it from the more traditional extraterritorial reach of national jurisdiction by one (home) state into foreign (host) domain. This nominal distinction is not meant to cloud the fact that both extraterritoriality and "reverse extraterritoriality" are merely two aspects of the same basic principle, but it seems useful to draw attention to the fact that in one case the extraterritorial reach originates in the home state, while in the other case ("reverse extraterritoriality") it originates in the host state.

Chapter IX.

CONTROL THROUGH MERGER LEGISLATION

1. Applicability of Antitrust and the 'Effects' Doctrine

The majority of the discovery orders presenting jurisdictional difficulties between host states and foreign affiliates, as just reviewed, have arisen out of antitrust proceedings. The larger issue of antitrust legislation itself and its enforcement is a vast one, and much has already been written about the extra-territorial application of such legislation, particularly as exercised by the United States, home of a long antitrust tradition.

While antitrust legislation is itself an extensive subject, its primary aim is to protect competition, not to control the operations of foreign enterprises. It has, in fact, traditionally been directed by a government at its own national enterprises, whether those enterprises operate purely domestically or as multinationals; and, in the latter case, the control may be exercised exterritorially when anti-competitive 'effects' of corporate concentrations abroad are felt within the 'home' territory.[1]

It is clear, of course, that the pioneering antitrust laws, the U.S. Sherman and Clayton Acts,[2] have expressly applied to foreign as well as interstate commerce since their inception; but the control envisaged in 1890 at the time the Sherman Act was drafted, even as it related to foreign commerce, was not designed to be exercised over foreign firms but rather over U.S. firms operating in foreign markets. In the early days of the Sherman Act, the territorial principle of jurisdiction seems to have been generally respected and monopolistic collusions were treated by the U.S. legal authorities with more-or-less official indifference when arranged and implemented outside the country.[3] "The hardy company which ventured to expand by entering into foreign trade was given

1. For control to be exercised, however, the effects must be "substantial", "direct" and "intended" (see *United States* v. *Aluminum Company of America and others (Alcoa),* 148 F.2d 416 (2d Cir. 1945).

2. Sherman Antitrust Act, 15 U.S.C. § 1 *et seq.;* Clayton Act, 15 U.S.C. § 12 *et seq.*

3. See *American Banana Company* v. *United Fruit Company,* 213 U.S. 347 (1909).

practically a free hand, in the absence of some unlawful conduct in [the United States][4] or in territorial waters.[5] Joint ownership by American companies of a foreign subsidiary was approved;[6] international agreements with territorial restrictions were upheld;[7] and even outright monopolization was left undisturbed in one instance, where the acts of the American company were performed only abroad.[8] The courts ruled that [American] nationals were entitled to use whatever methods were necessary to conduct foreign trade.

> To hold otherwise would be, practically and commercially, to enjoin the steel trade of the United States from using the business methods which are necessary in order to build up and maintain a dependable business abroad, and if the Sherman Law were so construed, would itself be a restraint of trade[9]."[10]

Commerce "with foreign nations",[11] as expressed in the Sherman Act, would have originally referred to commerce carried on by a strictly American company doing business abroad; the wording of the Act, nonetheless, fortuitously left the way open to include any type of foreign commercial activity, with the result that MNE investment activity falls quite naturally within the scope of these early laws.

The point remains however that, traditionally, antitrust legislation has largely been directed through a national legal system toward locally incorporated enterprises, be they national concerns operating domestically or multinationally, or be they affiliates of foreign-based parents; and when the laws are applied with an extraterritorial reach, that reach has normally been exercised through the home parent company to its affiliates, rather than through a foreign affiliate incorporated in the host state to its parent company abroad. This being said, the occasional instance arises - and promises to do so increasingly - where the latter situation is true, i.e. where antitrust legislation is exercised extraterri-

4. *United States* v. *Sisal Sales Corporation,* 279 U.S. 268 (1927).

5. *United States* v. *Pacific and Arctic Company,* 228 U.S. 87 (1913).

6. *United States* v. *Keystone Watch Care Company,* 218 Fed. 502, 510 (E.D. Pa. 1915), *appeal dismissed* 257 U.S. 664 (1921).

7. *Thoms* v. *Sutherland,* 52 F.2d 592 (3d Cir. 1931).

8. *American Banana Co.* v. *United Fruit Co.,* loc. cit., *supra* note 3.

9. *United States* v. *United States Steel Corporation,* 223 Fed. 55, 114 (D.N.J. 1915), *aff'd,* 251 U.S. 417 (1920), cited in Van Cise, *Understanding the Antitrust Laws* (N.Y.: Practising Law Institute, c. 1955).

10. Turner, *Invisible Empires: Multinational Companies and the Modern World* (London: Hamish Hamilton, [1970]), at 14-15. [Notes 4-9 *supra* are from original text.]

11. Sherman Antitrust Act, loc. cit., *supra* note 2, sect. 1.

torially by the host, through a locally incorporated foreign affiliate ('reverse extraterritoriality'[12]), back to the parent company in the home state, as in the *Continental Can* case[13] which we shall look at in some detail in the following pages. This 'reverse extraterritoriality' is the only type of extraterritoriality which is pertinent to the present discussion where the primary interest is directed at host-state control over foreign affiliates operating within its territory.

Hence, any treatment of antitrust here - and it must be a limited one - will be confined to the most significant of those aspects in which the host state uses antitrust legislation specifically to control foreign multinational business activity within its borders, whether the actual exercise of control remains likewise within host borders or extends extraterritorially back to the parent company in the home state.

Neither territorial nor extraterritorial antitrust enforcement jurisdiction over a state's own national concerns, then, even when that enforcement affects the nationals or the national interests of another state, is relevant to the present study. Likewise the effects doctrine, as normally applied, is not pertinent here in a study of host control over foreign multinational enterprises. This is in no way intended to imply that no control is exercised over foreign enterprises through the 'effects' doctrine. Such control is, in fact, being extended from both sides of the the Atlantic. While the doctrine was first established by a United States court in the 1945 *Alcoa* decision and has been applied extensively since as judicial precedent,[14] Germany has statutorily extended its competition rules to apply to all restraints of competition having effects on the domestic market, irrespective of whether the prescribed acts are committed territorially or extraterritorially.[15] The exercise of this statutory restriction can be seen in

12. See *supra* Chapter VIII note 153.

13. *Re Continental Can. Co., Inc.,* Commission Decision (72/21/EEC) of December 9, 1971, [1972] *Common Market Law Reports,* D11, 2 CCH *Common Market Reporter,* 9481 (1971); *Europemballage Corp. and Continental Can Co.,* v. *Commission of the European Communities,* 12 *Common Market Law Reports,* 199 (1973). In fact, subsequent to *Continental Can,* the EEC appears to be adopting the practice of considering the MNE as a single economic unit so as to apply extraterritorially the EEC competition rules under the rationale that acts of a foreign subsidiary within the Common Market are simultaneously acts of the non-EEC parent. (See e.g. *Instituto Chemioterapico Italiano Spa* v. *E.C. Commission,* 13 *Common Market Law Reports,* 309 (1974) (upholding the Commission's decision); *United Brands Co. and United Brands Continental BV* v. *Commission of the European Communities,* 21 *Common Market Law Reports,* 429 (1978); *Liptons Cash Registers* v. *Hugin Kassaregister,* 21 *Common Market Law Reports,* D19 (1978)).

14. See *infra* note 19 and accompanying text.

15. *Gesetz gegen Wettbewerbsbeschränkungen* [hereinafter cited as GWB], *in der Fassung der Bekanntmachung vom 24. September 1980, Bundesgesetzblatt* [BGB1] I S. 1761,§ 98(2).

practice in the current investigation by the *Bundeskartellamt* (Federal Cartel Office) of the effects on the German market of a reported cartel formed by Japanese machine manufacturers, the object of the investigation being to "take possible action" and to seek to impose fines.[16] Here, there is not even an element of German involvement in the cartel activities themselves, nor is there any Japanese direct investment involved.

Even the registration provisions can affect mergers which are consummated outside of German territory. Between 1 November 1978 and 31 March 1979, for example, 325 mergers were registered with the *Bundeskartellamt,* of which 28 occurred outside of West Germany.[17]

Where the German practice of the effects doctrine does have relevance in the present context is in cases where the *Bundeskartellamt* investigates the effects on the German market of enterprises outside its territory which have subsidiaries within its territory; but this, like the EEC practice mentioned above, involves some physical presence and will therefore be dealt with in more detail in the pages following.

An OECD Committee of Experts on Restrictive Business Practices reported in 1977 that the criterion of effects appears now to be accepted, to varying extents and degrees, in all OECD member countries with the exception of the Netherlands, the United Kingdom and Australia, and that this criterion is embodied in the legislation of Germany, Austria, Denmark, Spain, France, Sweden and Finland and has been recognized in the case law of Canada, Japan, Switzerland, the United States and the European Communities and attested by doctrine in Belgium.[18] This makes a very interesting study in its own right, and has already been the subject of a considerable legal literature. The 'effects' aspect of jurisdiction, however, implying the absence of actual physical presence, does not fall within our area of concern, *viz.* host state control over foreign enterprises within its borders, for obvious reasons. For one thing, the foreign enterprise reprehended under the doctrine need not be an MNE to be reached by such control. Secondly, taking as an example the United States

16. See "W. Germany Probes Alleged Japanese Cartel", *International Herald Tribune,* 7-8 March 1981, at 11.

17. See *Bundeskartellamt* Press Releases, reprinted in [1979] *Wirtschaft und Wettbewerb,* at 96, 164, 309, 386-387, as cited in Schnorr, (Notes): "Trust-Busting with a German Accent: The Control of Corporate Merger and Acquisition Activities Under Increasingly Aggressive West German Law", 19 *Virginia Journal of International Law* (1979), note 8 at 596.

18. See Organisation for Economic Co-operation and Development, *Restrictive Business Practices of Multinational Enterprises,* Report of the Committee of Experts on Restrictive Business Practices, Paris, OECD Publications, 1977, at 37.

where the effects doctrine originated,[19] the doctrine is primarily called upon when the 'effects' result from an agreement to which at least one home company is a party; and the action is then normally brought against the home component to the agreement, not against the foreign element.

In the landmark American *Alcoa* case,[20] in fact, where an international cartel arrangement between French, Swiss, British and Canadian aluminum producers was organized and concluded abroad and did not even directly involve a U.S. firm - although it did have a direct and intended effect upon U.S. commerce - the action was brought against the Aluminum Company of America (Alcoa), the *American* parent of the Canadian subsidiary involved in the agreement. Resort was made to *in personam* jurisdiction, though the court concluded that Alcoa, a majority of whose shareholders, moreover, were also shareholders of the Canadian subsidiary, was not, itself, even a member of the cartel.[21]

While one would have hoped that *Alcoa,* precedent-setting where 'effects' are concerned,[22] would have resolved the issue as to the enforceable applicability of the effects doctrine where *all* elements are foreign, unfortunately, due to the existence of the indirect domestic links involved in *Alcoa,* this question has still not been adequately clarified or put to the test.[23]

Yet, even if case law were to clarify the foreign application question, the answer could in no way presume to set up a distinction - with regard to 'effects' - between those foreign enterprises which are multinational and those which are simply foreign domestic firms operating within their own territory, albeit with effects abroad; nor would the extraterritorially located enterprise reached by (American, German or any other) antitrust laws through the effects doctrine automatically be thenceforward considered a multinational enterprise by implication, or the state affected classified as a 'host' state to that particular enterprise simply because the effects of the activities were felt within its

19. *United States* v. *Aluminum Company of America and others* (the *Alcoa* case), 44 F. Supp. 97; 148 F.2d 416 (2d Cir. 1945).

20. *Idem.*

21. The original contention that the U.S. firm, Alcoa, was a member of the conspiracy was subsequently abandoned.

22. *Alcoa* serves no longer as a vital precedent in other of its aspects (see e.g. *Berkey Photo, Inc.* v. *Eastman Kodak Co.,* 603 F.2d 263 (2d Cir. 1979), *cert. denied,* 48 U.S.L.W. 3532 (February 19, 1980); see also Robinson, "Recent Antitrust Developments - 1979", 80 *Columbia Law Review* (1980), at 1-13.

23. The failure of the 1980-1981 American antitrust suit against the giant oil cartel OPEC, on international law considerations related to the act of state doctrine, could be indicative of an answer to this question. (See *International Association of Machinists and Aerospace Workers* v. *The Organization of the Petroleum Exporting Countries (OPEC),* 477 F. Supp. 553 (C.D. Cal. 1980), *aff'd,* 649 F.2d, 1354 (9th Cir. 1981).

borders. 'Effects' is a long way from 'direct investment', and both the terms 'multinational enterprise' and 'host state' presuppose foreign direct investment. The very notion of 'host' state, by definition, implies the actual physical presence of at least some aspect of the enterprise within its borders.

Should there be physical presence, however - that is to say, should the state experiencing the 'effects' be concurrently 'host' to direct investment of the foreign enterprise causing the effects - the effects doctrine can indeed be germane to our area of concern, as evidenced by such cases as *Continental Can*[24] or *CIBA-Geigy*[25] which we shall shortly look at in greater detail. In the majority of such cases, however, jurisdictional competence relies not solely on 'effects', but also on some link of physical presence.

In the field of antitrust, or restrictive business practices, then, as regards host-state control over the foreign enterprise - over and above the normal subordinance of any locally incorporated concern to the laws of the state of incorporation - while there are some interesting cases involving market sharing or allocation,[26] foreign or international cartels,[27] exclusive purchasing agreements,[28] concerted boycotts,[29] discriminatory pricing,[30] etc., the two single most significant areas of legal conflict regarding MNE operatioons arise out of disclosure questions, as elaborated in the previous chapter, and out of 'merger' control, involving international 'combinations' or 'concentrations', to which we shall now turn.

24. See *supra* note 13; see also *infra*, Section 4 (d), esp. text accompanying note 50, *et seq.*.

25. *United States* v. *CIBA Corp.*, 1970 CCH Trade Cases, ¶ 73,269 (S.D.N.Y. 1970) [consent decree]. See also *infra*, Section 4 (c) (text accompanying note 46, *et seq.)*.

26. See e.g. *United States* v. *Imperial Chemical Industries, Ltd.*, 100 F. Supp. 504 (S.D.N.Y. 1951), 105 F. Supp. 215 (S.D.N.Y. 1952); *United States* v. *Timken Roller Bearing Co.*, 341 U.S. 593 (1951); *United States* v. *American Tobacco Co.*, 221 U.S. 106 (1911).

27. See e.g. *United States* v. *National Lead Co.*, U.S. 319 (1947); *United States* v. *Watchmakers of Switzerland Information Center, Inc.*, 1963 CCH Trade Cases ¶ 70,600 (S.D.N.Y. 1963); *United States* v. *Aluminum Co. of America*, 148 F.2d 416 (2d Cir. 1945).

28. See e.g. *Continental Ore Co.* v. *Union Carbide and Carbon Corp.*, 370 U.S. 690 (1962).

29. See e.g. *Interamerican Refining Corp.* v. *Texas Maracaibo, Inc.*, 307 F. Supp. 1291 (D.Del. 1970).

30. See e.g. *Re Pittsburgh Corning Europe,* Decision of the Commission of the European Communities (72/403/EEC), 23 November 1972, 12 *Common Market Law Reports* (1973), D2.

2. Purpose of Anti-Combines Laws

Excessive concentration of economic power has been said to be one of the most ominous threats posed by big business in the world today. Although such concentration, nationally, is in reality no less menacing from powerful domestic firms than it is from multinational concerns,[31] in the case of the latter it is once again the fact that the 'economic power' originates and is directed from abroad that magnifies the concern beyond that experienced with regard to purely domestic firms, and turns the spotlight onto the MNEs.

The protection of competition is one of the most effective weapons against such undue concentrations of economic power, as witnessed in part by the fact that in the United States, historically averse to economic concentration in any form, the Justice Department enforcement of the Sherman and Clayton Acts[32] has concerned itself solely with the protection of competition,[33] in its dealings with both foreign and interstate commerce, throughout the history of the Acts. In terms of control over foreign MNE affiliates, this type of 'protection' translates most frequently into 'merger' or 'combines' control, normally embodied in antitrust or anti-monopoly laws. While the term "merger" is commonly used in Europe to mean corporate acquisitions or combinations of various forms, in American law it is a legalistic 'term of art' for a particular form of combination ("statutory merger"), among many others; hence, a general usage of the term here could be misleading and cause confusion of analysis. There will, therefore, be greater recourse to more general terms such as "combinations", "concentrations", acquisitions", etc.; and in those instances where the term "merger" is used, it is to be generally understood in its broader sense, to mean simply the combining of two commercial companies, though the stricter legalistic sense is included within the broader meaning.

3. American *v.* European Practice

The American and European - or even Canadian - experience in antitrust legislation and practice have historically been strikingly different, if not to say, in the case of Europe, diametrically opposed. This is simply a reflection of the

31. See e.g. Davidow, "Recent Developments in International Antitrust", 10 *Akron Law Review* (1977), at 606.

32. Loc. cit., *supra* note 2.

33. See Fugate, "An Overview of Antitrust Enforcement and the Multinational Corporation", 8 *Journal of International Law and Economics,* (1973), at 2.

fact that the historical and economic conditions which gave rise to EEC merger practice are totally different from those which inspired the American laws.[34] The Americans have a long-standing and deep-seated distrust of 'bigness' in business, and as early as 1890 this distrust was manifested legally in the very first antitrust legislation, embodied in the Sherman Act, even before the specific anti-merger provisions of the 1914 Clayton Act appeared. The Canadians, though they first enacted their Combines Investigations Act in 1889, did not include trusts, monopolies and mergers under the proscribed activities until 1910. In Europe, there has not only been very little pre-occupation, historically, with the issue of antitrust in general, but combinations and concentrations have actually been actively encouraged in the last fifteen or so years by the EEC, mainly in order to better meet the competition from large firms entering the European market from abroad. It was thought that by integrating, unifying and combining, European firms would be enabled ultimately to 'multinationalize' more effectively in their own right, and thus to take a more active part in overseas investment of their own.

Perhaps the strongest single non-legal stimulus to this unification trend was supplied by Servan Schreiber's *Défi américain*[35] which appeared in 1967 and encouraged corporate integration as a response to the "challenge" of the American multinationals. 'Mergers' were seen as a way of attempting to provide an economic counterweight to the at-that-time massive influx of American direct investment flowing, largely through MNE expansion, into the European market.

Legal justification for such a move was already embodied in Article 220 of the Rome Treaty[36] which provides that "member states shall, as far as necessary, enter into negotiations with each other with a view to ensuring for the benefit of their nationals...the possibility of mergers between firms or companies which are subject to different domestic laws...." The Treaty provision at the time of drafting was not anticipating the fostering of mergers substantively, but was merely aimed at eliminating some of the 'red tape' involved in trans-border combinations between members states. It is also noteworthy that at the time of the drafting of the Rome Treaty, no special attention was given to mergers in terms of their *control,* and consequently the Treaty contains no

34. See e.g. Norton, "The European Court of Justice Judgment in *United Brands:* Extraterritorial Jurisdiction and Abuse of a Dominant Position", 8 *Denver Journal of International Law and Policy, (1979), at 383.*

35. Translated as *The American Challenge,* (London: Hamish Hamilton, 1968).

36. Treaty Establishing the European Economic Community (with Annexes and Protocol). Done at Rome, on 25 March 1957 [hereinafter cited as the Treaty of Rome]; reprinted in 295 U.N.T.S. 23.

provision which would correspond to Section 7 of the Clayton Act and deal specifically with mergers and acquisitions. It is clear that strengthening of competition meant something different to a European government than it did to an American government. To the former it meant enhancing its competitive advantage in meeting competition from abroad; to the latter it meant the avoidance of monopolistic and oligopolistic associations which would disrupt the internal economic well-being.

The European attempt at 'trans-frontier mergers' has, however, not been entirely successful. For one thing, it was not fully taken into account that such combinations can generate difficulties of their own, in the area of, for example, internal control and co-ordination.[37] Furthermore, a trans-frontier combination - whatever form it takes - inevitably results in the amalgamation of one firm into another, if acquisition of control is effected through the transfer of assets, and, consequently, in the total disappearance of one nation's firm. This is not a very favourable incentive for the particular firm which loses its independent national identity - in fact, its very existence as a separate economic unit - even if its legal form is retained.[38]

Non-legal elements, such as national pride or corporate honour enter in to lend resistance to such combinations which might economically be sound and sensible moves. One author recounts that:

> [t]he concern felt in France about the proposed merger of Citroen with Fiat arose largely from a sentimental distaste that the national name might no longer be clearly identified with a prestigious product. Whether Citroen could benefit from the increased research capabilities and more efficient production which the merger promised, even whether it would flourish as a part of a transnational entity and fail under the national banner - these matters seemed, so far as one could tell from the newspaper reports, beside the point.[39]

While the European attempt at 'trans-frontier mergers', then, has not produced much in the way of case studies on combines control, there have been a number of interesting cases involving 'transnational mergers' between continents; and as, in general, combinations between enterprises of different na-

37. See Tugendhat, *The Multinationals* (New York: Random House, 1972), at 69.

38. See Schmitthoff, "The Multinational Enterprise in the United Kingdom", in Hahlo, ed., *Nationalism and the Multinational Enterprise: Legal Economic and Managerial Aspects* (Dobbs Ferry, N.Y.: Oceana, 1973), at 35.

39. Rubin, "Multinational Enterprise and National Sovereignty: A Skeptic's Analysis", 3 *Law and Policy in International Business* (1971), at 22.

tionalities are directly relevant to a study of control of MNEs, in that such combinations (1) may create new multinational firms, and (2) may involve the strengthening of already-existing MNEs,[40] it is the control over such 'transnational mergers' which constitutes the last area of host-state control over the operations of multinationals within the limits of the present work. This topic itself and all its antitrust implications - just as the 'effects' question mentioned above - could easily be a study in its own right, and we must be cautious to limit our treatment here to the immediate object in view, namely, control over combinations in whatever form, as they specifically relate to host control over foreign affiliates.

4. Model Types of MNE Mergers

For instance, we could envisage four different types of international 'merger' situations (see Figure 1):

Situation I: State X is host to company *b*, an affiliate of a multinational enterprise (*B*) with its *siège* in State Y, 'merges' with company *A/a*, a national of State X (it is irrelevant whether *A/a* is or is not itself a multinational); the merger is deemed by State X to contravene its competition laws; the merger is dissolved in State X.

Situation II: Parent company (*A*), a multinational with its *siège* in State X has an affiliate *(a)* in State Y; a company (*B/b*) (it is irrelevant whether *B/b* is an national of State X, Y, or Z, or whether it is or is not itself a multinational) in State Y 'merges' with foreign company *a*; this merger is deemed by State X to contravene its competition laws, on the grounds that such merger will have detrimental effects (e.g. will hamper competition) in State X, although the merged company itself is located in State Y; the merger is dissolved in State X.

Situation III: Two national companies (*B* and *C*), with their *sièges* in State Y, 'merge' legally under the laws of State Y. It is directly relevant that the firms are multinationals, since, as a part of the merger plan of *B* and *C* in State Y, the corresponding subsidiaries *b* and *c in State X likewise merge. The merger of b* and *c* is deemed by State X to contravene its competition laws; the merger of *b* and *c* is challenged by State X.

Situation IV: parent company (A), a multinational with its *siège* in State X, has an affiliate (*a*) in State Y; a company (*B/b*) (it is irrelevant whether *B/b* is or is not a multinational) in State Y 'merges' with foreign affiliate *a*; this

40. Markert, "Anti-Monopoly Legislation in Europe", in Hahlo, ed., op. cit., *supra* note 38, at 283.

FOUR TYPES OF 'MERGER' SITUATIONS INVOLVING MNEs

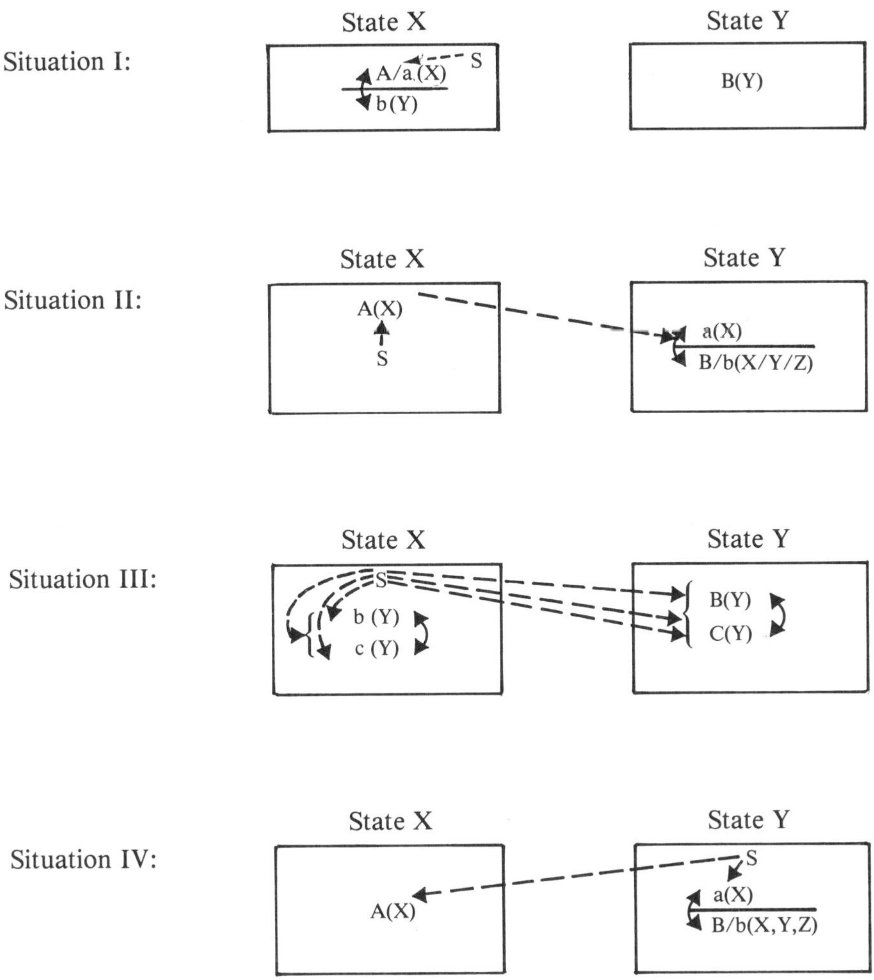

Figure 1

S = state government
A = parent company
a = affiliate
A/a = Enterprise as a whole (parent and affiliate(s))
(X) = state of incorporation of parent
- -➔ = challenge to merger
⇄ = merger

merger is deemed by State Y to contravene its competition laws; the merger is dissolved in State Y.

a. Merger Situation I: strict territorial principle

While the first type of situation has resulted in some interesting multinational cases, it does not represent a technique of host state control over a foreign affiliate, for the reason that, once 'merged', the foreign entity loses its foreign identity and no longer has a separate existence. If the merger is prevented before its consummation, the restraint is normally directed at the national company of State X, and not at the foreign company, or if the restraint is directed also at the foreign entity, its treatment under the law of State X is strictly in conformity with the territorial principle, and in no way differs from the treatment it would receive as a national company of State X.

Take, for example, the *Bayer-Monsanto* case.[41] Bayer, the German multinational chemical company, entered into a joint-venture agreement with Monsanto, an American firm, assuming the name "Mobay". In the U.S., joint ventures, along with other forms of partnerships, fall equally prey to the antitrust laws as do mergers in the technical sense, when such joint ventures or partnerships are deemed (in the U.S., by the Antitrust Division of the Department of Justice) to jeopardize free competition in (U.S.) markets. The joint venture already tends to be looked upon by the Antitrust Division as a 'quasi-merger' and is not allowed to be used as a cloak to camouflage abuses of competition policy. The Bayer-Monsanto partnership, nonetheless, met with no governmental opposition when it was effected in 1954. By 1962, however, Mobay had captured 50 per cent of the U.S. market for the production and sale of various products used in the manufacture of polyurethane, and consequently the partnership came to the attention of the American Antitrust Division. A legal battle ensued. Eventually, in 1967, a consent decree was issued, the partners were obliged to separate, and Monsanto ended up selling out to Bayer its share of Mobay.

Although this case involved a foreign affiliate, there is no reason to believe that the same action would not have taken place had both partners been domestic firms. Moreover, it was the American partner which sold out of Mobay. And the issue in this type of 'merger' situation is one of preserving competition, not one of controlling activities of a foreign enterprise.

41. *United States* v. *Monsanto, Farbenfabriken Bayer AG and Mobay Chemical Co.,* 1967, CCH *Trade Cases,* ¶ 72,001 (W.D. Pa. 1967).

The same could be said of the *British Petroleum Company-Standard Oil Company of Ohio* 'merger' case,[42] which, while the transaction was instigated by the foreign BP company, was brought against Sohio, the American party to the transaction; and when, subsequent to a consent decree which precluded the combination, the reaction in the U.K. indicated a feeling of having been discriminated against as a foreign company, the then Assistant Attorney General, (later Judge) McClaren, responded by assuring the European Institutional Investor Conference that "there is no hidden purpose in the Antitrust Division's objection to a particular foreign firm transaction: we apply the law in exactly the same manner in which it is applied in wholly domestic situations."[43]

The *Gillette-Braun* case[44] is another case in point, in which the U.S. Justice Department objected to the acquisition by the Gillette Company, the largest American domestic producer and distributor of 'wet shaving' instruments, of the German company Braun, A.G., the third largest European manufacturer of 'dry shaving' instruments, the contention being that, due to an exclusive distributorship and licensing arrangement between Braun and Ronson Corporation, Gillette's domestic competitor, competition in the U.S. market would be "substantially lessened", as per Section 7 of the Clayton Act,[45] and Braun would be eliminated as a potential competitor in that market. Eventually the terms of the acquisition were modified by consent decree, the major provision of which was the creation of a new 'spin-off' company which would provide a competitive counterweight to the strengthened Gillette Company. Here, of course, again, though the transaction was of an international character, the action was brought against the domestic firm exclusively.

b. Merger Situation II: extension of jurisdiction through home parent to foreign affiliate

Likewise, in Merger Situation II, the directive to dissolve the combination

42. *United States* v. *The Standard Oil Company, et. al.,* 1970 CCH Trade Cases, ¶ 72, 988 (N.D. Ohio, 1970) [consent decree].

43. This comes from an address by Richard McClaren entitled "International Investment and the U.S. Antitrust Laws", London, England, December 1, 1969, cited in Fugate, op. cit., *supra* note 33, at 6.

44. *United States* v. *Gillette Company,* 40 Fed. Reg. 27265 (1975); 5 Trade Reg. Rep. (1976-1 Trade Cases) ¶ 60,691, at 67,996 (D.C. Mass. December 30, 1975); 5 Trade Reg. Rep. (1975-2 Trade Cases) ¶ 60,651, at 67,838 (D.C. Mass. December 30, 1975); see also King, "International Operations: Current Antitrust Environment", in 8 *Case Western Reserve Journal of International Law* (1976) at 452 *et seq.;* also Fugate, op. cit., *supra* note 33, at 5.

45. Clayton Act, loc. cit., *supra* note 2, sect. 18.

(or, as the case may be, to prevent it before it is actually realized) is directed from the home government to a domestic affiliate, though, in this case, located abroad. Thus, while the host state may be ill-disposed to having decisions made outside its territory which affect business concerns within its territory in a way which may conflict with its own economic policy, the main issue in such situations is one of the extension of jurisdiction from the home state through subsidiaries into the territory of the host, and not one of host control over a foreign MNE.

The third and fourth types of merger situation, however, are responsive to the issue at hand, namely, the exercise of host state control over a foreign MNE. The two situations described, however, differ in one or two fundamental aspects which can perhaps best be made apparent through a look at some actual cases.

c. Merger Situation III: territorial principle with foreign ramifications

The classic case of the third type of 'merger' situation is the *CIBA-Geigy* case.[46] In this case, two diversified Swiss chemical companies legally merged in the home state, resulting in a corresponding combination of the firms' respective U.S. subsidiaries. This mirror-merger, so to speak, ran afoul of the U.S. antitrust laws. In this case, a compromise settlement was reached, in a consent decree, whereby the U.S. subsidiaries' merger was tempered by certain conditions such as, *inter alia,* compulsory patent licensing, divestiture of certain properties, and the setting up of a third ('spin-off') company in the field to counter the anti-competitive consequences of the combination.

This is clearly a case of host control over affiliates of foreign MNEs; yet here again, the foreign firms cannot be said to have been subjected to any more severe restrictions than those to which purely domestic firms acting independently would have been. In fact, due to the foreign link in the *CIBA-Geigy* case - and international principles of comity (or simply considerations of reciprocity) - the two corporations were, if anything, dealt with more leniently than would purely domestic firms have been under similar conditions.

Moreover, while the court, through its jurisdiction *in rem,* and by voluntary submission and consent to this jurisdiction on the part of the foreign-based parties (the Swiss firms CIBA Ltd. and J.R. Geigy S.A.), named as defendants not only the local subsidiaries, CIBA Corporation and Geigy Chemical Cor-

46. *United States* v. *CIBA Corp.* 1970 CCH Trade Cases, ¶ 73, 269 (S.D.N.Y. 1970) [consent decree].

poration, but also their Swiss parents,[47] the problem nonetheless - legally and jurisdictionally - remained a local one, to be dealt with in domestic courts and on the territorial principle.

d. Merger Situation IV: 'reverse extraterritoriality'

In Merger Situation IV, however, jurisdictional powers are extended even further. Situation IV combines aspects of the territorial principle of Situations I and III with aspects of the extraterritorial principle of Situation II; but in each aspect there is a significant distinction. In Merger Situation I, the restraints are directed by the home government, territorially, at its own national enterprise; in Merger Situation II, the restraints, while extraterritorial, are likewise directed at the home government's own national enterprise; in Merger Situation III, while the restraints are, in contrast, directed by the *host* government at *foreign*-based local subsidiaries, this is done still strictly on the territorial principle; in Merger Situation IV, on the other hand, the restraints may also be directed territorially against the locally incorporated foreign affiliate, but may even be extended, extraterritorially ('reverse extraterritoriality'[48]), to a *parent* company in the *home* state. This presents a different jurisdictional exercise altogether.

The classic example of a rather more complex version of this last type of merger situation is the celebrated EEC case involving the American company, Continental Can. This is the one Common Market case addressing foreign mergers.[49] In *Re Continental Can Company,*[50] the EC Commission interpreted Article 86 of the Rome Treaty to prohibit a combination between an American-based (i.e. non-EEC member) subsidiary of Continental Can Company and a Dutch (i.e. EEC member) company, contending that Continental Can, by indirectly 'merging' with a potential competitor through its wholly owned domestic subsidiary, was abusing its "dominant position", assumed already to be held in the "relevant market".

The facts of the *Continental Can* case[51] are somewhat complex (see Figure

47. Ibid., I [Jurisdiction] & II [Definitions] (F), at 89,067.

48. See *supra* Chapter VIII, note 153.

49. See Wittman, "International Mergers Under Section 7 of the Clayton Act and Article 86 of the Common Market Treaty of Rome: A Comparative Perspective", 18 *Washburn Law Journal* (1979), at 512.

50. Decision of the EC Commission (72/21/EEC) of 9 December 1971, J.O. 17/25 (1972) E.C.; 2 CCH *Common Market Reporter* ¶ 9481 (1971).

51. See *supra* note 13; also *Décision de la Commission du 9 décembre 1971 relative a une*

BASIC ELEMENTS INVOLVED IN THE CONTINENTAL CAN 'MERGER' TRANSACTION

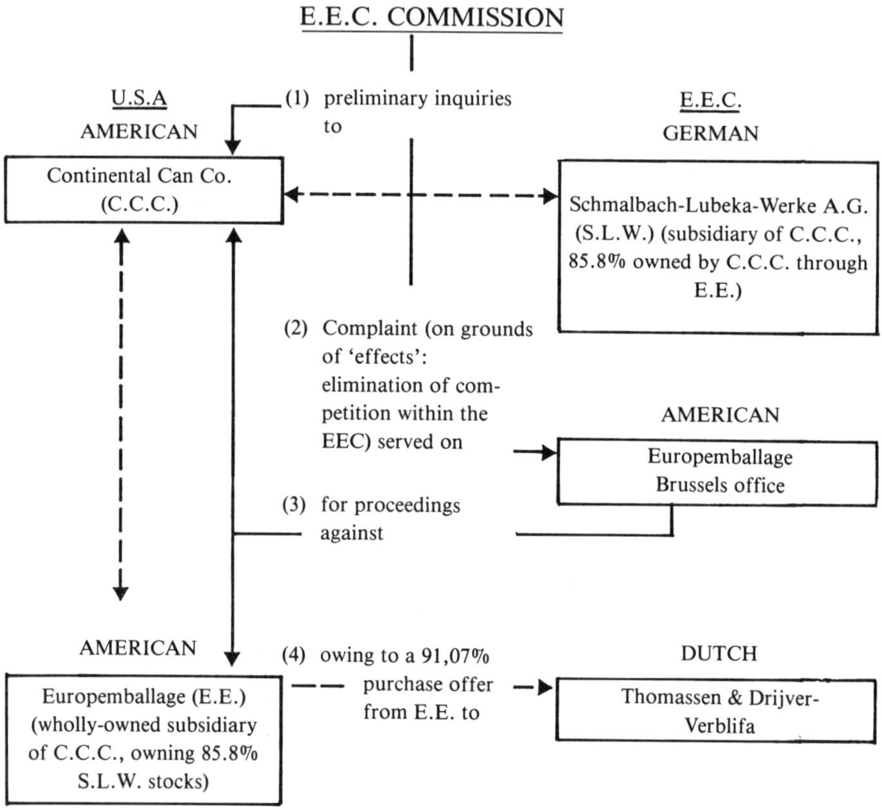

Figure 2

2), and as it is a landmark case in the development of European (Community) antitrust law, and of EC 'merger' control in particular, it deserves our closer attention.

Continental Can Company, Inc. ("Continental Can"), an American enterprise with its *siège* in New York, and the world's largest producer of metal containers as well as being an important producer of other packaging materials and packaging machinery, purchased in February 1969 a controlling interest in the German Schmalbach-Lubeka Werke ("Schmalbach"), the largest producer of light metal containers in continental Europe. By the end of the year, Continental Can had gradually acquired ownership of 85.8 per cent of the German firm's share capital. Continental Can then entered into negotiations with an English firm, The Metal Box Company, Ltd. ("Metal Box"), with the aim of setting up, in Delaware, a European container holding company involving ultimately Metal Box, its Italian subsidiary Superbox, and two licencees of Continental Can: The Dutch Thomassen & Drijver-Verblifa ("Thomassen") and the French Carnaud et Forges de Basse-Indre ("Carnaud"). Metal Box and Continental Can would be expected to transfer their related European interests, including their shares in Schmalbach and Thomassen, to the holding company "Europemballage," which would then, with share capital supplied by Continental Can from additional stock purchases in Europemballage, purchase the outstanding stock in Thomassen. The result would be a 'merger' between Continental Can and Thomassen, effected through the holding company, Europemballage Corporation, and would assure Continental Can's effective control, through Europemballage, over the leading container producers in the Common Market.

Carnaud, for its own business reasons, declined the offer to participate in the holding company; Metal Box, on the other hand, agreed; and Continental Can went ahead and, in February 1970, incorporated in Delaware the new wholly owned subsidiary Europemballage Corporation, with offices in New York and Brussels, to which it transferred all its European holdings,[52] the most significant of which being those in Schmalbach. Europemballage then tendered its offer to Thomassen, which was made public on March 16, 1970. Within a month, the Commission had notified all parties concerned that the transaction could come into conflict with Article 86 of the Treaty of Rome. Metal Box

---

procédure d'application de l'article 86 du traité CEE (IV/26811 Continental Can Company), E.C. J.O. L7/25 (1972). [The French text is the only authoritative text ("le seul faisant foi")]; for an English translation see 11 *International Legal Materials* (1972) (English translation reproduced from CCH *Common Market Reporter,* Supp. No. 178, 1972), at 316 *et seq.*

52. These included a 10% holding in Thomassen, an 85.8% holding in Schmalbach, and a 1.3% holding in Superbox.

thereupon temporarily withdrew from the arrangement, pending the outcome of possible Commission proceedings, with the result that, in April 1970, Europemballage, wholly owned by Continental Can, acquired a 91.07 per cent interest in Thomassen, effectively concluding the transaction.

Continental's realization of the 'merger' transaction produced immediate repercussions in the EEC. The very next day proceedings were instituted by the Commission, under Regulation 17,[53] against both Continental Can and Europemballage. The ensuing investigation culminated in a finding that Continental Can, by combining with Thomassen, the largest producers of metal containers in the Benelux countries,[54] and already exercising a dominant position through its subsidiary, Schmalbach, contravened the abuse-of-a-dominant-position prohibition in Article 86 of the Rome Treaty by eliminating potential competition in the relevant market and hence affecting trade between member states of the Community.

Continental Can, contending inconsistencies and points of error in the Commission's judgement, made an appeal to the European Court of Justice, and, in February 1973, the Court, while upholding the basic legal arguments of the Commission,[55] found on the facts for Continental Can on grounds that:

> Where the E.C. Commission bases a decision under Article 86 EEC on the elimination or near elimination of competition, it must give reasons that are sufficient in law to justify it, or at least must prove that competition was so substantially impaired that the remaining competitors could not constitute an adequate counterweight. Where such burden of proof is not discharged the resultant decision will be annulled.[56]

Hence the decision of the Commission was reversed on the finding that the Commission had failed to meet its burden of proof to establish that Continental Can enjoyed a dominant position in the "relevant market" and that the combination effectively eliminated competition.

The Commission was nonetheless not without its own victory in principle as regards significant legal arguments advanced in the case. It was substantially vindicated in its position by the Court holding, with reference to substantial increases in "market control", that:

53. Regulation 17, 5 E.C. J.O. 204 (1962), Art. 3, para. 1.; 1 CCH *Common Market Reporter,* 2401 (1971).

54. *Décision de la Commission du 9 décembre 1971...,* op. cit. *supra* note 51.

55. See text accompanying note 57 *infra.*

56. 12 *Common Market Law Reports* 199 (1973), at 201.

> Article 86(2) EEC applies not only to practices which may cause a prejudice to consumers directly but also to those that cause such prejudice through interference in the structure of actual competition which is mentioned in Article 3 (f) EEC. There may therefore be abusive behaviour if an undertaking in a dominant position strengthens that dominant position so that the degree of market control achieved substantially obstructs competition, i.e., so that the only undertakings left in the market are those which are dependent on the dominant undertaking as regards their market behaviour. The strengthening of the position of an undertaking may be abusive and prohibited by Article 86 EEC regardless of the means or methods whereby it has been achieved, if it has the above-mentioned effects.[57]

A substantial increase in latitude of application of Article 86 was thus assured by the Court, which went further to assert that:

> Regardless of fault, it may be considered to be abusive under Article 86 EEC if an undertaking has such a dominant position that the objectives of the Treaty are frustrated by a substantial change in the supply structure which seriously jeopardizes the consumer's freedom of action in the market. This is necessarily the case if competition is almost eliminated.[58]

Multinational enterprises intending to enter the market of the Community by acquisition, merger or other form of combination, or to enhance their position within that market by those means, have since the decision found themselves confronted by restraints greater than had been the case prior to that judgment.[59]

One author[60] contends that, while the case in question does indeed serve to

57. *Idem.*

58. *Idem.*

59. For further comment on the significance of this case to EEC 'merger' control, see *inter alia,* Korah, "The Control of Mergers under Article 86 of the Rome Treaty: Continental Can", 26 *Current Legal Problems* (1973); Hurwitz, "The Impact of the Continental Can Case On Combinations and Concentrations Within the Common Market", 25 *Hastings Law Journal* (1973-1974); Guyénot, "La décision 'Continental Can' de la Commission C.E.C. et la naissance du droit anti-trust européen", 91 *Zeitschift für Schweizerisches Recht,* (1972); Adler and Belman, "Anti-merger Enforcement in Europe - Trends and Prospects", 8 *Journal of International Law and Economics* (1973); Haubert, "Continental Can - New Strength for Common Market Anti-Trust", (Comments), 11 *San Diego Law Review* (1973).

60. de Richemont, "L'épineux problème du contrôle des firmes multinationales", *Revue du Marché Commun* 1974, at 497-506.

demonstrate the susceptibility of a foreign firm to the laws of an international market of which it is not, itself, a member ("l'obligation de respecter les règles d'un marché international dont elle ne font pas partie"), the main issue is not really one of extraterritoriality at all, since the presence of the subsidiary within the Community calls into play the normal international law rules of jurisdiction, namely the territorial principle affirmed by the Permanent Court of International Justice in the *Lotus* case[61] and consistently upheld in subsequent decisions. In Monsieur de Richemont's own words:

> En réalité, il s'agit ni plus ni moins que de l'application du principe de territorialité qui a été retenue dans l'affaire du 'Lotus', par la Cour Permanente de Justice Internationale, ainsi que par une jurisprudence constante des Juridictions américaines, et qui est approuvée d'une façon générale par la Doctrine.[62]

But the deficiency in the above observation, in the opinion of the present writer, is the lack of significance attributed to the fact that the action was brought against the American parent, as well as against its American subsidiary, and not against the locally incorporated subsidiary within the Common Market as would be more normally consistent with the territorial principle. There is clearly an exercise of 'reverse' extraterritorial jurisdiction on the part of the Commission, even if the channel of the extraterritorial reach was, in this case, ultimately a local office (in Brussels) of the foreign parent's (U.S.) subsidiary. There is no reason to assume that in the absence of the Brussels office no complaint would have been served on the American parent and its subsidiary, since the preliminary Commission enquiries were sent directly by letter and telex to Continental Can in New York. The fact that the ultimate complaint was served on the Brussels office was most likely more a matter of convenience than of legal necessity. The Commission's final decision, moreover, was directed at "Continental Can Company, Inc. à New York".[63]

Whatever jurisdictional novelties the present case may present, there can be no question that of utmost significance in *Continental Can* is the broad interpretation of Article 86, in the sense that in the instant case it was construed by the Commission to condemn the very act of concluding a combination by a 'dominant' company - if not the very dominance in itself[64] - as an abuse, totally

61. *Case of the "S.S. Lotus"* [1927], P.C.I.J., ser. A, No. 10.

62. de Richemont, op. cit., *supra* note 60, at 501-502.

63. See *Décision de la Commission, du 9 décembre 1971,* loc. cit., *supra* note 51, *Arrêté,* Art. 3, at L7/39.

64. See Vogelenzang, "Abuse of a Dominant Position in Article 86; The Problem of Causality and Some Applications," 13 *Common Market Law Review* (1976), at 70.

independent of any morally improper behaviour performed by the firm in question, or of any identifiable harm to consumers, whereas a strict literal interpretation would require that both a dominant position and an abuse of that position must exist to constitute an offense under Article 86, and would even imply the need for a causal relationship between the dominance and the improper conduct.

The Commission, in *Continental Can,* defined the notion of dominant position as follows:

> ...des entreprises sont en position dominante lorsqu'elles ont une possibilité de comportements indépendants qui les met en mesure d'agir sans tenir notablement compte des concurrents, des acheteurs ou des fournisseurs; qu'il en est ainsi lorsque, en raison de leur part de marché, ou de leur part de marché en liason notamment avec la disposition de connaissances techniques, de matières premières ou de capitaux, elles ont la possibilité de terminer les prix ou de contrôler la production ou la distribution pour une partie significative des produits en cause; que cette possibilité ne doit pas nécessairement découler d'une domination absolue permettant aux entreprises qui la détiennent d'éliminer toute volonté de la part de leurs partenaires économiques, mais qu'il suffit qu'elle soit assez forte dans l'ensemble pour assurer à ces entreprises une indépendance globale de comportement, même s'il existe des différences d'intensité de leur influence sur les différents marchés partiels....[65]

After having established the existence of a dominant position according to the above definition, the Commission, despite its position that even a monopoly does not, *per se*, necessarily constitute a violation of Article 86, nonetheless insisted that it is an infraction "pour une entreprise en position dominante de renforcer cette position par concentration avec une entreprise concurrente occupant elle-même une forte position dans la même zone économique....étant en outre précisé que l'infraction a été consommé au motif que ladite concentration a eu pour effet d'éliminer la concurrence....Dès lors, la position dominante qui a pour effet de fausser la concurrence dans une zone peut devenir cause d'exploitation abusive au sens de l'article 86."[66]

Hence we have the judgment that when a dominant position is strengthened through 'merger' (*concentration*), resulting in a distortion of competition in the relevant market, the dominant position itself may be regarded as abusive.

It is difficult to reconcile logically the two positions that (1) a monopoly will

65. E.C. J.O L7/25 (1972), II.B. 3, at L7/35.
66. Guyénot, op. cit., *supra* note 59, at 164.

not necessarily violate Article 86, and that (2) a dominant position distorting competition may be regarded as a violation. What monopoly does not enjoy market dominance; or what monopoly does not distort competition? It would appear that there is an attempt to preserve in theory the 'letter' of the law, while, in practice, altering the 'spirit'. The alteration of the 'spirit' is undoubtedly necessary and justifiable, this interpretation of 'abuse' having been upheld by the Court of Justice on appeal, even while finding for Continental Can on the facts; and this concept, although otherwise expressed, is evident also in current practice of other industrialized states. But clinging to the 'letter' for what would seem to be for mere appearance or appeasement purposes, by theoretically shielding monopolies, would seem to this writer to constitute an inconsistency which only weakens the credibility of the EEC's competition policy.

The key may lie in the following citation from the Commission Decision, wherein it is declared that:

> l'achat d'une participation majoritaire dans une entreprise concurrente par une entreprise ou un groupe d'entreprises détenant une position dominante, peut, dans certaines circonstances, constituer une exploitation abusive de cette position;....[67]

With the words "peut, dans certaines circonstances", the Commission seems to be taking care to retain at least a semblance of flexibility in its application of Article 86 - a flexibility which it may also use to neutralize the apparent illogicality alluded to above, and to retain the prerogative to consider mergers on a case-by-case basis, which of course is advisable and expedient.

It has been suggested that, while the Commission maintains that a dominant position, in itself - or even its extreme manifestation, a monopoly - does not always and automatically provoke condemnation under Article 86 as abusive (as it would certainly do under Article 2 of the U.S. Sherman Act), in actual fact it indirectly arrives at a practical result amounting to just that, when, in the *Continental Can* case, for example, it affirms that "l'acquisition par Continental d'une participation majoritaire dans [Thomassen] a pour effet de supprîmer la concurrence entre [Thomassen] et [Schmalbach] dans cette zone d'action concurrente pour les types d'emballage visés,"[68] when virtually on that basis alone it condemned the acquisition.

67. E.C. J.O. L7/25 (1972), II. C. 22, at L7/37.
68. Guyénot, op. cit., *supra* note 59, at 165.

In the words of another author, approvingly referring to Professor Joliet's opinion[69] on the matter, "Professor Joliet convincingly asserts that the concepts of dominant position in EEC competition law and of monopoly power in American law are functionally equivalent concepts."[70]

Hence, in addition to *Continental Can's* significance in affirming the power of the EC Commission to enforce its interpretation of Article 86 of the Rome Treaty on enterprises of non-member states and to extend, by 'reverse extraterritoriality', its jurisdiction to the foreign parent, the relatively new orientation in 'merger' control practice within the EEC has rapidly extended beyond the literal parameters of Article 86, so that the prospective MNE entrant into the Common Market area by means of merger or acquisition must reckon with the fact that the concentration itself - where at least one market-dominant firm is involved - runs the risk of being condemned as abusive.

This naturally generates a further uncertainty as to whether, in future, the purview of Article 86 might be further expanded to condemn as abusive a combination *creating* a market-dominant position. This is only one step beyond *Continental Can.*

Further development of the concept of market dominance came out of another EEC case, *United Brands Company and United Brands Continental BV* v. *EC Commission* (*United Brands* case);[71] but while this case exemplifies emerging EEC practice regarding the notion of abuse of a dominant position and extraterritorial extension of jurisdiction of Community antitrust laws, it is not the present intention to look at the case in detail, as it does not involve an international merger. One point is worth making here, however, and that is that *United Brands*, in substantially easing the concept of dominance, magnified the anti-acquisition powers established by the *Continental Can* case.[72]

The one immutable proscription under Article 86 is the effect of reducing competition.[73] The conduct leading to that effect, or any causal relationship between dominance and the conduct, is no longer relevant. This is all certainly

69. Joliet, *Monopolization and Abuse of Dominant Position: Study of the American and European Approaches to the Control of Economic Power* (The Hague: Nijhoff (1970)), passim.

70. Hurwitz, op. cit., *supra* note 59, at 507.

71. *United Brands Co. and United Brands Continental BV* v. *Commission of the European Communities,* Court of Justice of the EC, Case No. 27/76, Feb. 14, 1978, CCH *Common Market Reporter* [Transfer Binder: Court Decisions 1977-1978] ¶ 8429, on appeal from a prior decision by the European Commission, CCH *Common Market Reporter* [Transfer Binder: New Developments 1976-1978], ¶ 9800.

72. For an analysis of the *United Brands* decision, see Norton, op. cit., *supra* note 34; also Swan, "EEC United Brands Decision: Can Chiquita Banana Find Happiness in Europe?", 7 *California Western International Law Journal* (1977), at 385 *et seq.*

73. Haubert, *op. cit., supra* note 59, at 240.

new ground for the EEC, but is not new in concept; antitrust legality of all Euro-acquisitions in the United States rests strictly on the competitive consequences.[74]

The *Continental Can* case thus marks the beginning of an EEC merger policy based on Article 86 (and some would include Article 85)[75] of the Rome Treaty; this merger 'law' is predominantly dependent on policy rather than statute.[76] A growing preoccupation with merger control of a statutory nature, however, has since been demonstrated by the fact that, five months after the *Continental Can* decision, the Commission of the European Communities drafted a regulation,[77] which it submitted to the Council of Ministers, for stemming the anti-competitive effects of the increasing number of corporate concentrations by requiring prior notice to the Commission for acquisitions and mergers involving companies with sales volume levels over a designated amount,[78] thus exposing such combinations to possible intervention on the part of the Commission. Of particular interest is the fact that this proposed Regulation on Concentrations, if it were to be applied in its present form, would operate on the basis of the acquisition or enhancement of the mere power to alter the competition structure of the market, independent of any actual or probable abuse of that power. The assessment of this 'power' would be based on such considerations as "economic and financial" strength of the enterprises involved and the structure of the relevant markets. Basically, all criteria on which a merger would be judged center upon its ability to affect competition within the Common Market (Article 1) and the growth of *actual or potential* international competition (Commission's Memorandum to the Council). While the proposed combines regulations have still not been adopted by the Council, due to three unresolved issues[79] and considerable interpretational difficulties, they

74. See Rowe, "Antitrust Aspects of European Acquisitions or Joint Ventures in the United States" (paper presented at the Cologne Conference on "The U.S. Antitrust Laws/Die U.S. Antitrust Gesetze: the legal implications for those entering or operating in the U.S. market," under the auspices of the Practising Law Institute of New York in co-operation with the German-American Lawyers Association, Bonn, the American Chamber of Commerce in Germany, Frankfurt am Main, and the Studienvereinigung Kartellrecht e.V. Wiesbaden, June 1979), at 7; *also* CCH *Common Market Reporter: Doing Business in Europe,* para. 31,045. [New Developments, 1978].

75. See Wittman, op. cit., *supra* note 49, at 526.

76. Hawk, "Antitrust in the EEC - The First Decade", 41 *Fordham Law Review* 229 (1972), at 231, as cited in Ibid., at 524.

77. Proposal for a Regulation (EEC) of the Council on the Control of Concentrations Between Undertakings, 16 E.C.O.J. (No. C92) 1 (1973), 12 *Common Market Law Reports* (1973), D205.

78. Ibid. (Proposal for a Regulation) art. 4(2), at 3-4, 12 *Common Market Law Reports,* at D209.

79. See Wittman, op. cit., *supra* note 49, at 532. See also CCH *Common Market Reporter*

represent a further formulation of the tougher EEC position on mergers, as do the EEC plans for tightening up antitrust regulation of state-controlled companies.[80] At the same time, however, such regulations would have the advantage of eliminating some of the uncertainty for the MNE as to the legality of projected merger transactions.

Whether or not the proposed regulations will be adopted in their present form is uncertain, but the adoption of some form of Common Market merger control is extremely likely.

It has been suggested[81] that there are currently five systems which could serve as a model for an EEC Regulation: 1) the Canadian system (criminal prohibition); 2) the American system (civil prohibition); 3) the British system (administrative intervention against mergers contrary to the public interest); 4) the European Coal and Steel Community Treaty[82] (administrative authorization of undertakings above a specified size); and 5) the Japanese system (notification with administrative discretionary authority to preclude combinations with anti-competitive effects). Such regulations would endow the Commission with prior-restraint powers, and would have the force of law and allow the imposition of sanctions.[83] The OECD Committee of Experts on Restrictive Business Practices reports that, once a system of merger control is introduced, the European Communities' "highly sophisticated antitrust law...will be among the most comprehensive legislations in the world.[84]

5. Emergence of New Competition Policy and Legislation

Elsewhere in the industrialized world new competition policy is also taking shape. As the subject of the present work is not one of comparative law, the individual legislation of each industrialized state will not be elaborated here in depth. Moreover, the EEC itself has determined that the degree of diversity in

---

[1973-75 Transfer Binder] ¶ 9779; EC Commission, *Seventh Report on Competition Policy,* EEC 43 (1978).

80. See e.g. "EEC Plans Antitrust Crackdown on State-Controlled Companies", *International Herald Tribune,* October 25, 1979, at 1:1.

81. See Wittman, op. cit., *supra* note 49, at 533.

82. Treaty Instituting the European Coal and Steel Community, done April 18, 1951, 261 U.N.T.S. 140.

83. Wittman, op. cit., *supra* note 49 at 534.

84. Organisation for Economic Co-operation and Development, *Restrictive Business Practices of Multinational Enterprises,* op. cit., *supra* note 18, at 61.

merger procedures among European Community members demands some harmonization before any effective regulation of trans-frontier mergers can be achieved. It is in fact to this end that several Directives have been drafted by the EEC on the harmonization of these national laws, a step which it sees as a prerequisite to any effective regional co-operation in this area.

Already, certain legislative and policy trends are discernable, however, not only within the European Community as a whole, but also in certain of the individual member states, as well as in United States federal practice. As the United States and Germany have the most developed antitrust systems, more emphasis is given to these two nations' legislation on competition policy than to that of other countries falling within the scope of the present study; nonetheless, as national legislation on merger control is indeed on the increase in a number of countries, and tends to reflect United States and Community practice and to underscore the tendency we have seen toward stricter control over transnational mergers, we shall note briefly, in passing, some of the legislation illustrative of the current direction.

Canada, for example, in the mid-1970's enacted new anti-combines legislation[85] amending the Combines Investigation Act[86](Canada's version of the U.S. Sherman Act) providing, *inter alia,* powers to regulate mergers. The Act's predecessor[87] was first enacted in 1889, and has been known as the Combines Investigation Act since 1910,[88] at which time trusts, monopolies and mergers were first included as prohibited activities. The Act has, since 1889, been a criminal prohibitory statute, and, as such, has provided no regulatory powers. A significant feature of the amended Act is that, while under the Act's former provision mergers (and monopolies and conspiracies) were proscribed only when they constituted an excess or abuse, under the amended Act there is no need to prove that the combination, if effected, would eliminate or be likely to eliminate competition in the relevant market. In the exact words of the new provision which follows Section 32 of the established Act:

> (1.1) For greater certainty, in establishing that a conspiracy, combination, agreement or arrangement is in violation of subsection (1), it shall not be necessary to prove that the conspiracy, combination, agreement

85. An Act to amend the Combines Investigation Act and the Bank Act and to repeal an Act to amend an Act to amend the Combines Investigation Act and the Criminal Code, *Statutes of Canada,* (1974-75-76) c. 76.

86. R.S.C. 1970, c. C-23 (1970); c. 10 (1st Supp.); c. 10 (2nd Supp.).

87. An Act for the Prevention and Suppression of Combinations formed in the Restraint of Trade, 1889, c. 41.

88. The Combines Investigation Act, 1910, c. 9.

or arrangement, if carried into effect, would or would be likely to eliminate, completely or virtually, competition in the market to which it relates or that it was the object of any or all of the parties thereto to eliminate, completely or virtually, competition in that market.[89]

For the combination to be prohibited, it is presumably sufficient, under the amended Act, that it be deemed by the Restrictive Practices Commission to be contrary to the public interest of Canada, or, more specifically, to be judged to have a detrimental effect on the state of competition in Canada.

Another interesting new feature of the amended Act is the power granted to the Commission to prohibit the implementation of foreign judgments, foreign laws, or foreign court orders or government directives[90] which could detrimentally distort competition in Canada or oppose the public interest - provisions which were clearly motivated by MNE activity involving foreign-owned and controlled subsidiaries.

In general, the amended Act provides more flexible machinery for regulating combinations, particularly by removing the onus of proof from the Crown, which heretofore was disinclined to undertake the economic analysis necessary to determine undue concentration within the economic structure. Even so, the Combines Investigation Act, more a "technical legal matter" than the result of a distrust of big business as in the United States, is more limited in its terms than the broadly applied American antitrust statutes, and its enforcement has equally been far less severe.[91]

West Germany, as well, already possessing the most rigorous antitrust laws in Western Europe,[92] continues to strengthen its controlling powers over combinations and abuse of market dominating positions, and did so significantly in a major revision in 1973 of its Law against Restraints of Competition (*Gesetz*

89. The Combines Investigation Act, as amended, loc. cit., *supra* note 85, § 32 (1.1).

90. Ibid. §§ 31.5, 31.6, 32.1.

91. See Baker, "Antitrust Conflicts Between Friends: Canada and the United States in the Mid-1970's", 11 *Cornell International Law Journal,* (1978), at 171; also, Lenrow, "Foreign Direct Investment in the United States: Possible Restrictions at Home and a New Climate for American Investment Abroad", 26 *American University Law Review* (1976)", at 124. See generally, Henry, "Anti-monopoly Legislation in Canada", in Hahlo, op. cit., *supra* note 38, at 289 *et seq.*

92. See e.g. *Kartellverordnung vom 2. November 1923; Gesetz gegen Wettbewerbsbeschränkungen* [GWB] of July 27, 1957; *Gesetz zur Änderung des Gesetzes gegen Wettbewerbsbeschränkungen vom 15. September 1965,* BGBl 1965 I S.1363; *Zweites Gesetz zur Änderung des Gesetzes gegen Wettbewerbsbeschränkungen,* BGBl 1973 I S.917; *Drittes Gesetz zur Änderung des Gesetzes gegen Wettbewerbsbeschränkungen vom 28. Juni 1976,* BGBl 1976 I S.1697; *Viertes Gesetz zur Änderung des Gesetzes gegen Wettbewerbsbeschränkungen vom 26. April 1980,* BGBl 1980 I S.458; *Gesetz gegen Wettbewerbsbeschränkungen in der Fassung vom 24. September 1980,* BGBl I S.1761. See also Schnorr, op. cit., *supra* note 17, at 602, 630-1.

gegen Wettbewerbsbeschränkungen [GWB][93]). The 1973 Amendment Act (*Zweites Gesetz zur Änderung des Gesetzes gegen Wettbewerbsbeschränkungen*[94]) not only tightened notification requirements for various forms of concentrations and stiffened the originally proposed rules on merger controls, but more importantly introduced *preventive* merger controls, and generally increased the merger control powers of the Federal Cartel Office (*Bundeskartellamt*). Since the 1973 Amendment Act, two additional antitrust amendments (*Kartellnovelle*) have been adopted[95] which even further intensified control over mergers and surveillance of market-dominating enterprises.[96] The latest of these amendments, the merger and market-dominance regulations of which entered into force on February 28, 1980, not only further tightened existing merger control

93. *Idem.* (See GWB, September 1980 version.)

94. *Idem.* (*Zweites Gesetz zur Änderung des Gesetzes gegen Wettbewerbsbeschränkungen*) loc. cit., *supra* note 92.

95. *Viertes Gesetz zur Änderung des Gesetzes gegen Wettbewerbsbeschränkungen vom 26. April 1980,* BGBl 1980 I S.458. See Rauschenbach, "Die Entwicklung des Deutschen Kartellrechts 1977", *Neue Juristische Wochenschrift* [*N.J.W.*], Heft 5, 1978, at 190 [hereinafter cited as "Kartellrecht 1977"]; also Rauschenbach, "Die Entwicklung des deutschen Kartellrechts im Jahre 1978", *N.J.W.,* Heft 15, 1979, starred note at 737 [hereinafter cited as "Kartellrecht 1978"]; Bechtold, "Die Entwicklung des deutschen Kartellrechts im Jahre 1979, *N.J.W.,* Heft 23, 1980, at 1265; *Mehr Wettbewerb ist Möglich* [First Bi-Annual Report by the Monopolies Commission], *Monopolkommission, Hauptgutachten* [I] *1974/1975* (Baden-Baden: Nomos Verlag, 1977); "The First Bi-Annual Report of the Monopolies Commission", English summary printed in 15 *German Economic Review* (1977), pp. 155-174; *Fortschreitende Konzentration bei Großunternehmen* [Second Bi-Annual Report by the Monopolies Commission], *Monopolkommission, Hauptgutachten* [II] *1976/1977* (Baden-Baden: Nomos Verlag, 1978; "West Germany: Monopolies Commission" [concerning the Second Report of the Commission], 13 *Journal of World Trade Law* (1979), pp. 448-462; *Fusionskontrolle bleibt Vorrängig* [Third Bi-Annual Report by the Monopolies Commission], Monopolkommission Hauptgutachten [III] 1978/1979 (Baden-Baden: Nomos Verlag, 1980).

96. For comment on the latest *Kartellnovelle* and the more recent trends in German merger control (*Fusionskontrolle*) in general, see e.g. ibid. (Bechtold); also Mestmäcker and Richter, eds., "Competition Policy: German and American Experience - A Symposium", *Zeitschrift für die gesamte Staatswissenschaft,* Heft 3 (1980), pp. 387-407; also Kaiser, "Fusionskontrolle oder Fusionsverbot?: Die Vermutungstatbestande des Entwurfs der IV. GWB-Novelle", *Wirtschaft und Wettbewerb* Jahrgang 28, Heft 6, 1978, at 344 *et seq.*; "Anhaltender Konzentrationstrend in Deutschland: Jahresbericht des Bundeskartellamtes", *Neue Zürcher Zeitung,* June 6, 1979 at 16; "Zur Diskussion um den Entwurf für ein neues Kartellgesetz: Aktive Kartellpolitik als Entwicklungsforderung" (Gerster), *Neue Zürcher Zeitung,* August 17, 1979, at 11; "Zur Diskussion um den Entwurf für ein neues Kartellgesetz: Das amerikanische Wettbewerbsrecht (Gurley), *Neue Zürcher Zeitung,* September 7, 1979, at 14; "Um die Fusionskontrolle wird weiter gepokert", *Frankfurter Allgemeine Zeitung,* December 3, 1979, at 13; "Börsenaufsichtsbehörde: Mitspracherecht bei Fusionen", *Frankfurter Allgemeine Zeitung,* December 12, 1979, at 12; "Kartellnovelle 'kein grosser Wurf': Einstimmige Verabschiedung im Wirtschaftsausschuss", *Frankfurter Allgemeine Zeitung,* January 25, 1980, at 11; "Fusionsstatistik sagt nicht alles", *Frankfurter Allgemeine Zeitung,* February 19, 1980, at 12.

criteria and facilitated the *Kartellamt*'s control over planned or anticipated combinations, but also introduced new sanctions for abuses and increased by tenfold the maximum amount of fines imposable for violations. It is Sections 23, 23a, 24 and 24a that deal directly with the regulation of mergers, "mergers" being defined to include a broad spectrum of corporate combinations (*Zusammenschlüsse*): merger, acquisition, consolidation and joint-venture activities, and "[a]ny other combination of enterprises as a result of which one or several enterprises are able directly or indirectly to exercise a controlling influence on another enterprise."[97] (It is interesting to note the significance of 'control' in the German definition of a 'merger'.)

In brief, Section 23 regards compulsory registration for certain mergers, Section 23a deals with presumptions of market dominance, Section 24 concerns the prohibition of certain types of mergers, and Section 24a sets out pre-merger notification requirements.

Significant among the features under the amended law is the fact that enterprises contemplating mergers will, by virtue of newly introduced paragraph 23a, face new obstacles in the form of statutory presumptions of market dominance (*Marktbeherrschungsvermutungen*).[98] Based upon criteria of individual (monopolistic) or combined (oligopolistic) market share percentages and determined annual sales-figure levels, it is *assumed, a priori,* that the proposed merger of companies meeting such criteria will secure or strengthen a dominant position simply on the strength of meeting these threshold criteria. There is a rebuttal clause, but the burden of proof rests totally upon the enterprises involved to show that substantial competition will remain unhampered following the merger or that an oligopoly (*Gesamtheit der Unternehmen*) will have, in relation to its usual competitors, no undue competitive advantage, or "paramount market position" (*überragende Marktstellung*). The word "undue" competitive advantage is important here. As regards the MNEs, for example, there is no question that their vast experience and know-how in areas of management, finance, research and production normally affords them an advantage over any competitors without the equivalent capacity. The key question is, at what point does competitive advantage become an 'undue' advantage?

In cases where the competitive advantage reaches the point of unfair competition, it is clearly unlawful, and not only German laws but other national and regional laws as well as international regulations exist for dealing with it.

97. GWB §23(2) (5), translation taken from Organisation for Economic Co-operation and Development, *Guide to Legislation on Restrictive Business Practices* (1977), D1.O at 14.

98. GWB §23a.

In U.S. law, for example, under Section 5 of the Federal Trade Commission Act, unfair methods of competition in commerce, and unfair or deceptive acts or practices in commerce, are declared unlawful. Unfair competition is also declared unlawful by the earlier Sherman Act of 1890[99] and other U.S. antitrust legislation. Regionally, the EEC has proscribed unfair competitive practices, under Articles 85 and 86 of the Rome Treaty,[100] and at least one legal practitioner[101] has even attempted to establish a link between unfair competition and dominant position under Article 86 of the Treaty, although admitting that not every act of unfair competition constitutes an abuse of a dominant position.[102] On the international level, the International Chamber of Commerce has recently created a new Commission on Ethical Practices, to deal with any instances of unethical conduct on the part of MNEs which do arise. The ICC has also pointed out[103] that irregular practices, where they exist, are in no way peculiar to MNEs – i.e. this challenge of undue competitive advantage is one presented by indigenous industries as well, which, through natural growth and graduation into mass production methods and possibilities of bulk purchase, pose their own threat to the smaller local producer.

Of particular interest in the German legislation is the fact that the mere expectation or 'anticipation' (*Erwartung*) that a merger will achieve or strengthen a market dominating position suffices to prohibit the combination (§24(1)). And that expectation must not even necessarily be immediately fulfilled; the *Bundeskartellamt* can prohibit amerger which has only a possible *eventual* effect on competition through market dominance where a market-dominating position is not an *ipso facto* result of the merger (§24(1)).[104]

At least one court, however, has interpreted the 'anticipation' (*Erwartung*) of a strengthening of market dominance to rely on immediacy of the strengthening as well as on direct causal relationship between the merger and the strengthening, that being the *Kammergericht* in the *GKN-Sachs* case.[105] Yet in the

99. Sherman Antitrust Act, 15 U.S.C. §§ 1 *et seq.* (amended 1937, 1955).

100. Treaty of Rome, loc. cit., *supra* note 36.

101. Vogelenzang, op. cit., *supra* note 64, at 76-77.

102. It should also be kept in mind that the law of unfair competition is not the same as that against restrictive business practices (antitrust); the law of unfair competition is aimed at protecting the competitors, while antitrust law is aimed at protecting competition itself (cf. *idem*).

103. See ICC Doc. No. 191/91: "Second Session of the U.N. Commission on Transnational Corporations", at 5.

104. See *Business International*, "Europe's Rules of Competition (1976)", at 130-131, as cited in Schnorr, op. cit., *supra* note 17, at 615.

105. See *infra* note 117 and accompanying text, and quote accompanying note 125.

Zementmahlanlage decision[106] the *Bundeskartellamt,* affirmed by the *Kammergericht,*[107] prohibited an already-concluded acquisition, even though the market share of the acquisitor dropped in each of two consecutive years following the merger, on the basis that Section 24(1) of the GWB speaks of *future* strengthening of a dominant position, and that therefore temporary fluctuations in an enterprise's market share would not counterbalance the anticipated long-range effect of an acquisition.

This illustrates not only the importance of interpretation, but the role played by the concept of *Erwartung*. Even in calculating the appropriate registration fee for foreign mergers affecting the German market, the *Bundeskartellamt* relies solely on the *anticipated* impact in Germany of such mergers.

It is of particular interest that the German 1980-amended GWB embodies the prohibition principle of the U.S. approach along with the regulatory (or control-of-abuse) principle of the EEC rule of reason. The German law still does not go as far as the U.S. law which conclusively proscribes even the conclusion of monopolies or any other form of restrictive arrangement; while the German GWB expressly prohibits certain types of concerted agreements - unless they come under the numerous exceptions allowed - the legislative technique of German enforcement differs significantly from the American. The German law technically allows such agreements to be entered into, but then holds them to be of no effect (*unwirksam*) where an anti-competitive influence is 'anticipated'.[108]

Of interest as well is the fact that already prior to the rebuttal clause introduced in 1980 by paragraph 23a(2), the *Bundeskartellamt's* special power to dissolve or prohibit any concluded or proposed combination that would create or strengthen a market dominating position (*marktbeherrschende Stellung*)[109] was stayed if it could be demonstrated by the firms in question that the combination would in fact have a beneficial effect on competition which would outweigh any disadvantages otherwise caused by the resultant market dominance:

> Ist zu erwarten, dass durch einen Zusammenschluss eine marktbe-

106. Decision of December 22, 1976, *Bundeskartellamt* [BKartA], [1977] *Wirtschaft und Wettbewerb Entscheidungsammlung* [WuW/E] 585, BKartA 1667.

107. Judgment of March 15, 1978, *Oberlandesgericht* [OLG] Berlin, [1978] WuW/E 205, OLG 1989.

108. See GWB § 1; also Grendell, "The Antitrust Legislation of the United States, the European Economic Community, Germany and Japan", 29 *International and Comparitive Law Quarterly* (1980), at 77.

109. See CCH *Common Market Reporter: Doing Business in Europe,* ¶ 23,510C [1980].

> herrschende Stellung entsteht oder verstärkt wird, so hat die Kartellbehörde die in den folgenden Bestimmungen genannten Befugnisse, es sei denn, die beteiligten Unternehmen weisen nach, dass durch den Zusammenschluss auch Verbesserungen der Wettbewerbsbedingungen eintreten und dass diese verbesserungen die Nachteile der Marktbeherrschung überwiegen.
>
> Liegen die voraussetzungen des Absatzes 1 vor, so untersagt das Bundeskartellamt den Zusammenschluss.... Ein vollzogener Zusammenschluss, den das Bundeskartellamt untersagt hat, ist aufzulösen, wenn nicht der Bundesminister für Wirtschaft die erlaubnis zu dem Zusammenschluss erteilt.[110]

In this particular provision of the Act, the contrast to the official EEC position is marked. This is particularly noteworthy in that the German law and its *travaux préparatoires* influenced in many of its aspects the drafting of both the EEC competition regulations and their subsequent administration.[111] By the literal terms of the Rome Treaty, as we have seen, for a combination to be prohibited or dissolved within the EEC, a dominant position must not only already be deemed (1) to exist, but additionally (2) to be abusive, or improperly exploited, and (3) to have the potential ability to affect trade between member states. In other words, while the prohibiting powers of the Rome Treaty's Article 86 presuppose a dominant position, its abuse, and the collective effect upon member states, and only where all three ingredients appear is there justification - strictly under the Treaty terms - for prohibiting or dissolving a combination, the West German provision can prohibit or dissolve a combination which merely is expected to create or strengthen the dominating position, irrespective of the presence or absence of indications of intended abuse of that position. The emphasis on the words "*literal terms* of the Rome Treaty" and "*strictly* under the Treaty terms", in speaking of the EEC position above, is not fortuitous, because the point is, as we have seen in the *Continental Can* case discussed earlier, it was held by the European Court of Justice that a merger *as such* can constitute an abuse if it but strengthens an already-existing market dominating position. There still remains the significant difference, however, that under the EEC rules - regardless of what is to be construed as an 'abuse' -

110. *Gesetz gegen Wettbewerbsbeschränkungen,* loc. cit., *supra* note 92, at 246, §§ 24 (1) & (2). For cases based on this concept, see *infra* notes 117-123 and accompanying text.

111. Mueller and Schneider, *Gesetz gegen Wettbewerbsbeschränkungen: Deutsch-Englische Textausgabe,* Frankfurt am Main, Fritz Knapp Verlag [c. 1973], "Introduction", at 5.

the dominant position must already exist in the relevant market, which is not the case under the German law which applies not only to the strengthening of a dominant position but also to its creation.

Hence, in both substantive provisions and statutory techniques, the German and the EEC regulations differ from one another, though the statutory techniques are similar to the extent that both Germany and the EEC employ a 'conduct' approach, in contrast to the 'structural approach' of the United States,[112] and that the German law, like the EEC rules, is also susceptible to interpretation. But while the Rome Treaty has a reasonably wide scope for interpretation, owing to its fairly broad general provisions, the German Act sets dow specific, detailed rules, even if primarily merely in the area of notification procedures and prohibitions and the elaboration of what constitutes a merger, market dominance, etc. German courts are correspondingly obliged to hold more strictly to the statutory language in applying the law which embodies an opposition to the very existence of the dominant position *per se,* whereas the European Court of Justice has been obliged to assume wider interpretative authority concerning the broad competition rules of the Treaty of Rome, resulting in the Treaty's provisions being interpreted in such a way that the strengthening of a dominant position was itself considered to be an abuse of that position, as evidenced in *Continental Can.* Nonetheless, while this represents a rather broad construction of 'abuse', the abuse - however interpreted -is still necessary in order to enforce an Article 86 prohibition; this is not true of the German law or interpretative practice.

While it would have appeared likely from what we have seen in the *Continental Can* judgment that the EEC position on mergers was approaching the German one, there has been little to substantiate this supposition in practice over the last decade, despite the fact that the subsequent "prior notice" regulation proposed by the EC Commission for increased regulation of concentrations would give further (legal) sanction and support to the position taken in *Continental Can*, and would appear to indicate an official position on the part of the EEC in the direction of increased control over the actual creation or strengthening of a dominant position through acquisition or merger, rather than waiting until an 'abuse' - strictly or broadly interpreted - occurs.

Continental Can, incidently, was also influential in an interpretation of Section 50 of the Australian Trade Practices Act of 1974-1977, in a significant acquisition/merger case, *Trade Practices Commission* v. *Ansett Transport Industries Pty. Ltd.* (the *Ansett* case),[113] regarding 'control' or 'dominance' of

112. See Grendell, op. cit., *supra* note 108, at 78.

113. *Trade Practices Commission* v. *Ansett Transport Industries Pty. Ltd.* (the *Ansett* case),

the 'relevant market', as discussed below.

Section 50 of the Australian Trade Practices Act picks up one step earlier even than the EEC or Germany in the acquisition-of-dominance (control) sequence; *viz.* while the EEC's Rome Treaty prohibits the *abuse* of a dominant position, and the West German *Bundeskartellamt* rules against mergers that *create* or *strengthen* a market-dominating position or are *expected* to create or strengthen such a position, Section 50 (1) of the Australian Trade Practices Act rules against acquisitions (or mergers) that would be *likely* to put the corporation *in a position* to control or dominate a market, but also, where that position is already deemed to exist, against acquisitions (or mergers) that would be *likely* to *strengthen substantially the power* to control or dominate, on the part of the corporation.

The *Ansett* case involved the proposed acquisition, in December 1977, of all capital shares of the Avis Rent-A-Car System Pty. Ltd. by Ansett Transport Industries (Operations) Pty. Ltd., a wholly owned subsidiary of Ansett Transport Industries Ltd. The acquisition was viewed as a merger of the 'conglomerate' or 'product-extension' type.[114] The Trade Practices Commission sought an injunction to prevent the acquisition of Avis by Ansett Operations, initiating proceedings in January 1978 under Section 80 of the Trade Practices Act. The issue was whether the merger would place Ansett, or "be likely to" place Ansett, "in a position to control or dominate" the relevant market, thus contravening Section 50 (1) (a) of the Trade Practices Act. The Court held to a strict interpretation of the provisions of the Act: "A corporation which, by the acquisition of shares in the capital of a body corporate, acquires a controlling interest in a body corporate which is in a position to control or dominate a market for services, thereby contravenes Section 50 (1) (a) of the Act...."[115] Hence the *Ansett* case is further evidence of the current trend to review a possible dominant position before it is created.

Although the instant case was decide under domestic law, and although the defendant was a home company, the *Ansett* case significantly reflects the influence in domestic law of precedents taken from the European Court of Justice, despite the latter being, further, a civil-law jurisdiction, the common-law-based Australian court having taken both *Continental Can* and *United Brands* into consideration in its decision.

Another significance of the *Ansett* case is that, while a domestic situation, it does involve a multinational enterprise, Avis; and, more importantly, it is the first court decision interpreting and enforcing Section 50 of the Australian

---

Federal Court, 13 June (1978) A.T.P.R. 17705.

114. See 52 *Australian Law Journal* (1978), Commercial Law Note, at 459. See also *infra* note 173.

115. Ibid., at 460.

Trade Practices Act, either in its 1977 wording or in its original 1974 formulation;[116] and there appears to be no reason why the precedent-setting interpretation accorded Section 50 on the national level will not in future be extended to similar cases involving mergers or acquisitions where the defendant is the foreign enterprise, rather than the domestic firm. While a continuity of interpretation of Section 50 ought to be reasonably predictable insofar as it is likely to continue to mean an in-depth review of any prospective concentration in all those aspects which relate to the capacity to attain or to promote a dominant position, with no obligation on the part of the Trade Practices Commission to wait to see if such a dominant position, once established, would be "abused", it will be interesting to see whether a correlative similarity will exist as regards the direction of the court's final judgment, which, in the instant case, found in favour of the defendant (the domestic firm), hence allowing the acquisition to proceed.

In this area of prejudging abuse of a dominant position, or, in practice, of tending to treat a dominant position *per se* as an abuse in its own right, a recent West German case furnishes us with an illustration of that country's evolving practice in this regard. The case in point is the widely publicized *GKN-Sachs* case[117] which was considered the test case for the German *Ressourcentheorie*[118] in merger control (the consideration of financial strength in determining market dominance), and is relevant to the present consideration in that it concerned an international merger which fell within the purview of Section 24(1) of the German cartel law (GWB).[119] In the *Sachs* decision the West German *Bundeskartellamt* prohibited the majority acquisition by "one of Britain's few important multinationals", Guest, Keen and Nettlefolds, Ltd. (GKN), of the German firm, Sachs AG, under the preventive merger-control provisions of

116. See *supra* note 114, at 458.

117. Case No. KVR 4/77 (KG), 21.2.78, *Neue Juristische Wochenschrift,* No. 27/78, at 1320; also as reported in *Bulletin of Legal Development,* 28 July 1978, No. 15, at 152. See also *Beschluss des Kammergerichts vom 1. Dezember 1976* - Kart. 51/76; WuW/E OLG 4/1977, at 1745 *et seq.* (Rauschenbach, in "Die Entwicklung des deutschen Kartellrechts 1977" [loc. cit., *supra* note 95], designates the *Sachs* case as the most important German antitrust case of 1977.) For a multidisciplinary analysis of related and overlapping business, economic, political and legal elements of the case, see Tillotson, "The *GNK-Sachs* Affair: A Case Study in Economic Law", 14 *Journal of World Trade Law,* (1980), at 39 *et seq.*

118. On the "Ressourcentheorie" in German antitrust law, see, *inter alia,* Rauschenbach, "Die Entwicklung des deutschen Kartellrechts in den Jahren 1975/1976", *Neue Juristische Wochenschrift,* Heft 48, 1 December 1976, at 2188; Kaiser, "Fusionskontrolle oder Fusionsverbot", op cit., *supra* note 96, at 353; "Ressourcenwürdung bei konglomeratem Zusammenschluss", WuW/E OLG 4/1977, at 1745 *et seq.*

119. Loc. cit., *supra* note 92.

Sections 24(1) and 24a(1) of the GWB, on grounds that Sachs' principle operating subsidiary, Fichtel and Sachs AG, held market dominance in its product line and that this dominant position would be strengthened through the projected combination of GKN and Sachs.

The *Bundeskartellamt* stood alone among the appropriate authorities in opposing the merger. The necessary consent had been obtained from the U.K. Office of Fair Trading, and in addition, the EC Commission's position, after an examination of the proposed combination in the light of Article 86 of the Rome Treaty, was that "on the basis of the facts known to the Commission, there [was] no case for it to oppose the proposed transaction."[120] The Commission similarly, in *Re The Merger of Guest, Keen and Nettlefolds Limited and Sachs AG,*[121] authorized the proposed GKN-Sachs combination under Article 66 of the European Coal and Steel Community Treaty in those areas falling within its sphere.

In its stance regarding the GKN-Sachs merger, the EEC showed no inconsistency with the *Continental Can* decision. The circumstances of the two cases, however, deviated considerably in certain key respects. In one respect, the GKN-Sachs merger situation was virtually the reverse of the position in *Continental Can*: in the latter, an enterprise with alleged dominance in West Germany acquired an enterprise within the Common Market which also was allegedly dominant (though the Commission's case failed owing to the inadequacy of proof of substantial market-distorting dominance), while in the former (*Sachs*), an enterprise with a dominant position in the West German market was agreeing to acquisition by an enterprise within the Common Market but *without* a dominant position, either in its primary market, the United Kingdom, or in West Germany.[122] Article 86 is strictly applicable only to mergers in which the *acquiring* company has a market-dominating position.[123]

Whatever the reasoning employed, there was no question as to the sanctioning of the merger by the EC Commission. Even prior to the Commission's approval, however, the *Bundeskartellamt* made its prohibitory ruling, stating, moreover, that its decision would not be affected by any forthcoming Commission finding regarding the applicability of ECSC Treaty Article 66 or EEC Treaty Article 86.

120. See [1977] *Common Market Law Reports,* D18, note 14; also *Bulletin of the European Communities* 7/8 (1976), at 31. See also European Commission, *6th Report on Competition Policy* (1977), at 64.

121. *Re The Merger of Guest, Keen and Nettlefolds Limited and Sachs AG* [1977] 1 *Common Market Law Reports,* D19.

122. See Tillotson, op. cit., *supra* note 117, at 51.

123. See e.g. *Trade and Industry*, 1 November 1973 (Annex H) (Markert).

Upon request from both the domestic and foreign firms, the Court of Appeals in Berlin (*Kammergericht*) reversed the prohibition decision, maintaining that a strengthening of the market-dominating position was not to be anticipated. The *Kammergericht* ruled that a merger between two companies may fall within Section 24 (generally, duty to give prior-notice to the authorities) even when such merger involves only one market-dominant enterprise, but it made an additional ruling that where market dominance is assumed under Section 22, the enterprise in question may appeal on evidence that competition will not essentially be affected or that, in relation to its competitors, it does not hold a paramount position.[124] This ruling was based on the earlier-mentioned feature of the 1973 amended German law, contained in Section 24(1), whereby if the parties can successfully demonstrate that the merger would improve competitive conditions sufficiently to outweigh any detrimental effects to the competitive structure of the relevant (domestic) market, the merger will be allowed to proceed.

Hence, while the *Kammergericht* affirmed the actual market dominance of the firm in question, it denied the 'anticipation' (*Erwartung*) of a strengthening of that position according to Section 24(1). It was held that to come under condemnation of Section 24(1), there must be concrete conditions that would result in all probability in an immediate strengthening of the dominating position; and that there must be a causal relationship between the combination and the strengthening of the market position:

> 'Die Prognose' (die Verstärkungserwartung) 'kann nicht abstrakt nach rein theoretischen Möglichkeiten angestellt werden. Insbesondere kann diese Eingriffsvoraussetzung nicht mit den Ergebnissen von Theorien, die keineswegs mathematisch starre Ergebnisse beinhalten und sich mit den wirtschaftlichen Verhältnissen ändern, automatisch als erfüllt angesehen werden. Die Anwendung des GWB ist fallbezogen. Für das Merkmal 'Erwartung' bedeutet das, dass sich abstrakte Möglichkeiten aufgrund bestimmter Umstände zu einem gesteigerten Grad von Wahrscheinlichkeit für einen zu erwartenden Erfolg verdichten müssen.'[125]

Here again, the operative issue was not the 'abuse' of a dominant position, but rather its strengthening alone; and the judgment was based solely on an interpretation of the *Erwartung* of a strengthened market dominance through the proposed merger.

124. See also *supra* note 110 and accompanying text.

125. Rauschenbach, "Die Entwicklung des deutschen Kartellrechts 1977", op.cit., *supra* note 95, at 187.

Here again also is evidence of the practical importance of interpretation of the German law, since, as mentioned earlier, there was no stipulation in the law that the 'anticipation' of a strengthening of market dominance needed to be immediate or in a causal relation to the merger itself.

In the *Kammergericht's* finding that such a strengthening of market dominance was not perforce to be anticipated in the relevant market, and the Court's consequent reversal of the *Bundeskartellamt*'s prohibition decision, there is a striking parallel with the EEC *Continental Can* decision handed down by the European Court of Justice in Luxembourg,[126] where recourse to appeal, upon invitation of the EC Commission, resulted in a reversal of the Commission's decision, in favour of the Continental Can Company, based on similar reasoning[127] (though the 'trade off' feature of the German law appears nowhere in EEC law other than in the proposed EEC regulation on concentrations).

The *GKN-Sachs* case does not end here, however. On further appeal, this time by the *Bundeskartellamt*, the *Bundesgerichtshof* overruled the lower appeal court's ruling, reinstating the original decision of the *Bundeskartellamt*. The *Bundesgerichtshof,* in affirming the original ruling and reversing that of the *Kammergericht,* relied on the 'expectation' or 'anticipation' (*Erwartung*) provision used by the *Kammergericht,* but came to the opposite conclusion, *viz.* that the merger *was* expected to strengthen Sachs' dominant position, and that the 'trade-off' exemption provided for in Section 24(1) was not applicable, Sachs having failed to adequately demonstrate that the merger would improve competitive conditions sufficient to "outweigh the detrimental effects of market domination." The *Bundesgerichtshof* relied also, *inter alia,* on the 1973 amendment of Section 22(1), under which the relative reduction of competition no longer depends on actual conduct in the market, but simply on alteration of market structure.

The German law still left a way open for an application to the West German Economics Minister (*Bundeswirtschaftsminister*) against the highest Appeal Court's decision, on the grounds that the proposed combination was in the German national and economic interest. Unlike the *Bundeskartellamt*, which is authorized to base its prohibitions only on considerations of domestic factors and internal competition policy, the *Bundeswirtschaftsminister,* in his capacity to override a prohibition order of the *Kartellamt* on appeal from the participating enterprises, is empowered to take into consideration the wider aspect of

126. See 11 *International Legal Materials* (1972), at 316. (English translation reproduced from CCH *Common Market Reporter,* Supplement No. 178 (January 18, 1972)).

127. See *supra* note 56 and accompanying text; also text following note 111.

Germany's competitiveness on foreign and international markets and its trading and investment position *vis-à-vis* other nations.[128] GKN, however, decided to forego this final option and instead sold its 25 per cent holding in Sachs AG to a German bank.

It appears clear from the *Kammergericht* ruling and from the possibility of recourse to the *Bundeswirtschaftsministerium* option that, in German practice, merger control and market dominance are interdependent, but that the distinction is maintained between the two, so that a dominant position *per se* does not perforce preclude an international (or other) acquisition.

It should be pointed out that the ruling of the *Bundesgerichtshof* in *GKN-Sachs* was more representative of the current German trend than the intermediate ruling of the *Kammergericht.* Even the 'trade-off' feature introduced by Article 24(1) of the 1973 Amendment Act,[129] or ultimate recourse to the *Bundeswirtschaftsministerum,* did not signify a trend towards a less rigid approach in the review of such combinations in West Germany at that time. In fact, there was evidence of discontent over the apparent ineffectiveness of the merger controls (*Fusionskontrolle*) - even as ostensibly strengthened by the 1973 Amendment Act - in the face of ever-increasing corporate concentration, as expressed, for example, in the West German *Handelsblatt* of March 13, 1979, reporting on the then-current Hearings regarding the merger control measures anticipated in the fourth *Kartellnovelle* which has since been made law by the 1980 Amendment Act:[130]

> Die Arbeitsgemeinschaft Selbständig Unternehmer (ASU) vertritt in ihrer Stellungnahme zum Hearing der 4. Kartellnovelle die Meinung, dass die Konzentrationsentwicklung in der Bundesrepublic 'nahezu ungebremst' sei.[131]

and in the *Frankfurter Allgemeine Zeitung* of the same date:

> Die Anhörung hat deutlich gemacht, dass die Wissenschaftler eine zum

128. This international-competition criterion for a public-good exemption based on the wider international-market considerations resembles the EEC and Japanese export exemptions which were similarly designed to promote their respective positions on the world market. (See Grendell, op. cit., *supra* note 108, at 79.)

129. Loc. cit., *supra* note 92.

130. *Drittes Gesetz zur Änderung des Gesetzes gegen Wettbewerbsbeschränkungen,* loc. cit., *supra* note 92.

131. "Kartell-Hearing: ASU: Fusionskontrolle noch immer lückenhaft", *Handelsblatt,* March 3, 1979, at 3.

> Teil weit über den Gesetzentwurf der Bundesregierung hinausreichende Verschärfung der Fusionskontrolle für erforderlich halten.[132]

It is little wonder, then, that, subsequent to *GKN-Sachs,* even more stringent legal measures were signed into law for the control of mergers and monopolies in West Germany. The effective enforcement of these merger controls has been demonstrated both by statistics[133] and by court decisions, though the application of the statutory presumptions of the GWB by German courts has not always been without criticism,[134] nor have some of the attempts at extraterritorial application of the German GWB been well received abroad.

A recent example of the latter situation is the *Firestone-Bayer* 'merger' case,[135] involving a combination of two French subsidiaries of American and German parents, respectively. Firestone France is a French-incorporated nearly wholly owned subsidiary of Firestone Tire and Rubber Company (Firestone U.S.A.); Bayer France, while incorporated under French law, is nearly 100 per cent owned by Bayer Foreign Investments Limited (Bayer Canada), a holding-company which in turn is nearly 100 per cent owned by Bayer AG, a German multinational enterprise. An Agreement comprising three contracts and involving all five firms was concluded on 17 June 1980 for the acquisition by Bayer France of the Synthetic Rubber and Latex Division of Firestone France. The related contracts concerned production, distribution, etc., for example, under Firestone U.S.A.'s production patent license, Bayer France was to supply a minimum of 80 per cent of the needs of Firestone U.S.A.'s European subsidiaries.

According to the provisions of the German GWB, all five concerns reported the agreement to the *Bundeskartellamt* which proceeded to prohibit the proposed merger/acquisition. Without going into further details of the ensuing proceedings other than to say that the prohibition order was reversed by the *Kammergericht* on appeal, it is interesting to note that France relied on her new *loi n°80-538 du 16 juillet 1980*[136] which proscribes the intervention from abroad in the nation's internal economic affairs as well as prohibiting, as we

132. "Monopolkommission will unabhängig bleiben: Gegen Beschwerderecht/Professoren: Fusionsverbote für 'Grosse'", *Frankfurter Allgemeine Zeitung,* at 11.

133. See Schnorr, op. cit., *supra* note 17, at 623.

134. See "Zum Verhältnis der Monopol- und der Oligopolvermutung in §22 Abs.3 GWB: Kritische Anmerkungen zur Entscheidung des Kammergerichts in der Sache 'Blei- und Silberhütte Braubach' vom 16.1.1980", 3 *Betriebs-Berater* (1981), pp. 149-153.

135. Decision of the *Kammergericht* (Berlin) of 26 November 1980 (Kart. 17/80; 18/80).

136. *Loi n° 80-538 du 16 juillet 1980, [1980] Journal Officiel* [J.O.], 1799.

have seen in the preceding chapter, the release of documents or other information pertaining to economic - business, industrial, financial - or technical activities which could be detrimental to France's sovereignty, security or national interests.

The grounds for the *Kammergericht's* overruling of the *Kartellamt's* prohibition order were: a) gross lack of material evidence and b) the consideration that the greatest portion of the merged activities was situated outside of Germany, while within Germany only an insignificant restriction of competition through the strengthening of a market-dominating position would result. Moreover, the French authorities themselves had approved the merger - even welcomed it for the benefits it seemed likely to secure for France; and the court found no meaningful or genuine link as understood under generally accepted rules of international law, nor did it view such a prohibition as compatible with the non-intervention principle in international law.

Hence it was ruled by the *Kammergericht* that the prohibition of a merger, through the acquisition of assets, directly affecting only foreign parties and having only a marginal effect on the local market, constitutes a violation of the general principles of international law and customary international law which, according to Article 25, Section 2 of the German *Grundgesetz* (Basic Law) are a part of German municipal law and, while not having priority over its constitutional law, do prevail over such laws as the GWB.

Firestone-Bayer is the first *Kartellamt* case in which a 'merger' prohibition order was considered in the light of its compatibility with international law.

Worth mentioning briefly in this context are two other cases in which the German *Bundeskartellamt* investigated the effects within Germany of mergers consummated outside its territory between enterprises which had subsidiaries within the German market. One of these was the merger of two American companies, Colgate Palmolive and Helena Rubenstein, each of which had German subsidiaries but which, in this case, were ultimately deemed not to affect a relevant German market.[137] The other investigation involved the merger of two Dutch firms, also with subsidiaries in Germany but which on the other hand were deemed to be strong competitors in the relevant market and were thus temporarily restrained by an order of the *Bundeskartellamt* from concluding the merger.[138] In these cases, the merger of the parent companies was considered to constitute a merger of the subsidiaries, as per Section 23(3) of the GWB,

137. See Markert, "Recent Developments in German Antitrust Law", 43 *Fordham Law Review* (1975), at 715.

138. Decision of May 3, 1978 *(Kartoffelstärke), Bundeskartellamt,* [1978] WuW/E 598 BKartA 1716.

which is reminiscent of the *CIBA-Geigy* case[139] mentioned earlier.

While none of these attempts resulted in definitively preventing the mergers in question, they have obvious serious implications for foreign MNEs, which could find themselves thus subject to extraterritorial merger controls under the German GWB, with the possible prohibition or dissolution which that implies. MNEs are specifically included in Sections 17 and 18 of the *Aktiengesetz* (German Companies Act)[140] under the denominations *abhängige und herrschende Unternehmen* (controlled and controlling enterprises) and *Konzern und Konzernunterhehmen* (combine and affiliated enterprises), and are referred to in Section 23(1) of the GWB which stipulates that if one party to a merger is a member of such a corporate combine, whether in a controlling or in a controlled capacity, then *each* member of the combine or affiliated enterprise is considered a participant in the merger. This clearly brings both the parent and the affiliated members of a multinational corporate group even more comprehensively within the express extraterritorial reach of the German competition laws. It should be mentioned, however, that while members of a foreign merger affecting competition within the German market are susceptible to administrative and quasi-criminal proceedings in German courts, the resulting sanctions cannot be enforced in Germany.[141] This did not, on the other hand, prevent the *Bundeskartellamt* from imposing substantial filing fees on mergers which were entirely foreign and had only a minimal effect on the German market,[142] or from requiring registration of a foreign (U.S.) parent under GWB Section 23(1) when its wholly owned subsidiary planned to acquire essentially all the assets of an unrelated (U.S.) company, on the grounds that, although the parent of the acquiring firm as well as the acquired firm were both totally foreign, they were competitors in the same German market.[143]

It is interesting to note that the Germans sometimes face acquisition obstruction in their own attempts at international acquisitions. It was made public in April 1979, for instance, that, for the second time in less than a year, proposed acquisitions of Allegheny-Ludlum Chemetron pigments division by West German firms were curtailed. In the same period, Bayer's Rhinechem unit was precluded from acquiring Chemetron's pigments division; subsequently

139. See *supra* note 46 and accompanying text.

140. *Aktiengesetz* of 6 September 1965 BGBl 1965 I S.at 1089. in the version of 1 July 1976.

141. See CCH *Common Market Reporter: Doing Business in Europe* ¶ 23,521. (1980).

142. See e.g. the judgment *(Computer)* of the *Kammergericht* (Berlin) of June 3, 1977, *Kammergericht* [1978] WuW/E 501, OLG 1951; see also Schnorr, op. cit., *supra* note 17, at 612.

143. See the judgment of the *Kammergericht* (Berlin) of April 5, 1978 *(organische Pigmente), Kammergericht* [1978] WuW/E 709, OLG 1993; see also Schnorr, op. cit., *supra* note 17, note 8 at 596.

BASF-Wyandotte's bid for the division was challenged by U.S. government officials. The Federal Trade Commission claimed that the acquisition would make BASF the third largest seller of organic pigments in the United States, thus obstructing competition and tending to create a monopoly. A spokesman at BASF's U.S. headquarters insisted, however, that the German firm would continue to defend its projected acquisition,[144] and, in 1980, it succeeded.

It is significant that Germany, which exercises the least control over incoming foreign direct investment of perhaps any West European nation, has the strictest merger and monopoly controls. A similar observation could be made as regards the United States. In both cases, the controls are correspondingly not aimed against foreign enterprises, but rather at preserving competition, whether the competition be threatened from foreign or from domestic sources. Another similarity between American and German practice resides in the fact that both the U.S. and Germany have criminal and civil penalties for corporate and/or individual violations for their antitrust laws, in contrast to the EEC which has a civil penalty only against the corporation.[145]

The similarity of the German and the American antitrust policies, in fact, led to the signing of an Executive Agreement between the two governments,[146] which took effect on September 11, 1976, for mutual co-operation in this area and in restrictive business practices in general, primarily as regards exchange of information for facilitating enforcement.

In Britain, as typical of the European states, there in no statutory provision that monopolies *per se* are contrary to public policy or that a practice restrictting competition is automatically contrary to the public interest.[147] Legislation on the subject, however is not lacking. In addition to the 1973-enacted combines control legislation, the Fair Trading Act 1973,[148] which repealed and replaced the Monopolies and Restrictive Practices (Inquiry and Control) Act 1948[149] and the Monopolies and Mergers Act 1965[150] in respect to monopolies

144. See "U.S. Challenges BASF's Purchase", *International Herald Tribune,* April 19, 1979, at 7.

145. See Grendell, op. cit., *supra* note 108, at 67.

146. *Agreement between the Government of the United States of America and the Government of the Federal Republic of Germany Relating to Mutual Cooperation Regarding Restrictive Business Practices,* October 23, 1976, BGBl 1976 II S.1711; CCH *Common Market Reporter: Doing Business in Europe* ¶ 23,529 [1976]; 27 U.S.T. 1956, T.I.A.S. No. 8291; 5 CCH *Trade Regulation Reports,* ¶ 50,283.

147. CCH *Common Market Reporter: Doing Business in Europe,* ¶ 40,059 [New Developments, 1980].

148. Fair Trading Act 1973 c. 41.

149. Monopolies and Restrictive Practices (Inquiry and Control) Act 1948, 11 & 12 Geo. 6, c. 66.

150. Monopolies and Mergers Act 1965 c. 50 (See Fair Trading Act 1973 c. 41, Schedule 13.)

and mergers, and which amended the Restrictive Trade Practices Act 1956 and 1968,[151] a further controls legislation, the Competition Act 1980,[152] came into force on 4 April 1980.

While the 'merger' process' in the United Kingdom is still a matter of some political debate, and while the prohibitions are still not as rigorous as those of a number of other nation-states, notably the United States, Germany and Australia, and despite the 1980 Competition Act - which further broadens the investigatory powers of the U.K. Office of Fair Trading in the area of anti-competitive practices[153] but which has been widely criticized for, *inter alia,* its "irrelevance" in a time of widespread recession and its lack of definition of the concept of 'anti-competitive practice'[154] - the Fair Trading Act 1973 remains "the most comprehensive and most complex of all competition legislation enacted in Britain"[155] and hence merits closer attention.

The 1973 Act reiterated, with some modifications, many of the provisions of the Monopolies and Mergers Act 1965, but distinguished between the political natures of monopolies (now regarded as 'non-political') and mergers (still regarded as containing some 'political' elements),[156] and renamed the Monopolies Commission as the Monopolies and Mergers Commission.[157] Among other capacities of the Commission, one of its primary functions is "to report on any question that may be referred to it with respect to...the (possible) creation of a merger situation qualifying for investigation."[158] Here the notion of prior-notice is clearly discernable, as it is in Section 64(1) of the Act:

> A merger reference may be made to the Commission by the Secretary of State where it appears to him that it is a fact (or may be the fact) that two or more enterprises (the 'relevant enterprises') - of which one is carried on in the United Kingdom or by or under the control of a body corporate incorporated in the United Kingdom - have ceased to be distinct enterprises and that either (a) as a result, a specified market share has been

151. The Restrictive Trade Practice Act 1956 c. 68. The Restrictive Trade Practices Act 1968 c. 66. (See Fair Trading Act 1973 c. 41, Schedule 12.)

152. Competition Act 1980 c. 21.

153. See CCH *Common Market Reporter: Doing Business in Europe* ¶ 40,076 [New Developments, 1980]; see also Chapter VIII *supra* note 37 and accompanying text.

154. See *Idem* (CCH *Common Market Reporter: Doing Business in Europe*)

155. Ibid. [1975], ¶ 24,007; see also ¶ 24,011 [1975] and ¶ 31,045 [New Developments, 1978].

156. See ibid., ¶ 24,007. [1975].

157. *Idem.*

158. Ibid., ¶ 24,007A.

achieved or (b) the value of the assets taken over exceeds £5 million.[159]

Of interest in addition to this prior-notice feature is that Section 65 of the Act takes express cognizance of the concept of "control":

> For the purposes of that part of the Act relating to mergers generally, any two enterprises will be regarded as ceasing to be distinct enterprises if either (a) they are brought under common ownership or "common control" (whether or not the business to which either of them formerly belonged continues to be carried on under the same or different ownership or control) or (b) either of the enterprises ceases to be carried on at all and does so in consequence of any arrangements or transactions entered into to prevent competition between the enterprises. [Footnotes omitted][160]

"Common control" is identified in Section 65(2)(c) of the Act as referring to enterprises which are either:

> (a) enterprises of interconnected bodies corporate, or (b) enterprises carried on by two or more bodies corporate of which one and the same person or group of persons has control, or (c) an enterprise carried on by a body corporate and an enterprise carried on by a person or group of persons having control of that body corporate.[161]

Notwithstanding the stringent and comprehensive nature of the Fair Trading Act, several more subsequent developments indicate the trend to tighten even further the U.K. merger controls, one being a legal measure and two being non-legal guidelines. The legal measure is the Protection of Trading Interests Act 1980 which has as its object to limit the amount of information provided to foreign (U.S.) antitrust investigators and of preventing foreign (U.S.) judgments from being enforced in Britain.[162] This effort to shield British companies from U.S. court subpoenas and judgments is, as noted in the preceding

159. Fair Trading Act 1973 c. 41, sect. 64(1).

160. Ibid., §§ 65(1), (2) (c).

161. Ibid. § 65 (2) (c).

162. Protection of Trading Interests Act 1980 c.11, [1980] Statutes Annotated 2, at 11. See also "Stand on U.S. trust laws", *The Daily Telegraph* (London), October 5, 1979, at 21; "Antitrust: New Imperialism", *International Herald Tribune,* November 6, 1979, at 4; "The Protection of Trading Interests Bill", *Law Society Gazette,* December 5, 1979.

chapter,[163] in openly declared retaliation against U.S. antitrust decisions which have had direct effects on British companies.

The first of the non-legal measures is the City Code on Takeovers and Mergers.[164] The Code, now in its fourth edition, was issued by the City Working Party, a body originally established by the Governor of the Bank of England in 1959, and "represents the collective opinion of those professionally concerned in such matters on a range of business standards."[165] The Code, while playing "a vital role in U.K. competition and antitrust matters", neither has nor seeks to have the force of law.[166] The other non-legal guideline was a Labour-government Green Paper[167] which recommended a slightly tightened U.K. policy on corporate mergers, stressing that competition was the primary goal of such a policy, and which advocated setting up machinery for a more frequent investigation of such combinations. The Paper also noted that, due to the greater degree of concentration of industry in Britain than in other EEC member states, it is conceivable that the EC Commission could act to prohibit combinations that would be permissible under present and proposed British law. Hence it is clear that, when agreement is reached among EEC member states as to the Commission's functional role concerning Community merger control policy, certain aspects of U.K. merger legislation will - at least if preliminary proposals are implemented - need to undergo amendment.[168]

Even Japan, in spite of its traditional and cultural incompatibility with a strong antitrust position, notwithstanding its post-war adoption of a law[169] codifying the major American antitrust acts and court decisions up to that date - a law which is repeatedly revised[170] to allow mergers and other forms of concerted conduct and to introduce numerous exceptions - is beginning to show signs of a shift in that quarter, with stronger enforcement of the existing legislation and stepped-up antitrust activity through its Fair Trade Commis-

163. See *supra* Chapter VIII, text accompanying note 91.

164. The City Code on Takeovers and Mergers, as revised. Issuing Houses Association, London, April 1976.

165. CCH *Common Market Reporter: Doing Business in Europe,* para. 24,015 [1976].

166. *Idem.*

167. "A Review of Monopolies and Mergers Policy: A Consultative Document," Cmnd. 7198, HMSO London, May 1978. (In Britain, a Green Paper is a consultative document, offered as grounds for discussion before the introduction of a White Paper, which is a finalized statement of government, or proposed legislation. See ibid., para. 31,045 [New Developments, 1978].

168. See ibid., (CCH Comm. Mkt. Rep.: *Doing Business in Europe*), ¶ 31,045 [New Developments, 1978] and ¶ 24,018 [1976].

169. Law No. 54, April 14, 1947.

170. See e.g. Law No. 214, June 1949; Law No. 259, September 1953; see also Ariga and Rieke, "The Antimonopoly Law of Japan and its Enforcement", 39 *Washington Law Review* (1964), at 445.

sion,[171] the agency created by the Anti-monopol Law to enforce its provisions. This heightened interest in antitrust enforcement was already in evidence in 1971, according to a lecture delivered at the Symposium on International Business of that year,[172] in which it was reported that "[t]here are ... indications that the Japanese Anti-monopoly Law, which is based largely on the American antitrust laws and which has not been applied particularly strenuously in the past, may be applied with increasing vigor to increase its effectiveness as a device for controlling the activities of foreign investors in Japan."[173]

The fundamental motivation of Japan's policy, and the reason for its many exemptions, is to promote expansion of selected domestic industries in order to make them more competitive internationally and, as just seen, to control incoming foreign investment, while controlling abuses within their own domestic free market. The EEC and Germany share this regulatory method with Japan, giving them an advantage over the U.S. enterprise, which has no access to an international-competitive-advantage exemption. The Japanese Law - originally probably the most stringent antitrust statute ever enacted, based as it was on a conglomeration of U.S. models - while still, like the U.S. laws, prohibitive rather than regulative in form, has come, through its many amendments, to rest on a balance of the primary concepts of 'substantial restraint' and 'public interest'.[174] Hence, when a "substantial restraint of competition" has been established, the conduct is technically deemed to be illegal *per se*, but due to the necessity to show that the conduct is also "contrary to the public interest", the rule of reason comes into play. Thus in practice, the approach is basically the same as that of the control-of-abuse technique of the EEC and Germany.[175]

The United States itself, already the most active enforcer of antitrust of any nation, in 1976 enacted the Hart-Scott-Rodino Antitrust Improvements Act,[176]

171. See von Mehren and Gold, "Multinational Corporations: Conflicts and Controls", 11 *Stanford Journal of International Studies* (1976), at 24.

172. Symposium on International Business in 1971 - Problems and Solutions of Private Investors Abroad, conducted by the International and Comparative Law Center of the Southwestern Legal Foundation in Dallas, Texas, June 16-18, 1971.

173. Calhoun and Brumder, "Japanese Laws Relating to Foreign Investment in Japan", in *Private Investors Abroad - Problems and Solutions in International Business in 1971* (New York: Matthew Bender, 1971), at 24-25.

174. Antimonopoly Law No. 54 of April 14, 1947, Art. 2(5), (6).

175. See Grendell, op. cit., *supra* note 108, at 67, 82-83, 86.

176. Hart-Scott-Rodino Antitrust Improvements Act of 1976, Pub. L. No. 94-435, 90 Stat. 1390.

with its premerger notification rules;[177] and it shows signs of tightening up even more on certain types of mergers heretofore largely exempt from controls, if the Anti-Conglomerate Mergers Bill[178] is any indication. This legislation, if passed, would bring the more loosely controlled conglomerate-type mergers more into line with the strictly controlled horizontal and vertical mergers,[179] thus making them more vulnerable to legal challenge.[180]

None of this legislation represents, however, a deviation from the United States' cornerstone policy of applying impartially its antitrust laws without preference between domestic and foreign firms.[181] Of course the test of such policies is not their expression in principle but their application in practice. One indication of the principle's application can be seen in the fact that over a ten-year period (1967-1977) only one large merger out of every 100 between American and foreign firms was challenged under the U.S. antitrust laws, which was the same percentage as that applying to equivalent mergers generally in the United States.[182]

The same policy is observable as regards foreign acquisitions.[183] In fact, the U.S. antitrust laws actually tend to favour foreign investors since:

> Typically, an acquiring European firm is not a competitor (or a supplier or customer) of the acquired U.S. firm. Hence, a Euro-acquisition is less likely than an acquisition by an American firm to cause the prohibited impairment competition. Thus, U.S. petro-giant Atlantic-Richfield could not, but British Petroleum could, acquire Sinclair Oil's assets. Likewise, West Germany's Tengelmann Group evidently can, but Safeway clearly could not, buy America's Great A&P Tea Company.* And

177. See *Premerger Notification Compliance Guide: An explanation of the application and operation of the premerger notification rules implementing the Hart-Scott-Rodino Antitrust Improvements Act of 1976,* prepared by the Premerger Notification Office of the Federal Trade Commission's Bureau of Competition, September 18, 1978.

178. U.S. Bill S-600, "Small and Independent Business Protection Act of 1979", still pending at the time of writing.

179. Horizontal mergers are mergers between firms dealing in the same products in the same markets; vertical mergers are mergers between firms which supply goods or services or parts in the same production line in the same market; conglomerate mergers are mergers between companies with different product lines, either indirectly related or totally non-related, in either the same or in different markets.

180. See "Wall Street's rush to beat the new merger rules", *The Economist,* March 17, 1979, at 113.

181. See Davidow, op. cit., *supra* note 31, at 603.

182. Ibid., at 607.

183. See Rowe, op. cit., *supra* note 74, at 4.

* According to a top Antitrust Division enforcement official, "Justice Dept. merger

West Germany's Henkel can control Clorox, which Proctor & Gamble lost under an antitrust decision by the U.S. Supreme Court.[184]

Former Chairman of the Section of Antitrust Law of the American Bar Association, Frederick M. Rowe, sees the rising tide of Euro-investment in the United States as a sharp reversal of the "American challenge" of the 1960's, and the current *Drang nach Westen* as a possible "rediscovery of America by European enterprises...of historic dimensions."[185]

In French law, the U.S. type of "statutory merger", or direct legal amalgamation between companies of different nationalities, is virtually unknown. A foreign MNE cannot, therefore, plan to directly absorb a French company in this manner,[186] though nothing prevents it from indirectly acquiring the domestic French company through a French subsidiary. This is not due to prohibitive antitrust controls on the part of the French, however; French legislation relating to competition has historically shown greater concern for price controls than for the prevention of monopolies or corporate concentrations *per se,*[187] the latter, in fact, even being encouraged among national firms in order to better meet the competition in world markets.[188]

Even though in 1977, under the influence of membership in the EEC, the French Government enacted a new law[189] with prior notification requirements to control economic concentrations and suppress abuses of dominant positions,[190] the legislation concerns only concentrations in French territory and

---

enforcement has often promoted opportunities for foreign corporations to acquire American commercial firms and thus enter the U.S. market. In general, we have welcomed and encouraged such entries because it did not involve the elimination of direct competition as a sale to a domestic competitor would." Joel Davidow, Antitrust, International Mergers and International Joint Ventures, in Proceedings of the First Annual Fordham Corporate Law Institute - International Antitrust (1975). [Note from original text.]

184. Rowe, op. cit., *supra* note 74, at 3. (Frederick Rowe is former Chairman of the Section of Antitrust Law, American Bar Association.) See *FTC* v. *Proctor & Gamble,* 386 U.S. 568 (1967). See also Tillotson, op. cit., *supra* note 117, at 61-67.

185. Rowe, op cit., *supra* note 74, at 1. See also CCH *Common Market Reporter: Doing Business in Europe* ¶ 40,033 [New Developments, 1980].

186. Leleux, "France, Belgium, European Economic Community and the Multinational Enterprise", in Hahlo, op. cit., *supra* note 38, at 107.

187. CCH *Common Market Reporter: Doing Business in Europe,* ¶ 23,001 [1979] also ¶ 30,967 [New Developments, 1978].

188. See e.g. ibid., ¶ 22,615 [1981] and ¶¶ 30,879 and 30,967 [New Developments, 1978].

189. *Loi n° 77-806 de 19 juillet 1977,* [1977] J.O. 2833.

190. See also CCH *Common Market Reporter: Doing Business in Europe,* ¶ 23,016 [1979].

will have consequently no effect on combinations with foreign multinationals.[191] Moreover, the 1977 law does not signify a change in French merger policy, in that corporate combinations and concentrations are neither prohibited nor discouraged; they are in fact still thought to be beneficial, in many cases, for France's competitive position in international trade and investment. The French law, like the German and EEC rules, is regulatory rather than prohibitory, and provides for penalties in cases of unlawful agreements impairing competition and of abuse of dominant positions. While its strict territorial application means that only those foreign subsidiaries will be affected which by virtue of their incorporation in France fall under the law, it is significant that it applies not only to individual enterprises but also to groups of enterprises and that the definition of a 'concentration' revolves around the power to "exercise, directly or indirectly... any influence so as to control or even affect the management or operation" of these one or several enterprises.[192] Here once again we are reminded of the importance of the control and management factor.

Of particular interest among the types of injunctive action imposable by the French Minister of Economy and Finance is the not unusual practice of subjecting an enterprise proposing - or already constituting - a concentration to conditions that it is thought will promote sufficient economic and social benefit to compensate for any impairments of competition.[193] This 'bargaining' practice is being increasingly resorted to in Germany as well.

There has been some dissatisfaction expressed by certain elements in the *Assemblée Nationale* that the 1977 French rules are too limited, due to their inapplicability to non-resident MNEs and to certain types of mergers. If this dissatisfaction spreads, possible expansion of the rules to apply more broadly to MNEs can be expected in the future.

If one takes into account both legislative and case-law practice as regards antitrust controls (and it is possible, in case law, to single out actions specifically involving MNEs), it would appear that everywhere in the industrialized world, to a greater or lesser degree, depending on historical, cultural, political, economic, legal and other traditions, the direction is becoming oriented toward stricter control over combinations in general, and away from the notion of actual *abuse* of a dominant position to one of mere *creation,* or *existence* or *enhancement* of such a position, if not, as in the amended German law, simply the *anticipation* of the creation or strengthening of market dominance or, as in the Australian legislation, the mere *likelihood of the capability* of dominating a market.

191. Ibid., ¶ 30,967 [New Developments, 1977].
192. Ibid., ¶ 23,016 [1979].
193. Ibid., ¶ 23,016C [1979].

This direction, in fact, simply brings international antitrust practice more in line with what has been the position in American antitrust all along. American antitrust has a history of combatting restraints on competition *before* they reach detrimental proportions. The *likelihood* of a merger or acquisition resulting in a lessening of competition has long sufficed as grounds to prevent the conclusion of such a transaction. As commented in the Senate Report on the 1950 Amendment to the antimerger section (Section 7) of the Clayton Act, "[t]he words 'may be' have been in Section 7 of the Clayton Act since 1914. The concept of *reasonable probability* conveyed by these words is a necessary element in any statute which seeks to arrest restraints of trade in their incipiency and before they develop into full-fledged restraints violative of the Sherman Act." [Emphasis supplied.][194]

In a 1964 acquisition case against Alcoa, this 'reasonable probability' concept led the court to rule that even Alcoa's intended acquisition of less than 1.5 per cent of a competing company's market share "*seems* to us *reasonably likely* to produce a substantial lessening of competition within the meaning of Section 7." [Emphasis supplied.][195] Nonetheless, the dissimilar goals underlying the American and European antitrust legislation are still reflected in the fact that in, for example, EEC, German and British national competition laws, as we have seen, there are no *per se* unlawful monopolies or restrictive arrangements; while in U.S. antitrust law there is a conclusive presumption of *per se* illegality as regards monopolization and other anti-competitive behaviour, for which not even a defence of ultimate benefit to the economy or society would mitigate the illegality. It should be added here that, where restrictive intent of an arrangement is less evident, even the American laws allow a rebuttable presumption of illegality, though the burden of proof rests with the defendant for establishing the conduct's legality. This rule of reason also allows judicial exemptions for some arrangements falling outside of the *per se* illegal combinations which, while in some measure restrictive, contribute some benefit to the overall economy.[196] While the 'overall economy' here still does not allow for considerations of a global competitive position as does the practice of, for example, Germany, France and Japan, there appears to be some limited application of the general European rule of reason in this area, which justifies concerted arrangements where there is some transcendent economic or social benefit. It must not be forgotten, however, that this European concept of the rule of

194. Senate Report No. 1775, 81st Cong., 2d Sess. 6 (1950); *U.S. Code Cong. & Adm. News,* 4298 (1950).

195. *United States* v. *Aluminum Co. of America,* 377 U.S. 271, 280 (1964).

196. See Grendell, op. cit., *supra* note 108, at 70.

reason includes even outright monopolies and other restrictive arrangements conclusively illegal under U.S. laws, and that under the EEC concept, there is a presumption of legality of an arrangement, with the burden of proof on the government to establish illegality.

Other new initiatives[197] in American antitrust legislation have been observable beginning on a large scale in 1979, primarily as a result of the report to the President of a National Commission for the Review of Antitrust Laws and Procedures of January 1979.[198] The most important of these, for merger control, which has actually been signed into law is the Antitrust Procedural Improvements Act of 1980[199] which, *inter alia,* amends certain provisions of the Antitrust Civil Process Act,[200] as well as Title 28 of the United States Code[201] and certain provisions of the Clayton Act.[202]

The most significant of the changes brought about by the new Act for the present context is that relating to merger control under Section 7 of the Clayton Act which, prior to the amendment, concerned only mergers between "corporations". Through the substitution of the word "corporation" by the word "person", the application of Section 7 has been expanded to include such non-incorporated enterprises as partnerships and joint ventures. Moreover the addition, after the words "engaged in commerce", of the phrase "or in any activity affecting commerce" clearly broadens even further the reach of Section 7's application as regards combinations.

Although American antitrust legislation uses different terminology, and is more likely to speak of lessening of competition than of strengthening of a dominant market position, the ultimate outcome is essentially the same, or, at least, increasingly so. The word "increasingly" is used intentionally here so as not to obscure the fact mentioned earlier that traditionally - and indeed still, to a large extent - the European (and Japanese) attitudes toward merger policies have been vastly different from, if not to say contrary to, the American attitude, even if for no more significant reason than that the historical, politi-

197. See e.g. Hölzer, "Neuere Initiativen zum US-Antitrust - Ein Überblick - ", 30 *Wirtschaft und Wettbewerb* (1980), pp. 728-740.

198. National Commission for the Review of Antitrust Laws and Procedures, Report to the President and the Attorney General, Washington, D.C., 22 January 1979.

199. Antitrust Procedural Improvements Act of 12 September 1980, printed in CCH *Trade Regulation Reports* No. 445 of 16 September 1980, at 25. Cf. Conference Report, "Antitrust Procedural Improvements Act of 1980", printed in CCH *Trade Regulation Reports* No. 50 of 25 August 1980, at 418.

200. Antitrust Civil Process Act, 15 U.S.C. § 1311; 76 Stat. 548.

201. Cf. H.R. 4047 of May 10, 1979 with S.309, 96th Cong., 1st Sess., (1979).

202. Clayton Act, 15 U.S.C. § 15, Sects. 4, 4A, 4C, 5(a)).

cal and economic - and hence legal - realities have vastly differed between the American and the European experience. As we have seen, domestic legislation on anti-combines enforcement, responding individually - as Europe has begun to do collectively - to each member country's own economic and legal tradition, continues to develop and be exercised according to respective national policies; but increasing evidence of EEC influence, and a resultant commonality of direction in this regard, is clearly emerging. Moreover, the fact that the EC Commission has begun interpreting its Article 86 (Rome Treaty) to apply to mergers and acquisitions by market-dominant enterprises and has drafted a prior-notice Directive for proposed mergers and acquisitions is concrete indication of a heightened interest in anti-combines enforcement in general.

It is interesting to note how rapidly the European antitrust climate has undergone this shift. As recently as 1973, the following observation appeared in an article in the *Journal of International Law and Economics:*

> To the European multinational industrialist, it would be understandably disquieting even to suggest that the American experience under Section 7 [of the Clayton Act] might someday be transported across the Atlantic. The idea that a merger or acquisition would be prohibited merely because it *may* substantially lessen competition would surely be disturbing....[203]

This statement is already clearly outdated.

It may still be true that the EEC has some way to go to equal the American preoccupation with antitrust enforcement, but this widespread tightening of anti-combines control is indeed an interesting development, and indicates that, while the underlying motives for such control still differ between the various states, particularly between America and Europe, and while combines-control legislation is certainly not reserved to only those combinations involving a foreign element, it is decidedly proving an increasingly strong tool in the hands of the host state - American or European - for exercising control over the operations of foreign MNE affiliates.

6. International Tentatives

International initiatives are also observable in the area of restrictive business

203. Adler and Belman, op. cit., *supra* note 59, at 32.

practices, notably those within the framework of the United Nations and the Organisation for Economic Co-operation and Development (OECD). The efforts of the United Nations in this area have culminated in the adoption of a "Set of Multilaterally Agreed Equitable Principles and Rules for the Control of Restrictive Business Practices Having Adverse Effects on International Trade..." ("Principles").[204] This Set of Principles was elaborated by the United Nations Conference on Restrictive Business Practices convened[205] under the auspices of the United Nations Conference on Trade and Development (UNCTAD), and was based on the work of the Third *Ad Hoc* Group of Experts on Restrictive Trade Practices. Of particular interest, especially with a view to the national tendencies we have just seen as regards 'merger' control, is the definition of restrictive business practices:

> "Restrictive business practices" means acts or behaviour of enterprises which, through an abuse or acquisition and abuse of a dominant position of market power, limit access to markets or otherwise unduly restrain competition, having *or being likely to have* adverse effects on international trade, particularly that of developing countries, and on the economic development of these countries, or which through formal, informal, written or unwritten agreements or arrangements among enterprises have the same impact.[Emphasis supplied.]

Reflecting this definition is a "principle" addressed to enterprises (Section D, para. 4) - expressly including multinational enterprises ("transnational corporations") - requesting them to refrain from, *inter alia,* "mergers, takeovers, joint ventures *or other acquisitions of control,* whether of a horizontal, vertical or a conglomerate nature" [emphasis supplied],[206] "when, through an abuse or acquisition and abuse of a dominant position of market power, they ...[fall under the above-cited definition of restrictive business practices]".[207] In this connection, the Principles stipulate that: "Whether acts or behaviour are abusive or not should be examined in terms of their purpose and effects in the actual situation...",[208] going on to elaborate what that means in the context of the developing countries.

204. UNCTAD document TD/RBP/CONF/10, Annex; U.N. document A/C.2/35/6 of 23 October 1980, Annex [hereinafter cited as UNCTAD Principles]. For remarks on the disclosure provisions of the UNCTAD Principles and Rules see Chapter VIII *supra*, text accompanying notes 62-65.

205. By resolution 33/153 of 20 December 1978.

206. UNCTAD Principles, Sect. D, para. 4(c).

207. UNCTAD Principles, Sect. D, para. 4.

208. UNCTAD Principles, Sect. D, para. 4, note.

It has been remarked[209] that although the Principles and Rules are described as "multilaterally agreed", they still contain some wide areas of disagreement between representatives of the major economic groups involved. The Principles have been seen by some as less of a code for competitive practices than as a tactical step on the part of the developing countries to restrain competition from foreign private international business and to aid in the campaign for the New International Economic Order, or as an effort by some representatives of socialist states "to impose [their] anticompetition, antiprivate business principles in the trappings of principles to regulate 'restrictive business practices' ".[210] It is indeed difficult to argue that the political considerations do not outweigh the legal ones where the definition of abusive behaviour is left so open to situational interpretation that it could, as one writer expressed it, "be read to include any action by a large international company that is claimed by a developing country to adversly affect its trade and development",[211] and where the definition of "restrictive business practices" stressing effect on trade and developing countries is a test in determining whether conduct is a restrictive business practice."[212]

Hence, not only is there a reinforcement of the concept of the central role of *control*, and of that of the *likelihood* of adverse effects, but also there is provision for a very broad interpretive scope based on situational considerations. The notions in the "principle" addressed to enterprises are reiterated among the "principles" addressed to states, in which, *inter alia*, states are urged to "adopt, improve and effectively enforce appropriate legislation..." (Section E, para. 1), based on the criteria enunciated in the definition and in Section D, paragraph 4 just discussed.

At the same time, the UNCTAD Principles also stipulated that "[t]he provisions of the Set of Principles and Rules should not be construed as justifying conduct by enterprises which is unlawful under applicable national or regional legislation" (Section C(i), para. 5). Thus, both provisions reinforce the importance of control at the national (and regional) level.

Section G(i) provides that an International Group of Experts operating within the framework of a Committee of UNCTAD will supply the institutional machinery for administering and overseeing the activities, but again urges that states which have accepted the Set of Principles and Rules should

209. Gill, "The UNCTAD Restrictive Business Practices Code: A Code for Competition?", 13 *International Lawyer* (1979), at 607.

210. See ibid., at 614, 617.

211. Ibid., at 611.

212. Davidow, "The UNCTAD Restrictive Business Practices Code", 13 *International Lawyer* (1979), at 591.

take appropriate steps at the national or regional level to meet their commitment to these Principles. A review procedure is provided in Section G(iii) whereby in 1985 a UN Conference, under the auspices of UNCTAD, will review the Principles and Rules in all their aspects.[213]

The final version of the text stated that the "principles and rules for enterprises, including transnational corporations", applied to all enterprises, private or state,[214] whereas at one stage in the drafting process there was no agreement as to whether actions by state-owned enterprises would fall under the provisions of the Principles and Rules, and the Group of 77, representing the developing countries, was also strongly proposing that preferential treatment should be afforded to their national enterprises.[215] It would have been difficult to sustain a position which did not recognize that local national firms as well as state-owned enterprises are equally capable of perpetrating abuses as are multinational enterprises.

One thing is clear as regards the UNCTAD Principles and Rules: given the significant discrepancies among the different economic sectors representing diverse economic policies, objectives, political and legal systems and approaches to competition generally, it is not to be expected that any international code can successfully eliminate the difficulties and inherent differences, or even achieve a common acceptance of the role of competition, as long as the fundamental underlying disagreement on objectives remains unaltered.

Turning now to the OECD initiatives, it should be recalled that the OECD's preoccupation with the question of restrictive business practices in general, and mergers in particular, is not altogether new. Even prior to the 1969 OECD-sponsored Cambridge International Conference on Monopolies, Mergers and Restrictive Business Practices at which it was recommended that OECD's Committee of Experts on Restrictive Business Practices undertake a study on such practices as are engaged in by multinational enterprises, the Organisation had already begun to produce recommendations and reports in this field. The Committee was also invited to contribute to the drafting of the 1976 Guidelines for Multinational Enterprises[216] discussed earlier.

The only direct reference to mergers in the 1976 Guidelines, however, is found in the recommendation that enterprises should: "While conforming to

213. See also U.N. document A/Res/35/63 of 16 December 1980, para. 2.

214. UNCTAD Principles, Sect. B(i), paras. 2, 6.

215. Gill, op. cit., *supra* note 209, at 609.

216. Declaration of 21st June 1976 by Governments of OECD Member Countries on International Investment and Multinational Enterprises, Annex: "Guidelines for Multinational Enterprises", Organisation for Economic Co-operation and Development, Paris (1976).

official competition rules and established polices of the countries in which they operate, [r]efrain from actions which would adversely affect competition in the relevant market by abusing a dominant position of market power, by means of, for example,...anti-competitive acquisitions....''[217]

Of greater interest in the present context, then, is the Committee's report on mergers, published in 1975.[218] This report urges OECD member states which have not already done so ''to consider the adoption of an effective system of merger control'' and suggests specific ''characteristics which might be taken into account in drawing up legislation namely:

i) a procedure for registering mergers, wherever this is felt necessary;
ii) a system to facilitate obtaining information about occurrence of major mergers, such as requiring their prior notification;
iii) minimum quantitative criteria below which mergers would not be subject to control;
iv) objective criteria or presumptions for use in evaluating mergers;
v) reasonable time limits for deciding initially whether to allow or challenge certain mergers.[219]

In 1977 the OECD Committee issued a report on the significant issues of competition policy and procedures relating to multinational enterprises,[220] through it noted the difficulty of assessing the impact of MNEs on the worldwide degree of concentration due to the fact that, because very few countries gather or publish data on mergers, there is a lack of sufficiently comprehensive information.[221] Nonetheless, supported by the extensive factual evidence and practical competition enforcement experience of nineteen member states and the EC Commission, the report succeeded in analyzing the effects of MNEs on competition, outlining the possibilities of applying relevant legislation to the activities of MNEs and recommending possible remedies to the problems identified. Among the wide range of proposals included are, *inter alia,* the creation of new information-gathering procedures – at the national and inter-

217. Ibid., at 15.

218. ''Mergers and Competition Policy'': Report of the Committee of Experts on Restrictive Business Practices, OECD Paris, 1975.

219. Ibid., para. 185.

220. Restrictive Business Practices of Multinational Enterprises: Report of the Committee of Experts on Restrictive Business Practices, OECD publication, Paris (1977), mentioned earlier in the context of the 'effects' doctrine (see *supra* text accompanying note 18).

221. Ibid., para. 86, at 26. The OECD, despite this obstacle, has maintained a practice of publishing annual reports on competition policy in member countries.

national levels - on the subject of MNEs; the development of international consultation, conciliation and arbitration procedures, or of voluntary codes or guidelines for enterprises and governments; and even the creation of a binding international antitrust law and an international agency with enforcement powers.

While suggesting that, "at the international level action may mainly be taken by governments and by international organizations", the emphasis remains on action by national governments themselves - either at the international level in the form of bilateral or multilateral agreements, arrangements or formal treaties,[222] or at the national level in the form of domestic legislative action which, the report suggests, "is [p]robably the most effective [m]easure to solve or mitigate the problems identified in this report."[223] The OECD recommendation expressly states that a merger control system should apply to domestic and multinational enterprises alike.[224]

Among the Report's concrete suggestions for action, those directly related to mergers are contained in paragraphs 210 and 211. Paragraph 210 suggests the introduction of a workable system of merger control or the strengthening of an already-introduced but not effectively functioning merger control system, based on the criteria of the 1975 OECD Committee's report on mergers listed above;[225] Paragraph 211 makes a similar suggestion as regards a workable abuse control procedure or legislation against existing or attempted monopolization.

The suggestions for action also refer the member states back to the 1967 Recommendation concerning co-operation between member countries on restictive business practices affecting international trade, and to the 1973 Recommendation regarding a consultation and conciliation procedure on such practices.[226] In 1978, the OECD Council adopted a Recommendation regarding the co-operation of member countries in the field of restrictive business practices in general, which, as it was adopted by all members, shows a common interest in this increasingly important area of MNE activity.

222. Ibid., para. 205, at 60.

223. Ibid., para. 197.

224. Ibid., para. 198.

225. See *supra* note 218.

226. OECD Doc. C(73) 99. A significant feature of this Recommendation is that unresolved disputes between two states may be submitted for reconciliation to the OECD's Committee of Experts, comprising antitrust enforcement officials from 22 OECD countries.

Chapter X.

CONTROLS OVER OPERATIONS RESULTING IN DISINVESTMENT

Before we move completely out of the realm of control over operations into that of the cessation of operations, or "disinvestment", which is the subject of the following chapter, it is worth looking very briefly at two legal control techniques which actually begin as host controls over operations, but have either the potential or the avowed intent of finishing as *de facto* disinvestment techniques. One of these is that of contract renegotiation, and the other is that referred to as the 'fade-out' (or 'phase-out') formula.

This brings us for the first time squarely before the whole question of 'disinvestment', and provides an appropriate juncture for distinguishing between the concepts of 'voluntary' and 'involuntary' disinvestment, prior to considering the two techniques just mentioned.

1. Voluntary *v.* Involuntary Disinvestment

Clearly, voluntary or involuntary here relates to the 'will' of the corporate enterprise, and not that of the host, so that 'voluntary' disinvestment implies a decision on the part of the enterprise to withdraw its presence, or cease operations, while 'involuntary' disinvestment implies a decision on the part of the host government to effectively remove the foreign presence, either by demanding its physical withdrawal or by actually taking over operations, ownership and/or management control.

Since we are concerned, in the present study, not with the motivating will of the MNE, but with that of the host state as exercised over the MNE, our discussion will naturally concentrate on 'involuntary' disinvestment - i.e., that initiated and executed at the will of the host state.

In some circumstances, however, the line between 'voluntary' and 'involuntary' can become sufficiently blurred as to obscure the responsibility of the host government and the actual source of the motivating 'will.' Such is sometimes the case in contract renegotiation.

2. Contract Renegotiation

As our purpose here is not to go into the finer points of the contract renegotiations themselves, but simply to recognize such renewed bargaining as a further control exercised over MNE affiliates which are already established and operating within a host state, a few observations should suffice.

a. Shift in bargaining position

The renegotiation of contracts at the initiation of the host involves the recognition by the recipient government that a foreign affiliate, once it is established in a particular location, with the accompanying commitment in the form of vast expenditures of resources and time in launching production and training local staff, will not, without substantial difficulty and loss, uproot and remove elsewhere. Capitalizing upon this knowledge, some governments have been prompted to change the conditions under which the company is allowed to continue operations, after that company has been in production for some years.

In principle, renegotiation should only be resorted to when there has been a fundamental change of circumstance, and should be aimed at re-establishing a mutually advantageous balance between the contracting parties - in the present context, betweeen the host government and the MNE. As expressed by one writer:

> Les circonstances changeantes...peuvent conduire a reviser les contrats passé entre un État et une compagnie privée. Seuls les changements de nature fondamentale ou substantielle peuvent être invoqés et l'objectif final ne doit pas être nécessairement une amélioration à tout prix de la position du pays-hôte. Avant de recourir aux mesures unilatérales, c'est le devoir des deux parties de renégocier et l'on doit rechercher l'équivalence mutuelle des avantages contractuels.[1]

In practice, the fundamental-change-of-circumstances condition may be used by the host as a pretext, where an actual substantial change - dependent as that is upon subjective interpretation - would in fact be difficult to substantiate. (If one were to draw an analogy here with *rebus sic stantibus* in

1. Rouhani, "Renégociation des contrats entre états et investisseurs privés", 1 *Revue Juridique et Politique, Indépendence et Coopération* (1975), at 93.

treaty law, it is worth noting that no case has ever been proved.) The 'mutual-advantage' stipulation is also more than likely to be weighted on the side of the host state, for reasons already mentioned. The formulation of the above citation is surprisingly transparent in its underlining of this fact, where it states: "...l'objectif final ne doit pas être *nécessairement* une amélioration *à tout prix* de la position du pays-hôte." [Emphasis supplied]. This statement along with that which follows: "*Avant de* recourir aux mesures unilatérales..." [emphasis supplied], is a clear indication of what is probably the case in actual practice, *viz.* that the final objective normally *is* to improve the position of the host state, and that the measures *do* tend, ultimately, to weigh unilaterally[2] on the side of the host government. If this were not generally the case, it is unlikely that the host would initiate such renegotiations. It is widely known that while the MNE may be allowed a large measure of autonomy as long as it is making a critical contribution which cannot be gained through other channels, as that contribution diminishes, local control inreases.[3] Skills, technology and know-how which may have been all on the side of the investing enterprise at the time of entry have gradually been transferred to local personnel at the host's insistence, and the way has also been paved for competitors to enter the market, which also contributes to diminishing the bargaining strength of the initial investor. Even the process of integration of an MNE's affiliates, with each other and the parent company, which would seem to enhance the enterprise's bargaining power *vis-à-vis* governments in such matters as location of production and marketing efforts, is counterbalanced by the fact that "the higher the degree of integration among affiliates of the enterprise, the more one affiliate becomes a 'hostage to government', because interference with its operation can quickly affect the entire multinational enterprise."[4] Thus, in the developed as well as in the developing world, with the passage of time, the balance of power - and consequently the bargaining strength - of the MNE *vis-à-vis* the host shifts predictably from corporate advantage to local control.[5] Multinational oil companies furnish a prime example of enterprises which have found themselves subjected by their hosts to severe pressure to renegotiate the

2. The very legal nature of the MNE precludes its "taking measures", in the legal sense, against a state.

3. United Nations, *Multinational Corporations in World Development,* U.N. publication ST/ECA/190, New York, 1973, at 38.

4. Behrman, *National Interests and the Multinational Enterprise* (Englewood Cliffs, N.J.: Prentice-Hall, 1970), at 7.

5. See Moran, *Multinational Corporations and the Politics of Dependence: Copper in Chile* (Princeton, N.J. Princeton University Press, 1975); also Kindleberger, *International Economics,* 4th ed., (Homewood, Ill.: Richard D. Irwin, 1968), at 399.

terms of their concessionary contract, undercutting their positions in a number of ways.[6] Among the 'classic' contracts of those enterprises operating in the Persian Gulf, not one has remained unchanged.[7] The oil companies involved rarely reacted swiftly to the revision demands, but in most instances they ultimately accepted amendments which were often radical.[8] While many of these "contract revisions", when one considers the unilateral measures of Iran, Iraq and Algeria, for example, amounted to *de facto* nationalizations, we can find an interesting example, within the industrialized nations, of oil-concession contract renegotiations which all but constituted nationalization, though care was taken to preserve the outward form of negotiation. Reference here is to the North Sea oil renegotiations of the mid-1970's in Great Britain.

In 1975, 60 per cent of the assets of the commercial oil fields in the North Sea were in foreign companies' hands. The need for a rapid and thorough exploration in a high risk area had prompted the Government to encourage investment and to dole out licences on lenient terms beginning in 1964. After ten years, the terms of the licensing agreements were virtually unchanged.[9] By that time, however, the uncertainty and high-risk elements of the undertaking had been supplanted by profitable oil production; and under such conditions:

> officials are apt to pay little heed to the fact that the corporation has lost substantial sums in vain efforts in other countries so that its overall profitability is not exceptional. They also ignore the fact that it might have lost substantial sums if the...endeavor had not turned out as it did. The company may retain some bargaining counters by way of external connections in credit and marketing aspects, as well as the country's hopes for expansion, but its position clearly suffers from the increasing options [the host state] possesses.
>
> It is idle to try to freeze the position of the parties for long periods to conditions that become so out of date. Either parties will include renegotiation provisions in their contracts or they will act as if they were there.[10]

In the case of the North Sea oil operations, the latter was true: There was an abrupt and radical change of policy subsequent to the 1974 elections which

6. Vafai, "Conflict Resolution in the International Petroleum Industry", 5 *Journal of World Trade Law* (1971), at 427. See also Rouhani, op. cit., *supra* note 1, at 95-96.

7. See Rouhani, op. cit., *supra* note 1, at 95.

8. *Idem.*

9. See "North Sea Oil: Survey", *The Economist,* July 26, 1975, at 16, 18.

10. Vagts, "Coercion and Foreign Investment Rearrangements", 72 *American Journal of International Law,* (1978), at 22.

returned the Labour Government to office; new legislation was introduced (in accordance with the terms of the Government's July 1974 White Paper[11]), designed to ensure greater state participation in, and control over, "commercially proven"[12] North Sea exploition. By the end of 1975, three major bills had been enacted to this end. A key provision contained in one of the resulting acts, the Petroleum and Submarine Pipelines Act[13] enacted on November 12, 1975, called for the establishment of the British National Oil Corporation (BNOC), with the objective of securing majority (51 per cent) state participation in North Sea production. With the Norwegian state-participation policy as an example, Part 2 of the Act introduced changes to the model clauses set out in Schedule 4 of the Petroleum Regulations of 1966 (as amended by the Petroleum Regulations of 1971), containing the terms and conditions upon which both landward and seaward production licences had been issued. The changes in the model clauses included, generally, conditions relating to royalties, disclosure and control.[14]

In contrast to the Norwegian policy, however, the British Act's contractual amendments were not confined to future agreements,[15] but were also expected to affect existing agreements. Among other powers extended under the Act was that granted to government authorities to revoke an authorization regarding type, capacity and general location of refineries, issued by the Secretary of State, if the company concerned underwent a change of control.[16] Further powers under the Act included the authority of the Secretary of State to authorize the BNOC to make payments out of the National Oil Account to licensees who agreed to the state participation scheme.[17] Incentives such as this were apparently deemed necessary due to the "voluntary" nature of "participation". It is this "voluntary" nature of the renegotiations which makes the 1975 Act and its relevant provisions of interest in the present context.

While the Government's "participation" scheme has been called outright "nationalization" by some,[18] and while certain of the Act's provisions have

11. See *Keesing's Contemporary Archives* 1974, [hereinafter cited as *Keesing* 1974] at 26628-26629.

12. *Keesing's Contemporary Archives* 1976, [hereinafter cited as *Keesing* 1976] at 27730.

13. Petroleum and Submarine Pipelines Act 1975 c.74. See generally Brenscheidt, "Petroleum Legislation in the North Sea Countries", 11 *Texas International Law Journal* (1976), at 296-299.

14. *Keesing* 1976, at 27728.

15. See e.g. "North Sea Oil: Survey", op. cit., *supra* note 9, at 18; Brenscheidt, loc. cit., *supra* note 13.

16. *Keesing* 1976, at 27729.

17. *Idem.*

18. See e.g. statement by Mr. Jo Grimond on behalf of the Liberal Party, *Idem.*

been said to depart "from all previous European practice in that the changes were retrospective and so represented a 'unilateral abrogation of existing rights without compensation...[and] a form of compulsory expropriation by the state just as any form of outright nationalization'",[19] the Government's insistence on the "voluntary" nature, in principle, of renegotiation, coupled with official and repeated government assurances that participation will involve "no loss"[20] (companies will be "financially neither better nor worse off"),[21] has managed to maintain the distinction between the "renegotiation" policy and technical "nationalization". Moreover, there was an appearance of retreat by the Government at an early stage, as regarded its 51 per cent stipulation, from its original solid stance on the issue, in exchange for other "rights", though official British spokesmen continued to maintain that the 51 per cent oil production participation remained the goal.[22]

In practice, while there was considerable resistance to the renegotiation proposals on the part of some of the major oil companies, and while the chairman of the powerful Exxon Corporation (and through Esso, one of the largest participants in North Sea operations[23]) stated that "when the Government said that participation was voluntary we took them at their word" and that Esso was "not volunteering" (and Britain's own Shell corporation shared this position),[24] by the time of the Government's allocation of the fifth round of offshore exploration licences, BNOC had succeeded in obtaining its desired 51 per cent share in all 44 'blocks' allocated.[25] This was not achieved without much hard bargaining - six months' bargaining in the cases of Shell and Esso[26] who perhaps had the most to lose, but also the most to offer. As reported by *The Economist*, in the midst of the negotiations: "A government cannot afford to exclude majors like Shell and Exxon, which have resisted participation, from the North Sea. The country needs their expertise and capital. The most the government could do is to put only a few blocks on offer until such companies toe the line."[27] Here we see an example of the continuing sig-

19. Statement by Mr. Patrick Jenkin, the Conservative spokesman on energy matters, *Idem*.

20. See e.g. "North Sea Oil: Survey", op. cit., *supra* note 9, at 18.

21. See e.g. *Keesing* 1976, at 27730; also "Participantomime", *The Economist,* February 7, 1976, at 75.

22. See e.g. Brenscheidt, op. cit., *supra* note 13, at 298; also *Idem* ("Participantomime").

23. *Keesing* 1976, at 27731.

24. *Idem.* Also "North Sea: Statesmen and oilmen", *The Economist,* November 20, 1976, at 128.

25. See "BNOC's chip off 44 Blocks", *The Economist,* February 12, 1977, at 103.

26. See e.g. "North Sea participation: Hollow agreement?", *The Economist,* January 8, 1977, at 91.

27. "North Sea oil: It's British", *The Economist,* March 6, 1976, at 86.

nificance, in shifting bargaining positions, of the relative strength of the state *vis-à-vis* the enterprise in terms of technological know-how and capital investment capabilities.

The Government was able to exert a more direct influence in its relative strength in negotiating with two other major American companies, Gulf Oil and the Continental Oil Company (Conoco), mainly owing to the fact that these two companies were already operating in partnership with the National Coal Board (Exploration) Ltd. which had become a subsidiary of BNOC immediately upon the establishment of the latter - i.e., the day the 1975 Act came into force - by provision of Section 13 of the Act.[28] The Government's negotiator in the transaction announced, in a written parliamentary answer on February 6, 1976, that: "These existing arrangements give BNOC full access to information and an effective voice in control [in Gulf and Conoco]. The new agreements with the companies build on this position."[29] Hence Gulf and Conoco had little left to lose by "renegotiating".

The greater operational, technological and financial independence of the larger Shell and Exxon corporations, which retained to them a stronger bargaining position, enabled these companies to negotiate over such details as the defining of "the national interest" as regards the exact circumstances in which the Government could withhold the oil that it otherwise promised to sell back to the companies. "The companies say a genuine crisis of national survival is one thing, but a simple change of heart by a subsequent minister is something else. They want to limit the conditions narrowly and stricly."[30]

Despite the major companies' bargaining strength, however, the energy secretary made it clear that in the fifth allocation of licences for North Sea exploration, only companies that had agreed to "participation" in principle would be offered more blocks, with full awareness that both Shell and Exxon wanted more blocks.[31] Esso and Shell eventually capitulated, even though one company man claimed that it was in the end little more than "a public relations exercise." The Government, for its part, while its energy department insisted that it had won real concessions in return, contented itself with remarking that "theoretical possession is better than no possession at all."[32] It is not insignificant that the American Oil Company (Amoco), the last big enterprise to resist the Government's scheme of "voluntary" state participation in existing fields, acquired no blocks at all.[33] The host government still prevails.

28. See also *Idem;* also "Pull up for a gallon of BNOC", *The Economist,* July 26, 1975, at 18.
29. Reported in *Keesing* 1976, at 27730.
30. "North Sea: Statesmen and oilmen", op. cit., *supra* note 24, at 129.
31. *Idem.*
32. See "North Sea participation: Hollow agreement?", loc. cit., *supra* note 26.
33. See "BNOC's chip off 44 blocks", loc. cit., *supra* note 25.

The *prima facie* coercive nature of the "renegotiating" process here is clear. What has not been called into question is whether a mere change of government or of economic policy should be regarded as a "fundamental change of circumstance" sufficient to justify a radical change in contract terms. On this subject surely a parallel can be drawn with *rebus sic stantibus* in international treaty law in that it is not every change of circumstance which allows recourse to a call for renegotiation, but only those changes which are *fundamental* or *substantial.*[34] Of course the difficulty is that to distinguish between a substantial and a non-substantial change of circumstances is inevitably a matter of interpretation, and therefore a subjective exercise; but surely in the case of a change of government, even with substantial consequences, where those consequences do not have direct and radical effects upon the actual conditions governing the original terms of the contract, they should not be invoked as circumstances justifying major contract revision. (Norway avoided difficulty here by a gradualist approach to licensing; it insisted on state participation only in cases of new agreements.[35])

Of course, a fundamental change of circumstances - either real or manufactured in the interest of the host - is not always a prerequisite to contract renegotiation. Periodical renegotiation may be written into the original agreement, or the contract or agreement may terminate according to its own terms or be legally abrogated by the host government; and most highly industrialized states do utilize their economic sophistication to anticipate renegotiation in the original agreement. Governments which have failed to anticipate renegotiation provisions in their contracts have, as noted above, sometimes seemed to proceed as if they were there. This tends to occur with greatest frequency in mineral-extracting industries.

b. Economic coercion by host state

It is perfectly legal for a host state to exact whatever conditions it wishes, not only at the moment of entry, but also for the continuation of business, as long as it does so according to the legal means available to it. Some legal observers,[36] however, feel that the host exactions can rise to the level of economic coercion

34. See Rouhani, op. cit., *supra* note 1, at 95.

35. See "North Sea Oil: Survey", op. cit., *supra* note 9, at 18; also Brenscheidt, op. cit., *supra* note 13, at 293-295.

36. See, *inter alia,* Vagts, "Coercion and Foreign Investment Rearrangements", op. cit., *supra* note 10, at 17 *et seq.*; also Hauser, speaking at the Panel Discussion on "International Law and

on the part of the host government *vis-à-vis* the MNE, and one such observer[37] specifically questions the legal basis for host exactions which require illegal acts on the part of the MNE (for example, illicit payments) as a condition for sustaining operations.

One might reason that there can hardly be economic coercion exercised against an MNE, since the enterprise can simply refuse to renew a contract if the terms are unfavourable. But one who reasons thus ignores the fact that unreasonable renegotiation terms, in themselves, can be a very definite form of economic coercion, particularly if they are used to force an MNE to effectively abandon its immovable assets to the host state without any obligation, on the part of the host government, to pay compensation under the law of state responsibility. In other words, while the investor "wants maximum 'stability' for what was probably a prudent investment when made and has been quite profitable in ensuing years," the host developing state "wants maximum freedom of action to 'improve' its own earnings from the investment from time to time, and eventually, if circumstances seem to it propitious, to take over the investment with a minimum of financial and political cost."[38] For example, contract revision between host and MNE may directly lead to a conveyance of property that on the surface appears to be an ordinary sale, but at a price which, at best, reflects only the diminished potential of the enterprise affiliate. This is then a form of government coercion.[39]

c. Unreasonable coercion resulting in disinvestment

In sum, terms offered in renegotiating a contract may be calculated to achieve the utmost limits in bargaining advantage, beyond which it is unprofitable for the enterprise to remain and carry on business. Or the government's terms may be so unreasonable as to actually exceed those limits making totally unprofitable and leaving the enterprise with no other alternative but to withdraw

---

Economic Intervention: Policing a Two-Way Street", 1975 International Law Weekend, sponsored by the Association of the Bar of the City of New York, and the American Branch of the International Law Association

37. *Idem* (Hauser).

38. "Two Perspectives on the Barcelona Traction Case: Nationality of corporate investment under Investment Guaranty Schemes - The Relevance of Barcelona Traction", (Editorial Comment: Metzger), 65 *American Journal of International Law* (1971), at 532.

39. Vagts, "Coercion and Foreign Investment Rearrangements", op. cit., *supra* note 10, at 17, 25.

altogether, or sell out at far greater loss. A 'coerced' or 'involuntary' disinvestment is thus accomplished by the host government, without, it would hope, the stigma or legal or moral obligations attached to an expropriation or other form of government 'taking' which traditionally carries with it compensation liability. This type of enforced disinvestment is a typical case of economic coercion exercised against the MNE by the host, and is no longer accepted without question as being exempt from state responsibility. There is a very fine line between government coercion and expropriation, and in most cases, economic coercion amounts to a 'distinguised' or 'de facto' expropriation and is now being recognized as such,[40] with the accompanying international responsibility and liability which that implies. An exception would be where the withdrawal is the normal outcome of "regulatory actions reasonably related to legitimate government objectives that are not arbitrary or themselves a violation of international law."[41] But when there is an "abrogation, repudiation, or impairment by a foreign government of its own contract with an investor", which is not caused "by the investor's own fault or misconduct"; and such governmental act "materially adversely affects the continued operation of the project"; such act can be designated as "expropriation".[42]

Disinvestment is obviously not the aim of the host in all contract renegotiation, but such renegotiation, whether in its milder or more extreme forms, is a powerful technique exercisable by a host state over MNE operations within its territory.

3. 'Fade-out' Formula

Another technique of host control over operations which could, in one sense, be said to fall somewhere between 'voluntary' and 'involuntary' disinvestment is that referred to as the "fade-out" (or "phase-out") formula. The 'fade-out' formula is a scheme which provides for the progressive transfer of ownership and/or control of an established foreign enterprise into the hands of the host state or its nationals and, as such, is not only a technique of control over foreign operations, but is at the same time a technique of programmed disinvestment enforced by the host state. It could be seen as 'involuntary' in the

40. The Overseas Private Investment Corporation (OPIC) for example, offers its insured investors confronted with a host government renegotiation the option of either accepting the new terms, which action is then regarded as "voluntary", or of refusing the renegotiated terms and falling back on its insurance rights, in obvious recognition on the part of OPIC of the expropriatory nature of the renegotiation.

41. Vagts, "Coercion and Foreign Investment Arrangements," op. cit., *supra* note 10, at 26.

42. As per U.S. Foreign Assistance Act of 1969, para. 238 (a).

sense that the operations and period of control over the initial investment are subject to specific host limitations which would not normally be agreed to by choice on the part of an MNE; yet it is 'voluntary' in the sense that the terms of disinvestment have been agreed to by the MNE as a primary condition of entry. It is, in essence, a compromise agreement from the standpoint of the enterprise, whose only alternative would likely be total exclusion of the proposed direct investment. For all legal and practical purposes, however, the 'fade-out' formula must be categorized as a 'voluntary' disinvestment technique, as it is an agreement voluntarily entered into by the investing enterprise prior to the actual establishment of operations, and the ultimate ownership and control intentions of the host government are clearly manifest.

The 'fade-out' formula, then, is a fully legal, non-compensable disinvestment technique which begins at entry, continues throughout the length of operations, and culminates in the total disinvestment of the foreign component and, as such, is of particular interest in the context of the present study. Since up to the present time, however, this technique has been one characteristically encountered in the developing rather than the industrialized economies, mention here will remain brief. The 'formula' is included herein for its interest as a technique which, while originating within a regional market in the developing world (the Andean Common Market), is not incompatible with investment practices in the developed markets, and could find its way into investment agreements within the developed economies.

The technique has not, however, yielded the anticipated degree of benefit hoped for by those states applying it thus far. It has (along with other restrictive foreign investment provisions of the Andean Pact) led to diminished foreign direct investment within the ANCOM and to Chile's consequent withdrawal from active participation in the Pact.[43] It has also faced criticism in the developed world. Harvard law professor Detlev Vagts sees possible unfortunate consequences for the host state resulting from the fact that, under the formula, the MNE must contemplate an investment "while simultaneously facing the prospect that at a given point in time it would have to cede its investment to the host or the host's nominee." Vagts fears that this would tend to encourage firms to select projects with a short pay-off period, "a strategy which would often be regarded by the host as exploitative."[44] Large corporations normally operate on long-term planning, with a lead time of ten or even twenty years or more for major operations and investments. The International

43. *Frankfurter Allgemeine Zeitung* of August 16, 1976, at 10, and of October 18, 1976, at 12.

44. Vagts, "The Host Country Faces the MNE", *Boston University Law Review* (1973) at 274-275.

Chamber of Commerce also has perceived the danger that the 'fade-out' formula "orientates investors toward quick returns and reduced inputs of new technology, which are unlikely to be in the best interests of host countries."[45] There is for the MNE, on the other hand, one advantage in this progressive disinvestment technique, and that is that the element of uncertainty and instability - so essential to an enterprise seeking opportunity for profitable utilization of its investment capital - is diminished, which is clearly not the case with contract renegotiation.[46] Yet the fact remains that it too readily leads to the dangers alluded to above for the host, while not even totally eliminating uncertainty and instability for the MNE, since even 'fade-out' agreements are not immune from the possible consequences of a change of regime or fundamental change of circumstances.

On the whole, then, this host control technique known as the 'fade-out' formula, while stretching over the entire period of operations of an enterprise within the host territory - from pre-entry to the moment of total disinvestment - and exemplifying a high degree of local control, has not rendered the results intended, or at least has not anticipated the inevitable consequences of its application.

4. Evaluation

While the 'fade-out' formula is clearly and openly a disinvestment technique, and while it has some 'involuntary' aspects, it can in no way be regarded as expropriatory, as long as the original terms of agreement are adhered to which were negotiated at the time of entry. The 'fade-out' formula, then, is a fully legal, non-compensable disinvestment technique, available to any host state which feels that the control advantages thereof outweigh the disadvantages of its exploitive potential.

The same cannot necessarily be said in the case of contract renegotiation, where the initial contract has of course been voluntarily entered into, but the subsequent renegotiation, as we have seen, may lead to consequences for the

45. "Multinationals", 40 *ICC Bulletin,* July-August 1974, at 1.

46. It has been remarked by Burns Weston that "unless you can instill a sense of confidence on the part of...corporate groups, in being secure in their transactions abroad, the whole international economic process will begin to fall down." [Round Table: "Toward More Adequate Diplomatic Protection of Private Claims: 'Aris Gloves', 'Barcelona Traction', and Beyond," (jointly sponsored with the Deutsche Gesellschaft für Völkerrecht), 65 *Proceedings of the 65th Annual Meeting,* American Society of International Law, Washington, D.C., April 29-May 1, (1971), at 339.]

foreign MNE affiliate which were not foreseen at the time of entry, including involuntary withdrawal coerced by the host and amounting to expropriation.

In the following chapter, we shall examine other means of coercive or 'involuntary' disinvestment as instigated and implemented by the host government *vis-à-vis* the multinational enterprise, considering 'involuntary' or coerced disinvestment as the ultimate control technique exercised by the host state over foreign MNE affiliates within its territory.

PART FOUR: TECHNIQUES OF RESTRICTIVE HOST-STATE CONTROL OVER FOREIGN MNEs: COERCED DISINVESTMENT

Chapter XI.

EXPROPRIATION: TRADITIONAL CONCEPTS IN TRANSITION

We have now looked at some of the major control techniques exercised by industrialized host states over foreign multinational enterprises from the time of application for entry through actual operations once the foreign MNE has gained entry and established itself within the host territory. We have noted that, prior to entry, the extreme form of control is total exclusion. Yet even at the other end of the investment spectrum, after entry has been granted and operations have been established, there still remains to the host the prerogative not only to continue to exercise control over those operations, but, again, to apply the extreme control form of total exclusion against the foreign firm - at this stage, however, by means of expropriation, nationalization, or other peremptory disinvestment techniques for eliminating a foreign corporate presence. The aim of this chapter is to examine this ultimate host-state control technique of peremptory or "involuntary" disinvestment as exercised by highly industrialized nations against foreign MNE direct investment within their territory.

1. Definitions

"Expropriation" and "nationalization" are reasonably straightforward concepts, traditionally coupled, at least in principle, with the notion of compensation, being undisguised direct government "takings" of private "wealth" (i.e. property and related acquired rights). Nationalization could be briefly described as the conversion of a private industry or enterprise into national property, administered by governmental agencies or organs, and expropriation as any government-initiated taking of private property (for present purposes, commercial property), movable and immovable, or simply the control of such property, whether that property remains then in the hands of the government or is subsequently transferred to other private hands, (normally in such cases, those of the state's own nationals).[1]

The distinction was elaborated further by Professor O'Connell who held, in fact, that "[t]he term 'nationalisation'...has no place in the language of international law," going on to explain that the term "is popularly employed to describe the process whereby certain industries or means of production, distribution or exchange are, in pursuance of social or economic policies, concentrated in public hands. Should the concentration take no more than the form of prohibiting private competition with governmental instrumentalities then the process is one of monopoly, and...international law does not protect liberties or privileges and hence imposes no duty with respect to them. However, should the process involve the transference from private to public ownership of movable and immovable property, debts and intangible things of value, then it is one of expropriation, and international law interests itself in the protection of foreign titleholders. The discussions on nationalisation by the *Institut de Droit International* in 1952[2] and the International Bar Association in 1954 assumed this distinction."[3]

As state practice tends to modify all such definitions, we shall avoid, here, going into further subtleties in the distinctions between "nationalization" and "expropriation", and rather treat them loosely together as a technique of involuntary[4] disinvestment by government or government-initiated takeover. The two terms are, in any case, often inappropriately applied and actually tend to differ from one another more in scope and extent than in juridical nature.[5] Hence, for the purposes of this study, since "[t]he doctrinal viewpoint of distinguishing 'nationalization' from 'expropriation' may indeed have little practical effect in the reality of international legal relations",[6] the distinctions are not of fundamental importance, our interest centering in the constructive taking of property, by whatever means, when the end result is the forced "dis-

1. See e.g. *Marguerite de Joly de Sabla (United States)* v. *Panama,* (1933), 6 *Reports of International Arbitral Awards,* at 366; 28 *American Journal of International Law* (1934), (Judicial Decisions), at 602. See also U.N. General Assembly resolution 3201 (S-VI), para. 3(e) regarding "the right to nationalization *or transfer of ownership to its nationals"* [emphasis supplied], United Nations, *Official Records of the General Assembly: 6th Special Session* (1974), *Plenary Meetings: Resolutions* (Supp. No. 1 (A-9559)), United Nations, New York, 1974.

2. *Annuaire,* 1952, at 251. [Note from original text.]

3. O'Connell, *International Law,* 2nd ed. (London: Stevens & Sons, 1970), Vol. II, at 769.

4. For a distinction between "voluntary" and "involuntary" disinvestment, see *supra* Chapter X (1).

5. See Wortley, *Expropriation in Public International Law* (Cambridge: University Press (1959)), at 36.

6. Domke, "Foreign Nationalizations: Some Aspects of Contemporary International Law", 55 *American Journal of International Law* (1961), at 588.

investment'' of a multinational enterprise. As much legal and political language continues to rely on the term "expropriation", however, that term will be used, where appropriate, along with the more general and flexible expressions: "taking," or "expropriatory taking"; and, other than where clarity or emphasis require, since "nationalization" is understood within the term "expropriation" while the reverse is not always true, we shall generally use "expropriation" or "taking" to encompass both concepts.

2. The Compensation Debate

Whatever the definitional distinctions, common to all types of expropriatory taking is that it rests upon (a) the property being amenable to the jurisdiction of the expropriating state, (b) the expropriation's being for a public purpose, and (c) its being non-discriminatory.[7] Compensation is also a key factor in expropriations of any type. And while it is settled law that the purpose, under both municipal and international law, must be social and economic and must be genuinely for the public good, and that the national interest must override private interests,[8] the additional traditionally accepted condition of the payment of adequate, prompt and effective compensation is becoming increasingly subject to various and contradictory interpretations. Compensation is clearly a matter for municipal law in cases where the taking of the property of a national is concerned, while the taking of alien property has been traditionally governed by international law standards. The latter assumption has become a heavily disputed topic since the most highly frequently expropriating states (the developing nations) have more recently held to the contention that compensation settlement in all expropriation cases, including those involving aliens, is a matter for domestic jurisdiction, without reference to international law. This has bred some confusion and uncertainty which is already discernable in the 1962 U.N. General Assembly resolution on permanent sovereignty over natural resources. In its Article 4 we read:

> Nationalization, expropriation or requisitioning shall be based on grounds or reasons of public utility, security or the national interest which are recognized as overriding purely individual or private interests, both domestic and foreign. In such cases the owner shall be paid appropriate compensation, in accordance with the rules in force in the State

7. See e.g. O'Connell, op, cit., *supra* note 3, at 776-777.
8. See note 9 *infra* and accompanying text.

> taking such measures in the exercise of its sovereignty and in accordance with international law. In any case, where the question of compensation gives rise to a controversy, the national jurisdiction of the State taking such measures shall be exhausted. However, upon agreement by sovereign States and other parties concerned, settlement of the dispute should be made through arbitration or international adjudication.[9]

Professor O'Connell has remarked that the above Resolution "is in substance no more than a restatement of customary international law, particularly in the matter of exhaustion of local remedies, but a restatement so deliberately ambiguous as to smother rather than elucidate the legal problems relating to expropriation." He sees the expression "appropriate compensation" as not necessarily meaning adequate compensation, but as possibly relying on such factors as "previous unjust enrichment", and the reference to settlement through channels of national jurisdiction as potentially inferring that compensation is a matter of domestic jurisdiction.[10] These notions have been perpetuated and reinforced in subsequent U.N. General Assembly resolutions, notably in Resolution 3201 (S-VI) of May 1974, the Declaration on the Establishment of a New International Economic Order,[11] and Resolution 3281 (XXIX) of July 1974, the Charter of Economic Rights and Duties of States,[12] as well as in the latest Formulations of the United Nations Code of Conduct for Transnational Corporations,[13] in each of which all reference to international law in matters of compensation has disappeared.

A most cogent and compelling argument was elaborated in the 1977 Arbitral Award of Dupuy in the *Texaco and Calasiatic* v. *Libya* case[14] on the issue of whether compensation is governed by international or municipal law standards. In his reasoning, Dupuy supported the customary international law nature of the earlier (1962) resolution which contains an international law reference in its compensation clause, while rejecting any international legal status

9. U.N. document A/RES/1803 (XVII) (December 19, 1962).

10. O'Connell, op. cit., *supra* note 3 at 792.

11. U.N.G.A. resolution 3201 (S-VI), op. cit., *supra* note 1.

12. United Nations, *Official Records of the General Assembly: 29th Session* (1974), Vol. I: *Resolutions* (Supp. No. 31 (A/9631), United Nations, New York, 1975 [hereinafter cited as United Nations Charter of Economic Rights and Duties of States]).

13. United Nations, "Transnational Corporations: Code of Conduct; Formulations by the Chairman," U.N. document E/C.10/AC.2/8, of 13 December 1978 [hereinafter cited as United Nations Code of Conduct: Formulations], para. 52, at 12.

14. *Texaco Overseas Petroleum Co. and California Asiatic Oil Co.* v. *The Government of the Libyan Arab Republic* (Award on the Merits, 19 January 1977), 53 *International Law Reports,* at 389 *et seq.* (translated from the original French).

of the later resolutions, which "as a practical matter rule out any recourse to international law and...confer an exclusive and unlimited competence upon the legislation and courts of the host country."[15] He makes this distinction on the basis of an examination of the circumstances under which the resolutions were adopted and an analysis of the provisions and principles which they embody. It is thus noted that the majority vote which favoured the text of the 1962 resolution evidenced the assent of a great many states, representing all geographic areas and all economic systems,[16] and that this broad consensus was felt to be directly attributable to the inclusion in the text of two references to international law, in particular in the field of nationalization.[17]

This could not be said of the later resolutions, which were supported by a majority of U.N. member states but none of which were those industrialized market-economy states which engage in the largest amount of foreign direct investment activity.[18] These later resolutions were characterized by serious disagreements between representatives of different economic and political sectors, and since the absence of any intrinsically binding force of U.N. General Assembly resolutions implies that a general consensus by member states is a prerequisite to establishing any possible "customary" legally binding nature, it is clear that a majority vote, unmitigated by reservations such as those made by a large number of industrialized states in connection with some of the above amendments, must be representative of all political and economic groups. Moreover, it must be emphasized that even a representative majority vote on a resolution does not *create* international law, it merely codifies or proclaims rules recognized by the community of nations. In other words, it simply confirms a custom "by formulating it and specifying its scope".[19] Or as expressed by Ambassador Castañeda, who was Chairman of the Working Group preparing the Charter of Economic Rights and Duties of States, such resolutions "do not create the law; they have a declaratory nature of noting what does exist".[20]

Hence, while the 1962 Resolution 1803 (XVII) seemed to Dupuy to reflect

15. Ibid., para. 82, at 485.

16. Ibid., para. 84, at 487. This resolution was passed in the General Assembly by 87 votes to 2, with 12 abstentions. It should be noted that the two negative votes were those of developed countries, *viz.* France and South Africa, and that the abstentions were on the part of Soviet bloc countries. However, as there is exclusively state ownership in the Soviet bloc in any case, nationalization with compensation is not an issue for that group.

17. Ibid., para. 84, at 488.

18. Ibid., para. 86, at 491.

19. Ibid., para. 86, at 491.

20. Ibid., para. 87, at 491.

the state of customary law existing in this field,[21] he could not regard the Charter, and other relevant resolutions relating compensation to the municipal law standard, as anything other than "a *de lege ferenda* formulation, which even appears *contra legem* in the eyes of many developed countries."[22]. Evidence of the continued irresolution of this and some of the surrounding issues in the international community can be found in the latest "Formulations" of the United Nations Intergovernmental Working Group on a Code of Conduct, presented in a paper following the Group's Sixth Session in January 1979.[23]

Predictably, in light of the expropriation provision set out in U.N. General Assembly resolution 3201 (S-VI)[24] and in the Charter of Economic Rights and Duties of States,[25] accepted as it was only with reservations by a large number of the industrialized states, the "Formulations" contain a carefully-worded but clear effort not only to dissociate the legality of expropriation from international law, but also to dissociate international law from the question of compensation altogether, as in the resolutions mentioned above. The exact statement is as follows:

> 52. In the exercise of their sovereignty, States have the right, acting in the public interest, to nationalize property in their territory. Fair and equitable treatment of transnational corporations by the countries in which they operate includes payment of just compensation in the event of nationalization or other taking of their property, such government action being undertaken under due process of law, in accordance with national laws, regulations and administrative practices without discrimination between enterprises in comparable situations and with full regard to international obligations and contractual undertakings to which States have freely subscribed.[26]

Paragraph 52, however, due to its controversial nature, required two pages of annexed "Comments on nationalization and compensation" to clarify it and the issues it embodies. This is some indication of the extent of the controversy on the international level. Out of these two pages of comments, dealing for the most part with international legal priciples and rules governing

21. Ibid., para. 87, at 492.
22. Ibid., para. 88, at 493.
23. United Nations Code of Conduct: Formulations, op. cit., *supra* note 13, para. 52, at 12.
24. U.N.G.A. resolution 3201 (S-VI), op. cit., *supra* note 1, para. 3(e).
25. United Nations Charter of Economic Rights and Duties of States, op. cit., *supra* note 12.
26. United Nations Code of Conduct: Formulations, loc. cit., *supra* note 23.

compensation questions, one point is of particular interest here, and that is the relevance of the domestic law of the nationalizing state in this regard. Paragraph 3(c) points out that:

> ...According to one view, [national law] is the only relevant law; international law either has no relevant rules or it provides that national law is the only law applicable. According to another view, international law also includes certain independent standards, which override or supplement national law in order to protect the aliens affected.[27]

In some cases, the international standard may be higher than the national legal standards, depending on the host country concerned, and would thus help to eliminate inconsistencies of treatment among the various nations.[28]

It is interesting to note that while the developing states have favoured the exclusion of an international law standard as regards the compensation issue, that same group of nations has generally favoured, from the drafters' earliest sessions, the view that the Charter of Economic Rights and Duties of States should be a legal instrument with binding force. There are those[29] who see as inconsistent a position which on the one hand advocates a new regime of binding rules of international law applicable to the conduct of multinational enterprises, while on the other hand insisting that only the national law of the host state shall apply to expropriation, with no reference to international law standards. It would seem unacceptable to exclude international law from one aspect of an issue and invoke it in related aspects of the same issue.

While this retreat from the international law standard as regards alien property rights is indeed disquieting, it is not the aim of the present work to presume to draw final conclusions as to which view is the 'valid' one. It is of interest simply to note that the differing views are reflected even in the latest analysis on the international level, and that the question remains unsettled.

27. Ibid., Annex, at 1.

28. See Metzger, "The Individual and International Law: Property Interests", in *Human Rights: Protection of the Individual Under International Law,* Proceedings of the Fifth Summer Conference on International Law, Cornell Law School, Ithaca, New York, June 18-20, 1964, at 184.

29. *Inter alia*, Komiya, "Report of the Group of Eminent Persons to Study the Impact of Multinational Corporations on Development and on International Relations", United Nations publication E/5500/Rev.1:ST/ESA/6, New York, 1974, at 122; Seidl-Hohenveldern, "The United Nations and Transnational Corporations", in Simmonds, ed., *Legal Problems of Multinational Corporations* (London: British Institute of International and Comparative Law, 1977), at 55.

3. Legality Link

One thing, however, is agreed, and that is that expropriation *per se* is not illegal under international law, provided the proper conditions are met. Those conditions enumerated earlier,[30] jurisdictional competence, public purpose and non-discrimination, as well as compliance with international obligations and contractual undertakings[31] are commonly recognized to govern expropriation legality. Basically only the question of whether prompt, adequate and effective compensation belongs - as it traditionally has - to the "proper conditions" remains to be resolved.

Resolving the issue will in no way be easy, as the differing views reflect a far deeper disaccord. As Mr. Justice Brennan commented even as far back as the *Sabbatino* case:

> The disagreement as to relevant international law standards reflects an even more basic divergence between the national interests of capital importing and capital exporting nations and between the social ideologies of those countries that favor state control of a considerable portion of the means of production and those that adhere to a free enterprise system. It is difficult to imagine...an area which touches more sensitively the practical and ideological goals of the various members of the community of nations.[32]

Among the several reasons for the U.S. Supreme Court's declining to adjudicate the merits of the now famous *Sabbatino* case - a decision which was subsequently much criticized - was its majority observation that "[t]here are few if any issues in international law today on which opinion seems to be so divided as the limitation on a state's power to expropriate the property of aliens."[33] The compensation issue, and its link to the legality of the taking, only adds to the already complex and controversial nature of the whole question of expropriation in international law.

4. Conclusion

As it is, in any case, not this issue of indemnity, other than its legality link, but

30. See text accompanying note 7 *supra*.

31. See e.g. United Nations, Code of Conduct: Formulations, op. cit., *supra* note 13, para. 52, at 12.

32. *Banco Nacional de Cuba* v. *Sabbatino, 376* U.S. 398 (1964).

33. Ibid., at 428.

rather that of the act of taking itself and the consequent expulsion of the foreign enterprise as such, or the *de facto* termination of its control over operations, which is our central concern, we shall not go further into the compensation debate here, realizing also full well that an early resolution of the issue canot be expected.

For the present, then, we can go no further than to say that "expropriation", subject to the proper conditions, is a perfectly acceptable control technique under international law, realizing at the same time that problems arise normally not with the expropriatory act itself but with the concomitant conditions, most frequently with questions of valuation of property and promptness of payment. It is indeed the compensation-related questions which are by far the most controversial and contested element involved in international expropriations.

Chapter XII.

"CREEPING EXPROPRIATION"

1. Defining the Perimeters

By far the greatest number of outright expropriation cases involves a developing state or communist or socialist state-run economy as expropriating host, with an industrialized state's enterprise as plaintiff. This considerably limits our discussion in the present context, as we have confined ourselves here, as throughout the work, to techniques applied by industrialized, free-enterprise host states to foreign direct investment within their territory. This automatically eliminates fuller treatment of such otherwise interesting cases as *Sabbatino*[1], *Anglo-Iranian Oil Company*[2], the Suez Canal nationalization, The Anaconda Company "Chileanization" arbitration and others where, even though industrialized states were involved, the acting government (the host) was not that of an industrialized but rather that of a developing state.

The numerous 'nationalizations' following World War II likewise have little relevance to the specific issue of industrialized host state control over foreign MNEs. First, the large majority of the nationalizations were carried out by newly "socialized" economies; and secondly, they - as well as those which were effected by free-enterprise industrialized states - were conditioned by political factors and by the special circumstances of war and post-war settlements, and were consequently largely negotiated according to the law of war, or at least a *lex specialis.* While it can be postulated that the "lump-sum" agreements which characterized most of the liability settlements involved, as perpetuated since in nearly all internationally negotiated compensation settlements, may possibly be regarded as a source of customary international law,[3] such post-war nationalizations themselves can hardly be regarded as general techniques of host state control over foreign MNE investments.

1. *Banco Nacional de Cuba* v. *Sabbatino,* 376 U.S. 398 (1964).

2. *Anglo-Iranian Oil Co.* (United Kingdom *v.* Iran), 1952 I.C.J. Reports p. 11.

3. Cf. White, "Nationalisation of Foreign Property", 55 *American Journal of International Law* (1961), at 183; van Hecke, "Nationality of Companies Analyzed", 8 *Netherlands Internation-*

Looking beyond the cases of outright expropriation, however, we discover that other more indirect means exist by which a government can divest alien interests of their direct investments. These alternative means of "disguised expropriation", or "constructive takings", tend to be applied as readily by the industrialized governments as by the developing states, the latter having, in many cases, actually learned these indirect taking techniques from the more economically sophisticated industrialized nations. Developments in this direction are taking on increasing significance in both the industrialized and developing worlds, and should not be overlooked.

In examining the subject of expropriation as any form of government taking of foreign commercial property or other acquired property rights, in the context of industrialized host state control techniques over foreign multinational enterprises, what is really significant - and is surely the trend of the future in "expropriation" measures, at least in industrialized states - are the various techniques used by developed nations to, in effect, implement what would amount to an expropriation, but without referring to it as such.

2. Terminology, Interpretation and Definitions

Current terminology itself reflects the avoidance of the classical concept of outright expropriation. In what would appear to be an attempt to avoid the associations connected with either the term "expropriation" or "nationalization", and perhaps the international responsibility which these terms imply, the use of such alternatives as "indigenization", "Mexicanization", "Chileanization", "Canadianization", etc., is on the increase. Furthermore, by emphasizing nationality or localness, the connotation is one of national public welfare, so as ostensibly to meet the requirement of "public purpose".

On the other hand, such terms as "de facto", "surreptitious", or "creep-

---

al Law Review (1961), at 236; Domke, speaking at Round Table: "Toward More Adequate Diplomatic Protection of Private Claims: 'Aris Glores', 'Barcelona Traction', and Beyond", (jointly sponsored with the Deutsche Gesellschaft für Völkerrecht), 65 *Proceedings of the 65th Annual Meeting* (1971), American Society of International Law, Washington, D.C., (September 1971), at 342-343; Weston, ibid., (Round Table), at 343-344; Flemming, ibid., (Round Table) at 345-346; Lillich, ibid., (Round Table), at 357; Lillich, "International Claims: Their Settlement by Lump Sum Agreements", in Sanders, ed., *International Arbitration: Liber Amicorum for Martin Domke,* (The Hague: Nijhoff, 1967), at 143, 154, note 40; "Two Perspectives on the Barcelona Traction Case: The Rigidity of Barcelona", (Editorial Comment: Lillich), 65 *American Journal of International Law* (1971), at 526-528; Dawson and Weston, " 'Prompt, Adequate and Effective': A Universal Standard of Compensation?" 30 *Fordham Law Review* (1962), at 727, 750.

ing'' expropriation indicate the recognition of more subtle forms of expropriation; and these and similar expressions are becoming increasingly popular for describing an indirect taking ''whose distinguishing characteristic usually involves, at once or over time, the denial of access to, use of, or benefit from wealth processes and institutions (rather than the deprivation of wealth itself) and/or the spoliation of values other than wealth but upon which the production, distribution, and consumption of wealth totally depend.''[4]

What this signifies is that the term ''expropriation'' is gradually taking on a considerably broader interpretation, within both the developing and developed world, to include various indirect means of taking over foreign assets or nullifying foreign control, in manifest recognition of the actual expropriatory effect of these indirect takings. By the recognition of other techniques of government-inspired takeovers as simply expropriation in disguise, the legality of the takeover can be scrutinized in the light of the international law governing expropriation, however much in flux some aspects of that law may be.

The urgency of arriving at reasonably precise basic definitions of ''takings'' or ''expropriations'' is becoming increasingly acute with the proliferation of bilateral treaties which guarantee the property of a state's nationals against expropriation other than for a public purpose and then only contingent upon payment of prompt and adequate compensation.[5] The importance of the interpretation of ''expropriation'' in such treaties is self-evident. This was recognized even back in the mid-1950's by the Committee on Foreign Law of the Association of the Bar of the City of New York in Hearings before the Committee on Foreign Relations of the United States Senate, in which it proposed that in future bilateral trade and navigation treaties it might be well to define the term ''taken'' in those provisions concerning expropriation or other ''taking of property''.[6]

Although the Committee did not go very far in carrying out its suggestion,

4. Weston, ''International Law and the Deprivation of Foreign Wealth: A Framework for Future Inquiry'', in Falk and Black, eds., *The Future of the International Legal Order,* Vol.II (Princeton, N.J.: Princeton University Press, 1970), at 76.

5. Cf. e.g. Treaties of Friendship, Commerce and Navigation between the United States and Ethiopia (1951), 206 U.N.T.S., 41, 68; between the United States and Iran (1955), 284 U.N.T.S. 93, 114; and between the United States and the Federal Republic of Germany (1957), 273 U.N.T.S. 3, 8; cf. also Art. 3 of Draft Convention on the Protection of Foreign Property, prepared by the Organisation for Economic Co-operation and Development (OECD Publication No. 23081, November 1967, OECD, Paris, 1967), [hereinafter cited as OECD Draft Convention]; reprinted in 7 *International Legal Materials* (1968), at 117 *et seq.*

6. *Hearings before the Senate Committee on Foreign Relations on Executives E, G,* and *H,* 84th Cong., 2d Sess., 15 (1956), as reported by Christie, ''What Constitutes a Taking of Property under International Law?'', *British Yearbook of International Law,* 1962, at 330.

the subsequent Harvard Draft Convention on the International Responsibility of States for Injuries to Aliens[7] and the American Law Intitute's *Restatement (Second) of the Foreign Relations Law of the United States,*[8] which relied heavily on the Harvard Draft in its provisions relating to economic injury to aliens, recognize and reflect the complex nature of the question. The Harvard Draft, for example, attempted to provide a definition in Article 10, paragraph 3(a) in stating that:

> A 'taking of property' includes not only an outright taking of property but also any such unreasonable interference with the use, enjoyment, or disposal of property as to justify an inference that the owner thereof will not be able to use, enjoy, or dispose of the property within a reasonable period of time after the inception of such interference.[9]

The definition could perhaps have benefitted from the insertion of the words "or controlling management" after the word "owner". Of course, as the owner(s) theoretically appoints the management, the effective control implications may be deemed to be implicit. But it must be said that the emphasis in the Harvard Draft distinctly inclines toward ownership control.

The emphasis rest not on ownership but rather on "effective control" in Article 1.13 of the (1975 form of) General Terms and Conditions used by the Overseas Private Investment Corporation (OPIC), which brings within the scope of "expropriation" "any action which...directly results in preventing...the Investor from effectively exercising its fundamental rights with respect to the Foreign Enterprise...or...the Foreign Enterprise from *exercising effective control* over the use or disposition of a substantial portion

7. Reprinted in part, by permission of the President and Fellows of Harvard College, in Sohn and Baxter, "Responsibility of States for Injuries to the Economic Interests of Aliens", 55 *American Journal of International Law* (1961), at 548 *et seq.* For the final version of the draft, see Convention on the International Responsibility of States for Injuries to Aliens [Final Draft with explanatory notes], Sohn and Baxter, reporters [hereinafter cited as Harvard Draft 1974], in Garcia-Amador, Sohn and Baxter, *Recent Codifications of the Law of State Responsibility for Injury to Aliens* (New York: Oceana, 1974), at 208.

8. American Law Institute, *Restatement of the Law (Second): Foreign Relations Law of the United States* (St. Paul, Minn.: American Law Institute Publishers, 1965) [hereinafter cited as *Restatement].*

9. Harvard Draft (1974), op. cit., *supra* note 7; also in earlier drafts reprinted in part in Sohn and Baxter, "Responsibility of States for Injuries to the Economic Interests of Aliens", op. cit., *supra* note 7, at 553; also cited in Christie, loc. cit., *supra* note 6. The notion of "unreasonable" is also embodied in Art. 1 of the OECD Draft Convention, loc. cit., *supra* note 5. See also ibid., notes 6(a) (b) (i), 7 (Notes and Comments to Article 1).

of its property or from constructing the Project or operating the same" [emphasis supplied].[10]

A precise definition of "expropriatory action" is at least as critical in the OPIC context as it is in the many bilateral treaties of friendship, commerce and navigation, since any foreign-government action falling outside the terms of the definition is excluded from insurance recovery.[11]

Both of the above sets of standards stress the right of exercising effective control over the use, enjoyment and disposition of property. In the OPIC formulation, the operative words are "effective control over...property"; in the Harvard Draft, the operative words are "unreasonable interference", and this clearly should apply not only to unreasonable interference with ownership, but also to unreasonable interference with control and management of an enterprise. In the following pages we shall, in turn, consider both types of "unreasonable interference" with effective control, *viz.* unreasonable interference with ownership control, and unreasonable interference with management control.

3. Unreasonable Interference with Ownership: "Canadianization"

First let us look at an example of unreasonable interference with ownership[12] by an industrialized state, so assessed by a lawyer who is a national of the state in question, namely Canada, with its recent "Canadianization" program.

"Canadianization", in a word, implies a special brand of nationalization aimed at bringing foreign corporations under Canadian public and private control. The policy was motivated by a concern over the extent of foreign (particularly American) ownership and managerial control represented by multinational enterprises in the Canadian economy.

One of the chief vehicles through which this policy was to be implemented is the Canada Development Corporation (CDC) whose main purpose, as summarized by the Commons Committee on External Affairs and National Defence,

10. OPIC (234 KGT 12-70), extracted from a citation in Steiner and Vagts, *Transnational Legal Problems,* 2nd Edition (Mineola, New York: The Foundation Press, 1976), at 474-475. See also Vagts, "Coercion and Foreign Investment Rearrangements", 72 *American Journal of International Law* (1978), at 26.

11. See ibid. (Steiner and Vagts), at 473.

12. By stipulating membership of a majority of resident nationals on the Board of each company, management "interference" is also involved. But what this really amounts to is interference with the usual prerogative of the owners to designate a majority of the Board – i.e., for the purpose here, it interferes with ownership.

> should be that of a large holding company with entrepreneurial and managerial functions; it should assume a leadership role in Canada's business and financial community in close cooperation with existing institutions; it should help to organize consortia of investors domestic and foreign to carry out large projects beyond the capacity of a single institution, while throughout maintaining a clear Canadian presence.
>
> Its main purpose would not be to buy back Canadian businesses now owned by Americans.[13]

The key phrase in the first paragraph is: "maintaining a clear Canadian presence." The first sentence of the following paragraph is a strong indicator of the likelihood of the very purpose it ostensibly decries.

Canadianization measures include both provincial and federal legislation aimed at ensuring a certain proportion of national shareholders in each public corporation, a majority of resident nationals on the board of each company, and other similar requirements.

Another vehicle for implementing Canadianization has been the amended Income Tax Act[14], first made public in the Budget Speech of 14 June 1971, then passed by the House of Commons on 17 December 1971, "assented to" on 23 December 1971, and in full effect since 1 January 1972. Tax reductions under this Act were extended to corporations with "a degree of Canadian ownership"[15], and were thus meant to encourage Canadian ownership participation. Canadian lawyers Feltham and Rauenbusch, writing in 1973, announced that "[u]nder the new tax legislation...the incentive to Canadianize will be continued." But their own assessment of its merits was revealed by the subsequent remark: "Now is the time to recognize that this effort to 'Canadianize' industry through the tax system is fruitless and that we should expunge the ill-conceived wrinkle from the tax system."[16] A year later the same two lawyers wrote: "It is generally agreed that this effort to 'Canadianize' industry through the tax system has been fruitless."[17]

13. *Eleventh Report of the Standing Committee on External Affairs and National Defence Respecting Canada-U.S. Relations,* Second Session, 28th Parliament (September 1970) ("Wahn Report"), at 134.

14. *Revised Statutes of Canada* [1952], c. 148, as partially repealed by 1970-71-72, c. 63, s.l, and as otherwise amended.

15. Ibid., s. 212(3).

16. Feltham and Rauenbusch, "Canada and the Multinational Enterprise", in Hahlo, ed., *Nationalism and the Multinational Enterprise: Legal, Economic and Managerial Aspects* (Dobbs Ferry, New York: Oceana Publications, Inc., 1973), at 77.

17. Feltham and Rauenbusch, "Economic Nationalism", in Macdonald, et al., eds., *Canadian Perspectives on International Law and Organization (Toronto:* University of Toronto Press, (c. 1974)), at 909.

There has, in fact, been a diminishing of interest and a growing disenchantment with Canadianization in general. In addition to the overriding economic and other non-legal factors which have contributed to this disenchantment, the Canadians have conscientiously and exemplarily reviewed their own "Canadianization" policy in the light of international law, and in so doing have recognized the discriminatory nature of the program. An astute and perceptive analysis in this regard has been made by one Canadian lawyer, E. James Arnett, who holds the following "fundamental initial distinction" to be essential to a comprehension of the problem:

> [A] sovereign state has virtually unlimited rights to prevent aliens from entering into its territory and to prevent the acquisition by aliens of rights, whether respecting property or otherwise, in its territory. However, once an alien has entered or has acquired rights within the territory of the host state then certain definite obligations are imposed upon such state by international law, the breach of which will be enforceable by diplomatic efforts, international adjudication or otherwise.[18]

Foreign investors, then, with their "acquired rights" guaranteed by international law, are entitled to expect certain minimum standards on the part of the host state. Arnett cannot conceive of the Canadian Government simply confiscating foreign commercial interests. He does not rule out, however, "expropriation with compensation". Here he already begins the association of "Canadianization" with "expropriation", and expropriation with compensation remains "indeed possible" under international law.

The problem arises with the application of the principle of non-discrimination, which principle he agrees is an absolute condition of lawful expropriation. Citing both the OECD Draft Convention of 1967 on the Protection of Foreign Property[19] regarding the illegality of "*de facto* discrimination", and Professor O'Connell who reiterates the rule which "goes back to Vattel and has been sanctioned by many tribunals" that "[w]hen the nationals of only one State are selected for expropriation this is *a fortiori* illegal discrimination, which likewise perhaps exposes the motivation...,"[20] Arnett reasons that "*[p]rima facie* this would appear to prohibit any kind of 'Canadianization' of foreign enterprises already established in Canada."[21]

18. Arnett, "Canadian Regulation of Foreign Investment: The Legal Parameters," 50 *Canadian Bar Review* (1972), at 234. See also *Restatement,* op. cit., *supra* note 8, at 508.

19. OECD Draft Convention, loc. cit., *supra* note 5.

20. O'Connell, *International Law,* 2nd ed. (London: Stevens & Sons, 1970), Vol. II at 780.

21. Arnett, op. cit., *supra* note 18, at 236.

While Arnett's arguments are sound, they perhaps lose some force by his resort to Vattel's rule relating to discrimination based on nationality. It is evident that the CDC measures are aimed at reducing the dominant American presence in Canadian industry, as obvious from the inverted statement by the Commons Committee on External Affairs and National Defence, *inter alia,* cited earlier[22]; but as this is indirect, and nowhere officially stated, it does not perhaps provide the strongest argument upon which to base the claim that Canadianization is contrary to international law on grounds of discrimination. Even if one were to deny any discrimination against specifically American companies as opposed to foreign companies in general, the discriminatory nature of the Canadianization program would still remain an issue. This is clear when one recalls that discrimination under international law has three aspects: (1) discrimination against a legal or natural person on account of his alien status, (2) discrimination against aliens of one particular nationality, and (3) discrimination against aliens generally, once they have entered into the host territory and/or lawfully acquired property interests therein.[23] Hence, Arnett's argument could perhaps gain force by relying more on the third of the aspects enumerated above, though in fact the second can likewise be seen to be applicable.

It is important to note, as set forth in Section 166(2) of the American Law Institute's *Restatement (Second) of the Foreign Relations Law of the United States,* that discrimination against an alien consists in "treating the alien differently from nationals or from aliens of a different nationality *without a reasonable basis for the difference*" [emphasis supplied].[24] This recognition that there do exist "reasonable" bases for differential treatment (of aliens in general *vis-à-vis* nationals) is important, and is expanded upon in the *Restatement* as follows:

> *a. Reasonable basis for different treatment.* International law does not require that an alien be accorded all the privileges of a national. If the basis for different treatment is reasonable in the light of the legitimate interests of the state, it is not discriminatory within the meaning of this Section. International law imposes no duty on a state to permit aliens to enter its territory or to acquire interests in property subject to its jurisdiction. It may, therefore, impose a great variety of conditions on

22. See text accompanying note 13 *supra.*

23. See *Restatement,* op. cit., *supra* note 8, § 166 and Comment, at 507-508. Cf. the OECD Draft Convention (op. cit., *supra* note 5) Note 8(e), (Notes and Comments to Article 1) which enumerates *four* different forms of discrimination as regards the treatment of property.

24. *Idem* (*Restatement*).

> such entry or acquisition as to substantive matters such as ownership or exploitation of natural resources, ownership of land, engaging in commercial activities, practicing professions, ownership of domestic corporations, etc. The only criterion as to the reasonableness of such conditions is the international standard of justice defined in Section 165(2).[25] However, if an alien has lawfully entered the territory for a purpose lawful at the time of entry, or lawfully acquired an interest in property subject to the jurisdiction of the state, hardship on the alien must be taken into account in determining the reasonableness of new restrictions....[26]

Without going into the finer distinctions between "just" and "unjust" discrimination,[27] it is clear that even if there does exist, "a reasonable bisis for the less favorable treatment of the alien", which precludes such treatment being unlawful on grounds of discrimination under the rule stated in Section 166, this still does not lend legality to conduct attributable to a state that forbids an alien to engage in previously lawful gainful activity (*Restatement,* Section 196(1)) unless either:

> (1)...
> (a) the alien receives reasonable notice and opportunity to engage in other gainful activities or to depart from the territory of the state, [or]
>
> (b) the prohibition is promulgated for bona fide reasons of public policy of the state and is equally applicable to nationals and to aliens similarly situated....[28]

25. Section 165(2) of the *Restatement* (ibid., at 501) defines the international standard of justice as follows:
(2) The international standard of justice...is the standard required for the treatment of aliens by
(a) the applicable principles of international law as established by international custom, judicial and arbitral decisions, and other recognized sources or, in the absence of such applicable principles,
(b) analogous principles of justice generally recognized by states that have reasonably developed legal systems.

26. Ibid., at 508.

27. Cf. Moore, 6 *Digest of International Law* (1906), at 698 *et seq.*; OECD Draft Convention, loc. cit., *supra* note 5, Arts. 1 & 3; Council of Europe, Consultative Assembly, Opinion No. 39 (1963) on the OECD Draft Convention on the Protection of Foreign Property, reproduced in 3 *International Legal Materials* (1964), p. 133, at 137; Schwartzenberger, *Foreign Investments and International Law* (London: Stevens & Sons, 1969), at 163-164; Arnett, op. cit., *supra* note 18, at 236-237.

28. *Restatement,* op. cit., *supra* note 8, § 196 (1) (a) (b), at 589.

And as, in Subsection (1)(b), the prohibition must apply no more unfavourably to the alien than to a national similarly situated, and as this can clearly not be the case with Canadianization, the exception indicated in (1)(b) is not allowable.

One of the exceptions to the General Rule stated in Section 196 of the *Restatement* that "[c]onduct attributable to a state that forbids an alien to engage in previously lawful activity is wrongful under international law" is where:

> (c) under the law and practice of the state in effect when the prohibiton becomes effective there is reasonable provision for the determination and payment of just compensation.
>
> (2) Failure of a state to pay just compensation under the circumstances indicated in Subsection (1)(c) is wrongful under international law.

The above arguments would seem to strengthen the implication of Arnett's argument that "any policy of 'rolling-back' existing foreign investment in Canada will run afoul of the prohibition against discriminatory expropriation."[29]

Arnett thus concludes, and rightly so in the opinion of the present writer, that while international law would not prevent Canada from prohibiting further MNE investment, any actual taking of existing foreign property in Canada which is "(a) unjustifiable on the grounds of overriding public policy, (b) discriminatory, or (c) unaccompanied by prompt and adequate compensation", would be a breach of international law. "Hence", he submits, "virtually all the calls for 'Canadianization' or 'roll-back' involve illegality because they are by definition discriminatory. Furthermore, even if such legislation can be framed in such a way as to be non-discriminatory, care must be taken to meet the minimum international standards relating to compensation."[30]

4. Unreasonable Interference with Management: 'Mitbestimmung'

An "expropriation" or "taking", however, as we have already remarked, is not limited to takeovers of mere ownership rights. In full awareness of the present-day diminished relevance of nominal ownership in control considera-

29. Arnett, op. cit., *supra* note 18, at 237.
30. Ibid., at 244.

tions, other than where it is the owner himself whose right to manage his own enterprise[31] is interfered with, it may well be that the assumption of managerial control is a sufficient "taking" to constitute expropriation giving rise to a claim for full compensation.[32] This is based on the premise that "the most fundamental right that an owner of property has is the right to participate in its control and management."[33]

It is precisely in this regard that the expropriatory nature of 'co-determination' or *Mitbestimmung* (the priciple of the representation of non-shareholder workers in decision-making and management) has in recent years received so much attention in the Federal Republic of Germany and in those states doing business in the West German market or planning their own co-determination legislation. This issue was particularly publicized by the landmark decision of the West German Constitutional Court *(Bundesverfassungsgericht)* on March 1, 1979[34] regarding the constitutionality of the co-determination law *(Mitbestimmungsgesetz)* of 1976.[35] Whether *Mitbestimmung* is compatible with the West German "Basic Law" *(Grundgesetz)* is not of course conclusive on the question of whether it is compatible with international law,[36] yet of specific interest to the present study are those relevant arguments which relate to the expropriatory nature of *Mitbestimmung* where the co-determination involves local nationals in the management of a foreign-owned and/or foreign-controlled MNE.

The decision of the *Bundesverfassungsgericht* of 1 March has spared us a lengthier discussion here in that the Court held the *Mitbestimmungsgesetz* of 1976 to be constitutional; according to that law, *Mitbestimmung* slightly favours the shareholders as against the work-force representation. This means that the co-determination is not on a full-parity basis (i.e. equal representation of both shareholder and work-force elements), which at least temporarily

31. "[T]he right of the owner to manage enterprise" has been seen, "from an examination of the cases and of the underlying realities, to be least subject to successful interference." (Christie, "What Constitutes a Taking of Property under International Law?", op. cit., *supra* note 6, at 333.)

32. Ibid., at 331.

33. Ibid., at 337. The notion of management as a property right has been codified in the OECD Draft Convention mentioned above which, in Art. I(a), provides that each Party to the Convention "shall not in any way impair the *management,* maintenance, use, enjoyment or disposal [of the property of the nationals of the other Parties] by unreasonable or discriminatory measures." [Emphasis supplied.]

34. See *Bundesverfassungsgericht, Neue Juristische Wochenschrift* 1979, at 669. See also (a) *infra* at 271.

35. *Mitbestimmungsgesetz* of 4 May 1976, BGBl 1976 I, S.1153.

36. See Wengler, "Parity Codetermination in West German Companies and International Law", 9 *Vanderbilt Journal of International Law* (1976), at 59.

allays the expropriation challenge from foreign shareholders in enterprises incorporated in the Federal Republic of Germany. Basing such a decision solely on factors of percentage of representation, however, would be to ignore the fact that there may be circumstances where even *Mitbestimmung* without full-parity representation (i.e. with a marginal majority on the part of the shareholders) may be deemed interference to a degree amounting to expropriation. It has been remarked that "[t]he fact that an alien employer is suddenly forced to take nationals of the local state on to his board of directors would not seem, by itself, to amount to expropriation. Nor would it seem to be expropriation if the alien owner were forced to take representatives of his labour force on to his board. There might even be circumstances where operating control over the enterprise might be completely taken from the alien owner without rendering the state liable even for 'damages' for use....Presumably [, however,] after a sufficient passage of time such action would amount to an expropriation....[37]

One need only consider the kind of situation where, as a result of co-determination, a company is no longer administered with a view toward earning dividends for the shareholders, but rather with the aim of operating at a loss in order to preserve jobs or even to induce the shareholders to sell out their shares at artificially depressed prices. Shares, after all, and the voting and other rights related thereto, constitute an 'investment', which has a right to protection.[38]

Certainly if the constitutionality question was raised before the German courts regarding a *Mitbestimmung* law where there was less than equal representation for the non-shareholder worker representation, there is an implicit recognition that "unreasonable interference" may exist even short of full parity. For the purposes of the present study, however, whether the representation of the non-shareholder work force is equal to that of the shareholders, or marginally in the minority, is of little importance, if it is agreed that what is deemed to constitute a constructive taking is "unreasonable interference"; the key, then, revolves around the interpretation of "unreasonable".

The early draft of the German Act provided for full-parity co-determination, and the American Chamber of Commerce in 1974 requested, on behalf of interested American investors, a legal opinion (*Gutachten*)[39] concerning the

37. Christie, op. cit., *supra* note 6, at 333-334.

38. See e.g. Treaty between the Federal Republic of Germany and Indonesia of November 8, 1968, *Bundesgesetzblatt* [BGBl] 1970 II S.492, in which shares are said to constitute an 'investment' within the meaning of the treaty (Art. 1), and the voting and election rights attached thereto are protected against expropriation and restriction (additional protocol to Art. 3).

39. Wengler, *Die Mitbestimmung und das Völkerrecht: Ein Gutachten über die Vereinbarkeit der Mitbestimmungsgesetzgebung in der Bundesrepublik mit dem deutsch-amerikanischen Han-*

compatibility of full-parity co-determination (*Mitbestimmung mit voller Parität*) with the German-American Treaty of Friendship, Commerce and Navigation of 1954.[40] While both the *Gutachten* and the court decision are based on a specific situation arising within the context of a treaty agreement, and thus cannot be seen as necessarily having general applicability in international law, some relevant inferences can nonetheless be drawn.

a. *Bundesverfassungsgericht* decision: international implications

As regards the *Bundesverfassungsgericht* decision of March 1, 1979, a more detailed look into the German *Mitbestimmungsgesetz* of 1976 and the particular constitutional articles in dispute and related complaints remain a domestic concern; but the judgment itself is of international importance for several reasons. First, a number of other Western European countries[41] had already introduced co-determination laws, though mostly with the workers in a slight minority position, and a number of others had plans to do so, including Switzerland, Great Britain and France,[42] all of which followed the West German case with close attention.

Secondly, international implications arise, as remarked earlier, where firms with alien ownership and control are concerned, as the rule applies to all companies established under the laws of the Federal Republic of Germany. Thus it extends to "West German companies whose stock is held exclusively, predominantly or partially by foreigners and foreign companies, so long as the 'controlled' German company has a work force of over 2000. Controlling foreign parent companies - which, after all, may have an organizational structure totally different from the German company in question - are themselves not affected....If, however, a foreign company controls several German companies, the work force of all of the companies is to be aggregated so that, if the total is more than 2000, the company most closely related to the central management of the combine may be subjected to the act, even if the work force

delsvertrag (Baden-Baden: Nomos Verlag [c. 1975]).

40. Treaty of Friendship, Commerce and Navigation between the United States of America and the Federal Republic of Germany of 29 October 1954 (entered into force 14 July 1956), 7 U.S.T. 1839, T.I.A.S. No. 3593.

41. *Inter alia,* the Netherlands, Norway, Luxembourg. (See Wengler, "Parity Codetermination in West German Companies and International Law", op. cit., *supra* note 36, at 42.

42. *Idem.*

of that particular company remains below 2000."[43] Here multinationality plays an obvious role in augmenting the vulnerability of a foreign company to the law of the host state.

Had the West German law under question provided for full parity co-determination, or if "unreasonable interference" had been shown to accompany even a less-than-full-parity worker representation, the question not only of German constitutionality but also of legality under international law where foreign investors were concerned, would have had to have been reviewed. Moreover, under Article 25 of the German Constitution,[44] general norms of international law are considered a part of German domestic law, allowing a challenge before the German Constitutional Court (*Bundesverfassungsgericht*) to the validity of any municipal law which is in possible conflict with those norms. Hence, if a German law is found by the *Bundesverfassungsgericht* to be in conflict with any principle of international law understood under Article 25, the German law in question is deemed unconstitutional (*verfassungswidrig*). In addition to general international law implications regarding expropriatory acts against alien property, Germany's commercial treaty relationships, such as the Treaty of Friendship, Commerce and Navigation of 1954 (FCN Treaty) with the United States[45] and the treaties for the mutual protection of capital investments (*Investitionsschutzverträge)* with numerous other states,[46]would have been brought into question.

b. The German *Gutachten*: international implications

While the German Court carefully avoided all reference to co-determination with full parity, the German *Gutachten* (legal opinion)[47] on the other hand, based on the original draft of the law which provided for *Mitbestimmung mit*

43. Wengler, "Parity Codetermination in West German Companies and International Law", op. cit., *supra* note 36, at 3.

44. *Grundgesetz für die Bundesrepublik Deutschland vom 23. Mai 1949* BGBl 1949 S.l). See especially, art. 25, 59(2), 100(2). For a more thoroughgoing analysis of the relation of German constitutional law with public international law, see Blockmann, *Grundgesetz und Völkerrecht* (Berlin: Duncker & Humblot, 1975).

45. Treaty of Friendship, Commerce and Navigation between the United States of America and the Federal Republic of Germany, loc. cit., *supra* note 40.

46. See West German *Bundesgesetzblatt* [BGBl]; for a listing and excerpts defining "expropriation" in each of the treaties, see Wengler, *Die Mitbestimmung und das Völkerrecht: Ein Gutachten,* op. cit., *supra* note 39, *Anlage 2,* pp. 101-108; also Wengler, "Parity Codetermination in West German Companies and International Law", *op. cit., supra* note 36, at 51-56.

47. *Idem (Die Mitbestimmung und das Vöerrecht: Ein Gutachten).*

voller Parität, found full-parity *Mitbestimmung* where aliens are involved to be an expropriatory "taking" contrary to international law. This finding was based on a number of considerations.[48] Firstly the German-American FCN Treaty of 1954, along with other FCN treaties[49] between the United States and third parties which affect the application of the German-American Treaty by virtue of the most-favoured-nation clause, contains the provision that nationals and companies of either party shall be permitted, within the territories of the other party, "to control and manage enterprises which they have established or acquired."[50]

Even more precise is the parallel provision in the Italian-American FCN Treaty of 26 September 1951, which stipulates that:

> [t]he nationals, corporations and associations of either High Contracting Party shall not be subjected to arbitrary or discriminatory measures within the territories of the other High Contracting Party resulting particularly in:
> (a) preventing their effective control and management of enterprises which they have been permitted to establish or acquire therein; or
> (b) impairing their other legally acquired rights and interests in such enterprises or in the investments which they have made, whether in the form of funds (loans, shares or otherwise), materials, equipment, services, processes, patents, techniques or otherwise.[51]

In addition to the express inclusion of "effective management" in both treaties, the *Gutachten* went further to state that even simply "control of the company means control of the *management* functions exercised by the competent organs of the company".[52] Moreover, since "such control by shareholders is exercised principally through their right to elect the organs of the

48. The ensuing analysis is condensed and excerpted from Wengler, "Parity Codetermination in West German Companies and International Law", op. cit., *supra* note 36, pp. 5-41.

49. See e.g. Treaty of Friendship, Commerce and Navigation between the United States of America and the Netherlands of 27 March 1956, Art. VII, containing the identical wording as that cited below (text accompanying note 50).

50. Treaty of Friendship, Commerce and Navigation between the United States of America and the Federal Republic of Germany of October 29, 1954 [1956], op. cit., *supra* note 40, Art. VII(1)(c).

51. Treaty of Friendship, Commerce and Navigation between the United States of America and Italy of 26 September 1951 [1961] 1 U.S.T. 131, T.I.A.S. No. 4685.

52. Wengler, "Parity Codetermination in West German Companies and International Law", op. cit., *supra* note 36, at 13.

company or to recall their officers through new elections[,[53] a]s an incident of the voting rights of the individual shareholder, the right to exercise such control constitutes a property right."[54] This is due to the fact that it is precisely this right which safeguards the shareholder's property interests:

> [T]he right to vote is a right which is inherent in and incidental to the ownership of corporate stock, and as such is a property right, and it follows that the stockholder cannot be deprived of it ....[55]

U.S. court decisions have also clarified that the voting right attached to a shareholding "cannot be encroached upon even by legislative or other action taken with the consent of the majority of shareholders, since this would constitute an expropriation of property without compensation."[56] As early as 1909 the Court of Appeals of New York ruled:

> [C]areless and improvident management might impair the value of the stock or utterly destroy it. The right to vote for directors therefore...is the right which gives the property value and is part of the property itself, for it cannot be separated therefrom....Without that right, as we may further assume,...[the stockholder's] property is not safe and may become of no value. To absolutely deprive him of the right to vote therefore is to deprive him of an essential attribute of his property....[57]

The German *Gutachten* extends that which in the above ruling applies to absolute deprivation, to the mere "diminution of the voting power of those shareholders who by virtue of ownership of a majority of the shares hold legal

53. "In the narrowest legal sense, control should mean possession of enough voting shares to elect a majority of the board of directors." Conard, Knauss and Siegel, *Enterprise Organization* 1063 (1972). "The law has always recognized the right of majority stockholders of a corporation to control its business and affairs, and a court of equity will never interfere with such control except for the very best of reasons." Gaines v. Gaines, 176 Okla., 583, 588, 56 P.2d 863, 868 (1936). [Note from the original text.]

54. Wengler, "Parity Codetermination in West German Companies and International Law", op. cit., *supra* note 36, at 13.

55. Ibid., at 12, citing Fletcher, *Cyclopedia of the Law of Private Corporations,* Sect. 2025 (1931-1933).

56. Wengler, "Parity Codetermination in West German Companies and International Law", op. cit., *supra* note 36, at 23-24.

57. *Lord* v. *Equitable Life Assurance Society,* 194 N.Y. 212, 226, 87 N.E. 443, 448 (1909), as cited in ibid., at 24.

control of the company'',[58] holding that such diminution suffices to constitute an expropriation within the meaning of the treaties.

Moreover, as the *Gutachten* points out, ''both American and German law severely restrict the possibilities of encroachment upon the voting rights that are by law attached to share ownership''[59] and ''[a]s property in the wider sense, the voting rights of the individual shareholder and the position resulting from the ownership of sufficient shares to ensure control are protected both against total expropriation or encroachments under the international treaties protecting investments.''[60] Furthermore, a restriction of such control through later laws is also irreconcilable with the treaties.[61]

Of even greater significance, however, is the observation that ''[t]he treaties' prohibition of restriction of the voting power of foreign investors, especially restrictions that impair the influence of the shareholders over the use of the property of the joint stock company, *conforms to the requirements of general international law* (at least as it is interpreted in the United States) *independent of the existence of the treaties themselves.*'' [Emphasis supplied.][62]

The *Gutachten* thus submitted that all those rights attached to shareholdings are general and inviolable ''property rights the deprivation or limitation of which would be a violation of international law''.[63]

In considering the general international law implications of the West German *Mitbestimmungsgesetz*, we shall profit from one additional portion of the *Gutachten's* analysis as excerpted here below:

> The findings of the Foreign Claims Settlement Commission of the United States...show clearly that...[a] 'taking of property' includes re-

58. Wengler, ''Parity Codetermination in West German Companies and International Law'', op. cit., *supra* note 36, at 20.

59. Ibid., at 14.

60. Ibid., at 18. N.B. also Idem note 33: ''German investments abroad can be insured in the Federal Republic against expropriation and 'encroachment amounting to expropriation' with payment of indemnities by the federal budget. According to the general regulations of the Ministry of Economics, it is a condition for such insurance that the investment be endowed with voting and control rights; no insurance shall be given 'if 50% or more of the capital or the voting rights are in foreign hands.' IIa *Handbuch der Entwicklungshilfe,* Sect. 62, Installment 11.''

61. Even socialist Yugoslavia constitutionally proscribes any change of law that would alter the status of foreign shareholders' rights from that existing at the time of investment. (*Ustav Socijalisticke Federativne Republike Jugoslavije* (Constitution) amend. XII, sect. 4 (1971) (Yugoslavia)); see Wengler, ''Parity Codetermination in West German Companies and International Law'', op. cit., *supra* note 36, at 45.

62. Ibid., at 20.

63. Ibid., at 32.

> strictions imposed on the owner which result in his no longer having 'control and management' of his property or other rights. As early as 1954, [one] decision...stated that 'taking of property' also takes place if the legal title formally remains with the claimant.[64] All acts depriving the owner of the right to administer or dispose of the property as well as depriving him of the enjoyment of the property or rendering this enjoyment de facto impossible constitute a 'taking' of property.[65]

> In a later decision, the Commission stated:

> It is clear that the claimant is precluded from the free and unrestricted use of his property and that the fact that record title...has not been transferred...is of little moment....Claimant's property has been 'taken'....[66]

While the issue we have been contemplating here is the expropriatory nature of co-determination, the above analysis also once more clearly demonstrates the key role of management control, the importance of which does not diminish even when that control is not directly administered by the owners themselves.[67] In other words, it could be said that the ultimate criterion of an international expropriation of a commercial enterprise is a host government's substantial interference (or "unreasonable interference") with the alien control or management of that enterprise - whether or not that control is directly linked with the ownership - to the point that the enterprise can no longer function independently in pursuit of the benefits, the enjoyment of which constitutes its very reason for existence.

5. Other Techniques of "Constructive Taking"

In addition to those already looked at, there are other techniques by which such debilitating interference is achieved, lending substance to the remark that

64. Claim of Michael and Nick Zuzich, Doc. No. 1196, November 24, 1954, cited in *Settlement of Claims by the Foreign Claims Settlement Comm'n and its Predecessors From Sept. 14, 1949 to March 31, 1955,* at 161. [Note from original text.]

65. Ibid. (Wengler), at 20-21.

66. Claim of *Albert Bela Reet,* Decision No. Hung. -1625 (1958), *Tenth Semiannual Report to the Congress for the Period Ending June 30, 1959,* at 61, as cited in Wengler, "Parity Codetermination in West German Companies and International Law", op. cit., *supra* note 36, at 20-21.

67. Cf. Harvard Draft, op. cit., *supra* note 7 and accompanying text.

"by the exercise of a little dialectic ingenuity a specific case can be so classified as to fall within a category of acts not liable to compensation."[68] While normal limitations prevent our going into additional techniques in greater detail, it is worth mentioning that among the various means of achieving disinvestment of a foreign MNE by a host government, beyond those just reviewed, figure such techniques as unreasonable taxation;[69] discriminatory legislation and administrative decrees; certain cases of zoning; the granting, in certain cases, of a monopoly by a government; prolonged 'temporary seizure'; unreasonable price ceilings which are not allowed to keep pace with inflationary trends; the rendering useless of property by the expropriation of other property so intimately connected with the first that it ceases to have any further value or function; the forced sale of alien property at a price which falls far short of the actual value of the property or of its real worth had its use not been interfered with by the state; the setting of local wages at prohibitively high rates; the appointment of custodians, managers or inspectors who substantially impair the free use by the alien of his premises and facilities; the appointment of a receiver to liquidate a commercial enterprise or other property; unreasonable contract renegotiation[70] or discriminatory contract termination; prohibition of gainful activity previously lawfully engaged in;[71] and any other means of such unreasonable interference with the property rights of the alien owner that he is effectively deprived of the use and beneficial enjoyment of his holdings.[72] It should also be kept in mind that the mere threat of a property deprivation may serve as effectively as any of the more outright techniques to force a liquidation or deprivation in fact.[73]

Burns Weston reminds us, moreover, that "[a] distinct categorization of deprivation strategies...can easily be deceiving. It would be wrong to assume that the various techniques employed are, and always remain, independent of each other. To the contrary, though they sometimes operate in isolation (particularly when diplomatic strategies are involved), they are most frequently employed in varying combination and sequence, especially when the so-called indirect approach is followed."[74] And while certain types of state interference,

68. Mann, "Outlines of a History of Expropriation", 75 *Law Quarterly Review* (1959), at 215.

69. See Council of Europe, Consultative Assembly, Opinion No. 39 (1963), loc. cit., *supra* note 27, at 136-137.

70. See *supra,* Chapter X(2).

71. See *Restatement,* op. cit., *supra* note 8, § 196, at 589-591.

72. See generally Christie, op. cit., *supra* note 6, especially pp. 322-329, 331. For additional techniques, cf. Weston, "International Law and the Deprivation of Foreign Wealth", op. cit., *supra* note 4, at 77-79.

73. Ibid., (Weston) at 77.

74. Ibid., at 80.

such as some of those enumerated above, will be considered as expropriatory acts whether or not they are labelled as such, other types of interference only become expropriatory when applied in combination. In other words, it may be only the combined effect of various forms of interference with the alien's beneficial use of his property which add up to an expropriation.[75]

This can tend to cloud the compensation issue, and it calls for a close examination of the question as to what constitutes the kind of taking that "brings into operation the widely recognized rule of international law that the property of aliens cannot normally be taken, whether for public purposes or not, without adequate compensation.[76] Some, such as Weston, deem all such constructive takings, by definition, to be "compensable events", by virtue of the law of state responsibility in international law under which compensation or other reparation has traditionally been required.[77] Weston, further declares the principle of compensation to be the central constituent of the law of state responsibility, to which indirect expropriation and all forms of constructive taking give rise.[78]

While it is clear that interference with alien property can amount to expropriation even where there is no explicit attempt to affect legal title, even in cases where the respondent state specifically disclaims any such intervention[79] (expropriation can conceivably be an unintended result of a governmental act), the actual application of the principle to concrete situations is often far less clear. Professor Christie lends his insight to the subject of takings of property under international law with the observation that:

> It is evident that the question of what kind of interference short of outright expropriation constitutes a 'taking' under international law presents a situation where the common law method of case by case development is pre-eminently the best method, in fact probably the only method, of legal development.[80]

75. See Christie, op. cit., *supra* note 6, at 337-338.

76. Ibid., at 307.

77. Weston, "International Law and the Deprivation of Foreign Wealth," op. cit., *supra* note 4, at 108.

78. See ibid., at 106, 108, 122, 128; cf. p. 121.

79. Christie, op. cit., *supra* note 6, at 309.

80. Ibid., at 338

It behooves us, then, to take a look at some actual international practice, and examine the evidence of at least one representative case in which a claim arose out of an indirect expropriatory act, and ended up before an international tribunal.

6. "Constructive Takings" before National Courts and International Tribunals

While national 'expropriation' laws normally have no direct bearing on the relevant international law rules, both private and public international law rules come into play in cases where the 'victim' of the expropriation (or 'nationalization') is a foreign firm. It is, in fact in the private international law context that most of the legal disputes over expropriation have taken place.

Internationally, while there have been numerous arbitrations and claims-commission cases dealing with expropriatory acts, throughout the history of the International Court of Justice there has not been a single 'expropriation' case which has proceeded to a judgment on the merits.[81] In the celebrated case of *Anglo-Iranian Oil Co.* v. *Jaffrate,*[82] which involved a discriminatory[83] taking of alien property without compensation, the forum was a municipal court of the corporate plaintiff's home state, although the legality of the expropriatory act in question was challenged on the basis of international law.

In this case involving a claim to title to oil, the expropriation issue rested on a much larger question, that of the legality under international law of the nationalization of the Anglo-Iranian Oil Company itself by the Persian Government. This nationalization represented an unquestionable breach of a government concessionary contract governed by international law and subject to arbitration in accordance with the contract itself. A claim, based not on those grounds but rather on the law of international responsibility, was brought before the International Court of Justice by the United Kingdom,

81. It should be noted here that the *Chinn* case [*The Oscar Chinn* case, P.C.I.J. 1934, ser. A/B, No. 63], decided by the Permanent Court of International Justice in 1934, while not considered at the time to be a case of expropriation by the Court (although Great Britain argued that there was indeed a taking of property rights in violation of certain treaties, as well as of international law, entitling its national, Mr. Chinn, to compensation), was not condemned by the Court even as an *indirect* taking. Such a case today, in the light of the growing recognition of indirect forms of government taking, might well be considered one of expropriation. The details of the case will be spared here, as Mr. Chinn's business did not represent a multinational enterprise.

82. *Anglo-Iranian Oil Co.* v. *Jaffrate (The Rose Mary),* [1953] 1 W.L.R. 246.

83. See ibid., at 251-252.

espousing the claim of its injured national company, on the allegation that the act was tortious for reasons of failure to compensate, discrimination, and *abus de droit*.[84] The merits of the case were never heard before the ICJ, as the Court denied *locus standi* on jurisdictional grounds. It is significant that while the company's cause was unsuccessfully espoused by the United Kingdom, its home state, before the International Court, the local court in *Anglo-Iranian* v. *Jaffrate* (though not located in the host state) found in favour of the expropriated company.

While the *Anglo-Iranian Oil Co.* case[85]essentially lies outside the scope of this study, as the expropriating state is not an industrialized country, it is nonetheless of interest for the instant argument to note that a case of this kind was brought before the International Court - a case in which, despite various and concerted efforts on the part of a government (U.K.) to raise the level of a commercial dispute legally to one between governments by attempting to establish implications of treaty relationships out of a private company's concessionary contract and by invoking other (Anglo-Persian) treaty links, the fact that the (U.K.) government failed to persuade the Court that the latter had jurisdiction illustrated the limitations on "translating into the realm of international law a contract to which two international persons are not directly parties."[86] In another case brought before the International Court of Justice involving commercial activity, the *Barcelona Traction* case,[87] while the Court did exercise jurisdiction, the (Belgian) government was unsuccessful in its attempts to obtain *locus standi* to protect the rights of its nationals who were shareholders in the "bankrupted" Barcelona Traction, Light and Power Company, on the basis of the fact that the protecting state was deemed not to be the 'national state' of the company and consequently to lack the capacity to exercise protection. Thus, while on different grounds, in neither case did the applying state gain *locus standi,* and up to the present, then, no judgment on the merits in an expropriation case has been issued by the International Court of Justice.

The fact that these cases were never judged on the merits, however, does not necessarily mean that the proceedings hold no interest or shed no light on the subject of "creeping expropriation" in international law. We have already indicated that *Anglo-Iranian* exemplifies the difficulties of government defence of its national private entrepreneurs on the international level. And while

84. See *Anglo-Iranian Co.* (United Kingdom *v.* Iran), *I.C.J. Reports* 1952, p. 11. See also Mann, *Studies in International Law* (Oxford: Clarendon Press, 1973), at 307.

85. *Anglo-Iranian Oil Co.* (United Kingdom *v.* Iran), *Idem.*

86. O'Connell, *International Law,* 2nd ed. (London: Stevens & Sons, 1970), Vol.I, at 204.

87. *Case Concerning the Barcelona Traction, Light and Power Company, Ltd., Judgment, I.C.J. Reports* 1970, p. 3, at 32.

Anglo-Iranian offers no further substantial contribution to the present discussion in that the nationalizing state was a developing state, *Barcelona Traction*, on the other hand, does hold considerable interest for the present study, for two reasons. First, none of the parties concerned (Canada, Belgium and Spain) were from the developing world or a state-run economy;[88] and, secondly, *Barcelona Traction* appears to be a model case of an "expropriation" under another guise, in this instance that of bankruptcy. Therefore, we shall look at the case in greater detail in the following pages.

7. "Disguised Expropriation": *Barcelona Traction*

Barcelona Traction[89] is perhaps the most obvious and renowned case before an international tribunal involving a multinational enterprise.[90] The case was brought by Belgium against Spain "on account of acts said to be contrary to international law committed by organs of the Spanish State,"[91] including "the deprivation of enjoyment of rights",[92] and leading to, according to Belgium, "the total spoliation of the Barcelona Traction group".[93] The facts of the case are as follows[94]:

The Barcelona Traction, Light and Power Company, Ltd. (Barcelona Traction), a Canadian holding company, was incorporated in 1911 in Toronto where it maintained its head office.[95] The purpose of the company was to create and develop an electric power production and distribution system in Catalonia, Spain, and to this end it formed a number of subsidiaries, three of which were incorporated under Canadian law and the remainder under Spanish law.

88. Judge Jessup pointed out that *Barcelona Traction* did not involve "any conflict between great capital-exporting States and States in course of development. Belgium and Spain are States which, in those terms, belong in the same grouping." (*Barcelona Traction* case, *Judgment, I.C.J. Reports* 1970, at 164.) See also 59 *American Journal of International Law* (1965), (Judicial Decisions), at 131 *et seq.*

89. *Barcelona Traction* case, loc. cit., *supra* note 87.

90. The Court makes two clear references to multinational enterprises: see *Barcelona Traction* case, loc. cit., *supra* note 87, para. 37 at 33, para. 89 at 47-48; see Rodley, "Corporate Nationality and the Diplomatic Protection of Multinational Enterprises: The *Barcelona Traction* Case," 47 *Indiana Law Journal,* (1971-1972), at 85-86.

91. *Barcelona Traction* case, loc. cit., *supra* note 87, at 6.

92. Ibid., at 12.

93. Ibid., at 13.

94. Ibid., at 7-10.

95. The Barcelona Traction Company has maintained a nominal presence in Toronto and continues to hold annual meetings. See Lutsky, "Barcelona Traction Holds Annual Vigil," *New York Herald Tribune,* August 2, 1979, at 7.

Purportedly, at all relevant times - and continuously since shortly after World War I - a very high percentage of Barcelona Traction's share capital was held by Belgian nationals - both natural and juridical persons.

Barcelona Traction had issued several series of bonds, some in pesetas but principally in sterling; the servicing of the bonds in both currencies was suspended in 1936 owing to the spanish civil war. In 1940 there was a resumption of interest payments on the peseta bonds - for which authorization of the Spanish exchange control authorities was required because the debt was owed by a foreign company - but authorization for the foreign currency transfers necessary to service the bonds issued in sterling was refused; consequently the payment of interest on the sterling bonds was never resumed.

In 1945 Barcelona Traction made three separate attempts at a compromise plan which would provide for the reimbursement of the sterling debt. Still the Spanish authorities persisted in their refusals to authorize foreign currency transfers, without which the debts on the bonds could not be honoured.

In February 1948 three Spanish holders of recently acquired Barcelona Traction sterling bonds - some evidence of whose "personal relationship with some [Spanish] governmental personalities" was later put forward by Belgium[96] - successfully petitioned a local Spanish court for a declaration of bankruptcy on grounds of failure to pay the interest on the bonds; and a judgment declaring the company bankrupt was given on February 12. As a result of certain provisions of the judgment, an interim receiver seized the assets of Barcelona Traction along with those of two of its subsidiaries. The commissioner in bankruptcy immediately dismissed the managers of the two subsidiary companies, who were then replaced by Spanish directors. Shortly thereafter the petitioners assumed control of the other subsidiaries as well.

Proceedings in Spain brought by the company and other interested parties to contest the bankruptcy judgment and the related decisions were unsuccessful.

In 1949 trustees in bankruptcy were appointed who effectuated the creation of new shares for the subsidiary companies, cancelling all shares located outside Spain. They further brought about the transfer of two of the head offices of the Canadian-based subsidiaries from Toronto to Barcelona. Finally, in 1951, the trustees procured legal authorization to offer for sale the entire corporate capital of the subsidiary companies in the form of the newly created shares. These shares were purchased at public auction by a newly formed Spanish company which thereupon acquired complete control of the enterprise located in Spain.

Out of these facts, five stand out as particularly significant in the context of the present study. The first is that a foreign currency transfer authorization

96. See *Barcelona Traction* case, loc. cit., *supra* note 87, at 159.

was denied, which recalls the host control technique of regulation of capital movements, which we have discussed in an earlier chapter,[97] and underlines the technique's partical effectiveness. The second is that a declaration of bankruptcy was secured against Barcelona Traction on grounds of Barcelona's failure to keep up interest payments, when the cause of the payment failure was the Government's action itself. As one writer expresses: "D'après le Gouvernement belge, le droit espagnol *exigeait* l'insolvabilité définitive du débiteur. Le juge de la faillite aurait donc commis un grave déni de justice puisqu'il s'est fondé sur la cessation de paiements de Barcelona Traction." [Emphasis supplied.][98] Whether or not a "grave déni de justice" was committed, the bankruptcy declaration was carried through, accomplishing, in effect, a 'disguised' or 'creeping' expropriation. The third specifically relevant fact is that the foreign management was dismissed, and Spanish directors appointed, which not only re-emphasizes the importance of management, but also recalls the similar manoeuvre as exercised by the French Government in the *Freuhauf-France* case.[99] The fourth particularly significant fact is that the original shares issued by the Barcelona Traction Company were arbitrarily invalidated by the Spanish Government and replaced by new shares which were later purchased by a Spanish company specially incorporated for that purpose. This indicates a possible discriminatory intent in the Government's action. The fifth fact of particular significance to the present study is the relocation of the head offices from Toronto to Barcelona, Spain, thereby completing, in combination with the previous two facts cited above (*viz.* the exclusive introduction of Spanish management and the issuance of new shares sold exclusively to Spanish purchasers), a total transfer of effective control from the foreign parent, or 'holding company', to nationals of the host state.

A series of litigations before numerous Spanish courts, and representations to the Spanish Government on behalf of Barcelona Traction by the British, Canadian, United States and Belgian Governments, failed to produce a satisfactory settlement, and the dispute was first referred (unilaterally by Belgium) to the International Court of Justice by an Application dated 15 September 1958. The subsequent course of proceedings in the ICJ - which was discontinued in April 1961 with a view to settlement out of court, that failed,[100] and which was thereafter renewed by Belgium's submission of a new

97. See *supra* Chapter VI.

98. Ridruejo, "La faillite en droit international privé," 133 *Receuil des Cours* 1971 (II), at 199.

99. See *supra* Chapter V(3)(a), especially text following note 66.

100. *Case Concerning the Barcelona Traction, Light and Power Company, Ltd.* (Belgium *v.* Spain), Order of 10 April 1961: I.C.J. Reports 1961, p. 9. See Briggs, "Barcelona Traction: The *Jus Standi* of Belgium," 65 *American Journal of International Law* (1971), at 328.

Application in June 1962, issuing in the Second Phase - covered a span of twelve years. It is not the aim here to go into details of either phase of the case, involving Spain's preliminary objections and other procedural and substantive points,[101] nor to fall to the temptation of getting caught up in the fascinating and controversial legal issues confronted during the extended proceedings, those for which the case is most often cited being the diplomatic protection of corporations and shareholders as juridical and natural persons and the many related questions of, *inter alia,* the right of a third state which is not the state of incorporation to bring a claim, the distinction between injury to the rights of a company and injury to the interests of shareholders, lifting the corporate veil to determine effective 'nationality',[102] the test of 'genuine link' as applied to corporate entities and, in general, the status and personality of a company in international law. The question of the general international law limitations on a host state's treatment of foreign investors, or of state responsibility, never came up for review.

It is precisely with this aspect of the matter that we have an interest here, and the extent to which the events leading up to Barcelona Traction's bankruptcy could be regarded as 'disguised' or 'creeping' expropriation. Every effort will be made to confine our discussion here to the issue at hand.

The Court's final judgement rendered on February 5, 1970 upheld Spain's third preliminary objection[103] that the Belgian Government lacked the necessary *jus standi* to pursue the claim,[104] based essentially on the grounds that an injury to shareholders' interests resulting from alleged injury to the rights of a company possessing the nationality of a third state does not constitute sufficient grounds for the exercise of diplomatic protection by the government of the foreign (majority) shareholders. Although the test of 'genuine link', according recognition to 'real and effective nationality' as applied in the *Nottebohm* case,[105] was raised, the Court declined to lift the corporate veil to determine the existence of a link between State and corporation on the basis of control, despite the fact that 80 per cent of the share ownership of the company

101. For a capsule of the significant features of the Judgment, see C.D. Wallace, "Barcelona Traction Case", in: Bernhardt (ed.), *Encyclopedia of Public International Law* [Installment 2 (1981)] p. 30.

102. See *supra* Chapter V (3)(c).

103. The first two preliminary objections - the first regarding Belgium's alleged incapacity to reinstitute proceedings, and the second contending the Court's lack of jurisdiction in the case - were rejected by the ICJ in a Judgment of 5 July 1964 which, at the same time, joined the third and fourth objections to the merits. The fourth objection was never pronounced upon.

104. Para. 102 of the Judgment.

105. *Nottebohm Case,* [1955] *I.C.J. Reports,* p. 7.

was held by Belgian nationals and represented an effective participation in management control as well as in capital investment. The Court similarly rejected any analogy with the *Nottebohm* case and any application of the 'genuine link' principle to the diplomatic protection of corporate entities.[106]

The Court's unexpected[107] judgment seems to have raised a host of complex issues and to have resolved almost none. Indicative of the lack of real unanimity underlying the ostensibly near unanimous judgment, and the controversial nature of some of the issues in question, is the fact that, out of fifteen concurring votes, nine of the judges (in addition to the sole dissenting judge, Judge *ad hoc* Riphagen) wrote separate opinions, three of which contained reasoning in rejecting the Belgian Government's claim which differed from that of the official majority opinion, and others of which, while subscribing to the principal reasons on which the Court based its judgment, qualified their concurrence, inevitably undercutting substantially the impact of the 'majority holding'.[108]

It has been suggested that the Court, in denying the *jus standi* of Belgium to pursue the claim and in further refraining from pronouncing on the fourth preliminary objection and the substantive merits of the case,[109] thereby left in question its will to uphold a state's claim on behalf of its nationals in their capacity as shareholders in international direct investments.[110] It also deprived

106. Para. 70 of the Judgment. But see, e.g., separate opinions of Judge Jessup, paras. 44-57, 80, and Judge Gros, paras. 22, 24.

107. "At a regional meeting of the American Society of International Law in March, 1969, on the topic 'International Claims: Their Settlement by Lump Sum Agreements,' none of the discussants anticipated the outcome in the case. Note, Regional Meeting of the Society at Syracuse, 63 *American Journal of International Law* 550 (1969). Furthermore, at the annual meeting of the Society that year every speaker on a panel entitled 'Nationality of Claims - Individuals, Corporations, Stockholders' agreed that the Court would ratify well-established past trends allowing shareholder claims. See 1969 Proceedings, Am. Soc. Int. Law 30-53." [Editorial Comment (Lillich), "Two Perspectives on the Barcelona Traction Case: The Rigidity of Barcelona", op. cit., *supra* note 3, Note 3 at 522.]

108. Round Table, op. cit., *supra* note 3 (Weston) at 349, 351; cf. also Higgings, "Aspects on the Case Concerning the Barcelona Traction, Light and Power Company, Ltd., 11 *Virginia Journal of International Law* (1970).

109. Other than to the extent that the question of Belgium's *jus standi* itself - Spain's third preliminary objection - was attached to the merits.

110. Other than in government claims for shareholders' protection in which the respondent state is also the state of incorporation and the corporation is incapacitated to the point of being unable to pursue local remedies. (See *Delagoa Bay Railway Co.* case (Great Britain *v.* Portugal), [1875], *Receuil des Arbitrages Internationaux,* Vol. 3 (1954), 596. See also Strupp-Schlochauer, *Wörterbuch des Völkerrechts,* Vol. 1, at 325.

itself of an opportunity to play a significant role in the clarification and development of international business litigation[111] and international economic relations, and of the process of customary prescription in international law,[112] or even simply in the "general international law obligations in the sphere of the treatment of foreigners" (Judge Fitzmaurice). While one view has it that the function of the Court is simply to state the law, an equally strong view holds that "there are compelling considerations of international justice and of development of international law which favour a full measure of exhaustiveness of judicial pronouncements in international Tribunals"[113] and, with specific reference to the instant case, that "[t]he more important function of the Court as the principal organ of the United Nations is to be found not only in the settlement of concrete disputes, but also in its reasoning, through which it may contribute to the development of international law".[114] We could surely have benefitted here, for example, from an expansion upon Judge Fitzmaurice's reference to the "general international law obligations in the sphere of the treatment of foreigners", particularly if it had led to a thorough consideration of what he also referred to as an action (on the part of the Spanish Government) which, to all appearances, "had the character of a disguised expropriation"[115] and, according to Judge Gros, represented "a sort of 'nationalization'".[116] Perhaps the Court would have given us more insight into whether that action was a breach of international law, as Belgium claimed, and, as such, was a control technique illegally exercised by the host (Spanish) Government. It is to this aspect of the case - that is, the expropriatory nature of the alleged 'bankruptcy' of the Barcelona Traction group - that we, essentially unaided by *obiter dicta,* must now turn our analysis.

111. See e.g. Notes: "Economic Internationalism v. National Parochialism: Barcelona Traction," 3 *Law and Policy in International Business* (1971), at 542.

112. Cf. Raman, "The Role of the International Court of Justice in the Development of International Customary Law", 1965 *Proceedings of the American Society of International Law,* at 177; Jenks, *The Prospects of International Adjudication* (London: Stevens and Sons, 1964), at 237-238; Lillich, "Two Perspectives on the Barcelona Traction Case: The Rigidity of Barcelona," op. cit., *supra* note 3, at 531; Round Table, op. cit., *supra* note 3 (Weston) at 352. Cf., however, a contrary point of view: ibid. (Caflish) at 352, (Seidl-Hohenfeldern) at 352; also Caflish, "The Protection of Corporate Investments Abroad in the Light of the Barcelona Traction Case", *Zeitschrift für ausländisches öffentliches Recht und Völkerrecht,* Band [Vol.] 31 (1971), at 196.

113. H. Lauterpacht, as cited in Judge Jessup's separate opinion, *I.C.J. Reports* 1970, p.3, at 161.

114. Separate opinion of Judge Tanaka, [1964] I.C.J. at 65.

115. *Barcelona Traction* case (Second Phase), loc. cit., *supra* note 87, at 106.

116. Ibid., at 274. Judge Gros pointed out that "the undertaking is today incorporated into the economy of Spain by a sort of 'nationalization' which, if it was effected by a misuse of legal procedure, constitutes a breach of international law as between the Parties."

The Spanish Government's takeover of the Barcelona Traction, Light and Power Company's Spanish-based assets was ostensibly on grounds of bankruptcy, pronounced by one of its own local courts. Belgium, however, had no difficulty in identifying the taking as expropriatory. The words "acts contrary to international law...including the deprivation of enjoyment of rights...", and the obligation of compensation attached, as used in the statements on behalf of the Belgian Government in the Application, and reiterated in the Memorial in the case's Second Phase, clearly imply expropriation, although the term is not explicitly used. The words are immediately reminiscent of those of Harvard Drafts 11, 12 and final of 1960, 1961 and 1974 respectively in which"...unreasonable interference with the use, enjoyment or disposal of property..." makes up part of the definition of a "taking of property."[117]

In *Barcelona Traction,* the incapacitating results of the Spanish Government's continued refusal to allow servicing of the sterling bonds would clearly seem to constitute an "unreasonable interference with the use, enjoyment, or disposal of [its] property." In its Application to the Court (Second Phase), the Belgian Government referred to "consequential damage" as well as to "incidental damage...including the deprivation of the enjoyment of rights."[118]

In an attempt to assess the expropriatory nature of the action leading to the "spoliation" of the Barcelona Traction group, it is useful to consider that action in the light of some international standards, including some of those referred to in earlier pages of this chapter.

The American Law Institute's *Restatement (Second) of the Foreign Relations Law of the United States,* by way of a set of criteria for determining when taking is wrongful under international law, states, in Section 185:

> The taking by a state of property of an alien is wrongful under international law if either
>
> (a) it is not for a public purpose,
>
> (b) there is not reasonable provision for the determination and payment of just compensation, as defined in Section 187,[119] under the law

117. Art. 10, paragraph 3(a): Harvard Draft No. 11, printed in 1960 *Proceedings of the American Society of International Law,* at 103; Harvard Draft No. 12, published by the Harvard Law School in 1961, Final Draft, op. cit., *supra* note 7. For Art. 10, paragraph 3(2), see text accompanying note 9 *supra.*

118. *Barcelona Traction* case (Second Phase)[1970], loc. cit., *supra* note 87, at 12.

119. In paragraph 187, compensation is defined in terms of "adequate", "prompt", and "effective."

> and practice of the state in effect at the time of taking, or
>
> (c) the property is merely in transit through the territory of the state, or has otherwise been temporarily subjected to its jurisdiction, and is not required by the state because of serious emergency.[120]

It would be difficult to justify the public purpose condition in the case of Barcelona Traction, in that as the Spanish Government, in January 1952, sold "the totality of the shares, with all the rights attaching to them, representing the corporate capital" at public auction, what had basically taken place amounted to an outright transfer of the ownership and control of the Barcelona Traction Company from foreign into local hands, and, even if the sale was concluded under genuine public-auction conditions, there could have been no guarantee to the Government that the new (local) owners would manage the company's business with any greater efficiency than had the previous (foreign) owners, or even with equal expertise. This being said, it must be recalled that 'public purpose' is extremely difficult to ascertain and that there is little authority in international law establishing any useful criteria for assessing a state's determination of its own public purpose. The shifting of nationalized property from public to private hands cannot *per se* negate the public purpose aspect of a taking. Moreover, the failure to prove public purpose has rarely, if ever, been sufficient grounds on its own for a taking to be held unlawful under international law.[121] Hence, on the basis of the public purpose condition, the Spanish Government's motives in the *Barcelona Traction* case, while they could be questioned, could scarcely be condemned.

As regards the just-compensation provision, there is no equivocation. No compensation was paid nor was any promise of future compensation offered. A token handful of Barcelona Traction shareholders resolutely meets annually in Toronto, with the hope that one day some form of compensation will be forthcoming.[122] Up to now there is no indication that their efforts will be rewarded.

Section 185(c) of the *Restatement* is clearly not applicable in the case of *Barcelona Traction,* but following the conditions of lawful expropriation set out in Section 185(a), (b) and (c) cited above, the *Restatement* makes separate reference to the issue of discrimination in the form of a "Comment" as follows:

120. *Restatement,* op. cit., *supra* note 8, at 553.

121. See e.g. *Idem.*

122. See "Barcelona Traction Holds Annual Vigil", loc. cit., *supra* note 95.

Comment:

a. Cross references...A taking of property is also wrongful under international law if it is in violation of an international agreement...or if it is discriminatory....[123]

This setting-apart of the non-discrimination condition should not be seen as a diminution of its importance. The Comment is in fact a cross-reference to a section (Section 166) devoted exclusively to the question of discrimination against aliens. The OECD Draft Convention on the Protection of Foreign Property[124] similarly emphasizes the discrimination issue as regards the taking of property by elaborating a separate "rule" on discrimination in its Notes and Comments to Article 1.[125] The OECD Draft Convention, approved by the Council of Europe,[126] in addition to expressly including "investments" as "property",[127] specifically covering "wrongful interference", "*indirect* deprivation" and "creeping expropriation",[128] and expressly stating its intention "to bring within its compass *any* measures taken with the *intent* of wrongfully depriving the national concerned of the substance of his rights and resulting in such loss",[129] and while enumerating the conditions of "public interest", "due process of law", non-discrimination and just, prompt and effective compensation,[130] nonetheless places a particular emphasis on "discriminatory measures".

Inter alia, it affirms that:

> Prohibition of discrimination is in accordance with the principles laid down by the Permanent Court of International Justice in the Case of Certain German Interests in Polish Upper Silesia, and the Case of Treatment of Polish Nationals in Danzig.[131]

123. *Restatement, op. cit., supra* note 8, at 553.

124. OECD Draft Convention, loc. cit., *supra* note 5.

125. Third rule: Exclusion of Unreasonable and Discriminatory Measures, ibid., Notes 6-8 (Notes and Comments to Article 1).

126. The European Council's approval of an earlier draft (see OECD Draft Convention, OECD publication No. 15636, December 1962, OECD, Paris, 1962, reprinted in 1-2 *International Legal Materials* (1962-1963), at 241 *et seq.*) was made subject to certain amendments proposed by the Legal Committee (see Council of Europe, Consultative Assembly, Opinion No. 39 (1963), loc. cit., *supra* note 27, para. 40, at 150).

127. OECD Draft Convention, op. cit., *supra* note 5, Art. 1, Note 2(a) (Notes and Comments to Article 1), Note 2 (Notes and Comments to Article 2).

128. Ibid., Note 4(b) (Notes and Comments to Article 3).

129. Ibid., Note 4(a) (Notes and Comments to Article 3).

130. Ibid., Art. 3; also Note 1(b) (Notes and Comments to Article 3).

131. Ibid., Note 8(b) (Notes and Comments to Article 1).

In addition, the commentary on the fundamental prohibition against discriminatory measures in international law embodied in the Draft Convention's first article states:

> For the very fact that the history of international relations abounds in examples of representations by Governments against measures of economic discrimination resulting in injury, implies the recognition of the principle that measures otherwise lawful, may be deprived of the protection of the law on the grounds of discrimination....It is immaterial whether the measure complained of is expressly or exclusively directed against the property of the national for whom redress is sought or is couched in general terms which bring such property within its scope. In other words 'de facto discrimination' is unlawful.[132]

This would appear to have direct applicability to *Barcelona Traction,* the proceedings of which, incidentally, were in progress at the time of drafting.

Professor O'Connell, also writing prior to the Court's final judgment in *Barcelona Traction,* but with obvious relevance to the case, lends his wisdom to the issue of discrimination:

> There is little doubt that if an alien is singled out for expropriation the State exceeds its powers in international law, though in most cases the discrimination will be less an autonomous head of wrongdoing than an index of non-public interest motivation.[133]

The principle of discrimination would appear reasonably manifestly to have been violated in the case of *Barcelona Traction,* both in the light of the above commentaries, and for reasons already expressed in connection with the public-purpose condition, namely that what effectively transpired was a *de facto* shift of control and ownership (including relocation of the *siège*) of a single selected enterprise from foreign to domestic domain. The discriminatory nature of the taking, manifest in the clear objectives of the persistent denial to authorize payments on the foreign-currency bonds, would be difficult to contest.

Relevant provisions regarding discrimination against foreign enterprises appear also in the numerous bilateral treaties of the treaty-of-friendship-and-navigation formula. Taking as an example the 1974 treaty of that name

132. Ibid., Note 8(b), (c) (Notes and Comments to Article 1).

133. O'Connell, *International Law,* 2nd ed. (London: Stevens & Sons, 1970), Vol.II, at 779.

between the Federal Republic of Germany and the United States,[134] we read in Article V, paragraph 3:

3. Keiner der beiden Vertragsteile darf unbillige oder diskriminierende Massnahmen ergreifen, durch welche die in seinem Gebiet von den Staatsangehörigen und Gesellschaften des anderen Vertragsteils rechtmässig erworbenen Ansprüche oder Interessen an den von ihnen errichteten Unternehmen oder an dem von ihnen durch Kapital oder durch ihr technisches Können, Wissen oder Geschick hierzu geleisteten Beitrag beeinträchtigt würden.

3. Neither Party shall take unreasonable or discriminatory measures that would impair the legally acquired rights or interests within its territories of nationals and companies of the other Party in the enterprises which they have established, in their capital, or in the skills, arts or technology which they have applied.

It is interesting here to note that, even in treating the subject of discrimination, the "legally acquired rights" are expressly stated to include not only capital, but also "skills, arts or technology," in other words, intangible property. As the Barcelona Traction Company's "bankruptcy" did not lead to liquidation but rather to a transfer of ownership and control into local, it follows that certain of the "skills" and "technology" of the foreign were preserved and transferred to the new owners.

Finally, one could assess the expropriatory nature of the Spanish Government's uncompensated act in *Barcelona Traction* against the latest "Formulations" by the United Nations Intergovernmental Working Group on a Code of Conduct for Transnational Corporations which states that:

> Fair and equitable treatment of transnational corporations by the countries in which they operate is to include payment of just compensation in the event of nationalization or other taking of their property, such government action being undertaken under due process of law, in accordance with national laws, regulations and administrative practices without discrimination between enterprises in comparable situations and with full regard to international obligations and contractual undertakings to which States have freely subscribed.[135]

134. Treaty of Friendship, Commerce and Navigation between the United States of America and the Federal Republic of Germany, loc. cit., *supra* note 40.

135. United Nations "Transnational Corporations: Code of Conduct; Formulations by the Chairman", U.N. document E/C 10/AC.2/8, of 13 December 1978, para. 52, at 12.

While controversy over the formulation and implications of some substantive aspects of the above paragraph has contributed to the delay in the completion of the Code in general, of immediate relevance in the present context is that, regardless of the current controversy over the various compensation issues, *Barcelona Traction* measured against even these latest formulated standards would, strictly speaking, equally find the Spanish Government wanting, not only on the basis of compensation but also *prima facie* on grounds of discrimination and failure to meet international obligations.

It is noteworthy that the condition of "public purpose", normally included as a prerequisite for legal expropriations, is totally absent from the U.N. "Formulations", unless implied under "international obligations". This is undoubtedly a reflection of the fact that the concept of public purpose is growing increasingly vague, to the point that its future usefulness is doubtful.[136] On the other hand, the position on "discrimination", so fundamental a principle in international law, is retained. Non-discrimination is one point upon which there appears to be universal agreement, at least in theory. This is emphasized in an Opinion by Lord McNair in which he stated that "[i]t is widely accepted that, at least in the field of expropriation, non-discrimination is an absolute condition of lawful expropriation."[137]

Considering together the above-discussed prerequisites for the legality of a taking under international law, Belgium's claim (and the opinions of Judges Fitzmaurice, Tanaka and Gros) as to the expropriatory nature of the Spanish Government's act *vis-à-vis* the Barcelona Traction Company would not appear unjustified.

The present discussion is not meant, however, to reflect any intent to single-handedly pass judgment on the actions of the Spanish Government in its dealings with the Barcelona Traction Company, actions which never reached the stage of being reviewed by the International Court. The intent is rather to highlight those elements of the action which might serve to illustrate the meaning of "illegal taking" under international law, or of "creeping" or "disguised" expropriation, where the case is one involving a multinational enterprise both incorporated and operating in a reasonably developed economy and a case, moreover, which found its way before the International Court of Justice.

136. See e.g. *Restatement,* op. cit., *supra* note 8, at 553.

137. Cited in Schwartzenberger, op. cit., *supra* note 27, at 120.

8. Conclusion

One could cite numerous and sundry assessments of the international law conditions for legal expropriation. We shall limit ourselves, in closing, to only one comprehensive formula, that of Professor O'Connell, which he has adopted from another writer, and which would seem to embody all the essential elements upon which the legality of expropriation in international law relies. The four conditions cited by O'Connell are the following:

> (a) The property must be amenable to the jurisdiction of the expropriating State.
> (b) The nationalisation must be motivated by some bona fide social or economic purpose.
> (c) There must be no discrimination against the property nationalised or its owners.
> (d) The nationalisation must be accompanied either by contemporaneous payment of adequate compensation or effective measures which ensure and make certain its prompt payment.[138]

In sum, the term "expropriation" can be seen to embody those conditions (public purpose, non-discrimination and compensation requirements), the absence of which would render the taking act unlawful. "Expropriation", under the foregoing terms, is a perfectly legal and acceptable technique, under domestic and international law, available to the host state for exercising the ultimate control over a foreign multinational affiliate within its territory - a control which goes beyond regulating operations to the very existence of the affiliate itself, and its continuing presence and productive activity. In other words, there is no limit upon the sovereign powers of a state to expropriate and thus eliminate the foreign commercial presence (in the present context, the MNE affiliate) from its territory. But rights carry with them responsibilities, and co-existent with the right to expropriate alien property are the prerequisites of non-discrimination and public good, and the international responsibility to compensate. Expropriation without prompt and adequate compensation is confiscation, and confiscation is contrary to international law.

Coupled with any serious discussion of direct or indirect expropriation, when its legality is at issue, is the question of state responsibility and the

138. Lord McNair, "The Seizure of Property and Enterprises in Indonesia", 6 *Nederlands Tijdschrift voor International Recht* (1959), as referred to in O'Connell, op. cit., *supra,* note 133, at 776-777.

protection of foreign investments, or as Judge Sir Gerald Fitzmaurice expressed it in his important Separate Opinion in the *Barcelona Traction* case, the "general international law obligations in the sphere of the treatment of foreigners."[139] In fact, one legal writer goes so far as to state that the "[i]ndirect deprivation of property under discriminatory restrictions or obligations imposed by legislative fiat, while not as dramatic as outright expropriation, may be the most serious problem faced by the foreign investor."[140] The present study does not concern itself with the problems of the (MNE) investor. Yet while it is basically the host state's control over the foreign MNE investor rather than the protection of the MNE investor from coercive acts of the host state which is at issue in the present study, it is nonetheless important to note that the expropriation issue is a two-sided one. It is not simply a question of the power of the host to exercise this degree of control over the MNE, but it is also a question of the extent of - i.e. limitations on - this power, as measured according to the international standards of state responsibility.

In short, 'expropriation' is a legally exercisable right of a host state, but it is not an unqualified right. Yet properly applied in accordance with universally accepted international law norms, it can be a powerful tool in the hands of the host state to eliminate undesired foreign MNE investment - and its potential economic influence - from within the host territory.

139. *Barcelona Traction* case, loc. cit., *supra* note 87, at 66.

140. Folsom, "The Taking by a State of the Property, Acquired Right, or Other Interest of a Foreign National, When No Contract is Involved," in *Rights and Duties of Private Investors Abroad* [Symposium], International and Comparative Law Center, Southwestern Legal Foundation, Dallas, Texas (New York: Matthew Bender, 1965), at 304.

PART FIVE: THE SCOPE FOR INTERNATIONAL CONTROLS

Chapter XIII.

NATURE OF INTERNATIONAL CODES AND GUIDELINES

1. Overview of Major Current Efforts at International Codes and Guidelines[1]

It may seem that, for a study which claims to make some statement about *international* control of the multinational enterprise, an inordinate amount of time has been devoted to *national* responses to the 'problem'; but ultimately, it may be precisely at the national level that the most effective control will be exercised, as too broad a base for control, for the sake of labelling it ''international'', may end up being no control at all, or illusory at best.

It is not the aim of the present study to launch into an in-depth analysis of the many aspects involved in the controversial issue of international legal controls. This would at this stage necessarily be a highly speculative investigation *de lege ferenda,* as there are, to date, no legally binding international controls over MNE activity, nor does such a development appear imminent, at present.

This is not meant to disparage efforts at international co-operation or attempts to come up with operable international 'guidelines' or 'codes of conduct' such as those being advanced by, *inter alia,* the United Nations (U.N. ECOSOC and U.N. Commission on Transnational Corporations), the Organisation for Economic Co-operation and Development (OECD), the Interna-

1. The present writer is indebted to Hans W. Baade for his comprehensive and up-to-date review of the significant current efforts among international bodies in the formulation of international codes and guidelines for MNE regulation, as presented in his background paper preparatory to the 1979 Bielefeld International Symposium on Legal Problems of Codes of Conduct for MNEs [hereinafter cited as Bielefeld Symposium]. Professor Baade's paper was entitled ''Codes of Conduct for MNEs: an Introductory Survey'', and provided much of the factual material constituting the present overview. (See Baade, ''Code of Conduct for Multinational Enterprises: An Introductory Survey'', background paper for the International Symposium on Legal Problems of Codes of Conduct for Multinational Enterprises, sponsored by the Zentrum für interdisziplinäre Forschung der Universität Bielefeld, July 16-18, 1979). Published as Hans W. Baade, *Codes of Conduct for Multinational Enterprises:* An Introductory Survey, in: Norbert Horn and E.R. Lanier (eds.), *Legal Problems of Codes of Conduct for Multinational Enterprises* (Frankfurt: Kluwer, 1980), Vol I [hereinafter cited as ''Codes of Conduct''].

tional Chamber of Commerce (ICC), the United Nations Conference on Trade and Development (UNCTAD), and the International Labour Organization (ILO). These guidelines and codes, however, are not of a legally binding nature and one more academic analysis of the common ground among such codes, their value as "soft law", or the obvious problems of their enforcement, could only be a superfluous addition to the extensive existing literature on the subject, as well as being, of necessity, very largely theoretical.

The numerous concentrated efforts by such international bodies as those mentioned above to devise operable international instruments are nonetheless clear evidence of the universal concern in this regard, and cannot and should not be ignored in any current study dealing with MNE regulation.

As anything even approaching an exhaustive survey or study of international aspects of control would be the subject for another entire volume, details or comparisons of the various codes must be avoided here. A few general remarks regarding international efforts are nonetheless in order.

Of signal importance regarding the above-mentioned international efforts at regulating MNE activity is that each group is fully cognizant of the other's work, and while a certain amount of overlap and parallel effort is inevitable, there is, for the most part, an attempt to avoid duplication. The prevalent desire is for co-operation. The preamble to the ILO Tripartite Declaration of Principles concerning Multinational Enterprises and Social Policy[2] (ILO Declaration), expressly acknowledges having been "informed of the activities of other international bodies, in particular the U.N. Commission on Transnational Corporations and the...OECD".[3] These two particular endeavors singled out by ILO still represent the two major control 'packages' receiving greatest attention by the international community in current MNE/home/host dialogue.

a. The United-Nations-family 'package' and related efforts

The ILO Declaration just mentioned deals strictly with those aspects of MNE conduct that relate to social policy in general and labour relations in particular, and already appears in its entirety as an Annex to a U.N. ECOSOC

2. International Labour Organisation, Tripartite Declaration of Principles concerning Multinational Enterprises and Social Policy, reprinted in 17 *International Legal Materials,* [hereinafter cited as ILO Declaration].

3. Ibid., at 423.

document concerning the U.N. Code of Conduct,[4] thus indicating the close interaction of the two. The ILO is, of course, a "specialized agency" (or "related agency") within the U.N. family, but specialized agencies have an independent status, and ILO studies on the impact of MNEs began well in advance of those by the U.N. Organization proper. Moreover, the ILO Declaration has already been adopted, while the U.N. Code is still in process of formulation.

The U.N. Code of Conduct proper is being formulated by a specially appointed Intergovernmental Working Group on a Code of Conduct as an undertaking of the U.N. Commission on Transnational Corporations,[5] itself a subsidiary organ ("advisory body") of ECOSOC, and with the substantive support of the U.N. Center on Transnational Corporations which functions as Secretariat to the Commission. At the moment of writing, the relevant draft of the Code, to the extent that it has been elaborated, is embodied in the January 1979 "Formulations by the Chairman".[6] The U.N. Code, in its definitive form, will surely make substantial reference to the ILO Declaration, though the drafters of the Code are effectively precluded - for practical purposes -from actually incorporating the lengthy Declaration into its text, due to the ILO's request in its letter of transmittal to the U.N. that the Declaration "neither be altered nor reproduced in parts only".[7]

UNCTAD, also part of the U.N. family, classified as a "subsidiary organ" but with "autonomous" functions, has established an Intergovernmental Group which has already gone some way in drafting a code of conduct on the transfer of technology.[8] Despite some potential overlap with the U.N. draft

4. United Nations, ECOSOC, "Transnational Corporations: Texts Relevant to an Annotated Outline Suggested by the Chairman of the Intergovernmental Working Group on the Code of Conduct", Report of the Secretariat of the Commission on Transnational Corporations, Intergovernmental Working Group of the Whole on the Code of Conduct, Third Session, New York, 6-10 February 1978, U.N. document E/C.10/AC.2/3 (January 26, 1978), Annex II.

5. Established by unanimous U.N. ECOSOC resolution 1913 (LVII) (E/RES/1913 (LVII)) of December 5, 1974. See also "Auf dem Weg zu einem Verhaltenskodex für Multis: Tagung der Uno-Kommission für transnationale Gesellschaften", *Neue Zürcher Zeitung,* May 30, 1979, at 10.

6. United Nations (ECOSOC) "Transnational Corporations: Code of Conduct; Formulations by the Chairman", U.N. document E/C.10/AC.2/8, December 13, 1978 [hereinafter cited as United Nations Code of Conduct: Formulations].

7. "Letter of transmittal by the ILO Deputy Director-General to the Secretary-General of the United Nations regarding the ILO Tripartite Declaration of Principles concerning Multinational Enterprises and Social Policy", November 16, 1977, reprinted in Commission on Transnational Corporations, "Texts Relevant to an Annotated Outline", Annex II (Doc. E/C.10/ AC.2/3, January 26, 1978, at 2).

8. See "UNCTAD V Ends Session in Manila, UNCTAD Information Unit, U.N. document TAD/INF/1079 of June 5, 1979, at 2, 14. See also U.N. document TD/L.173.

Code.[9] and some fundamental points of disaccord within the UNCTAD group itself delaying completion of its code,[10] the two are quite likely to appear contemporaneously.[11] UNCTAD has, further, as discussed in an earlier chapter,[12] formulated a code of conduct on restrictive business practices.[13] Clearly, the achievements of the various members of the U.N. family represent a more-or-less unified effort and will most likely be presented as an integrated whole.

The International Chamber of Commerce - the first to produce guidelines, which appeared in 1972 as the ICC Guidelines for International Investment (ICC Guidelines) - has kept close watch on the formulation of the U.N. Code, and has had an appreciable influence upon it. In fact, this 'input' function into the U.N. Code is one of the stated purposes of the Guidelines,[14] and the ICC has periodically submitted its views to the United Nations throughout the course of the latter's work on the formulation of its Code. The EEC and other regional and international bodies have also expressly been supplying input into the U.N. Code formulations.

The EEC is unique among the groups referred to above in that, within the limits of its legislative and enforcement jurisdiction, it has the authority to enact legally binding codes and to enforce compliance.[15] The EEC however has, up to now, as regard codes for MNEs, confined itself to activities of a recommendatory nature directed at the U.N. Formulations rather than utilizing its greater legal competence to initiate one more separate effort at codifying controls. We have already mentioned in previous chapters much of the EEC's current policy and relevant individual member-state legislation and practice surrounding MNEs, and since it has been the practice of the EEC Council to enact binding Community legislation only upon unanimous vote, the EEC will undoubtedly leave MNE code-drafting to those bodies already engaged in these activities.

b. The OECD 'package'

The one international organization which stands out as independent from

9. Ibid., (unnumbered) para. 9, at 13.

10. Ibid., (unnumbered) para. 1, at 2; (unnumbered) paras. 1-5, at 14.

11. See Baade, "Codes of Conduct", op. cit., *supra* note 1, at 20.

12. See *supra* Chapter IX(6).

13. "The Set of Multilaterally Agreed Equitable Principles and Rules for the Control of Restrictive Business Practices", U.N. document TD/RBP/CONF/10 of 2 May 1980.

14. International Chamber of Commerce, *Guidelines for International Investment,* ICC Publications, Paris, 1974, [hereinafter cited as ICC Guidelines], (unnumbered) paras. 5, 9, at 7, 8.

15. See e.g. Bowett, *The Law of International Institutions* (London: Stevens, 3d ed., 1975), at 185-189.

the United Nations group and related efforts is the Organisation for Economic Co-operation and Development (OECD), which adopted, in June 1967, its Declaration on International Investment and Multinational Enterprises,[16] along with four other instruments relating to the Declaration. Three of these related instruments are "Decisions" (on consultation procedures, national treatment, and international investment incentives and disincentives),[17] and the other is the "Guidelines for Multinational Enterprises" (OECD Guidelines), formally an Annex to the Declaration.[18]

Interestingly enough, this "integrated package", comprised of the five MNE-related instruments, comprehends three distinct legal categories[19] represented in (1) the Decisions, which, according to the OECD Convention,[20] are legally binding on all participating members (Article 5); (2) the Declaration, which, along with some member-state "considerations and understandings" prefacing the Guidelines, is not legally binding by virtue of the OECD treaty itself, but could be considered to be so in any aspect in which it expresses in convenient and systematic form some existing rule of general international law, or could become so by incorporation into a treaty duly ratified by OECD member states; and (3) the Guidelines, which are expressly stated within their own framework to be "not legally enforceable" (paragraph 6).

Our particular concern in the present context is with the Guidelines, and these, adopted on June 21, 1976, will undoubtedly continue to maintain an independent existence as distinct from the U.N. "package". Even the OECD Guidelines, however, have been a product of much the same climate of opinion as have been the U.N.-family Code Formulations. "Especially when it is recalled that the interests represented in the OECD are not so different from those shaping pertinent E.E.C. policies, it seems likely that the two basic sets [the U.N. Code and the OECD Guidelines] of international texts on MNE

16. Organisation for Economic Co-operation and Development (OECD), *Declaration by the Governments of OECD Member Countries and Decisions of the OECD Council on International Investment and Multinational Enterprises,* Paris, [1976], [hereinafter cited as OECD Declaration].

17. Organisation for Co-operation and Development, "Decisions of the Council on Inter-Governmental Consultation Procedures on the Guidelines for Multinationals"; "Decision of the Council on National Treatment"; and "Decision of the Council on International Investment Incentives and Disincentives", in *Idem.*

18. Organisation for Co-operation and Development, "Guidelines for Multinational Enterprises", [hereinafter cited as OECD Guidelines], Annex, OECD Declaration, loc. cit., *supra* note 16.

19. See Baade, "Codes of Conduct", op. cit., *supra* note 1, at 38-39.

20. Convention on the Organisation for Economic Co-operation and Development of December 14, 1960.

conduct will prove to be harmonious and mutually supportive''.[21]

2. Legal Aspects

a. Non-legally-binding character

The most pertinent common feature of all the codes and guidelines is their non-legally-binding character. Those which do not expressly state their non-legally-binding nature clearly acknowledge it. The two exceptions are those codes still in the drafting stage, namely, the draft U.N. Code, in which, in the Introductory Note, it is stated that ''the legal nature of the Code still has to be discussed'',[22] and the yet-to-be completed UNCTAD code on the transfer of technology,[23] for which a mandate reserves the questions of legal nature and implementation for later consideration.

There are two basic positions regarding this issue. One is known as the ''maximalist position'', and favours legally binding, internationally enforceable rules of conduct for MNEs. This position is adhered to generally by the international trade union movement and the developing nations. The other is the so-called ''minimalist position'', and promotes the notion of voluntary rather than legally enforceable guidelines. This position is predictably advocated by the international business community and generally by highly-capital-intensive industrialized nations.[24] Between these two poles is what has been termed a ''zebra code'', i.e., an instrument composed of both binding and

21. Baade, ''Codes of Conduct'', op. cit., *supra* note 1, at 58. See also generally Coolidge, et al., eds., *The OECD Guidelines for Multinational Enterprises: A Business Appraisal,* Washington, D.C., Institute for International and Foreign Trade Law, Georgetown University Law Center, [c. 1977]; also OECD, *Review of the 1976 Declaration and Decisions on International Investment and Multinational Enterprises,* Report by the Committee on International Investment and Multinational Enterprises to the OECD Council Meeting at Ministerial Level, 13th-14th June, 1979.

22. United Nations Code of Conduct: Formulations, op. cit., *supra* note 6, at 3.

23. Draft International Code of Conduct on the Transfer of Technology, United Nations document TD/CODE TOT/25 of June 2, 1980. It has been suggested that the UNCTAD code, if promulgated, could have certain model-law implications for those countries which have no law on the subject, or that such countries insist, administratively, that technology transfers to their country be in accordance with the code. (See Davidow, ''The UNCTAD Restrictive Business Practices Code'', *International Lawyer,* (1979), at 603.) See also Fikentscher, *The Draft International Code of Conduct on the Transfer of Technology,* published by the Max Planck Institute for Foreign and International Patent, Copyright, and Competition Law, Munich (Weinheim: Chemie, 1980).

24. See Baade. ''Codes of Conduct'', op. cit., *supra* note 1, at 56.

non-binding rules,[25] containing both "shall" and "should" clauses.[26] Such an instrument, it has been suggested, may find its way into customary international law, or even already be considered as a restatement thereof in certain of its provisions, particularly those addressed to states and phrased in legal terms.[27] This is still, however, somewhat speculative, so we shall concentrate here on the two major positions - 'minimalist' and maximalist' - mentioned above. What are the prospects for the two positions?

b. Prospects for the "minimalist position"

To support the institution of a universally applicable, legally binding international control system is to ignore the fact that not all governments on the one hand, nor all corporations on the other hand, share identical aims or interests. The fundamental acknowledgement of a divergence of political ideologies and economic policies is essential for an understanding of the nature and function of present or prospective international guidelines. Hence, even should those parties favouring the "minimalist position" (non-legally-binding controls) be doing so out of self-interest, they have the advantage that the above facts lend strong support to their postition. In other words, it is this very lack of uniformity of interests and intrinsic incompatibility of existing economic systems, along with the divergent levels or stages of industrialization and development (a) between different economic regions, (b) between individual states within those regions, and (c) even internal to the various states themselves at various stages in their development, that are perhaps the greatest and most obvious obstacles to any legally binding, globally applicable international regulatory agreement.

These disparities are universally recognized and need little elaboration, other than perhaps to point out that the problem lies not so much in differing long-range economic objectives between the developing and industrialized world, as in their immediate objectives, or, perhaps more significantly, simply in the fact that economic, political and sociological consequences arising out of business transactions among the developed nations are significantly different from those arising out of economic activities between the developed and the develop-

25. See e.g. Baade, "The Legal Effects of Codes of Conduct for Multinational Enterprises", 22 *German Yearbook of International Law* (1979), at 11 *et seq.* [hereinafter cited as "Legal Effects of Codes"].

26. See e.g. the Convention on a Code for Liner Conferences drafted under the auspices of UNCTAD, United Nations General Assembly resolution 3035 (XXVII), December 19, 1972.

27. See Baade, "Legal Effects of Codes", op. cit., *supra* note 25, at 24.

ing nations. This is due largely to the fact that in the industrialized world some equilibrium exists between incoming and outgoing direct investment, i.e. these nations tend to be simultaneously home and host to foreign direct investment; whereas the developing nations have, up to now, been almost wholly recipient (host) states rather than home states 'exporting' their own foreign investment. It is generally recognized that these two categories of investment activity require separate treatment for the reasons set out at the beginning of this study.

The ICC, for example, which includes a large number of developing states, bases the inability to conclude any form of binding 'code of conduct' or 'guidelines' in the area of restrictive business practices quite simply on the impossibility of taking into account "the diversity of national needs and objectives".[28] An ICC spokesman addressing the United Nations in 1976 summed up his organization's view of the situation as follows:

> Any 'Code of Conduct for transnational corporations' should not be binding, since the diversity of national situations makes it impossible to apply uniform rules to all countries.[29]

UNCTAD V, characterized by its well-known "Group of 77", meeting in Manila in May-June 1979, clearly reflected this diversity by dividing the participants into distinct regional or economic groupings. These groupings consisted of an "African Group", an "Asian Group", a "Latin American Group", a "Group B" (representing the western market-economy nations), a "Group D" (representing the Soviet-bloc, state-run economies), and China. Significantly, the Board recommended that all chairmen and vice-chairmen of the subject-oriented "Negotiating Groups" be nominated from the "Group of 77", "Group B" and "Group D".[30] In other words, the key position in each of the negotiating sessions was held by representatives of developing states, free industrialized states and communist-bloc states, the three major economic sectors to which we have alluded throughout.

Further precedents of differentiation are furnished both by the UNCTAD

28. ICC Document No. 225-1/67 Or., at 5. The ICC has nonetheless remained active in this field, a significant manifestation of which being its March 1981 special open meeting on the question of the extraterritorial application of antitrust laws (restrictive business practices).

29. "Multinationals: ICC Speaks to UN Session in Peru", *ICC Bulletin,* International Chamber of Commerce, Paris, March 1976, at 3.

30. United Nations Conference on Trade and Development, "Provisional Agenda for the Fifth Session of the United Nations Conference on Trade and Development", U.N. document TD/220, April 12, 1979, [hereinafter cited as UNCTAD V Provisional Agenda], at 7.

resolution 21 (II)[31] and by the U.N. General Assembly resolution 2626 (XXV),[32] para. 32, where the notion of non-reciprocal preferential arrangements for developing countries[33] is advanced - as it is throughout the EEC Lomé Convention, and in the latest GATT Tokyo Round[34] and UNCTAD V Session[35] - to make special provisions for the least developed and developing countries in an attempt, over the long term, to narrow the development gap between them and the developed states.

The division has been further incised as a result of the existence of a certain resistance on the part of the developing world to international law in general, which it is inclined to see as a tool of the industrialized nations for which it already harbours an underlying distrust. Evidence of this can be seen in the outcome and conclusions of the non-governmental Düsseldorf Conference on Multinational Corporations where, ironically enough, two separate panels meeting simultaneously - the one to consider the problems of investment control between developed nations, the other to consider the relationship between industrialized and developed nations - both arrived at similar conclusions (negatively disposed toward international controls) but for entirely different reasons. A Report on the Conference contains the observation that:

> the less developed nations would seem to fear that the international agency would seek to restrain their actions in regard to the foreign-based MNEs. And this attitude neatly balances the worry of business that any international agency would rather fetter than free the MNE.[36]

It has largely been between the time of the Düsseldorf Conference and the Bielefeld Symposium that the developing world, led by international labour, has begun to adhere most strongly to the "maximalist posi-

31. United Nations Conference on Trade and Development, resolution 21(II), March 26, 1968 (*Proceedings of the United Nations Conference on Trade and Development, Second Session,* Vol. I and Corr. 1 & 3 and Add. 1 & 2, Report and Annexes, [United Nations publication, Sales No. E 68 II, D 14]), at 38.

32. United Nations G.A. resolution 2626 (XXV), November 11, 1970.

33. In para. 56(5), a further distinction is made by granting special measures in favour of the "least developed" among the developing nations, reflecting the earlier UNCTAD resolution 21(II) and its related documents.

34. General Agreement on Tariffs and Trade, Document No. MTN/FR/W/20/Rev. 2. ("Different and more favourable treatment for developing countries, reciprocity by developing countries in trade negotiations, and their progressive fuller participation in GATT".)

35. UNCTAD V Provisional Agenda, op. cit., *supra* note 30, para. 15, at 4.

36. Rubin, "Report on the Düsseldorf conference on international controls on foreign investment", 7 *International Lawyer* (1973), at 826-827.

tion", since many of the codes and guidelines which have appeared during that period have clearly favoured their interests. Those developing states most concerned about the loss of sovereignty should nonetheless not lose sight of the fact that - as EEC member-states have already experienced - a certain loss of sovereignty is necessarily involved in the application of any binding agreement enforced by an international or even by a regional body. Those states must realize that international regulations can be as much of a compromise of sovereignty - or more so - as the commercial activities of foreign multinationals, which at least are subject to national regulation.

It is not only differing stages of development, but also fundamentally differing ideologies among nations and groups of nations which further serve to frustrate a meeting of the minds. Clearly, state-run economies are based upon a substantially different set of principles than are economies founded and run on a free-enterprise principle. In Eastern Europe, for example, the MNE can operate as such in only three states: Yugoslavia, Rumania and Hungary[37] (and only within certain specified limitations). The USSR itself and other communist-bloc countries[38] have made ever-increasing use of the joint venture - in partnership with state or private capital - as a means of entering the world market; yet even this limited entry by the Soviets into a wider economic system through the joint venture was publicly reproached as "revisionist" in a Press Release at the United Nations in 1975 - by the People's Republic of China, which significantly labelled such associations as "Moscow-brand 'transnational corporations'".[39]. Interestingly enough, China has just adopted its own law on joint ventures: "The Law of the People's Republic of China on Joint Ventures Using Chinese and Foreign Investment",[40] and has ceased attacking

37. Hellmann, "Countervailing Powers to the Multinational Corporation", in D. Wallace, ed., *International Control of Investment: The Düsseldorf Conference on Multinational Corporations* (New York: Praeger Publishers, 1974), at 59. But see Machowski, "Multinationale Unternehmen sozialistischer Länder", *Neue Zürcher Zeitung*, May 15, 1979, at 10.

38. See e.g. the Bulgarian Law on Joint Ventures of 25 March 1980 (English translation), published in 19 *International Legal Materials* (1980), pp. 992-1002.

39. Press Release, People's Republic of China, United Nations, September 9, 1975. It will be interesting to witness the further development of the Chinese attitude in these matters in view of the recent policy changes by the Chinese Government.

40. The Law of the People's Republic of China on Joint Ventures Using Chinese and Foreign Investment, adopted by the Second Session of the Fifth National People's Congress on July 1, 1979. Reproduced in 13 *International Legal Materials (1979)*, from the *Beijing Review*, No. 29 (July 20, 1979), at 24-26. The *Beijing Review* text of the Law was also distributed in Press Release No. 79/001 by the Embassy of the People's Republic of China at Washington, D.C. See also "Gesetzentwürfe im chinesischen Volkskongress", *Frankfurter Allgemeine Zeitung*, June 28, 1979, at 3. See also Torkert, "China's Joint Venture Law: A Preliminary Analysis", 12 *Vanderbilt Journal of Transnational Law* (1979), pp. 819-895.

Soviet economic policy as 'revisionist'. An interesting notion has been expounded by one author who writes:

> In one respect the enterprises within each Communist country can be viewed as one giant conglomerate enterprise directed at the top by political-economic unity of command. In Russia it could be called the USSR enterprise. And it is multinational in that its joint activities dovetail with other Communist country enterprises and, increasingly with Japan, Arab, African and other national enterprises.[41]

This, of course, is one rather novel interpretation, but is, indeed, thought provoking.

Realistically, given the general Communist view, any reconciliation between the state-run-economy concept and that of the industrialized western free-economy states leading to a uniform approach to international regulation is even more illusory than an agreement aspiring to solve the investment problems of both the developed and developing states under identical provisions.

The fact remains that, for the present, at least, there exists no legally binding agreement. Moreover, the general consensus, as reflected in the results of both governmental and non-governmental congresses, symposia and other international convocations, as well as in the relevant legal literature and study evaluations and assessments, is that actual universally applicable and legally enforceable international codes are simply not feasible in the present economic and political environment - an environment which shows no immediate promise of becoming more amenable to uniform treatment. Hence, for the time being and the foreseeable future, the "minimalist position" prevails.

c. Prospects for the "maximalist" position

The "maximalists", aware that there is little hope of a general international treaty to give the codes legal stature, are looking to other possible sources of international law to enhance the juridical status of their position. This has led to the promotion, almost exclusively by those interests adhering to the maximalist position, of the view that the U.N. Code at least, and certainly the

41. Tindall, *Multinational Enterprises: Legal and Management Structures and Interrelationships with Ownership, Control, Antitrust, Labor, Taxation and Disclosure,* (Dobbs Ferry, N.Y.: Oceana, 1975), at 238.

Charter of Economic Rights and Duties of States, may already be considered - or may over a (perhaps short) period of time come to be considered - customary international law.[42] This view is not so much based on the notion of 'instantaneous custom' as it is on what the maximalists see as the declaratory nature of these documents. As expressed by Ambassador Castañeda, who was Chairman of the Working Group preparing the Charter of Economic Rights and Duties of States, such resolutions "do not create the law; they have a declaratory nature of noting what does exist."[43] Important here, of course, is a consensus on "what does exist".

Predictably there is resistance to this view on the part of most of the industrialized states, which indeed, tend repeatedly to refer to the voluntary nature of the Code. Further, with regard to the Economic Charter, as a U.N. General Assembly resolution, there would be strong objection on the part of the same nations, on account of the 'one-state-one-vote' principle in the U.N. General Assembly,[44] to construing resolutions by that body as any sort of 'international legislation'.[45] The fact that U.N. General Assembly resolutions lack any intrinsically binding force implies that a general consensus by member states is a basic prerequisite to even contemplating any customary international legal nature of such resolutions. Even a majority vote representative of all political and economic groups does not of course *create* international law, though it may represent a codification or proclamation of rules recognized by the community of nations. And *should* a resolution become custom, it is in any case, not binding on dissenting states. The MNEs themselves, by compliance with the codes or guidelines, are clearly incapable of thereby transforming

42. For some contemporary views on the complexities of proving a "rule" has become custom, see generally, D'Amato, *The Concept of Custom in International Law* (Ithaca: Cornell University Press (1971), esp. pp. 41-44, 233-236, 246-263, 269-274; Thirlway, *International Customary Law and Codification* (Leiden: Sijthoff, 1972), esp. Chapter Four.

43. Cited in United Nations, *Official Records of the General Assembly: 29th Session* (1974), Vol.I: *Resolutions* (Supp. No. 31 (A/9631)), United Nations, New York, 1975 [hereinafter cited as United Nations Charter of Economic Rights and Duties of States], at 491.

44. This principle has for some years been consistently giving developing nations, and those other nations which tend to vote in the same block, a clear majority in voting on the resolutions favouring their interests, without a necessary consensus of all political and economic sectors represented.

45. See e.g. Tomuschat, "Die Charta der wirtschaftlichen Rechte und Pflichten der Staaten. Zur Gestaltungskraft von Deklarationen der UN - Generalversammlung." "The Charter of Economic Rigths and Duties of States. A New Legal Order of World Economy?" (Summary), in Mosler, ed. 36 *Völkerrecht als Rechtsordnung, Zeitschrift für ausländisches öffentliches Recht und Völkerrecht* (1976), at 491. For further comment on the resolutions and declarations of the United Nations General Assembly as a "legislative" activity, see Thirlway, op. cit., *supra* note 42, at 61-79.

them into customary international law, owing to their lack of full international legal personality.[46] Given these facts, and given the fact that 'custom' can become international law only in the absence of protest, the reservations expressed by a number of highly industrialized states to the Charter of Economic Rights and Duties of States, as well as constant references to its voluntary nature, would be difficult to ignore as a form of protest ('persistent objection') to the provisions of such documents ever becoming a source of international law.

The prospects for the "maximalist position" look doubtful, either by way of general international treaty or customary international law; but this debate is likely to continue.

d. General prospects

It may well be that by the time a workable consensus has been reached and an international control system - of whatever character - has been developed to where it can be effectively applied and enforced, that the 'threat' which generated it will have substantially diminished, or even ceased to be a 'threat', as a natural consequence of the ever-changing global economic landscape which is already displaying signs, in certain sectors, of a distinct shift in direction[47] and of an increasing tendency toward contractual arrangements[48] as

46. See Baade, "Legal Effects of Codes", op. cit., *supra* note 25, at 20, 22.

47. See e.g. "Auslandsinvestitionen in Amerika gestiegen", *Frankfurter Allgemeine Zeitung,* 29 August 1980, at 12; "Foreign direct investment in Germany DM 66.8 b end 1978", *Europe Agence internationale d'information pour la presse,* Luxembourg, 4 February 1981, at 17; "The new wave: Foreign capital investment in the United States - a survey", *The Economist,* 25 October 1980; "Deutsche Auslandsinvestitionen bzw. ausländische Investitionen in der Bundesrepublik Deutschland", *Archiv der Gegenwart,* 9 August 1980; CCH *Common Market Reporter: Doing Business in Europe* ¶ 40,033 [New Developments, 1980]; "Verstärkte Kapitalausfuhr aus Japan: Direktinvestitionen im Ausland auf Rekordhöhe", *Neue Zürcher Zeitung,* 6 September 1979, at 17; "Japan is Building Economic Empire in American West", *International Herald Tribune,* 3 August 1978, at 1 *et. seq.;* "Japanese Beachhead in California", *The New York Times,* Sunday edition, 21 August 1977, Section 3, at 1; "Look out - the Bristish are coming", *The Sunday Telegraph,* 27 February 1977, at 25; "Beecham expanding in North America", *Financial Times,* 9 March 1978 (Financial and Company News section).

48. That contractual arrangements are increasingly being resorted to as a solution to the growing restrictions on MNE foreign direct investment was stressed by George C. Kern, Jr., in private discussion, on the occasion of the June 1979 Cologne Conference on "The U.S. Antitrust Laws/Die U.S.-Anti-trust-Gesetze," presented by the Practising Law Institute of New York in co-operation with the German-American Lawyers Association, Bonn, the American Chamber of Commerce in Germany, Frankfurt am Main, and the Studienvereinigung Kartellrecht e.V., Wiesbaden.

opposed to the traditional forms of investment up to now characteristic of the MNE. This may already be an indication of the legal effect of an ever-tightening clampdown, through regulatory legislation, on MNE direct-investment activity.

To sum up, the real obstruction to universally applicable international legal controls is the general disparity between the various business and government interests globally represented, where cultural, political, economic and ideological differences all combine to make harmony of purpose among nations or economic groupings, in this regard, virtually unattainable in a form which is to have much practical impact.

3. Non-Legal Aspects

a. Non-legally-binding nature as a possible asset

Within code/guidelines discussions reigns the further debate as to whether, in actual practice, the fact that such instruments are *not* legally binding does not perhaps render them more effective than if they were legally binding, owing to the greater flexibility and specificity resulting from the non-necessity of the international consensus required for a legally enforceable instrument, among other similar arguments. While non-legal aspects of the codes are not central to our treatment here, a distorted picture could result if it were not pointed out that international codes and guidelines, despite their lack of legal enforceability, have not been without discernable and sometimes concrete effect.

b. Tangible non-legal effects

Of particular interest in this connection are two instances in which host governments have brought before the Committee on International Investment and Multinational Enterprise (CIME, or IME Committee) of the OECD, for "clarification", cases involving MNEs where the judgments handed down by local courts were considered by those governments to be unacceptable and in conflict with the 'letter' or at least the 'spirit' of the Guidelines.

In each case, specific action was consequently taken against the MNEs in question - action which had not, in either case, been a part of the final judgment in the respective national courts. One of these cases was the *Badger* case,[49] brought by the Belgian Government, and the other was the *Hertz* case,[50] brought by the Danish Government, both introduced on March 30, 1977. The *Badger* case involved the issue of co-responsibility of the parent company and its subsidiaries; the *Hertz* case involved the transfer of company personnel across national borders during a labour dispute. We shall avoid entering into the detailed facts of these domestic cases,[51] since at the stage at which they reached the international level their handling was extra-legal, and while the non-legal aspects are interesting and worthy of mention, the essential point to be brought out here is that these cases, called to the attention of the IME Committee of OECD by host governments, are illustrations of issues arising under the voluntary Guidelines which produced concrete and favourable results for those host states introducing the complaints. The Committee strictly limits itself to considering and clarifying the issues only - i.e. the general principles on which a debate was based, without any pretense of acting as a 'semi-court'. The Committee seeks no deviation from the practice of settling actual *cases* at the national or bilateral level, in domestic courts. It carefully avoids any references to 'fact-finding'; it debates 'issues' rather than 'cases'; and it aims at 'clarification' rather than 'interpretation'.

While a number of other cases have been brought before the IME Committee, all introduced by one of its advisory bodies, namely the Trade Union Advisory Committee (TUAC), the *Hertz* and *Badger* cases have up to the time of writing been the only two cases brought before the Committee by governments.

Of course OECD's CIME brings to mind also the ICC commercial arbitration service for conflicts arising in the course of international trade, as well as the International Center for the Settlement of Industrial Disputes (ICSID), as international bodies functioning to settle trade and investment conflicts, but we must not be sidetracked form the central theme here, which is not arbitration but regulation, or control, and the nature of international codes and guidelines.

49. The *Badger* case, Written Question No. 323/77 of June 29, 1977 (Mr. Van der Hek), and the Answer of the Commission, dated September 14, 1977, E.C.J.O. C. 246/17 and 18 (1977).

50. The *Hertz* case, EEC doc. 424/76, November 15, 1976; European Parliament, Resolution of November 16, 1976, E.C.J.O. C. 293/12 (1976); Debates, same date, at 46-51.

51. For a more detailed handling of the *Badger* and *Hertz* cases, see Blanpain, *The OECD Guidelines for Multinational Enterprises and Labour Relations: 1976-1979. Experience and Review* (Deventer: Kluwer, 1979).

4. Addressees

Every bit as significant for the effectiveness - legal or extra-legal - of the codes is the matter of to whom they are addressed. Just as national control legislation directed at MNE or other potential corporate abuse is of little effect when the actual management control centers are not pinpointed, so international codes or regulations - however well elaborated - are of little impact when the recommendations are not directed at parties with the will and capacity to carry them out effectively. Of prime importance, then, is that any international directives be addressed to the appropriate party. This may, in fact, vary according to the particular intent of any given set of guidelines, as there is no unanimous agreement as to the real function of codes and guidelines, and whom they are actually intended to protect.

It is noteworthy that, while the host state is the party most directly affected by the foreign investment, most of the Code provisions are directed either at the home state (ICC Guidelines: "The Investor's Country Should..."; ILO: "Governments of home countries should..."), or at the MNEs themselves (OECD: "Enterprises should..., should refrain from..."; ICC: "The Investor Should..."; ILO: "multinational enterprises should..."; U.N.: "Transnational corporations should..., should not..."). ICC and the ILO at least have included directives to the host as well (ICC: "The Host Country's Government Should..."; ILO: "Both host and home country governments should..."), addressing some provisions to two or to all three parties concerned (ILO: "All parties concerned... should...", "Governments, multinational as well as national enterprises should...").

Each major set of guidelines is constructed differently, reflecting the slightly different natures or objectives. The OECD Guidelines address only MNEs, and expressly state that they are to be regarded as "recommendations jointly addressed by Member countries to multinational enterprises operating in their territories, and that "[o]bservation of the guidelines is voluntary and not legally enforceable".[52]

The ICC divides its "Principles" into three separate categories: (1) those addressed to "The Investor"; (2) those addressed to "The Investor's Country's Government", and (3) those addressed to "The Host Country's Government". These guidelines are also expressly stated not to be a "rigid code of conduct".[53]

52. OECD Guidelines, op. cit., *supra* note 18, para. 6, at 12.

53. See Baade, "Codes of Conduct", op. cit., *supra* note 1, at 53.

The U.N. Code Formulations make it clear in the Preface that the treatment of principles and/or issues are divided into two groups, those related to the activities of MNEs, and those relating to their treatment. This would seem to imply that the addressees would be the MNEs on the one hand, and host states on the other. On examination of the text of the Code Formulations, one finds that paragraphs 1 through 44[54] are specifically addressed to MNEs ("Transnational corporations"), with only paragraphs 45 through 51 addressed to governments in general, not necessarily the host. The final four paragraphs, while mentioning both parties, indirectly address the MNEs. Of significance here, as mentioned earlier, is that the legal nature of the Code has been reserved to future discussion.

The ILO Declaration does not divide its provisions according to addressee, but rather to subject matter. Consequently the addressees, representing government, employer and labour, are scattered throughout. The subject headings are helpful, but it could perhaps be of greater utility to any of the parties consulting the Declaration, if the various addressees were likewise grouped together, to facilitate reference. The Declaration, as previously mentioned, is recognized to be non-mandatory.

Let us consider what relative effects can be expected from directives addressed to the various parties concerned.

a. Directives to home governments

First, in the present context, directives addressed to home governments concerning their multinational enterprises abroad can only mean greater exercise of extraterritorial jurisdiction, and hence, further penetration of foreign influence into host territory. This would undoubtedly tend to aggravate rather than to alleviate the present concerns.

Secondly, if an international directive provides that the home state do the regulating, the home state must apply uniform regulatory measures to every type of firm, from extractive industries to high technotronics, unless a system of exceptions is to be implemented; and then the question arises as to who determines those exceptions, the international body issuing the directives to the home states or the home states themselves, in which case international uniformity is immediately sacrificed and subjectivity re-enters.

Moreover, and even more importantly if the home state is directed to do the regulating, no differentiation can be made between various recipient (host)

54. With the exception of the several not yet formulated.

states. This may at first glance appear an ideal to be strived for. But the hosts themselves would soon find this unreasonable, if not intolerable. For one thing, it presupposes that all host states have identical national interests and economic needs, which simply is not a reflection of fact. Even if the international regulations were tripartite, in the sense that recognition of the substantial differences between industrial, developing, and state-run economies were reflected in the regulations governing them, this would still fail to deal with the fact that the national interests even within each group also vary considerably form one nation state to another. (Witness the frequent lack of unanimity within regional 'common markets'.[55] Such issues as what constitutes a 'key sector', or what particular technological, managerial, or other needs might be served by conditional entry requirements, or what constitutes the 'national interest', and similar issues, can only properly be determined by the individual national state hosting the investment, and not by the home state constrained to uniformly apply some internationally decreed standard, which it must then exert extraterritorially on its MNEs operating abroad.

b. Directives to MNEs

International directives addressed to the MNEs are certainly useful in the form of guidelines for good corporate citizenship; as binding codes, however, they would be less than optimal for several reasons. First, the multinational enterprises themselves are hit by regulations from both home and host governments. An international code aspiring to further regulate the multinationals would only add to the multitude of regulations already confronting them, and further aggravate international commercial relations.

An international code could indeed contribute to the avoidance of overlapping or conflicting legislative jurisdiction to alleviate the position of the MNE being subject to more than one jurisdiction when multiple jurisdiction means conflicting and mutually incompatible directives; but international directives to MNEs can clearly do nothing to ameliorate such conditions, as the MNEs themselves are powerless as regards jurisdictional questions, being neither general 'natural' nor 'artificial' subjects of international law as cur-

55. See, *inter alia,* Vagts, "The Host Country Faces the Multinational Enterprise", 53 *Boston University Law Review* (1973), at 276; "Chile Formally Quits Andean Market Pact", *International Herald Tribune,* November 1, 1976; Torem and Craig, "Developments in the Control of Foreign Investment in France", 70 *Michigan Law Review* (1971), at 300-311.

rently understood,[56] nor possessing "the power to participate directly in the norm-creating process."[57]

We would do well to reiterate here the aim of controls, as set out in an earlier chapter, *viz.* to minimize the detrimental effects and maximize the beneficial effects of MNE activity. This aim is a feature of every major 'code', 'guidelines', and 'declaration' on international MNE controls drafted in recent years.[58] The second element of this aim will not be achieved if all 'controls' relating to the MNE are uni-directional and end up by strangling such enterprises to the point where their beneficial contribution to economic rationalization and development are sacrificed.

Apropos, a 200-page report, with a further 200-page annex, has recently been published in Brussels,[59] revealing that multinationals are far more circumscribed by national, regional, and international regulations than they were even a few years previously. The report details the plethora of both international and purely EEC controls that have gradually and imperceptibly begun to restrict the freedom of action of the MNEs. Citing, *inter alia,* the EEC's fourth directive requiring standards of disclosure on MNEs' subsidiaries, its seventh directive aimed at demanding consolidated accounts from the MNEs, and its ninth directive creating a new legal basis for group liability of MNEs, the report warns that "it is the array of powers that the EEC Commission either possesses now or plans to acquire that stands out as the most formidable weapon multinationals have to face if they operate inside the Common Market."[60] As observed in a review of the report: "In effect, the multinational corporation is being tied down by strands of regulation, just as Gulliver was immobilised by the Lilliputians."[61] A similar type of metaphor was used by Thomas Enders, the then U.S. Assistant Secretary of State, before members of Congress and the European Parliament, when he remarked that: "the danger is that uncoordinated or excessive national and international regulation - particularly if aimed at potential rather than actual abuses - runs the risk of killing the goose which lays the golden egg."[62]

56. See generally Baade, "Individual Responsibility", in: Black and Falk, eds., *The Future of the International Legal Order,* Vol.4: *The Structure of the International Environment,* (Princeton, N.J.: Princeton University Press, 1970 [Vol.4, 1972]), pp. 290-327.

57. Baade, "Legal Effects of Codes", op. cit., *supra* note 25, at 16.

58. See *infra Chapter XIV,* notes 13-15 and accompanying text.

59. "Multinationals in the 1980s - trends in European regulation and international control", Agence Européen d'informations, Brussels, 1980.

60. "The EEC creeps up on the multinationals" (Merritt), *The Financial Times,* London, October 5, 1979, at 12, reviewing the Brussels report (*Idem*).

61. *Idem.*

62. Statement of Thomas O. Enders, Assistant Secretary of State, at a public hearing on the

Further, addressing directives to the MNEs fails to take full account of the semantic and definitional deficiencies. We discussed in an early chapter the difficulties of definition of a multinational enterprise, and remarked that no universally accepted legal definition of MNEs exists as yet. It is clear, then, that provisions aimed at "multinational enterprises" may fall short of their mark if it remains unclear as to just which enterprises fall under the category of "multinational".

The OECD Guidelines state specifically that "a precise legal definition is not required for the purpose of the guidelines".[63] This is true only due to the totally voluntary nature of the guidelines, and their "soft-law" character. In contrast to this, and reflecting the potentially different nature of the U.N. Code, is the statement that "[t]he need to define transnational corporations as well as some other fundamental concepts for the purposes of a code is recognized".[64] If a code is to be binding, a legal - or at least authoritative - definition is clearly called for, in order to identify the entities to be covered.[65]

But even a precise definition does not provide an adequate solution. Provided a legal definition were arrived at - and one such definition has been formulated independently by the Institut de Droit International, at its Oslo Session in 1977[66] - an enterprise operating internationally and wishing to avoid certain provisions of the Code could, if it were in its interest, so modify its operations as to fall just outside of the legal definition and thus outside of the

---

multinational corporation held jointly by members of Congress and the European Parliament, September 17, 1974, as cited in Sparkman, "The MNC and Foreign Investment", 27 *Mercer Law Review* (1976), at 385.

63. OECD Guidelines, op. cit., *supra* note 18, para. 7, at 12.

64. U.N. document E/C.10/AC.2/3, January 26, 1978, para. 24, at 10. For full title of document, see *supra* note 4.

65. See e.g. United Nations, *Transnational Corporations: Issues Involved in the Formulation of a Code of Conduct,* U.N. document E/C.10/18, para. 46.

66. Les entreprises formées d'un centre de décision localisé dans un pays et de centres d'activité, dotés ou non de personnalité juridique propre, situés dans un ou plusieurs autres pays, devraient être considérées comme constituant, en droit, des entreprises multinationales. [The French text is authoritative. English translation, furnished by I.D.I., follows:] Enterprises which consist of a decision-making centre located in one country and of operating centres, with or without legal personality, situated in one or more other contries should, in law, be considered as multinational enterprises.

Institut de Droit International, "Resolutions adoptées par l'Institut à la Session d'Oslo, 30 août - 8 septembre 1977: III. Les entreprises multinationales" (Deuxième Commission), (the French text is authoritative), as reproduced in *Institut de Droit International: Annuaire,* Vol. 57, Tome II, pp. 338-342, Sect. I, at 341.

reach of the regulations. Such a move is unlikely with a large and well-established multinational concern, but an enterprise just hovering on the borderline of becoming "multinational" by definition, could be tempted in this direction.

c. Directives to host governments

This leads us to another significant question, namely, how important is it that a multinaional firm be distinguished from a national firm for the purpose of regulation? It has been suggested that: "The so-called tensions between nation-states and multinational corporations are not very often different from those confronting government and business in the normal course of their mutual relations."[67]

It is true that certain control provisions could only relate to enterprises with a foreign control-center. Such provisions would include the protection of national security and key-sector areas. But are not many of the abuses which are named as MNE abuses just as apt to be perpetrated by a powerful domestic firm?

A small MNE (and there *are* small MNEs, unless the definition one selects includes a certain minimum size standard, which is not a very realistic criterion for establishing multinationality) is not likely to receive much criticism. It is generally a powerful MNE which becomes subject to attack. Is not a large and powerful domestic firm equally prone to exert undue pressures on its own government, lobby for its particular interests, which are not necessarily those of its government, or otherwise abuse the consumer by unfair competition and restrictive business practices? In the opinion of the present writer, it is the abuses themselves which should be attacked, whatever firm commits them, national or multinational;[68] and the host state would seem in the best position to assess those activities which are 'abusive' in the context of its own individual economy. Moreover, the very words "national interest" and "foreign enterprise" lose substantial significance outside of the national context.

If some potential abuses are exclusive to multinational activity, then of course a law should be enacted to curb that abuse, but that law should be enacted by the host state where the abuse has occurred. There would appear to be no need to specify that the law is to be applied exclusively to multinational firms, as then the definitional problems arises. The law should simply be directed

67. Rogers, "Multinational Corporations: A European View", in Blake, ed., 403 *The Annals of the American Academy of Political and Social Science,* (1972), at 65.

68. Two international codes reflect this view: the OECD Guidelines (op. cit., *supra* note 18, para. 9) and the ILO Declaration (op. cit., *supra* note 2, para. 11).

against the abuse. Firms which by their very legal structure are incapable of perpetrating the abuse will simply lie outside the applicability of the particular law.

Special care must of course be taken here, in conformity with the national treatment principle of international law, that the law is not of a discriminatory nature, and that, if it affects solely foreign enterprises, it is only in those allowed areas of the public interest and national security. There is clearly the danger, even so, that the 'public interest' can be stretched beyond all reasonable limits, as we have seen particularly in some cases relating to expropriation in the preceding chapters.

In short, it should not be "the multinational enterprise" which is under attack, but rather those results of operations - of MNEs or of strictly national enterprises - which have deleterious effects on the political, economic, cultural and/or natural environments. It is in the context of functioning national legal systems where this will hopefully be - and appears to be in the process of being - partially, if not substantially, achieved.

Consequently, it is the opinion of the present writer that any MNE-control regulations[69] in international codes, where the intent is any more than one of "guidance" in the strictest sense of the word, should consist mainly of directives to host governments to the end of harmonizing and rationalizing national legislation for controlling any abuses of power in corporate activity, as where this involves a foreign multinational enterprise, the control is best applied at its point of impact, its point of actual operations, namely the host state. For if the aim is to be served of making the MNE both efficiently productive and economically and technologically beneficial to the host state, surely a 'conflicting patchwork' of national controls will not serve this goal.[70] What is needed is a legal framework of effective national laws harmonized at least to an extent that companies can more easily initiate and conduct transnational operations[71] without the uncertainty and complexities of conflicting laws, and with the more stable environment for long-range and beneficial corporate planning that such a framework would provide.[72] No international code can achieve the aims sought unless it represents a reasonable balance of advantages and responsibilities for governments and corporations alike.[73]

69. As distinct from control limitations on the powers of host states in dealing with MNEs as aliens, which should also be included in any regulations regarding MNEs. See also *infra* note 85 and accompanying text.

70. See e.g. Tindall, op. cit., *supra* note 41, at 191-192.

71. See Tugendhat, *The Multinationals* (New York: Random House, 1972), at 91-92.

72. See Tindall, op. cit., *supra* note 41, at 228-229.

73. See Jenks, "Multinational Entities in the Law of Nations", in Jessup, *Transnational Law in a Changing Society;* Essays, Friedmann, ed. (New York: Columbia University Press, 1972), at 81-82.

Finally, the fact that the trend is moving in the direction of polycentric (host-country oriented)[74] management is another strong argument in favour of control being exercised by the host, in its capacity as not only the seat of operations, but, increasingly, the seat of management.

International guidelines addressed to the host states, then, (and it must not be forgotten that most industrialized host states are at the same time home states, but here we are concentrating on their capacity as host) would place the control at the locus of the potentially abusive act. Moreover, the enforcement and/or punitive machinery relating to the abuse - or at least to the local party to the abuse in cases where two or more different national units of a multinational enterprise are involved - would also be at the locus of the illegal act or abuse.

Support for this view from an international body is supplied by a resolution of the Institut de Droit International at its Oslo Session in 1977,[75] in which it was stipulated that for those enterprises which conform to the resolution's 'legal' definition of "enterprises multinationales",[76] "[i]l convient que soit progressivement élaboré un régime juridique...qu'il devrait en particulier sauvegarder la souveraineté et l'indépendance économique des États...."[77] While the recommendation that such "régime juridique" be implemented through "accords internationaux"[78] and that a study on the introduction of an "enregistrement international des entreprises multinationales" be undertaken,[79] the emphasis remains on safeguarding the sovereignty and economic independence of states.[80]

Further, the resolution provides that:

> 1. Pour la détermination de la loi applicable à la constitution, à l'organisation, au fonctionnement et à l'activité des divers éléments com-

74. See Perlmutter, "Some Architectural Problems of the Multinational Firm," 3 *Quarterly Journal of AISEC International* (1967), cited in *Yearbook of International Organizations,* 1968-1969, at 140; cf. also Perlmutter, "The Tortuous Evolution of Multinational Corporation," 3 *Columbia Journal of World Business* (1969), and Perlmutter, "L'entreprise internationale - trois conceptions," 23 *Revue économique et sociale* (1965), at 151 *et seq.*

75. Institut de Droit International, "Résolutions adoptées par l'Institut à la Session d'Oslo, 30 août - 8 septembre 1977: III. Les entreprises multinationales" (Deuxième Commission), (the French text is authoritative), as reproduced in *Institut de Droit International: Annuaire, Vol. 57, Tome II, pp. 338-342.*

76. Ibid., Sect. I. (See *supra* note 63).

77. Ibid., Sect. II.

78. Ibid., Sect. III: 1(a).

79. Ibid., Sect. III: 2(a).

80. Ibid., Sect. II.

posant l'entreprise multinationale, il doit être fait respectivement application des systèmes de solution de conflits de chaque for saisi. En ce qui concerne les activités des entreprises multinationales, il serait souhaitable que ces systèmes fussent progresivement harmonisés de manière à tenir compte, d'abord du pays où s'accomplissent ces activités, et en outre des pays ou celles-ci produisent des effets directs et immédiats.

2. Il est souhaitable que soit envisagée une harmonisation internationale progressive des règles de droit matériel relatives aux activités des entreprises multinationales, et que soient poursuivis les travaux d'élaboration de 'Codes de conduite' pour ces entreprises.[81]

Hence, while promoting "Codes of Conduct" for multinational enterprises, the general thrust of the resolution appears to be toward a "progressive international harmonization" within the choice of law system of each forum, wherein will be determined the law applicable as concerns MNE activities, "preserving the sovereignty and economic independence of states", rather than toward an actual globally applicable international regulatory agreement.

And finally, while recommending that "accords internationaux" be concluded for allocation of jurisdiction in matters of restrictive business practices in order to avoid overlapping jurisdiction or jurisdictional gaps, actual legislative, executive and judicial jurisdiction (to regulate, control and penalize in cases where the effects of such practices are of "un caractère intentionnel ou au moins prévisible, substantiel, direct et immédiat",) are to be based - at least in every case concerning restrictive business practices - on the locus where the delict is performed ("fondeée en tout cas sur le lieu où ces pratiques sont accomplies") and where its "direct and immediate effects" are felt.[82]

While considering the host as addressee, it would be well to make at least a passing comment on host-state limitations. Without continually recalling to mind that the present study has been focused upon control techniques exercised over the activities of multinational enterprises, one could easily develop the notion that a sort of 'cops and robbers' situation exists, where the 'good guys' are the regulating governments and the 'bad guys' are invariably the MNEs.[83] A very timely and useful study could be made concurrently on the extent to which the host states or other regulators should be limited or restrained from executing and exercising undue, excessive or unjustified 'controls' over the

81. Ibid., Sect. IV: 1,2.

82. Ibid., Sects. V, VI.

83. See e.g. "Multinationals: Bad guys do good" (ILO studies resulting in support for MNEs), *The Economist,* November 22, 1975, at 81.

MNEs. In other words, who is to control the controllers?[84] We have had a hint of some such excesses in the foregoing chapter on coerced disinvestment.

In considering international controls as a subject in themselves, one would really have to contemplate to what extent such controls should be seen as additional regulations on the MNE, already controlled from every side nationally, and conversely, to what extent they should be used to protect the interests of the multinational enterprises themselves[85] and to ease the many and various complexities confronting an enterprise doing business internationally.

Here, we are led into another realm of discussion entirely - that of protection of the foreign MNE investment against host-state coercive action which is not in conformity with the rules of international law. The delimitations of the present study have committed us to a consideration only of control *over* the MNE, and do not expand to include limitations on that control. If mention of the other side of the coin is totally neglected, however, an incomplete and deceptive impression could result.

84. See e.g. Schaffner, *Die Multinationalen Ausbeuter oder Triebkraft der Weltwirtschaft?* (Zürich: Edition Interfrom, 1974), at 23.

85. Little rationalized protection for MNEs exists, outside of foreign investment insurance schemes and access to certain international arbitral tribunals such as IBRD's International Center for the Settlement of Investment Disputes (ICSID). One notable effort at such protection is the Council-of-Europe-approved OECD Draft Convention on the Protection of Foreign Property, 1967, (Organisation for Economic Co-operation and Development, Draft Convention on the Protection of Foreign Property and Resolution of the Council on the Draft Convention, OECD Publication No. 23081 (November 1967), reproduced in 7 *International Legal Materials* (1963), at 117 *et seq.*)

Chapter XIV.

FUNCTION OF INTERNATIONAL CODES AND GUIDELINES

What should be, then, the functions of these controls exercised over the MNEs by host governments, under the guidance of international codes?

A certain amount of caution must be exercised in attempting to appraise what are properly national functions and what are more suitably international functions in controlling the MNE,[1] since the multinational enterprise is a political as well as an economic phenomenon, and legal 'answers' and categorizations cannot be expected to eliminate all the political consequences of MNE activity. Some evaluation as to the function of MNE-related controls, can nonetheless be made.

1. Protection of Beneficial Free-Flow of Private Investment Capital and Maintenance of Proper Balance of Benefits to MNE and Host Respectively.

This is perhaps the appropriate moment to make clear that when we speak of control on the national level, this is in no way to be construed to mean promotion of a state-run-economy concept. It does not mean, in other words, that the state should control the means of production, as in a socialized economy, but that the *regulation* of private enterprise should be a function of the individual nation-state, in an exercise of its national sovereignty in accordance with generally recognized principles of international law and in the interests of preserving the free movement of private investment capital which has, up to now, notwithstanding some well-publicized instances of abuse, been largely responsible for positive economic development and technological advancement on a global basis. As summed up by one legal writer, "[t]he free flow of capital and technology, as well as the free exchange of goods, is believed to

1. Brooke and Remmers, eds. *The Multinational Company in Europe, Some Key Problems* (London: Longman, 1972), at 109.

result in a more efficient allocation of the world's resources and an improvement in world economic welfare.''[2]

Another legal writer goes so far as to state that ''the advancement of aggregate global well-being *depends,* at least in part, upon an abundant flow of private foreign capital, which in turn depends upon stability of normative expectations...'' [emphasis supplied],[3]while at the same time admiting that ''it cannot be assumed that all such wealth will contribute to global well-being. Arguably only that foreign wealth which from economic, ecological, and other relevant points of view produces a net benefit to host countries is going to assist in this way. The fact remains, however, that world-wide economic growth cannot do without private foreign trade and investment''.[4]

This is not uniquely an industrialized-nation point of view. From the Düsseldorf Conference,[5] where the developing world was also represented, the following conclusion emerged:

> It was universally acknowledged (at the Conference) that foreign investment is still vital to the process of development and structural transformation in the developing world in order to provide capital, particularly high-risk capital as in natural resource exploration, to provide technology and to give access to and knowledge of international markets.[6]

In sum, ''[t]he free play of economic forces will, apart from a few exceptional cases, make the economic welfare of the whole world greater in the long run than any alternate arrangement of resources''.[7]

Hence, one function of 'controls' should be to protect the beneficial free-flow of private investment capital, and to maintain a proper balance between the benefits to the enterprise and those to the host state, cutting down on known abuses, through national regulations.

As remarked earlier, needs will vary not only from general economic sector to general economic sector, i.e. regionally, and not only from state to state

2. Ellis, ''United States Multinational Corporations: The Impact of Foreign Direct Investment on United States Foreign Relations'', 11 *San Diego Law Review,* (1973), at 3.

3 Weston, '' 'Constructive Takings' under International Law: A Modest Foray into the Problem of 'Creeping Expropriation' '', 16 *Virginia Journal of International Law* (1975), at 124.

4. Ibid., at 127.

5. See *supra* Chapter XIII: 2(b).

6. Stern, in D. Wallace, ed. *International Control of Investment: The Düsseldorf Conference on Multinational Corporations* (New York: Praeger Publishers, 1974), at 59.

7. Robinson, *The Structure of Competitive Industry* (Cambridge: James Nisbet and Co. & Cambridge University Press, 1958), at 141.

within one economic sector or region, i.e. nationally, but also within one particular state at different stages in its political and economic development. For example, certain sectors of the economy are liable to close and reopen to foreign investors as the host state concerned experiences various temporary political or economic crises.[8] These regional and national discrepancies and internal fluctuations can be reflected in regional and municipal legislation in a way that would be impossible under an international system, and this freedom must be maintained for the sake not only of national economic well-being, but also of the healthy international flow of capital world-wide.

2. Harmonization of National Laws in Certain Key Areas

A second function of international 'codes' or 'guidelines' directed at host governments should be one that we have spoken of throughout and that needs little further elaboration here - that of harmonizing national laws in the key areas of control over foreign direct investment, with allowance for diversities in regional and national needs and objectives. Some key areas for such harmonization would be, for example, certain aspects of antitrust legislation and its extraterritorial reach,[9] laws regarding illicit payments and other corrupt business practices,[10] and certain standards such as compensation in constructive takings of alien property; while areas left more to domestic prerogative would include controls on entry, key sector exclusions, reasonable tax incentives and disincentives, and other means of ensuring and safeguarding internal economic well-being and national security.

3. Coverage of Those Areas Inadequately Provided for under Municipal Law

A third function of any international guidelines should be to cover those areas which are inadequately provided for, or are not feasible or only ineffectively administrable uniformly under existing municipal systems. Among these might figure even some of those mentioned in the above paragraph, in

8. Brooke and Remmers, *The International Firm: A study of management across frontiers - trade and investment* (London: Pitman, 1977), at 60. A case in point would be the U.K. automobile manufacturing firm British Leyland's negotiations with Japanese car manufacturers to produce Japanese cars in the U.K. This would have been unthinkable ten years earlier.

9. See e.g. OECD Report of the Committee of Experts on Restrictive Business Practices: "Restrictive Business Practices of Multinational Enterprises", OECD, Paris, 1977, at 58.

10. See *infra* notes 11 and 12 and accompanying text.

cases where no laws yet exist to be 'harmonized' or where national standards are so diverse as to preclude any internationally recognizable norm - for example directives regarding compensation standards or illicit payments.

Some international support for binding codes or multilateral treaties in the area of corrupt practices can already be observed in association with certain of the code formulations.[11] Yet it is largely illusory to issue a guideline instructing multinational enterprises not to make illicit payments, when the MNE is operating in a host state where government officials openly or clandestinely exact such payments, or in host states where such payments constitute the traditional and accepted way of business. The MNEs would be the first to benefit from controls in this area. Such control cannot emanate from MNEs but must be exercised rather by governments, which have the power to penalize any breaches of the law.

It is not even sufficient that home governments make such payments illegal for their own multinationals operating abroad, unless all home governments enact - and enforce - such legislation. This is where the importance of harmonization of laws becomes particularly apparent. To date, for example, only the United States has made it a criminal offense for its enterprises to offer illicit payments in their business transactions abroad.[12] Since no European or other nations have followed suit, U.S. firms have been put at an obvious and costly competitive disadvantage *vis-à-vis* other foreign investors who continue to do business according to the means customarily expected of them in states which turn a blind eye to, or actively indulge in, such practices. So here again, while an international code would be useful for promoting a uniform international standard, it is to the host governments that international directives should be issued to the effect that no illicit payments are to be either exacted or accepted from foreign investors. Illicit payments is indeed one area in which a general treaty could alleviate some of the difficulties. Other areas might include accounting procedures and some aspects of restrictive business practices touching on extraterritoriality questions. Even so, if the provisions are not adequately enforced on the national level, nearest to the source of the difficulties, or if they merely duplicate what is already covered by municipal legislation, international solutions will be no improvement on national ones.

11. See e.g. International Chamber of Commerce, "Extorsion and Bribery in Business Transactions", Report adopted by the 131st Session of the Council of the ICC, November 29, 1977, Part II, Recommendations to Governments, Sect. I; also United Nations Economic and Social Council, *Report of the Committee on an International Agreement on Illicit Payments on its First and Second Sessions* (January 29-February 9 and May 7-18, 1979), U.N. document E/1979/104 of May 25, 1979.

12. United States Foreign Corrupt Practices Act of 1977, Pub. L. No. 95-213, 95th Cong. (December 19, 1977) [S. 305].

4. Overall Function

The overall function of international as well as of national control legislation as concerns the MNE, then, should be - to use the wording of the OECD Guidelines - to "encourage the positive contributions which multinational enterprises can make to economic and social progress and to minimize and resolve the difficulties to which their various operations may give rise."[13]

This statement, reiterated in the U.N. Code[14] and ILO Declaration,[15] expresses the general recognition that along with the difficulties which may arise from MNE operations, there is also a positive contribution resulting from these activities.[16] The task of "international" regulation then, is to maximize the benefits to the largest possible extent, and to minimize the difficulties to the greatest possible degree. This seems likely to be best accomplished by retaining to the individual states their sovereign powers and rights to protect their national interests, while allowing multinational business enterprises to manage their operations in a way that will maximize overall effectiveness in conformity with, and consistent with, their duties as responsible 'corporate citizens' and as responsible subjects of both municipal and international law.

Conclusion

In sum, then, it is submitted that - leaving aside the question of its legally binding nature - the most effective form of international regulation of multinational enterprises would be an international code or set of guidelines which would provide directives to host states (including limitations on host state

13. Organisation for Economic Co-operation and Development, "Guidelines for Multinational Enterprises", Annex, (OECD) *Declaration by the Governments of OECD Member Countries and Decisions of the OECD Council* on International Investment and Multinational Enterprises, Paris, [1976], para. 2, at 11. Cf.OECD Declaration, Secretary-General's Foreword to the Declaration, (unnumbered) para. 1, at 5.

14. United Nations (ECOSOC) "Transnational Corporations: Code of Conduct; Formulations by the Chairman", U.N. document E/C.10/AC.2/8 of December 13, 1978, at 13.

15. International Labor Organization, Tripartite Declaration of Principles concerning Multinational Enterprises and Social Policy, reprinted in 17 *International Legal Materials,* Preface, (unnumbered) para. 4 and para. 2.

16. The adherence to this statement on the part of the ILO would not appear to be merely for propaganda purposes, as evidenced by the published results of ILO studies carried out on the operations of MNEs, which resulted in some positive findings. (See e.g. *The Economist,* November 22, 1975, at 81, referring to the ILO studies resulting in support for MNEs.)

powers), in whose best interest it is, after all, that any abuses arising out of MNE activity be curbed and that all benefits arising therefrom be put to best advantage.

On the national level, as we have seen, a good deal of legislation already exists, the international harmonization of which, to a practical extent, could only be beneficial. Additionally, enforcement machinery already exists for the effective implementation of the controls.

Bilateral and multilateral agreement such as that between Germany and the United States in antitrust matters could also be a positive means of harmonization as well as having the binding force of the international law of treaties.

Any "international controls" should complement, not replace or override, national controls. States should retain full sovereignty over all activity - economic and otherwise - within their territory, subject, of course to international law norms. Outside of directives aimed at a general harmonization of national laws, a code of conduct or international set of guidelines should fulfill only that function which cannot better be filled on the national level. In the words of one writer, "the ideal of world controls is attractive, but it can easily become an excuse for postponing more realistic action."[17] After all, if the problems cannot be solved at the national level, it is illusory to imagine that they will be resolved at the international level.

17. Sampson, *The Sovereign State - The Secret History of ITT* (London: Hodder & Stoughton, 1973), at 270.

CONCLUSIONS

The alarm over multinational activity has been a healthy one. It has caused the MNEs themselves to look critically at their own operations and, where they are found wanting, to 'clean up shop'. The very fact of putting their activities into the spotlight and under international scrutiny may be doing more to bring them under control than any amount of international regulation. Studies such as those being carried on by the OECD, ICC, IBRD, ILO, UNCTAD, UNCTCIRC and others, as well as international congresses and symposia on the subject, while providing useful fora for discussion and bringing to light factual data useful in assessing both the negative and the positive impact of the multinationals, are still a long way from providing, or even seriously proposing, effective legal international enforcement machinery. This is not a criticism of those studies or efforts; it is simply stated as an indication of the inherent difficulty encountered by any body tackling the problem of legal international control of multinational enterprises.

As regards an actual universal international legal controls system, then, it is reasonable to conclude that, in light of the current international consensus, as evident from international conferences and symposia on the subject, as well as from contemporary practice in other areas which require international legal and political consensus, any prospects for the creation of a legally binding international instrument for the control of MNE activity look, for the immediately foreseeable future, dim.

The point is not, however, to belabour, or to waste time in regret over, the immediate unlikelihood of legally binding international MNE controls, but rather to look, as we have done throughout, for possible present alternatives on the national level, while continuing to pursue workable international solutions, where desirable. In looking for possible interim alternatives, we have seen that the multinational enterprise is indeed controlled from many sides, by existing domestic legislation, in the many states in which it carries on business, and that it does not - in fact cannot - run rough-shod and indiscriminately across borders, unfettered and undisciplined. It is controlled, increasingly, both directly by specific legislation, and indirectly by awakened public opinion.

This awakened public opinion has both itself been the result of, and resulted in, much of the international activity which we have been examining in the present study, in this whole area of control. Moreover, despite the non-legally-binding nature of 'Codes', 'Guidelines' and 'Declarations', these international efforts are of unquestionable importance for the light they shed upon the subject in general and for the fact that the varied points of view which are characterized by the different economic categories represented serve to show up all sides of that phenomenon known as the MNE, and lead to a fuller understanding of its many facets. Better understanding is clearly a key factor to bring to any serious consideration of whatever form of control can be envisaged for the future regulation of the MNE. In addition, it gives the multinational enterprise itself a mirror by which to contemplate its own reflection and to see where it comes up lacking. If it is wise, it will correct the deficiencies itself, in order to avoid excessive restrictions imposed from without. Many of the larger firms have already produced their own codes of good corporate conduct, some of which have actually served partially as models for international codes. While it would be of some interest to make a comparison of various codes and guidelines, this has not been the purpose of the present work, and will have to be left to a separate study.

The concentration of the present work has been on host-state controls over the foreign MNE on the private international law level, as exercised in international or transnational direct investment activity, reflected in the fact that, on the level of 'public' international 'codes' or 'guidelines', it is still the host government which is central to the effective exercise of control.

A summary of the conclusions of the present study must display two elements. The first concerns the nature of controls, and the second concerns their function. By way of conclusions regarding the nature of controls, it is submitted that the role of international regulations regarding the multinational enterprises should be an advisory or recommendatory one, but with the urgent and resolute aim of harmonizing domestic laws for application at the national level by each individual host government which is, after all, in the best position to assess its own public interest and national security requirements and where the greatest interest in economic sovereignty over undue foreign influence resides, and where machinery already exists for effective enforcement. It should also be re-emphasized here that such legislation, to be effective, will need to be responsive to the objective fact of the separation of ownership and management control, so that abuses are attacked where they originate, whether that be at the nerve-center of the enterprise's control system, or at the level of the foreign affiliate vested by the central management with broad or limited local decision-making powers. In other words, an effective legislative control structure must display a coincidence of external legal host control with internal management control.

Regarding the second - and directly related - element, the function of controls, it is further submitted that controls, as recommended by international 'guidelines' and implemented by municipal legislation of host governments, should be aimed at curbing the abuses not of multinational enterprises *per se,* as a selected target, but at all corporate abuses, regardless of whether they are perpetrated by national or by multinational enterprises. Otherwise - outside of obvious public interest and national security exceptions - there may be strong implications of non-compliance with the principles of non-discrimination and national treatment as guaranteed specifically under bilateral treaties such as the many friendship, commerce and navigation treaties, as well as under multilateral treaties such as the Treaty of Rome, and as called for under international law generally.

In sum, international guidelines should serve to harmonize national laws, to promote bilateral and multilateral treaties, to allay unnecessary fears and to bring about an awareness of genuine problem areas which will lead to effective host legislation, where such is lacking. These guidelines should be directly aimed at curbing the recognized abuses of national and international conduct, and will also make it incumbent upon the MNEs themselves to be on their good behaviour so as to avoid being 'controlled' out of existence.

In this way might that goal expressed by the major international bodies concerned with the issue of MNE control: to "encourage the positive contribution which multinational enterprises can make to economic and social progress and minimize and resolve difficulties which may arise from their various operations", be substantially achieved.

* * *

BIBLIOGRAPHY OF MATERIALS CITED

BOOKS AND MONOGRAPHS

Abraham, Neville. *Big Business and Government: The New Disorder.* London: Macmillan, 1974.

Adler, J., ed. *Capital Movements.*New York: Macmillan, 1967.

American Law Institute. *Restatement of the Law: Conflict of Laws.* St. Paul, Minn.: American Law Institute Publishers, 1934.

American Law Institute. *Restatement of the Law (Second) Conflict of Laws 2d.* St. Paul, Minn.: American Law Institute Publishers, 1971.

American Law Institute. *Restatement of the Law (Second) Foreign Relations Law of the United States.* St. Paul, Minn.: American Law Institute Publishers, 1965.

Arpan, Jeffrey S. *International Intracorporate Pricing; Non-American Systems and Views.* New York: Praeger, [1972].

Baade, Hans W. "Codes of Conduct for Multinational Enterprises: An Introductory Survey", in Norbert Horn and E.R. Lanier, eds., *Legal Problems of Codes of Conduct for Multinational Enterprises.* Frankfurt: Kluwer, 1980, Vol. I.

Baade, Hans W. "Individual Responsibility", in C.E. Black and R.A. Falk, eds. *The Future of the International Legal Order,* Vol. 4: *The Structure of the International Environment.* Princeton, N.J.: Princeton University Press, 1970 [Vol. 4, 1972].

Barnet, Richard J. and Ronald E. Müller. *Global Reach: The Power of the Multinationals.* London: Jonathan Cape, [1975].

Bathurst, M.E. et. al., eds. *Legal Problems of an Enlarged European Community,* (British Institute Studies in International and Comparative Law No. 6). London: Stevens and Sons, 1972.

Behrman, Jack N. *National Interests and the Multinational Enterprise: Tensions Among the North Atlantic Countries.* Englewood Cliffs, N.J.: Prentice-Hall, 1970.

Behrman, Jack N. *Some Patterns in the Rise of the Multinational Enterprise,* (Research Paper 18) [Chapel Hill, Graduate School of Business Administration, University of North Carolina, 1969].

Behrman, Jack N. *U.S. International Business and Governments.* New York: McGraw-Hill, 1971.

Berle, Adolf A. and Gardiner C. Means. *The Modern Corporation and Private Property.* Revised ed. New York: Harcourt, Brace and World, [c. 1968].

Bishop, William W., Jr. *International Law: Cases and Materials.* Boston: Little, Brown & Co., 1962.

Blanpain, R. *The OECD Guidelines for Multinational Enterprises and Labour Relations: 1976-1979. Experience and Review.* Deventer: Kluwer, 1979.

Blockmann, Albert. *Grundgesetz und Völkerrecht.* Berlin: Duncker & Humblot, 1975.

Bowett, Derek W. *The Law of International Institutions.* 3d ed. London: Stevens, 1975.

Brooke, M.Z. and H.L. Remmers. *The International Firm: A study of management across frontiers - trade and investment.* London: Pitman, 1977.

Brooke, Michael Z. and H. Lee Remmers, eds. *The Multinational Company in Europe; Some Key Problems.* London: Longman, 1972.

Brooke, Michael Z. and H. Lee Remmers. *The Strategy of Multinational Enterprise: Organization and Finance.* London: Longman, [1970].

Business International. *Management Monographs,* No. 18: "Pros and Cons of Joint Ventures Abroad". New York: Business International, 1964.

Calhoun, Alexander D., Jr. and George A. Brumder. "Japanese Laws Relating to Foreign Investment in Japan", in *Private Investors Abroad - Problems and Solutions in International Business in 1971.*New York: Matthew Bender, 1971.

Cary, W.L. and M.A. Eisenberg *Cases and Materials on Corporations.* 5th ed. unab'd 1980. (University Casebook Series). Mineola, N.Y.: Foundation Press, 1969.

Coing, H.C. "Germany and the Multinational Enterprise," in H.R. Hahlo, ed. *Nationalism and the Multinational Enterprise: Legal, Economic and Managerial Aspects.* Dobbs Ferry, N.Y.: Oceana, 1973.

Commerce Clearing House, *Common Market Reporter: Doing Business in Europe.* New York: Commerce Clearing House Publishers, 1976+.

Coolidge, Philip, George C. Spina and Don Wallace, Jr. eds. *The OECD Guidelines for Multinational Enterprises: A Business Appraisal.* Washington, D.C.: Institute for International and Foreign Trade Law, Georgetown University Law Center, [c. 1977].

D'Amato, A.A. *The Concept of Custom in International Law.* Ithaca: Cornell University Press, [1971].

Deppe, F. "Wissenschaftlich - technischer Fortschritt, internationale Konzerne und Supranationalität," in Manfred Kniper, ed. *Investitions-kontrolle gegen die Konzerne?* Reinbek bei Hamburg, Rowholt, 1974.

Dunning, John. *American Investment in British Manufacturing Industry.* London: Allen & Unwin, 1958.

Dunning, John, ed. *Economic Analysis and the Multinational Enterprise.* London: Allen & Unwin, 1974.

Eels, Richard. *Global Corporations.* New York: Interbook, 1972.

Falk, R.A. and C.E. Black, eds. *The Future of the International Legal Order.* Princeton, N.J.: Princeton University Press, 1970.

Feltham, Ivan R. and William R. Rauenbusch. "Canada and the Multinational Enterprise," in H.R. Hahlo, ed. *Nationalism and the Multinational Enterprise: Legal, Economic and Managerial Aspects.* Dobbs Ferry, N.Y.: Oceana, 1973.

Feltham, Ivan R. and William R. Rauenbusch. "Economic Nationalism," in R. St. J. Macdonald, et al., eds. *Canadian Perspectives on International Law and Organization.* Toronto: University of Toronto Press, [c. 1974].

Fikentscher, Wolfgang, *The Draft International Code of Conduct on the Transfer of Technology,* published by the Max Planck Institute for Foreign and International Patent, Copyright, and Competition Law, Munich. Weinheim: Chemie, 1980.

Fletcher, William M. *Cyclopedia of the Law of Private Corporations.* Chicago: Callaghan and Co., 1931-1933.

Folsom, Victor C. "The Taking by a State of the Property, Acquired Right, or Other Interest of a Foreign National, When No Contract is Involved," in *Rights and Duties of Private Investors Abroad* [Symposium], International and Comparative Law Center, Southwestern Legal Foundation, Dallas, Texas. New York: Matthew Bender, 1965.

Franko, Lawrence G. *Joint Venture Survival in Multinational Corporations.* New York: Praeger, 1971.

Fulda, Carl H. and Warren F. Schwartz. *International Trade and Investment, Regulation of* (1970), (University Casebook Series). Mineola, N.Y.: Foundation Press, 1970.

Garcia-Amador, F.V., Louis B. Sohn and R.R. Baxter. *Recent Codification of the Law of State Responsibility for Injuries to Aliens.* Dobbs Ferry, N.Y.: Oceana, 1974.

Glazer, Herbert. *The International Businessman in Japan.* Rutland, Vermont & Tokyo: C.E. Tuttle, 1968.

Hackworth, Green Haywood. *Digest of International Law,* Vol. 5 (1943). Washington, D.C.: U.S. Government Printing Office, 1940-1944.

Hadden, Tom. *Company Law and Capitalism.* World University, London: Weidenfeld and Nicolson, [c. 1972].

Hahlo, H.R., ed. *Nationalism and the Multinational Enterprise: Legal, Eco-*

nomic and Managerial Aspects. Dobbs Ferry, N.Y.: Oceana, 1973.

Hellmann, Rainer. "Countervailing Powers to the Multinational Corporation," in Don Wallace, ed. *International Control of Investment: The Düsseldorf Conference on Multinational Corporations.* New York: Praeger, 1974.

Henry, Q.C., D.H.W. "Anti-monopoly Legislation in Canada," in Hahlo, *Economic and Managerial Aspects.* Dobbs Ferry, N.Y.: Oceana, 1973.

Hymer, Stephen H. "The MNE and the Law of Uneven Development", in Jagdish N. Bhagwati, ed. *Economics and World Order from the 1970's to the 1990's.* New York: Macmillan, 1972.

Hymer, Stephen and Robert Rowthorn. "Multinational Corporations and International Oligopoly: The Non-American Challenge," in Charles P. Kindleberger, ed. *The International Corporation: A Symposium.* Cambridge, Mass.: MIT Press, [1970].

Institut de Droit International. *Annuaire,* Vol. 57, Tome II, Session d'Oslo 1977. Basel, Switzerland: S. Karger, 1978.

International Legal Center. *Law and Public Enterprise in Asia.* London: Praeger, [c. 1976].

Jenks, C. Wilfred. "Multinational Entities in the Law of Nations," *Transnational Law in a Changing Society,* Essays in honor of Philip C. Jessup, ed. by W.G. Friedmann, et al., eds. New York: Columbia University Press, 1972.

Jenks, C. Wilfred. *The Prospects of International Adjudication.* London: Stevens and Sons, 1964.

Joliet, René. *Monopolization and Abuse of Dominant Position: Study of the American and European Approaches to the Control of Economic Power,* Lièges Faculté de droit (Collection scientifique de la faculté de droit de l'Université de Lièges 31). The Hague: Nijhoff, [1970].

Keesing's Contemporary Archives, [Herbert C. Tobin and Robert Fraser, eds.], Vols. XX 1974, XXII 1976, XXV 1979.

Kindleberger, Charles P., ed. *The International Corporation: A Symposium.* Cambridge, Mass.: MIT Press, [1970].

Kindleberger, Charles P. *International Economics.* 4th ed. Homewood, Illinois: Richard D. Irwin, 1968.

Kolde, Endel J. *International Business Enterprise.* 2nd ed. Englewood Cliffs, N.J.: Prentice-Hall, [1973].

Kripke, Homer. *The SEC and Corporate Disclosure: Regulation in Search of a Purpose,* Law and Business, Inc., New York: Harcourt, Brace, Jovanovich, 1979.

Krüper, Manfred, ed. *Investitionskontrolle gegen die Konzerne?* Reinbek bei Hamburg, Rowholt, 1974.

Latty, Elvin. *Subsidiaries and Affiliated Corporations. A Study in Stockholders' Liability*. Chicago: Foundation Press, 1936.

Lea, Sperry and Simon Webley. *Multinational Corporations in Developed Countries: A Review of Recent Research and Policy Thinking*. Washington, D.C.: British-North American Committee, [1973].

Leleux, Paul. "France, Belgium, European Economic Community and the Multinational Enterprise," in H.R. Hahlo, ed. *Nationalism and the Multinational Enterprise: Legal, Economic and Managerial Aspects*. Dobbs Ferry, N.Y.: Oceana, 1973.

Lillich, R.B. "International Claims: Their Settlement by Lump Sum Agreements," in *International Arbitration: Liber Amicorum for Martin Domke,* P. Sanders, ed. The Hague: Nijhoff, 1967.

Lipstein, Kurt. *The Law of the European Economic Community*. London: Butterworth, 1974.

Mann, F.A. *Studies in International Law*. Oxford: Clarendon Press, 1973.

Marans, J.E., et al. (eds.). *Foreign Investment in the United States 1980: Legal Issues and Techniques*. Washington, D.C.: The District of Columbia Bar, [1980].

Markert, Kurt. "Anti-Monopoly Legislation in Europe," in H.R. Hahlo, ed. *Nationalism and the Multinational Enterprise: Legal, Economic and Managerial Aspects*. Dobbs Ferry, N.Y.: Oceana, 1973.

Metzger, Stanley D. "The Individual and International Law: Property Interests," in *Human Rights: Protection of the Individual Under International Law,* Proceedings of the Fifth Summer Conference on International Law, Cornell Law School, Ithaca, New York, June 18-20, (1964). South Hackensack, N.J.: Fred B. Rothman and Co., 1970.

Moore, John B. *Digest of International Law,* Vol. VI. Washington, D.C.: U.S. Government Printing Office, 1906.

Moran, Theodore. *Multinational Corporations and the Politics of Dependence: Copper in Chile*. Princeton, N.J.: Princeton University Press, 1975.

Mueller, Rudolf and Hannes Schneider. *Gesetz gegen Wettbewerbsbeschränkungen: Deutsch-Englische Textausgabe*. Frankfurt am Main: Fritz Knapp Verlag, [c. 1973].

Multinationals in the 1980s - Trends in European Regulation and International Control, Agence Européen d'informations, Brussels, 1980.

O'Connell, D.P. *International Law*. 2nd ed. Vol. II. London: Stevens and Sons, 1970.

Okita, S. and T. Miki. "Treatment of Foreign Capital: A Case Study of Japan", in J. Adler, ed. *Capital Movements*. New York: Macmillan, 1967.

Phatak, Arvind V. *Evolution of World Enterprises.* [New York: American Management Association, 1971].

Robinson, E.A.G. *The Structure of Competitive Industry.* Cambridge: James Nisbet and Co. & Cambridge University Press, 1958.

Rolfe, Sidney and W. Damm, eds. *The Multinational Corporation in the World Economy; Direct Investment in Perspective.* New York: Praeger, 1972.

Ross, Howard. "An Attempted Summing Up," in H.R. Hahlo, ed. *Nationalism and the Multinational Enterprise: Legal Economic and Managerial Aspects.* Dobbs Ferry, N.Y.: Oceana, 1973.

Rubin, Seymour J. "The International Firm and National Jurisdiction," in Charles P. Kindleberger, ed. *The International Corporation: A Symposium.* Cambridge, Mass.: MIT Press, [1970].

Said, Abdul A. and Luiz R. Simmons, eds. *The New Sovereigns: Multinational Corporations as World Powers.* Englewood Cliffs, N.J.: Prentice-Hall, 1975.

Sampson, Anthony. *The Sovereign State - The Secret History of ITT.* London: Hodder and Stoughton, 1973.

Sanders, P., ed. *International Arbitration: Liber Amicorum for Martin Domke.* The Hague: Nijhoff, 1967.

Schaffner, Hans. *Die Multinationalen - Ausbeuter oder Triebkraft der Weltwirtschaft?* Zürich: Edition Interfrom, 1974.

Schmitthoff, Clive M. "Group Liability of Multinationals," in K.R. Simmonds, ed. *Legal Problems of Multinational Corporations.* London: The British Institute of International and Comparative Law, 1977.

Schmitthoff, Clive M. "The Multinational Enterprise in the United Kingdom," in H.R. Hahlo, ed., *Nationalism and the Multinational Enterprise: Legal, Economic and Managerial Aspects.* Dobbs Ferry, N.Y.: Oceana, 1973.

Schmitthoff, Clive M. "The Role of the Multinational Enterprise in an Enlarged European Community," in M.E. Bathurst, et al., eds. *Legal Problems of an Enlarged European Community,* (British Institute Studies in International and Comparative Law No. 6). London: Stevens and Sons, 1972.

Schwartz, Louis B. *Free Enterprise and Economic Organization,* 3rd ed. 2 vols.: 1. Concentration and Restrictive Practices; II. Regulation of Entry, Rules and Discrimination, (University Casebook Series). Mineola, N.Y.: Foundation Press, 1966.

Schwartzenberger, G. *Foreign Investments and International Law,* 8th ed. London: Stevens and Sons, 1969.

Seidl-Hohenfeldern, Ignaz. "The United Nations and Transnational Corporations," in K.R. Simmonds, ed., *Legal Problems of Multinational Corporations.* London: British Institute of International and Comparative Law, 1977.

Servan-Schreiber, Jean-Jacques. *The American Challenge.* London: Hamish Hamilton, 1968.

Simma, Bruno. *Das Reziprozitätselement in der Entstehung des Völkergewohnheitsrechts.* München/Salzburg: Wilhelm Fink Verlag, 1970.

Simmonds, Kenneth R. "Foreign Investment, The International Law Standard, and the Multinational Corporation - An Overview," in K.R. Simmonds, ed. *Legal Problems of Multinational Corporations.* London: The British Institute of International and Comparative Law, 1977.

Simmonds, Kenneth R., ed. *Legal Problems of Multinational Corporations.* London: The British Institute of International and Comparative Law, 1977.

Stein, Eric. *Harmonization of European Company Laws: National Reform and Transnational Coordination.* Indianapolis: Bobbs-Merrill, 1971.

Steiner, H. and D. Vagts. *Transnational Legal Problems.* 2nd ed. Mineola, N.Y.: The Foundation Press, 1976.

Stopford, John M. and Louis T. Wells, Jr. *Managing the Multinational Enterprises: Organization of the Firm and Ownership of the Subsidiaries.* London: Longman, 1972.

Strupp, Karl and Hans-Jurgen Schlochauer. *Wörterbuch des Völkerrechts,* Vol. 1 (zweiter Auflage). Berlin: Verlag Walter de Gruyter, 1960.

Symposium on International Business in 1971 - Problems and Solutions of Private Investors Abroad. International and Comparative Law Center of the Southwestern Legal Foundation, Dallas, Texas, June 16-18, 1971.

Thirlway, H.W.A. *International Customary Law and Codification.* Leiden: Sijthoff, 1972.

Tindall, Robert E. *Multinational Enterprises: Legal and Management Structures and Interrelationship with Ownership, Control, Antitrust, Labor, Taxation and Disclosure.* Dobbs Ferry, N.Y.: Oceana, 1975.

Transnational Law in a Changing Society, Essays in honor of Philip C. Jessup, ed. by W.G. Friedmann, et al. New York: Columbia University Press, 1972.

Tugendhat, Christopher. *The Multinationals.* New York: Random House, 1972.

Tunc, Andre. "Multinational Companies in French Law," *Law and International Trade,* Festschrift für Clive M. Schmitthoff, ed. by Fritz Fabricus. Frankfurt: Athenaum Verlag, 1973.

Turner, Louis. *Invisible Empires: Multinational Companies and the Modern World.* London: Hamish Hamilton, [1970].

United States Department of Justice, Antitrust Division, *Antitrust Guide for International Operations,* (revised March 1, 1977), 1977.

Vagts, Detlev F. "Law and Accounting in Business Associations," in *International Encyclopedia of Comparative Law,* (Vol. XIII: "Business and Private Organizations"). Dobbs Ferry, N.Y.: Oceana, 1972.

Vagts, Detlev F. "The United States of America and the Multinational Enterprise," in H.R. Hahlo, ed. *Nationalism and the Multinational Enterprise: Legal, Economic and Managerial Aspects.* Dobbs Ferry, N.Y.: Oceana, 1973.

Van Cise, Jerrold G. *Understanding the Antitrust Laws.* New York: Practising Law Institute, c. 1955.

Vaupel, J.W. and J.P. Curhan. *The Making of Multinational Enterprise.* Boston: Harvard Business School, 1969.

Vernon, Raymond. "Future of the Multinational Enterprise", in Charles P. Kindleberger, ed. *The International Corporation: A Symposium.* Cambridge, Mass.: MIT Press, [1970].

Vernon, Raymond. *Sovereignty at Bay; The Multinational Spread of U.S. Enterprises.* London: Longman, 1971.

Wallace, Cynthia D. "Barcelona Traction Case", in Bernhardt, ed. *Encyclopedia of Public International Law* [Installment 2 (1981), p. 30].

Wallace, Don Jr. *International Control of Investment: The Düsseldorf Conference on Multinational Corporations.* New York: Praeger, 1974.

Wengler, Wilhelm. *Die Mitbestimmung und das Völkerrecht: Ein Gutachten über die Vereinbarkeit der Mitbestimmungsgesetzgebung in der Bundesrepublik mit dem deutsch-amerikanischen Handelsvertrag.* Baden-Baden: Nomos Verlaggesellschaft, [c. 1975].

Weston, Burns H. "International Law and the Deprivation of Foreign Wealth: A Framework for Future Inquiry," in R.A. Falk and C.E. Black, eds. *The Future of the International Legal Order,* Vol. II, Princeton, N.J.: Princeton University Press, 1970.

Willey, H. David. "Direct Investment Controls and the Balance of Payments," in Charles P. Kindleberger, ed. *The International Corporation: A Symposium.* Cambridge, Mass.: MIT Press, [1970].

Wilson, Robert Renbert. *The International Law Standard in Treaties of the United States.* Cambridge, Mass.: Harvard University Press, 1953.

Wilson, Robert Renbert. *United States Commercial Treaties and International Law.* New Orleans, La.: Hauser Press, [c. 1960].

Wortley, B.A. *Expropriation in Public International Law.* Cambridge: Cambridge University Press, [1959].

Zinn, K.G. "Möglichkeiten der Machtkontrolle von Superkonzernen durch internationale Organisationen und nationale Regierungen," in *Investitionskontrolle gegen die Konzerne?,* M. Krüper, ed. Reinbek bei Hamburg: Rowholt, 1974.

PERIODICALS, REPORTS AND PAPERS

Abi-Saab, Georges. "The International Law of Multinational Corporations," 2 *Annals of International Studies* (1971).

Adler, Howard Jr. and Murray J. Belman. "Antimerger Enforcement in Europe - Trends and Prospects," 8 *Journal of International Law and Economics* (June 1973).

Akehurst, Michael. "Jurisdiction in International Law," 46 *The British Yearbook of International Law* (1972-1973).

American Society of International Law. "Should Investment Capital Stay Home? A Canadian-U.S. Dialogue": *Proceedings of the 68th Annual Meeting* (1974), Washington, D.C. (c. 1975).

Andrews, Gregory E. "An Evaluation of the Need for Further Statutory Controls on Foreign Direct Investment in the United States," 8 *Vanderbilt Journal of Transnational Law* (1974).

Angelo, Homer D. "Multinational Enterprise," 125 *Receuil des Cours* (1968 III).

"Anhaltender Konzentrationstrend in Deutschland: Jahresbericht des Bundeskartellamtes," *Neue Zürcher Zeitung,* June 6, 1979, p. 16.

Annuaire de L'Institut de Droit International, Vol. 2 (1929).

Arnett, E. James. "Canadian Regulation of Foreign Investment: The Legal Parameters," 50 *Canadian Bar Review* (1972).

"Arnold Toynbee: Are Businessmen Creating a New Pax Romana?," *Forbes,* April 15, 1974, p. 70.

"Auf dem Weg zu einem Verhaltenskodex für Multis: Tagung der Uno-Kommission für transnationale Gesellschaften," *Neue Zürcher Zeitung,* May 30, 1979, p. 10.

"Auslandsinvestitionen in America gestiegen," *Frankfurter Allgemeine Zeitung,* August 29, 1980.

Baade, Hans W. "Code of Conduct for Multinational Enterprises: An Introductory Survey," background paper for the International Symposium on Legal Problems of Codes of Conduct for Multinational Enterprises, sponsored by the Zentrum für interdisziplinare Forschung of the University of Bielefeld, July 16-18, 1979.

Baade, Hans W. "The Legal Effects of Codes of Conduct for Multinational Enterprises," 22 *German Yearbook of International Law* (1979).

Baker, Donald I. "Antitrust Conflicts Between Friends: Canada and the United States in the Mid-1970's," 11 *Cornell International Law Journal* (1978).

Barnes III, Louie Burton. "State Regulation of Foreign Investment," 9 *Cornell International Law Journal* (1975).

Bechtold, R. "Die Entwicklung des Deutschen Kartellrecht im Jahre 1979," *Juristische Wochenschrift,* Heft 23, 1980.

Behrman, Jack N. "Industrial Integration and the Multinational Enterprise," in D.H. Blake, ed., "The Multinational Corporation," 403 *The Annals of the American Academy of Political and Social Science,* (1972).

Behrman, Jack N. "The Multinational Enterprise and United States Foreign Economic Policy," 52 *Indiana Law Journal* (1977).

Blake, David H., ed. "The Multinational Corporations," 403 *The Annals of the American Academy of Political and Social Science,* (1972).

"BNOC's chip off 44 Blocks," *The Economist,* February 12, 1977, p. 103.

"Börsenaufsichtsbehörde: Mitspracherecht bei Fusionen," *Frankfurter Allgemeine Zeitung,* December 12, 1979, p. 12.

Bonney, William H. "Foreign Investment Review Act," 13 *Alberta Law Review* (1975).

Borton, Richard C. and James M. Goss. "Control of MNCs' Foreign Activities," 15 *Washburn Law Journal* (1976).

Brenscheidt, Michael H. "Petroleum Legislation in the North Sea Countries," 11 *Texas International Law Journal* (1976).

Briggs, Herbert W. "Barcelona Traction: The *Jus Standi* of Belgium," 65 *American Journal of International Law* (1971).

Bringezu, Volker. "Parent-Subsidiary Relations under German Law," 7 *International Lawyer* (1973).

Business International, Roundtable for Chief Executive Officers, Jamaica, January 6-10, 1971.

Caflish, Lucius C. "The Protection of Corporate Investments Abroad in the Light of the Barcelona Traction Case," 31 *Zeitschrift für ausländisches öffentliches Recht und Völkerrecht* (1971).

Carroll, Mitchell B. "Taxation of U.S.-Based Transnational Corporations," 27 *Mercer Law Review* (1976).

Carroll, Terence M. "Securities and Exchange Commission," in "Administrative Survey: October 1975 to September 1976: IV Investment Regulation," *Law and Policy in International Business* (1977).

"Chile Formally Quits Andean Market Pact," *International Herald Tribune,* November 1, 1976, p. 4.

"China ebnet den Weg zu 'Joint Ventures': Gesetz gestattet Kapitalbeteiligungen und Transfer von Gewinnen", *Süddeutsche Zeitung,* 9 July 1979, p. 15.

Christie, G.C. "What Constitutes a Taking of Property under International Law?," *British Yearbook of International Law: 1962.* London: Oxford University Press, 1964.

Church, Frank. "The Multinational Enterprise," (Foreword), 11 *San Diego Law Review* (1973).

Clausen, A.W. "The Internationalized Corporation: An Executive's View," in D.H. Blake, ed., "The Multinational Corporation," 403 *The Annals of the American Academy of Political and Social Science* (1972).

"Commercial Law Note," 52 *Australian Law Journal* (1978).

"Continental Can - New Strengths for Common Market Anti-Trust," (Comment), 11 *San Diego Law Review* (1973).

"The Continental Challenge," *The Economist,* February 4, 1978, p. 78.

Craig, William L. "Application of the Trading with the Enemy Act To Foreign Corporations Owned by Americans: Reflections on *Fruehauf* v. *Massardy,"* 83 *Harvard Law Review* (1970).

Davidow, Joel. "Antitrust, International Mergers and International Joint Ventures," *Proceedings of the First Annual Fordham Corporate Law Institute - International Antitrust* (1975).

Davidow, Joel. "Recent Developments in International Antitrust," 10 *Akron Law Review* (1977).

Davidow, Joel. "The UNCTAD Restrictive Business Practices Code," 13 *International Lawyer* (1979).

Davidow, Joel. "U.S. Antitrust and Doing Business Abroad: Recent Trends and Developments," paper delivered at the Conference on Antitrust Aspects of International Terrorism, Chapel Hill, North Carolina, September 28, 1979.

Dawson, Frank G. and Burns H. Weston. " 'Prompt, Adequate and Effective': A Universal Standard of Compensation?" 30 *Fordham Law Review* (1962).

"Der Investor sollte sich willkommen fühlen," *Frankfurter Allgemeine Zeitung,* November 22, 1979, p. 13.

"Deutsche Auslandsinvestitionen bzw. ausländische Investitionen in der Bundesrepublik Deutschland," *Archiv der Gegenwart,* August 9, 1980.

"Discovery in Great Britain: The Evidence (Proceedings in Other Jurisdictions) Act," 11 *Cornell International Law Journal* (1978).

Dolzer, Rudolph. "Notstandsrecht in den Vereinigten Staaten von Amerika und seine Reform" ("Stellungnahmen") 40 *Zeitschrift für ausländisches öffentliches Recht und Völkerrecht,* (1980).

Domke, Martin. "Foreign Nationalizations: Some Aspects of Contemporary International Law," 55 *American Journal of International Law* (1961).

Done, Kevin. "Beecham expanding in North America," *Financial Times:* Financial and Company News section, March 9, 1978.

"Economic Internationalism v. National Parochialism: Barcelona Traction," (Notes) 3 *Law and Policy in International Business* (1971).

"EEC Plans Antitrust Crackdown on State-Controlled Companies," *International Herald Tribune,* October 25, 1979, p.l.

Ellis, Clarke N. "United States Multinational Corporations: The Impact of Forcign Direct Investment on United States Foreign Relations," 11 *San Diego Law Review* (1973).

"Ende britischer Kapitalverkehrskontrollen," *Neue Zürcher Zeitung,* October 25, 1979, p. 11.

"England jetzt ohne Devisenkontrollen," *Frankfurter Allgemeine Zeitung,* October 24, 1979, p. 13.

Evans, Alona E. "Self-Executing Treaties in the United States of America," *British Yearbook of International Law* 1953.

Fallon, Ivan. "Look out - the British are Coming," *Sunday Telegraph* (London), February 27, 1977, p. 25.

Farnsworth, Clyde H. "Tax Loophole for Multinationals," *New York Times,* 21 August 1977, Section 3, p. 1.

Fayerweather, John. "The Internationalization of Business," in D.H. Blake, ed., "The Multinational Corporation," 403 *The Annals of the American Academy of Political and Social Science* (1972).

Feliciano, F.P. "Legal Problems of Private International Business Enterprises: An Introduction to the International Law of Private Business Associations and Economic Development," 118 *Receuil des Cours* (1966 III).

"Foreign Direct Investment in Germany DM66.8 b End 1978," *Europe Agence internationale d'informations pour la presse,* Luxembourg, February 4, 1981.

"Foreign Relations Law," 8 *Vanderbilt Journal of Transnational Law* (1974).

"Freedom for Capital Movement," 40 *International Chamber of Commerce Information* (Paris) (1974).

Friederich, Blair Phillips. "Criteria for Self-Executing Treaties" (Comment), *University of Illinois Law Forum* (Summer 1968).

Fugate, Wilbur F. "An Overview of Antitrust Enforcement and the Multinational Corporation," 8 *Journal of International Law and Economics* (June 1973).

"Fusionsstatistik sagt nicht alles," *Frankfurter Allgemeine Zeitung,* February 19, 1980, p. 12.

Gerster, Richard. "Zur Diskussion um den Entwurf fur ein neues Kartellgesetz:

Aktive Kartellpolitik als Entwicklungsforderung," *Neue Zürcher Zeitung,* August 17, 1979, p.11.

"Gesetzentwürfe in chinesischen Volkskongress," *Frankfurter Allgemeine Zeitung,* June 28, 1979, p. 3.

Gill, David, "The UNCTAD Restrictive Business Practices Code: A Code for Competition?", 13 *International Lawyer* (1979).

Gordon, Edward. "Extraterritorial Application of United States Economic Law: Britain Draws the Line," 14 *International Lawyer* (1980).

Gordon, William C. "Tests for Determining the Status of a Treaty Provision as Domestic Law" (Comment), 48 *Michigan Law Review* (1950).

Grendell, Timothy J. "The Antitrust Legislation of the United States, the European Community, Germany and Japan," 29 *International and Comparative Law Quarterly* (1980).

Griffin, Joseph P. "The Power of Host Countries over the Multinational: Lifting the Veil in the European Economic Community and the United States," 6 *Law and Policy in International Business* (1974).

Gurley, Franklin L. "Zur Diskussion um den Entwurf für ein neues Kartellgesetz: Das amerikanische Wettbewerbsrecht," *Neue Zürcher Zeitung,* September 7, 1979, p. 14.

Guyénot, Jean. "La décision 'Continental Can' de la Commission C.E.E. et la naissance du droit antitrust européen," 91 *Zeitschrift für Schweizerisches Recht* (1972).

Harvard Draft No. 11, printed in 60 *Proceedings,* American Society of International Law (1960).

Haubert, William H. III. "Continental Can - New Strength for Common Market Anti-Trust," (Comments), 11 *San Diego Law Review* (1973).

Hauser, Rita. Panel Discussion. "International Law and Economic Interrelations: Policing a Two-Way Street," 1975 International Law Weekend, Association of the Bar, City of New York, and American Branch, International Law Association, New York, New York, 1945.

Hawk, Barry E. "Antitrust in the EEC - The First Decade," 41 *Fordham Law Review* (1972).

Hayden, P.R. and J.H. Burns, "Canadian Foreign Investment Review Act," 21 *Practical Lawyer* (1975).

Hodges, J.W. "The Trading with the Enemy Act of 1917 foreign-based subsidiaries of American multinational corporations: a time to abstain from restraining," 11 *San Diego Law Review* (1973).

Hölzer, Heinrich. "Neuere Initiativen zum U.S. Antitrust - Ein Überblick -", 30 *Wirtschaft und Wettbewerb* (1980).

Hurwitz, James D. "The Impact of the Continental Can Case On Combinations and Concentrations Within the Common Market,'' 25 *Hastings Law Journal* (1973-1974).

Institut de Droit International. *Annuaire.* Basel, Switzerland: S. Karger, 1952.

International Herald Tribune, October 9-10, 1976, p. 11.

International Law Association. *Report on the 52nd Conference of the International Law Association* (1966).

''The International Uranium Cartel: Litigation and Legal Implications,'' 19 *Texas International Law Journal* (1979).

Jennings, R.Y. ''Extraterritorial Jurisdiction and the United States Anti-trust Laws,'' 33 *British Yearbook of International Law* (1957).

Kaiser, Joseph H. ''Fusionskontrolle oder Fusionsverbot?: Die Vermutungstatbestande des Entwurfs der IV. GWB-Novelle,'' 28 *Wirtschaft und Wettbewerb,* Heft 6 (1978).

''Kartell-Hearing: ASU: Fusionskontrolle noch immer lückenhaft,'' *Handelsblatt,* March 3, 1979, p.3.

''Kartellnovelle 'kein grosser Wurf': Einstimmige Verabschiedung im Wirtschaftsausschuss,'' *Frankfurter Allgemeine Zeitung,* January 25, 1970, p.11.

King, H.T. Jr. ''Foreign Restrictions on U.S. Investment,'' 11 *San Diego Law Review* (1973).

King, H.T. Jr. ''International Operations: Current Antitrust Environment,'' in 8 *Case Western Reserve Journal of International Law* (Spring 1976).

Kolde, Endel J. ''The Administrative Structure of International Business with Special Reference to Foreign-Based Affiliates,'' 22 *University of Washington Business Review* (1963).

Korah, Valentine. ''The Control of Mergers under Article 86 of the Rome Treaty: Continental Can,'' 26 *Current Legal Problems* (1973).

Kotkin, Joel. ''Japan is Building Economic Empire in American West,'' *International Herald Tribune* (Paris), August 3, 1978, p. 1.

Kozyris, Ph. John. ''Equal Joint-Venture Corporations in France: Problems of Control and Resolution of Deadlocks,'' 17 *The American Journal of Comparative Law* (1969).

''La Grande-Bretagne abolit tous les contrôles,'' *Le Monde* (Paris), October 25, 1979, p. 42.

Lenrow, Jay Laurence. ''Foreign Direct Investment in the United States: Possible Restrictions at Home and a New Climate for American Investment Abroad,'' 26 *American University Law Review,* (1976).

Lichtenstein, Cynthia Crawford. ''Current Proposals for Marshalling Data on and Disclosure by Multinationals,'' 11 *International Lawyer* (1977).

Liebman, Howard. ''Taxation of Foreign Source of Income: Implications of

C.C.A. Inc.,'' 17 *Harvard International Law Journal,* (1976).

Lillich, R.B. ''Two Perspectives on the Barcelona Traction Case: The Rigidity of Barcelona,'' (Editorial Comment), 65 *American Journal of International Law* (1971).

Linde, Stephen A. ''Regulation of Transfer Pricing in Multinational Corporations: An International Perspective,'' 10 *Journal of International Law and Politics* (1977).

Lindsay, Robert. ''Japanese Beachhead in California,'' *New York Times,* Sunday edition, August 21, 1977, Section 3, p. 1.

Litvak, I.A. and C.J. Maule. ''The Multinational Corporation: Some Economic and Political Legal Implications,'' 5 *Journal of World Trade Law* (1971).

Lutsky, Irvin. ''Barcelona Traction Holds Annual Vigil,'' *New York Herald Tribune,* August 2, 1979, p. 7.

Machowski, H. ''Multinationale Unternehmen sozialistischer Länder,'' *Neue Zürcher Zeitung,* May 15, 1979, p. 10.

McNair, Lord. ''The Seizure of Property and Enterprises in Indonesia,'' 6 *Nederlands Tijdschrift voor International Recht* (1959).

Mann, F.A. ''The Doctrine of Jurisdiction in International Law,'' 111 *Receuil des Cours* (1964).

Mann, F.A. ''The Dyestuffs Case in the Court of Justice of the European Communities,'' 22 *International and Comparative Law Quarterly* (1973).

Mann, F.A. ''Outlines of a History of Expropriation,'' 75 *Law Quarterly Review* (1959).

Markert, Kurt. ''Recent Developments in German Antitrust Law,'' 43 *Fordham Law Review* (1975).

McClaren, Richard. Address. ''International Investment and the U.S. Antitrust Laws,'' London, December 1, 1969.

Meessen, M. ''Das Mitbestimmungsurteil des Bundesverfassungsgerichts,'' *Neue Juristische Wochenschrift,* April 25, 1979, p. 833.

Meng, Werner. ''Neuere Entwicklungen im Streit um die Jurisdiktionshoheit der Staaten im Bereich der Wettbewerbsbeschränkungen'', 41 *Zeitschrift für ausländisches öffentliches Recht und Völkerrecht* (1981).

Merritt, Giles. ''The EEC creeps up on the multinationals,'' *Financial Times* (London), October 5, 1979, p. 12.

Mestmäcker, E.J. and R. Richter, eds. ''Competition Policy: German and American Experiences - A Symposium,'' *Zeitschrift für die gesamte Staatswissenschaft,* Heft 3 (1980).

Metzger, Stanley D. ''Two Perspectives on the Barcelona Traction Case: Nationality of Corporate Investment under Investment Guaranty Schemes -

The Relevance of Barcelona Traction," (Editorial Comment) 65 *American Journal of International Law* (1971).

Modelski, G. "The Corporation in World Society," in 22 *Yearbook of World Affairs* (1968).

"Monopolkommission will unabhängig bleiben: Gegen Beschwerderecht/ Professoren: Fusionsverbote für 'Grosse'", *Frankfurter Allgemeine Zeitung,* March 13, 1979, p. 11.

"Multinational Business Enterprises," prepared by A.J.N. Judge, *Yearbook of International Organizations,* 1968-69.

"Multinationals," 40 *International Chamber of Commerce Bulletin* (1974).

"Multinationals: Bad guys do good," *The Economist,* November 22, 1975

"Multinationals: ICC Speaks to UN Session in Peru," *International Chamber of Commerce Bulletin* (1976).

"Nat West predicts a boost for Investors," *The Guardian,* November 5, 1979.

"New Era for the Multinationals," *Business Week,* July 6, 1974.

"The New Wave: Foreign capital investment in the United States - a survey," *The Economist,* October 25, 1980.

"North Sea oil: It's British," *The Economist,* March 6, 1976.

"North Sea Oil: Survey," *The Economist,* July 26, 1975.

"North Sea participation: Hollow agreement?," *The Economist,* January 8, 1977.

"North Sea: Statesmen and oilmen," *The Economist,* November 20, 1976.

Norton, Joseph J. "The European Court of Justice Judgment in United Brands: Extraterritorial Jurisdiction and Abuse of a Dominant Position," 8 *Denver Journal of International Law and Policy* (1979).

Onga and Rieke. "The Antimonopoly Law of Japan and its Enforcement," 39 *Washington Law Review* (1964).

Onkelinx, Ivo T. "Conflict of International Jurisdiction: Ordering the Production of Documents in Violation of the Law of the Situs," 64 *Northwestern University Law Review* (1969-1970).

Ozawa, T., "Technology Imports and Direct Foreign Investment in Japan," 7 *Journal of World Trade Law,* (1973).

Parker, Paul S. "Foreign Relations Law," (Recent Decisions) 8 *Vanderbilt Journal of Transnational Law* (1974).

"Participantomime," *The Economist,* February 7, 1976.

Perlmutter, Howard V., "Some Architectural Problems of the Multinational Firm," 3 *Quarterly Journal of AISEC International* (1967), cited in *Yearbook of International Organizations, 1968-69.*

Perlmutter, Howard V. "The Tortuous Evolution of Multinational Corporations," 3 *Columbia Journal of World Business* (1969).

Perlmutter, Howard V. "L'entreprise internationale - trois conceptions," 23 *Revue économique et sociale* (1965).

"The Protection of Trading Interests Bill," *Law Society Gazette,* December 5, 1979.

"Pull up for a gallon of BNOC," *The Economist,* July 26, 1975.

Raman, K.V. "The Role of the International Court of Justice in the Development of International Customary Law," in American Society of International Law, *Proceedings of the 65th Annual Meeting,* Washington, D.C., 1965.

Rauschenbach, G. "Die Entwicklung des deutschen Kartellrechts 1977," *Neue Juristische Wochenschrift,* Heft 5, February 1, 1978, p. 190.

Rauschenbach, G. "Die Entwicklung des deutschen Kartellrechts im Jahre 1978," *Neue Juristische Wochenschrift,* Heft 15, April 11, 1979, p. 737.

Rauschenbach, G. "Die Entwicklung des deutschen Kartellrechts in den Jahren 1975/1976," *Neue Juristische Wochenschrift,* December 1, 1976, p. 2188.

Reese, Knut. "Multinational Companies and the Nation State," 28 *Studia Diplomatica* (1975).

"Ressourcenwürdigung bei konglomeratem Zusammenschluss," 4 *Wirtschaft und Wettbewerb/Entscheidungsammlung [des Oberlandesgerichts] zum Kartellrecht* (1977), p. 1745.

Richmont, Jean de. "L'épineaux problème du contrôle des firmes multinationales," *Revue du Marché Commun* 1974.

Ridruejo, J.A. Pastor. "La faillite en droit international privé," 133 *Receuil des Cours* (1971 II).

Riedweg, A.J. "The Extra-territorial Application of Restrictive Trade Legislation – Jurisdiction and International Law," in International Law Association, *Report on the Fifty-First Conference* (1965).

Robinson, Stanley D. "Recent Antitrust Developments - 1979," 80 *Columbia Law Review* (1980).

Rodley, Nigel S. "Corporate Nationality and the Diplomatic Protection of Multinational Enterprises: The *Barcelona Traction* Case," 47 *Indiana Law Journal* (1971-1972).

Rogers, Paolo N. "Multinational Corporations: A European View," in D.H. Blake, ed., "The Multinational Corporation, 403 *The Annals of the American Academy of Political and Social Science,* (1972).

Rosenberg, Herman. "Weighing the Power of the Multinationals," [book-review of A.A. Said and L.R. Simmons, *The New Sovereigns: Multinational Corporations as World Powers*] (Englewood Cliffs, N.J.: Prentice-Hall, 1975, 11 *Stanford Journal of International Studies* (1976).

Rouhani, Tuad. "Renégotiation des contrats entre Etats et investisseurs privés," 1 *Revue Juridique et Politique, Independance et Cooperation* (1975).

Round Table: "Toward More Adequate Diplomatic Protection of Private Claims: 'Aris Gloves', 'Barcelona Traction', and Beyond" (jointly sponsored with the Deutsche Gesellschaft für Völkerrecht), American Society of International Law, 65 *Proceedings of the 65th Annual Meeting* (1971).

Rowe, Frederick M. "Antitrust Aspects of European Acquisitions or Joint Ventures in the United States," paper presented at the Cologne Conference on "The U.S. Antitrust Laws/Die U.S. Antitrust Gesetze: the legal implications for those entering or operating in the U.S. market," under the auspices of the Practising Law Institute of New York in co-operation with the German-American Lawyers Association, Bonn, the American Chamber of Commerce in Germany, Frankfurt am Main, and the Studienvereinigung Kartellrecht e.V. Wiesbaden, June 1979.

Rubin, Seymour J. "The Multinational Enterprise at Bay," 68 *American Journal of International Law* (1974).

Rubin, Seymour J. "Multinational Enterprise and National Sovereignty: A Skeptics Analysis," 83 *Law and Policy in International Business* (1971).

Rubin, Seymour J. "Report on the Dusseldorf conference on international controls on foreign investment," 7 *International Lawyer* (1973).

Rugman, Alan M. "The Results of Foreign Investment in Canada," 11 *Journal of World Trade Law* (1977).

Safarian, Albert. "Country of Ownership and Performance of the Firm," 44 *Economic Record* (1968).

Schmidt, Dominique. "La Protection des entreprises nationales contre les prises de contrôle par des sociétés multinationales étrangères," 21 *Rivista delle Società* (1976).

Schmitthoff, Clive M. "Multinational Enterprise," 121 *New Law Journal,* (1971).

Schmitthoff, Clive M. "Multinationals in Court," *Journal of Business Law* 1972.

Schnor, Thomas. "Trust-Busting with a German Accent: The Control of Corporate Merger and Acquisition Activities under Increasingly Aggressive West German Law," 19 *Virginia Journal of International Law* (1979).

Schweitzer, Thomas A. "The United Nations as a Source of Domestic Law: Can Security Council Resolutions Be Enforced in American Courts?," 4 *Yale Studies in World Public Order* (1978).

Simmonds, Kenneth R. "Is the World Going More Multinational?," Internationalization of Business, Paper read at the Society of Business Economists Conference at Churchill College, Cambridge, 1971.

Skol, A.G. and C.H. Peterson. "Export Control Laws and Multinational Enterprises," 11 *International Lawyer* (1977).

Sohn, L.B. and R.R. Baxter. "Responsibility of States for Injuries to the Economic Interests of Aliens," 55 *American Journal of International Law* (1961).

"Some Guiding Principles of Good Corporate Behaviour for Subsidiaries in Canada of Foreign Companies," *Trade and Commerce* 1967.

Sparkman, John. "The Multinational Corporation and Foreign Investment," (Case Note), 27 *Mercer Law Review* (1976).

Squartini, P. "The EEC and the Multinational Enterprise," paper read at the International Conference on Legal Problems of Multinational Enterprises, the British Institute of International and Comparative Law, London, September 1976.

"Stand on U.S. trust laws," *Daily Telegraph* (London), October 5, 1979, p. 21.

Stanford, J.S. "The Application of the Sherman Act to Conduct Outside the United States: A View from Abroad," 11 *Cornell International Law Journal* (1978).

Swan, C.S. "EEC United Brands Decision: Can Chiquita Banana Find Happiness in Europe?" 7 *California Western International Law Journal* (1977).

"Tax a Deterrent for U.S. Firms," *International Herald Tribune* (Paris), October 3, 1978, p. 9.

Thiesing. "Antitrust and International Law as Viewed from the United States and the European Common Market," 25 *Record N.Y.C.B. Association* (1970).

Tillotson, John, "The GKN-Sachs Affair: A Case Study in Economic Law," 14 *Journal of World Trade Law* (1980).

Tomuschat, Christian. "Die Charta der wirtschaftlichen Rechte und Pflichten der Staaten. Zur Gestaltungskraft von Deklarationen der UN - Generalversammlung," 36 *Völkerrecht als Rechtsordnung, Zeitschrift für ausländischer öffentliches Recht und Völkerrecht* (1976).

Torem, Charles and William Laurence Craig. "Developments in the Control of Foreign Investment in France," 70 *Michigan Law Review* (1971).

Torkert, Preston M., "China's Joint Venture Law: A Preliminary Analysis," 12 *Vanderbilt Journal of Transnational Law* (1979).

"U.K. Removes Foreign Exchange Curbs," *International Herald Tribune* (Paris), October 24, 1979, p. 1.

"Um die Fusionskontrolle wird weiter gepokert," *Frankfurter Allgemeine Zeitung,* December 3, 1979, p. 13.

"U.S. Challenges BASF's Purchase," *International Herald Tribune* (Paris), April 19, 1979, p.7.

Vafai, John. "Conflict Resolution in the International Petroleum Industry," 5 *Journal of World Trade Law* (1971).

Vagts, Detlev. "Coercion and Foreign Investment Rearrangements," 72 *American Journal of International Law* (1978).

Vagts, Detlev. *"The Host Country Faces the Multinational Enterprise,"* 53 *Boston University Law Review,* (1973).

Vagts, Detlev. "The Multinational Enterprise: A New Challenge for Transnational Law," 83 *Harvard Law Review* (1970).

van Hecke, G.A. "Nationality of Companies Analyzed," 8 *Netherlands International Law Review* (1961).

Vernon, Raymond. "Economc Sovereignty at Bay," *Foreign Affairs,* October 1968.

"Verstärkte Kapitalausfuhr aus Japan: Direktinvestitionen im Ausland auf Rekordhöhe," *Neue Zürcher Zeitung,* September 6, 1979, p. 17.

Vogelenzang, P. "Abuse of a Dominant Position in Article 86; The Problem of Causality and Some Applications," 13 *Common Market Law Review* (1976).

von Mehren, Robert B. and Martin E. Gold. "Multinational Corporations: Conflicts and Controls," 11 *Stanford Journal of International Studies* (1976).

Walker, Herman, Jr. "Modern Treaties of Friendship, Commerce and Navigation," 42 *Minnesota Law Review,* (1958).

"Wall Street's rush to beat the new merger rules," *The Economist,* March 17, 1979.

Wengler, Wilhelm. "Parity Codetermination in West German Companies and International Law," 9 *Vanderbilt Journal of International Law* (1976).

"West Germany: Monopolies Commission," 13 *Journal of World Trade Law* (1979).

"West Germany Probes Alleged Japanese Cartel," *International Herald Tribune,* (Paris) March 7-8, 1981, p. 11.

Weston, Burns H. " 'Constructive Takings' under International Law: A Modest Foray into the Problem of 'Creeping Expropriation'," in 16 *Virginia Journal of International Law* (1975).

White, G. "Nationalisation of Foreign Property," 55 *American Journal of International Law* (1961).

Wilkinson, Theodore. "International Accounting: Harmony or Disharmony," *Columbia Journal of World Business,* March-April 1969.

Wilson, Robert Renbert. "A Decade of New Commercial Treaties" (Editorial Comment), 50 *American Journal of International Law* (1956).

Wittman, Joseph I. "International Mergers Under Section 7 of the Clayton Act and Article 86 of the Common Market Treaty of Rome: A Comparative Perspective," 18 *Washburn Law Journal,* (1979).

Wood, Jeffrey and Victor M. Carrera. "The International Uranium Cartel: Litigation and Legal Implications," 14 *Texas International Law Journal* (1979).

Yoshino, M.Y. "Toward a Concept of Managerial Control for a World Enterprise," 11 *Michigan Business Review* (1966).

"Zum Verhältnis der Monopol- und der Oligopol- vermutung in §22 Abs. 3 GWB: Kritische Anmerkungen zur Entscheidung des Kammergerichts in der Sache 'Blei- und Silber- hütte Braubach' vom 16.1.1980," 3 *Betriebs-Berater* (1981).

DOCUMENTS AND OTHER OFFICIAL PUBLICATIONS

Canadian Government, Privy Council, *Foreign Ownership and the Structure of Canadian Industry. Report of the Task Force on the Structure of Canadian Industry* ("Watkins Report"), (Ottawa, 1968).

Canadian Government, *Foreign Direct Investment in Canada* ("Gray Report"), Information Canada, (Ottawa, 1972).

Canadian Government, *Eleventh Report of the Standing Committee on External Affairs and National Defence Respecting Canada-U.S. Relations,* 28th Parliament, Second Session (Ottawa, 1970).

European Communities, Commission, *Third General Report on the Activities of the Community* (1960).

International Chamber of Commerce, ICC Document No. 225-1/67 Or.

International Chamber of Commerce, Commission on Taxation, ICC Document No. 180/136, 30.I.1974.

International Chamber of Commerce, Commission on Ethical Practices, "Draft Report on Ethical Practices in Commercial Transaction," ICC Document No. 192/36, March 14, 1977.

International Chamber of Commerce, Commission on Ethical Practices, *Recommendations to Combat Extortion and Bribery in Business Transaction,*ICC Publication No. 315. (Report adopted by the 131st Session of the Council of the ICC, November 29, 1977.)

International Chamber of Commerce, *Guidelines for International Investment,* ICC Publications, Paris, 1974.

International Chamber of Commerce, Special Committee on Multinational Enterprises: "Multinational Enterprises and their Role in Economic Development," ICC Document No. 191/81 or.

International Labour Organisation, *Tripartite Declaration of Principles concerning Multinational Enterprises and Social Policy,* International Labour Office, (Geneva, 1977).

Japan, Ministry of Finance and Foreign Department, International Finance Bureau, Bank of Japan, *Manual of Foreign Investment in Japan* (1974).

Organisation for Economic Co-operation and Development, *Declaration on International Investment and Multinational Enterprises by the Governments of OECD Member Countries* (21st June 1976), OECD Publications (Paris, 1976).

Organisation for Economic Co-operation and Development, *Draft Convention,* OECD Publication No. 15636, (Paris, December 1962).

Organisation for Economic Co-operation and Development, *Draft Convention on the Protection of Foreign Property and Resolution of the Council on the Draft Convention,* OECD Publication No. 23081, (Paris, November 1967).

Organisation for Economic Co-operation and Development, "Declaration on International Investment and Multinational Enterprises by the Governments of OECD Member Countries" (21st June 1976), published in: *International Investment and Multinational Enterprises,* OECD Publications, Paris, 1976.

Organisation for Economic Co-operation and Development, *International Investment and Multinational Enterprises,* OECD Publications, Paris, 1976.

Organisation for Economic Co-operation and Development, *Merger and Competition Policy,* Report of the Committee of Experts on Restrictive Business Practices, OECD Publications, Paris, 1975.

Organisation for Economic Co-operation and Development, *Restrictive Business Practices of Multinational Enterprises,* Report of the Committee of Experts on Restrictive Business Practices, OECD Publications, Paris, 1977.

Organisation for Economic Co-operation and Development, *Review of the 1976 Declaration and Decisions on International Investment and Multinational Enterprises,* Report by the Committee on International Investment and Multinational Enterprises to the OECD Council Meeting at Ministerial Level, 13th-14th June, 1979, OECD Publications, Paris, 1979.

United Kingdom, Department of Trade, *Disclosure of Interests in Shares: A Consultative Document,* London, August 11, 1980.

United Kingdom, Government of, *The Impact of Foreign Direct Investment of the United Kingdom* (Steuer Report), prepared by M.D. Steuer, et al., HMSO, London, 1973.

United Kingdom, Government of, "A Review of Monopolies and Mergers Policy: A Consultative Document," Cmnd. 7198, HMSO London, May 1978.

United Nations Conference on Trade and Developments, "A Set of Multilaterally Agreed Equitable Principles and Rules for the Control of Restrictive Business Practices," UNCTAD Document No. TD/RBP/CONF/10, May 2, 1980; also Annex; also No. A/C.2/35/6 October 23, 1980, Annex.

United Nations Conference on Trade and Development, "UNCTAD V Ends Session in Manila, UNCTAD Information Unit, UNCTAD Document No. TAD/INF/1079, June 5, 1979.

United Nations Conference on Trade and Development, *Proceedings of the United Nations Conference on Trade and Development, Second Session,* Vol. I and Corr. 1 & 3 and Add. 1 & 2, Report and Annexes, U.N. publication, Sales No.: E.68.II.D.14 (New York, 1968).

United Nations Conference on Trade and Development, "Provisional Agenda for the Fifth Session of the United Nations Conference on Trade and Development," UNCTAD Document No. TD/220, April 12, 1979.

United Nations, *Multinational Corporations in World Development,* U.N. Publication E/5500/Rev.1; St/ESA/6, Sales No. E.74.II.A.5, New York, 1974.

United Nations, Commission on Transnational Corporations, Second Session, Lima, 1-12 March 1976, "National Legislation and Regulations Relating to Transnational Corporations," U.N. Document No. E/C.10/8.

United Nations, Commission on Transnational Corporations, Intergovernmental Working Group Report on the Formulation of a Code of Conduct, Third Session, New York, 25 April - 6 May 1977, Agenda item 5. U.N. Document No. E/C.10/31 (May 4, 1977).

United Nations, Commission on Transnational Corporations, Intergovernmental Working Group on the Formulation of a Code of Conduct, "Transnational Corporations: Code of Conduct; Formulations by the Chairman," U.N. Document No. E/C.10/AC.2/8, (December 13, 1978).

United Nations, "Commission on Transnational Corporations. Report on the First Session (March 17-28, 1975)" Economic and Social Council, Official Records: Fifty-Ninth Session, Supplement No. 12, U.N. Document No. E/5655, E./C. 10/6.

United Nations, "Commission on Transnational Corporations: Report on the Second Session" (March 1-12, 1976), U.N. Document No. E/5782, E/C. 10/16.

United Nations, *The Impact of Multinational Corporations on Development and on International Relations,* U.N. publication E/5500/Rev.1; ST/ESA/6., Sales No.E.74.II.A.5 (New York, 1974).

United Nations, *Multinational Corporations in World Development,* U.N. Publication ST/ECA/190, Sales No. E.73.II.A.11, (New York, 1973).

United Nations, "Report of the *Ad Hoc* Intergovernmental Working Group on the Problem of Corrupt Practices on Its First, Second, Third and Resumed Third Sessions," U.N. Document E/6006 (July 5, 1977).

United Nations, "Report of the Committee on an International Agreement on Illicit Payments on its First and Second Sessions," (January 29 - February 9 and May 7-18, 1979), U.N. Document E/1979/104 (May 25, 1979).

United Nations, *Summary of the Hearings Before the Group of Eminent Persons to Study the Impact of Multinational Corporations on Development and on International Relations,* U.N. publication ST/ESA/15, Sales No. 1975. I.5 (New York, 1979).

United Nations, "Transnational Corporations: Issues Involved in the Formulation of a Code of Conduct," U.N. Document No. E/C.10/18.

United Nations, "Transnational Corporations: Texts Relevant to an Annotated Outline Suggested by the Chairman of the Intergovernmental Working Group on the Code of Conduct," Report of the Secretariat of the Commission on Transnational Corporations, Intergovernmental Working Group of the Whole on the Code of Conduct, Third Session, New York (February 6-10, 1978), U.N. Document No. E/C.10/AC.2/3.

United States, Department of Commerce, *Foreign Investment in the United States* (1976).

United States, Federal Trade Commission, *Premerger Notification Compliance Guide: An explanation of the application and operation of the premerger notification rules implementing the Hart-Scott-Rodino Antitrust Improvements Act of 1976,* prepared by the Premerger Notification Office of the Federal Trade Commission's Bureau of Competition, September 18, 1978.

United States, Congress, *Hearings before the Senate Committee on Foreign Relations on Executives E, G,* and *H,* 84th Cong. 2d sess., 15 (1956).

United States, Congress, Senate Committee on Banking, Housing, and Urban Affairs, *Report to the Securities and Exchange Commission on Questionable and Illegal Corporate Payments and Practices,* 94th Cong. 2d sess. 3-5 (1976).

United States, National Commission for the Review of Antitrust Laws and Procedures, *Report to the President and the Attorney General,* Washington, D.C., January 22, 1979.

TABLE OF CASES

INDEX

Abbreviations used in index

CIME = Committee on International Investment and Multinational Enterprise
ECOSOC = UN Economic and Social Council
ECSC = European Coal and Steel Community
EEC = European Economic Community
FCN = friendship, commerce and navigation
FRG = Federal Republic of Germany
FTC = US Federal Trade Commission
GATT = General Agreement on Tariffs and Trade
ICC = International Chamber of Commerce
ILO = International Labor Organization
IME = International Investment and Multinational Enterprise
MNE = Multinational enterprise
LDC = less-developed country
OECD = Organisation for Economic Co-operation and Development
SEC = US Securities and Exchange Commission
UK = United Kingdom
UN = United Nations
UNCTAD = UN Conference on Trade and Development
UNCTC/IRC = UN Commission on Transnational Corporations/ Information and Research Centre
UNESCO = United Nations Educational and Scientific Organization
US = United States